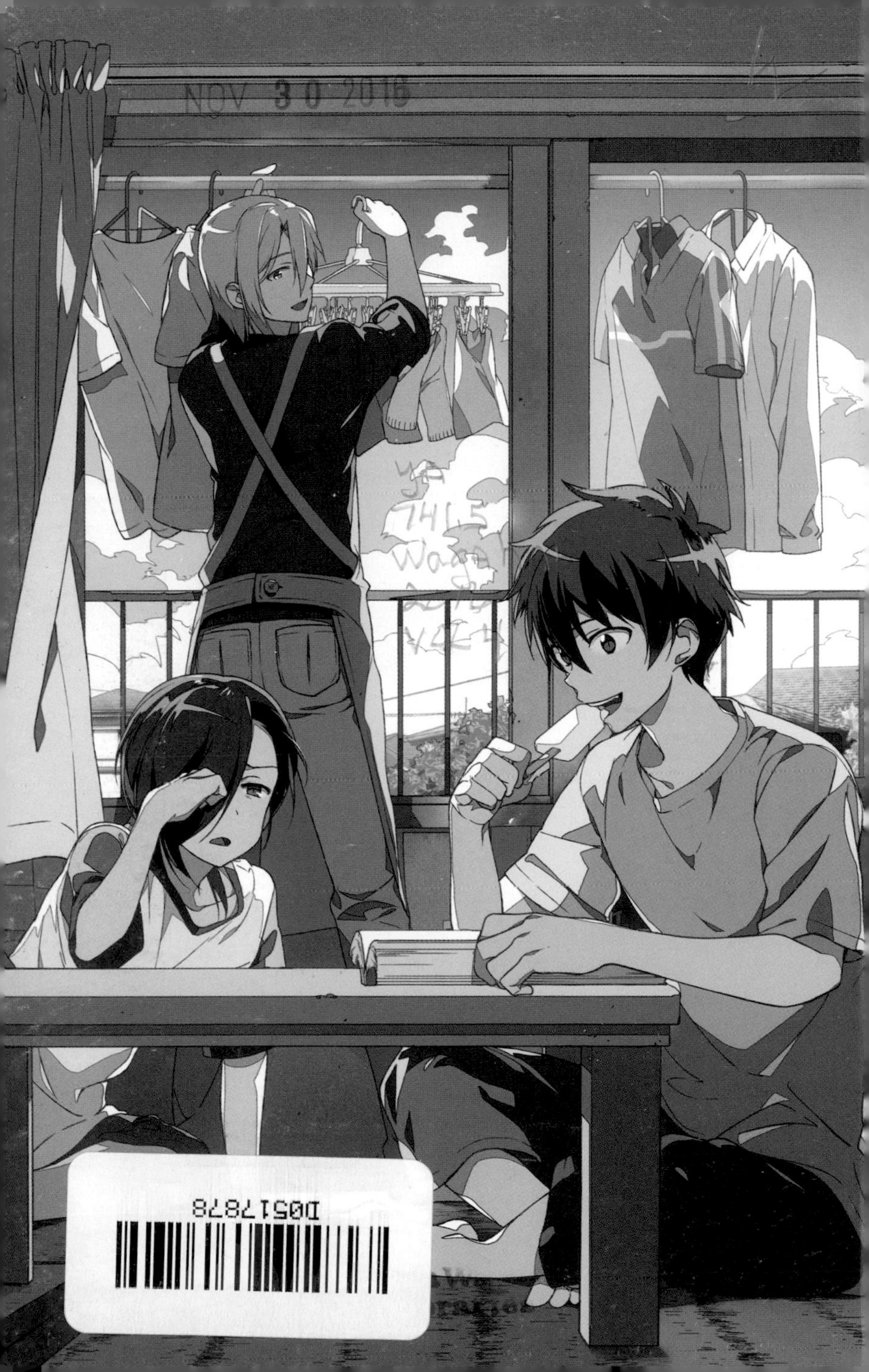

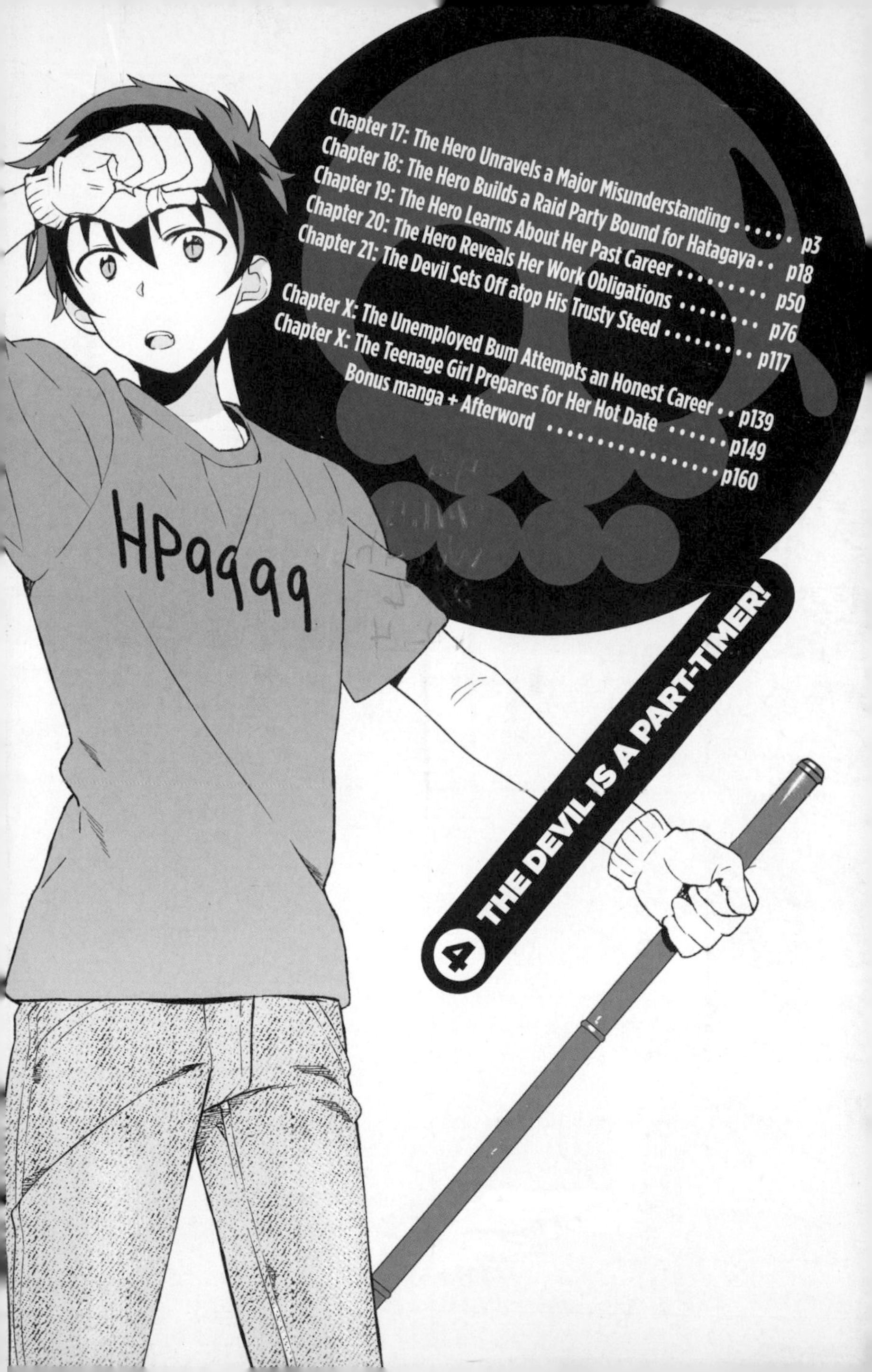

# THE DEVIL IS A PART-TIMER! 4

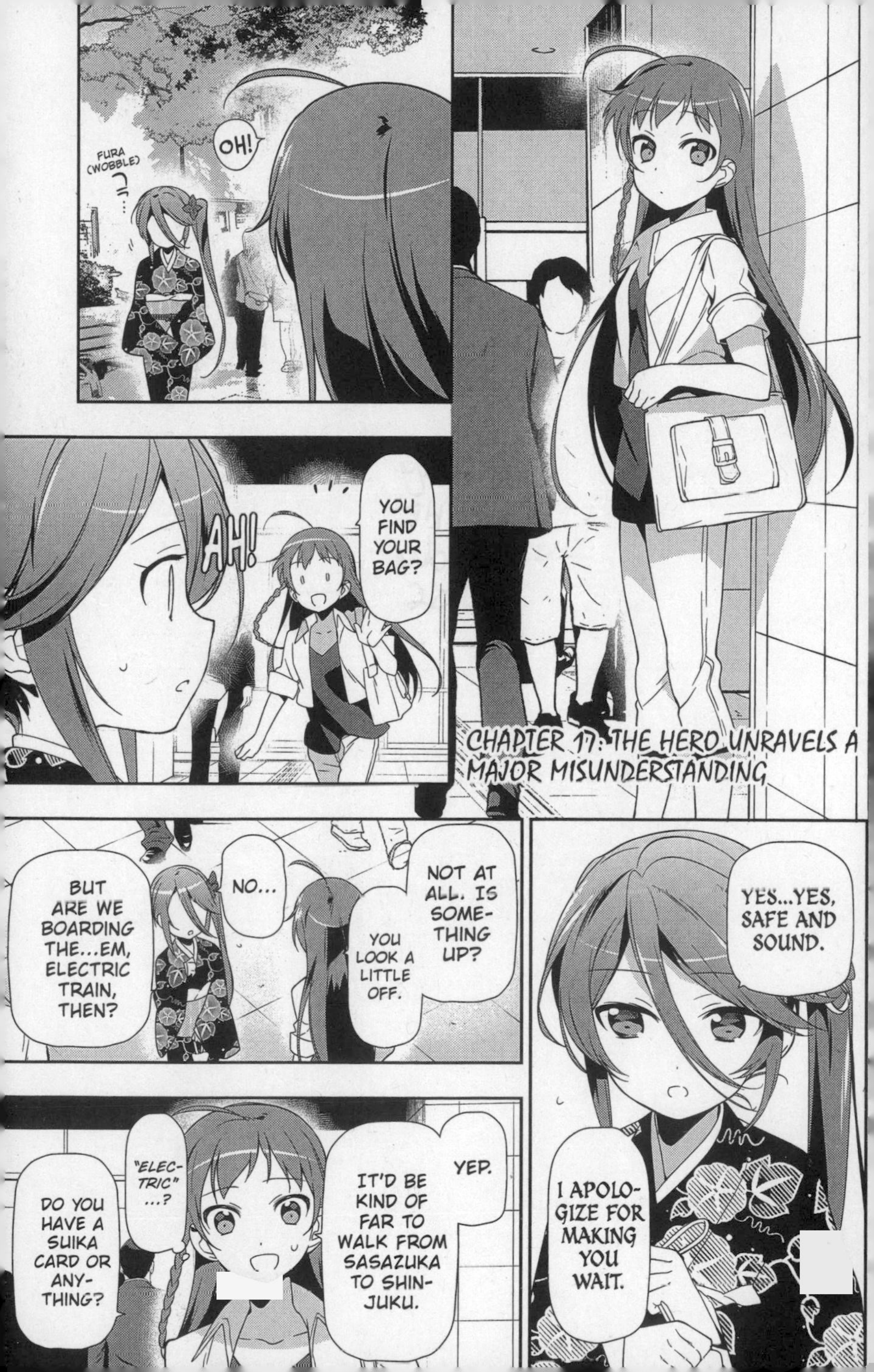
CHAPTER 17: THE HERO UNRAVELS A MAJOR MISUNDERSTANDING
OH!
FURA (WOBBLE)
YOU FIND YOUR BAG?
AH!
YES...YES, SAFE AND SOUND.
I APOLOGIZE FOR MAKING YOU WAIT.
NOT AT ALL. IS SOMETHING UP?
YOU LOOK A LITTLE OFF.
NO...
BUT ARE WE BOARDING THE...EM, ELECTRIC TRAIN, THEN?
YEP.
IT'D BE KIND OF FAR TO WALK FROM SASAZUKA TO SHINJUKU.
"ELECTRIC" ...?
DO YOU HAVE A SUIKA CARD OR ANYTHING?

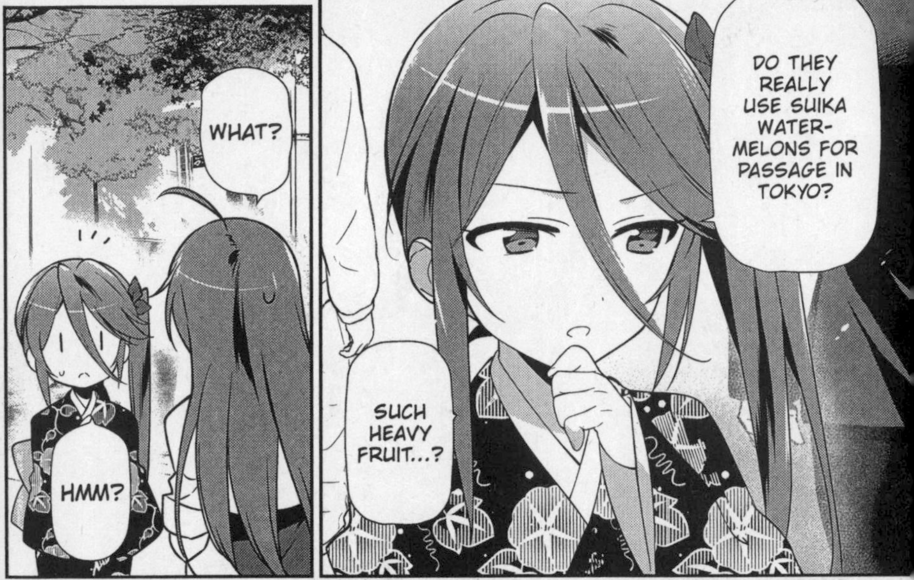
DO THEY REALLY USE SUIKA WATER-MELONS FOR PASSAGE IN TOKYO?
SUCH HEAVY FRUIT...?
WHAT?
HMM?

*NOTE: "SUIKA" MEANS "WATERMELON" IN JAPANESE, AND IS ALSO THE TERM FOR THE REFILLABLE CARDS USED BY THE TOKYO TRANSIT SYSTEM.*

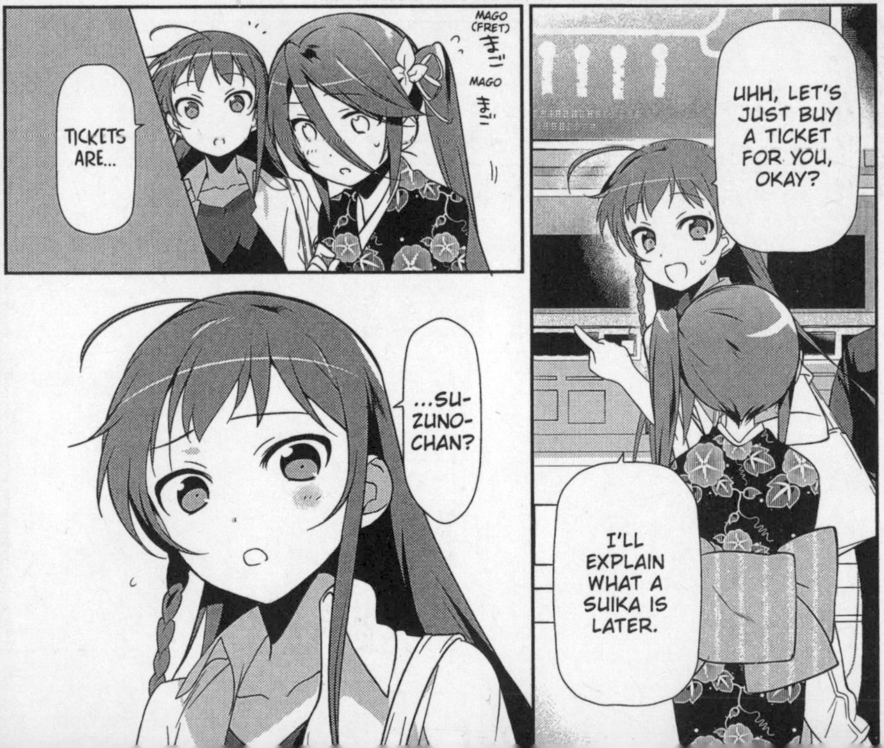
UHH, LET'S JUST BUY A TICKET FOR YOU, OKAY?
I'LL EXPLAIN WHAT A SUIKA IS LATER.
MAGO (FRET) まご
MAGO まご
TICKETS ARE...
...SU-ZUNO-CHAN?

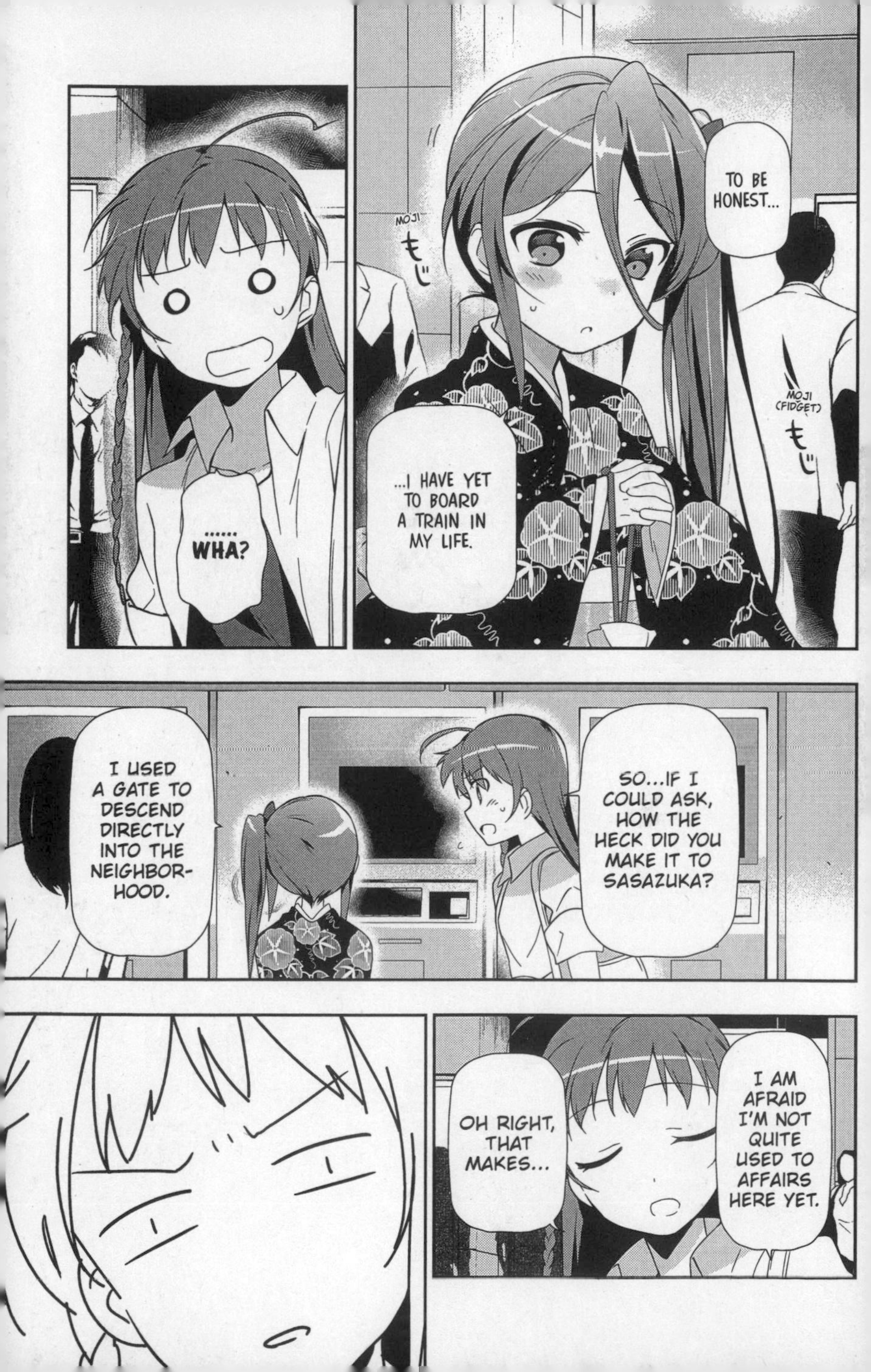
TO BE HONEST...
MOJI (FIDGET)
もじ
MOJI
もじ
...I HAVE YET TO BOARD A TRAIN IN MY LIFE.
...... WHA?
SO...IF I COULD ASK, HOW THE HECK DID YOU MAKE IT TO SASAZUKA?
I USED A GATE TO DESCEND DIRECTLY INTO THE NEIGHBORHOOD.
I AM AFRAID I'M NOT QUITE USED TO AFFAIRS HERE YET.
OH RIGHT, THAT MAKES...

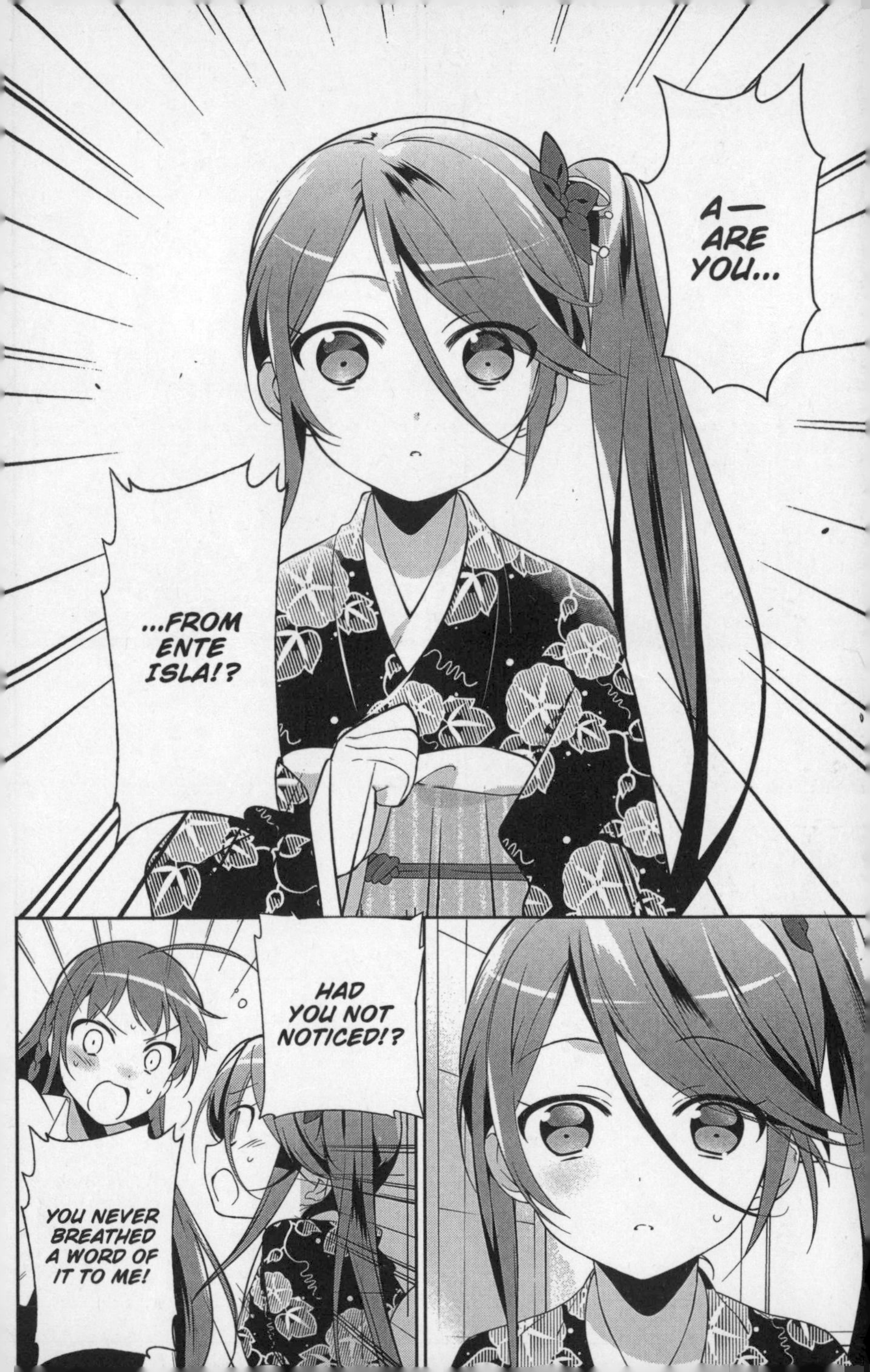
A—
ARE YOU...
...FROM ENTE ISLA!?
HAD YOU NOT NOTICED!?
YOU NEVER BREATHED A WORD OF IT TO ME!

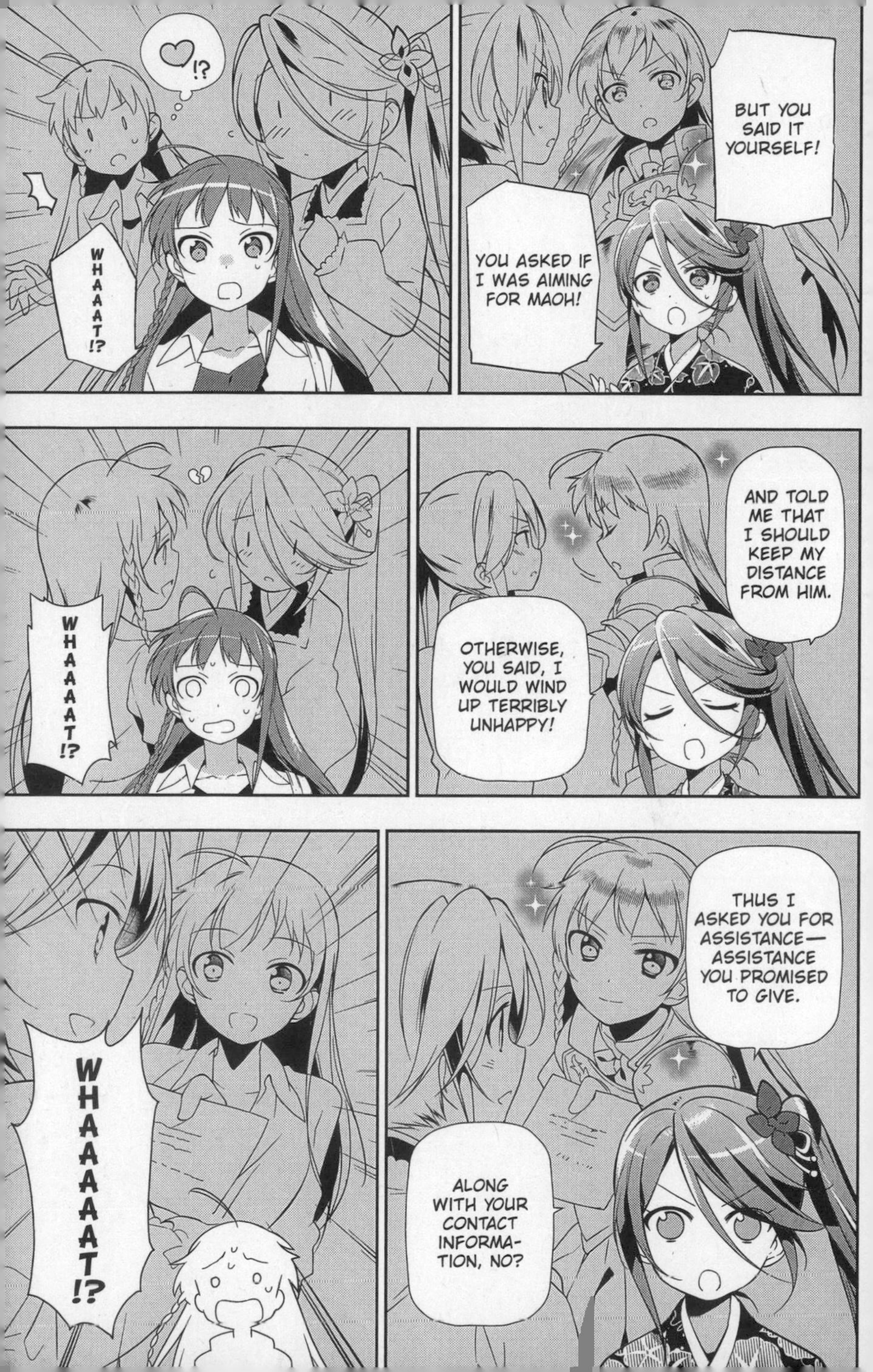
BUT YOU SAID IT YOURSELF!
YOU ASKED IF I WAS AIMING FOR MAOH!
!?
WHAAAT!?
AND TOLD ME THAT I SHOULD KEEP MY DISTANCE FROM HIM.
OTHERWISE, YOU SAID, I WOULD WIND UP TERRIBLY UNHAPPY!
WHAAAAT!?
THUS I ASKED YOU FOR ASSISTANCE—ASSISTANCE YOU PROMISED TO GIVE.
ALONG WITH YOUR CONTACT INFORMATION, NO?
WHAAAAAT!?

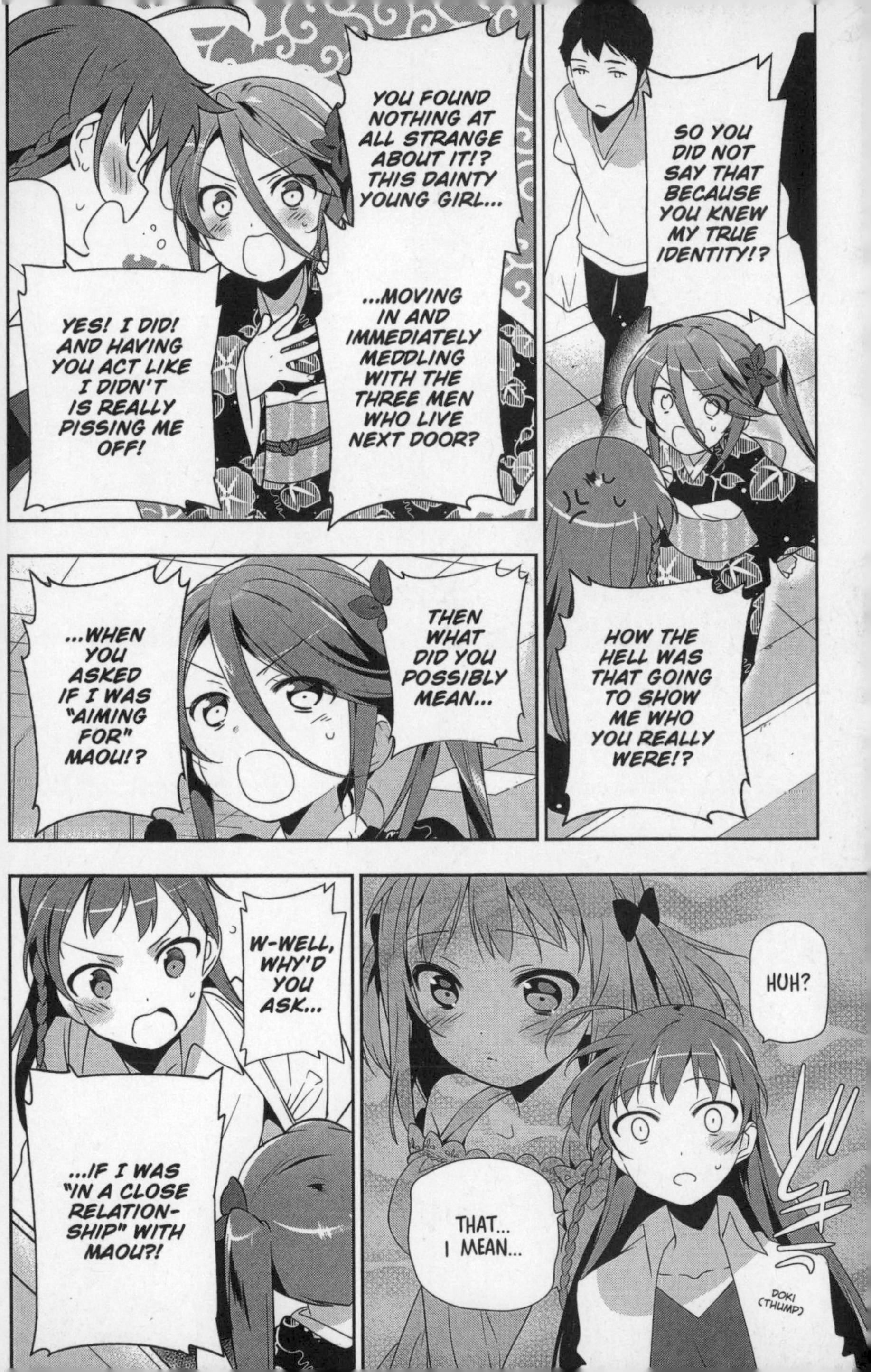
SO YOU DID NOT SAY THAT BECAUSE YOU KNEW MY TRUE IDENTITY!?
HOW THE HELL WAS THAT GOING TO SHOW ME WHO YOU REALLY WERE!?
YOU FOUND NOTHING AT ALL STRANGE ABOUT IT!? THIS DAINTY YOUNG GIRL...
...MOVING IN AND IMMEDIATELY MEDDLING WITH THE THREE MEN WHO LIVE NEXT DOOR?
YES! I DID! AND HAVING YOU ACT LIKE I DIDN'T IS REALLY PISSING ME OFF!
THEN WHAT DID YOU POSSIBLY MEAN...
...WHEN YOU ASKED IF I WAS "AIMING FOR" MAOU!?
HUH?
THAT... I MEAN...
DOKI (THUMP)
W-WELL, WHY'D YOU ASK...
...IF I WAS "IN A CLOSE RELATION-SHIP" WITH MAOU?!

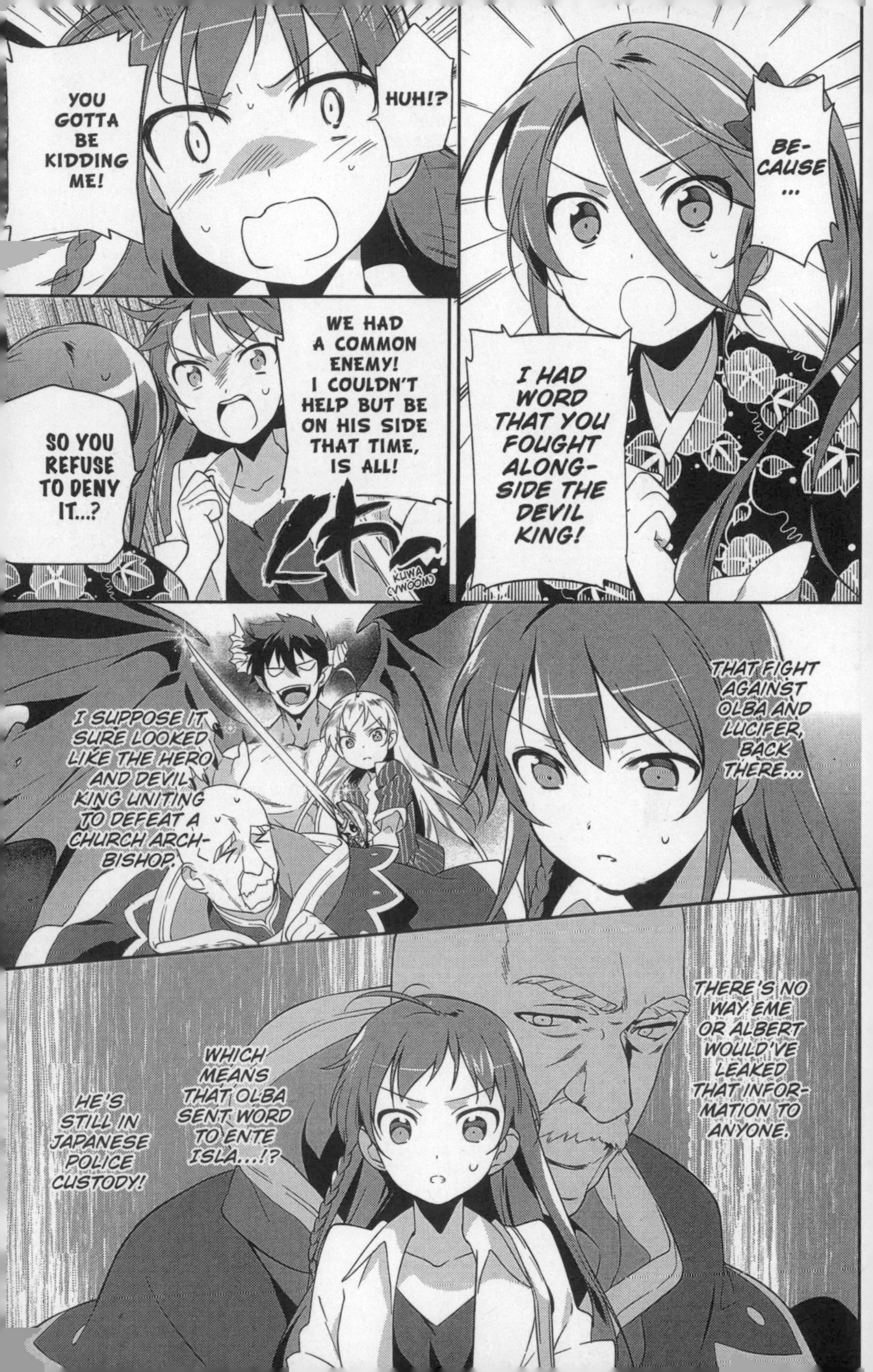
BE-CAUSE...
I HAD WORD THAT YOU FOUGHT ALONG-SIDE THE DEVIL KING!
HUH!?
YOU GOTTA BE KIDDING ME!
WE HAD A COMMON ENEMY! I COULDN'T HELP BUT BE ON HIS SIDE THAT TIME, IS ALL!
KUWA (VWOOM)
SO YOU REFUSE TO DENY IT...?
THAT FIGHT AGAINST OLBA AND LUCIFER, BACK THERE...
I SUPPOSE IT SURE LOOKED LIKE THE HERO AND DEVIL KING UNITING TO DEFEAT A CHURCH ARCH-BISHOP.
THERE'S NO WAY EME OR ALBERT WOULD'VE LEAKED THAT INFOR-MATION TO ANYONE.
WHICH MEANS THAT OLBA SENT WORD TO ENTE ISLA...!?
HE'S STILL IN JAPANESE POLICE CUSTODY!

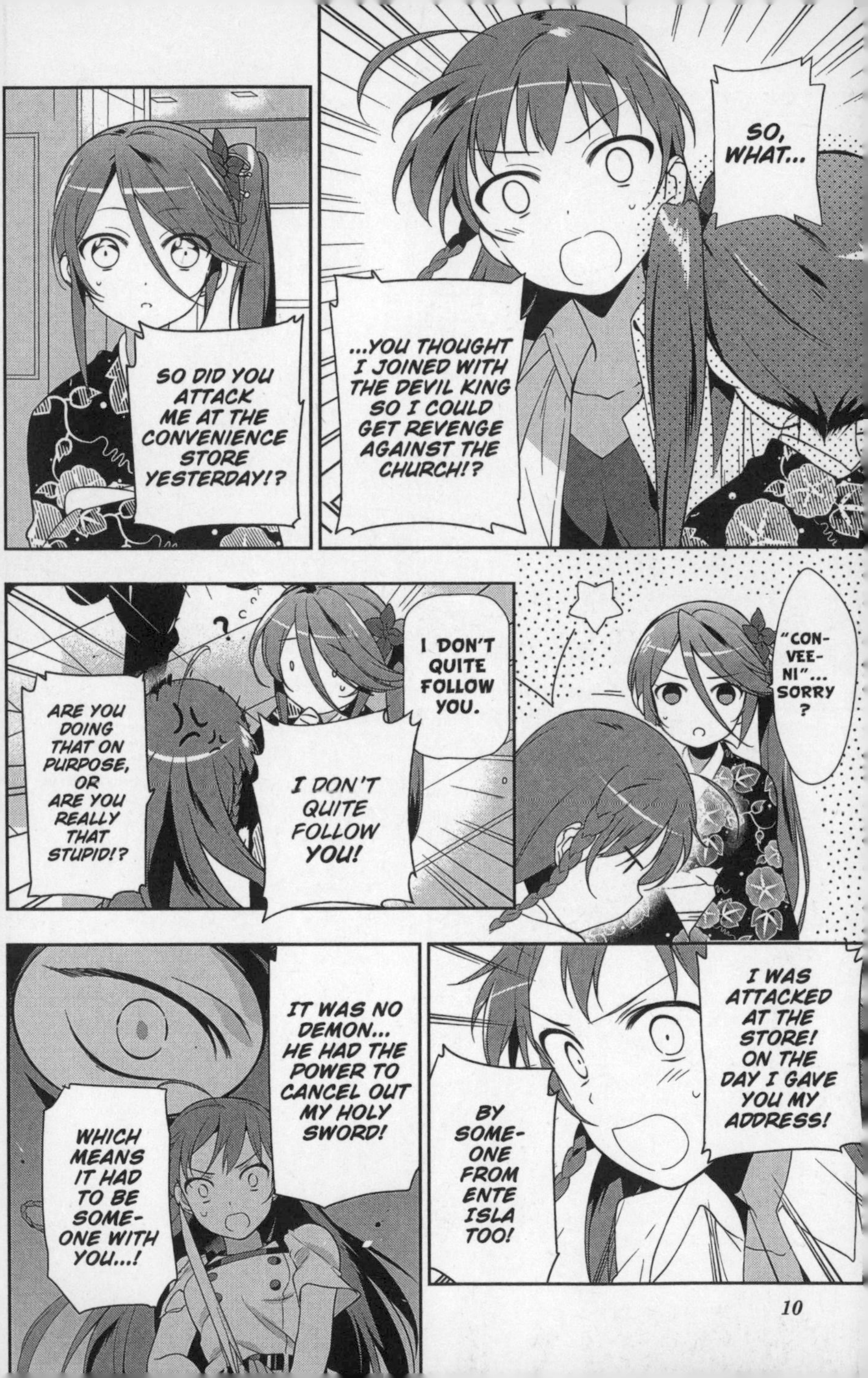
SO, WHAT...
...YOU THOUGHT I JOINED WITH THE DEVIL KING SO I COULD GET REVENGE AGAINST THE CHURCH!?
SO DID YOU ATTACK ME AT THE CONVENIENCE STORE YESTERDAY!?
“CON-VEE-NI”... SORRY?
I DON'T QUITE FOLLOW YOU.
I DON'T QUITE FOLLOW YOU!
ARE YOU DOING THAT ON PURPOSE, OR ARE YOU REALLY THAT STUPID!?
I WAS ATTACKED AT THE STORE! ON THE DAY I GAVE YOU MY ADDRESS!
BY SOME-ONE FROM ENTE ISLA TOO!
IT WAS NO DEMON... HE HAD THE POWER TO CANCEL OUT MY HOLY SWORD!
WHICH MEANS IT HAD TO BE SOME-ONE WITH YOU...!

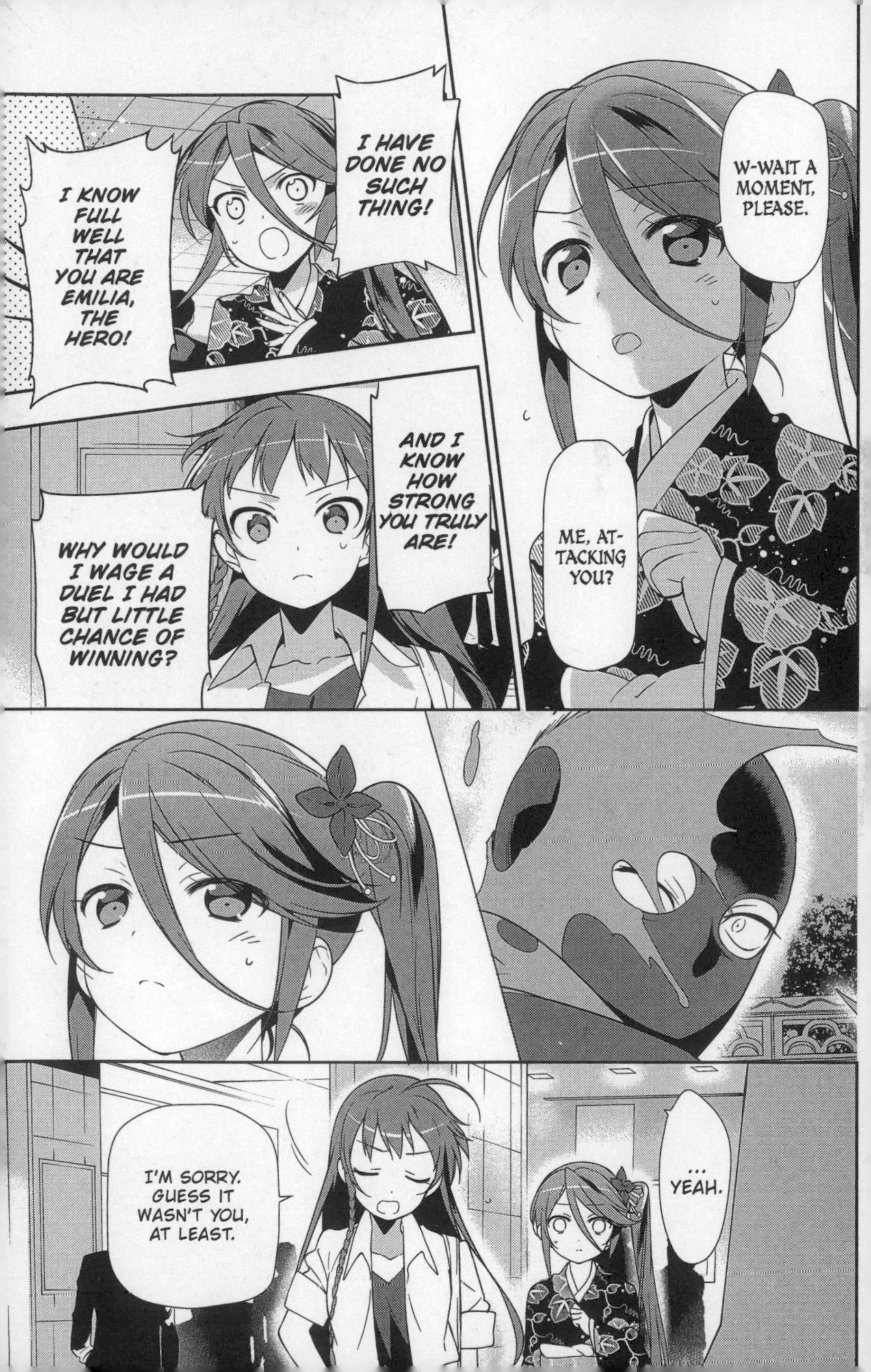
W-WAIT A MOMENT, PLEASE.
ME, AT-TACKING YOU?
I HAVE DONE NO SUCH THING!
I KNOW FULL WELL THAT YOU ARE EMILIA, THE HERO!
AND I KNOW HOW STRONG YOU TRULY ARE!
WHY WOULD I WAGE A DUEL I HAD BUT LITTLE CHANCE OF WINNING?
... YEAH.
I'M SORRY. GUESS IT WASN'T YOU, AT LEAST.

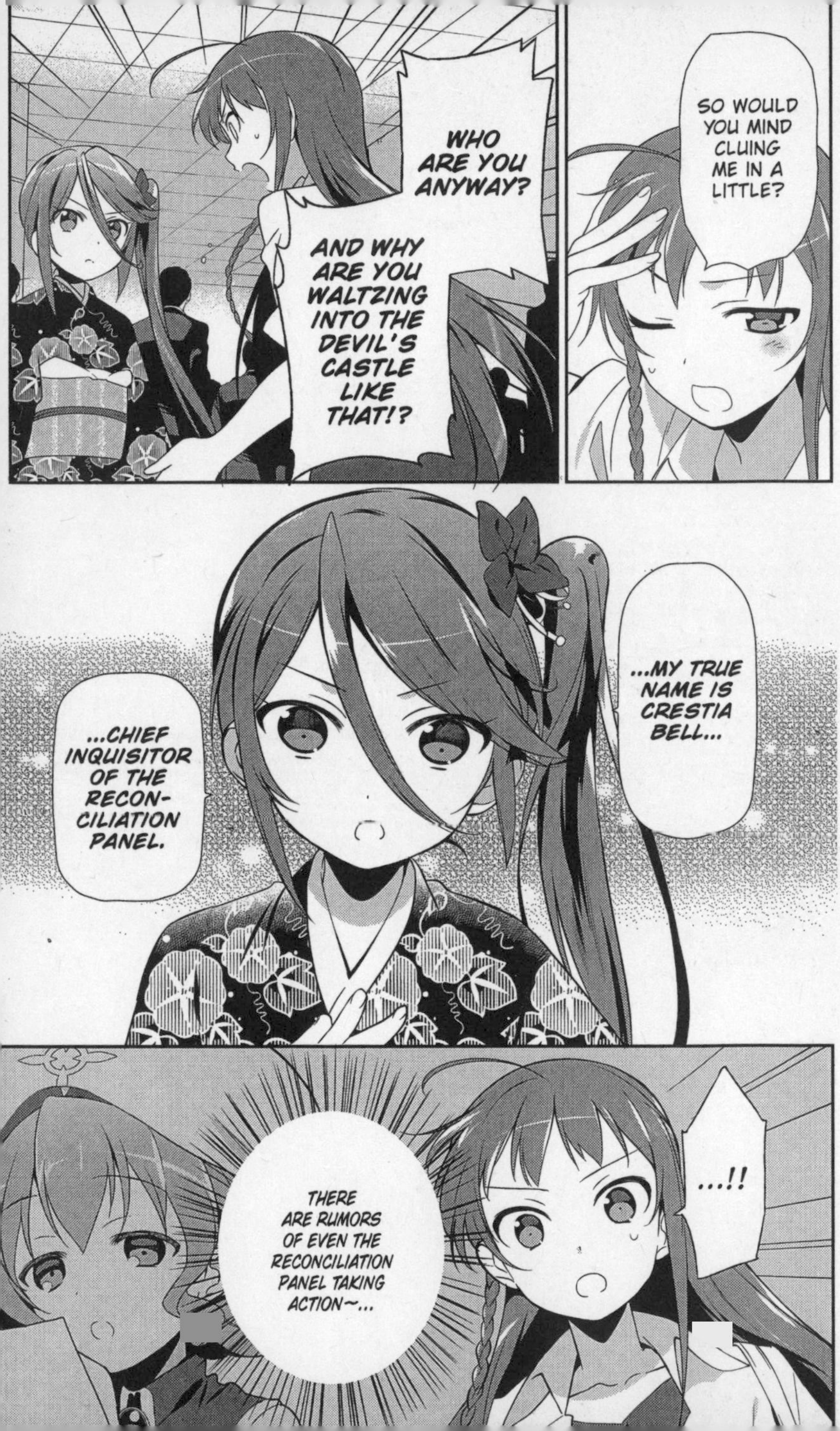
SO WOULD YOU MIND CLUING ME IN A LITTLE?
WHO ARE YOU ANYWAY?
AND WHY ARE YOU WALTZING INTO THE DEVIL'S CASTLE LIKE THAT!?
...MY TRUE NAME IS CRESTIA BELL...
...CHIEF INQUISITOR OF THE RECON-CILIATION PANEL.
...!!
THERE ARE RUMORS OF EVEN THE RECONCILIATION PANEL TAKING ACTION~...

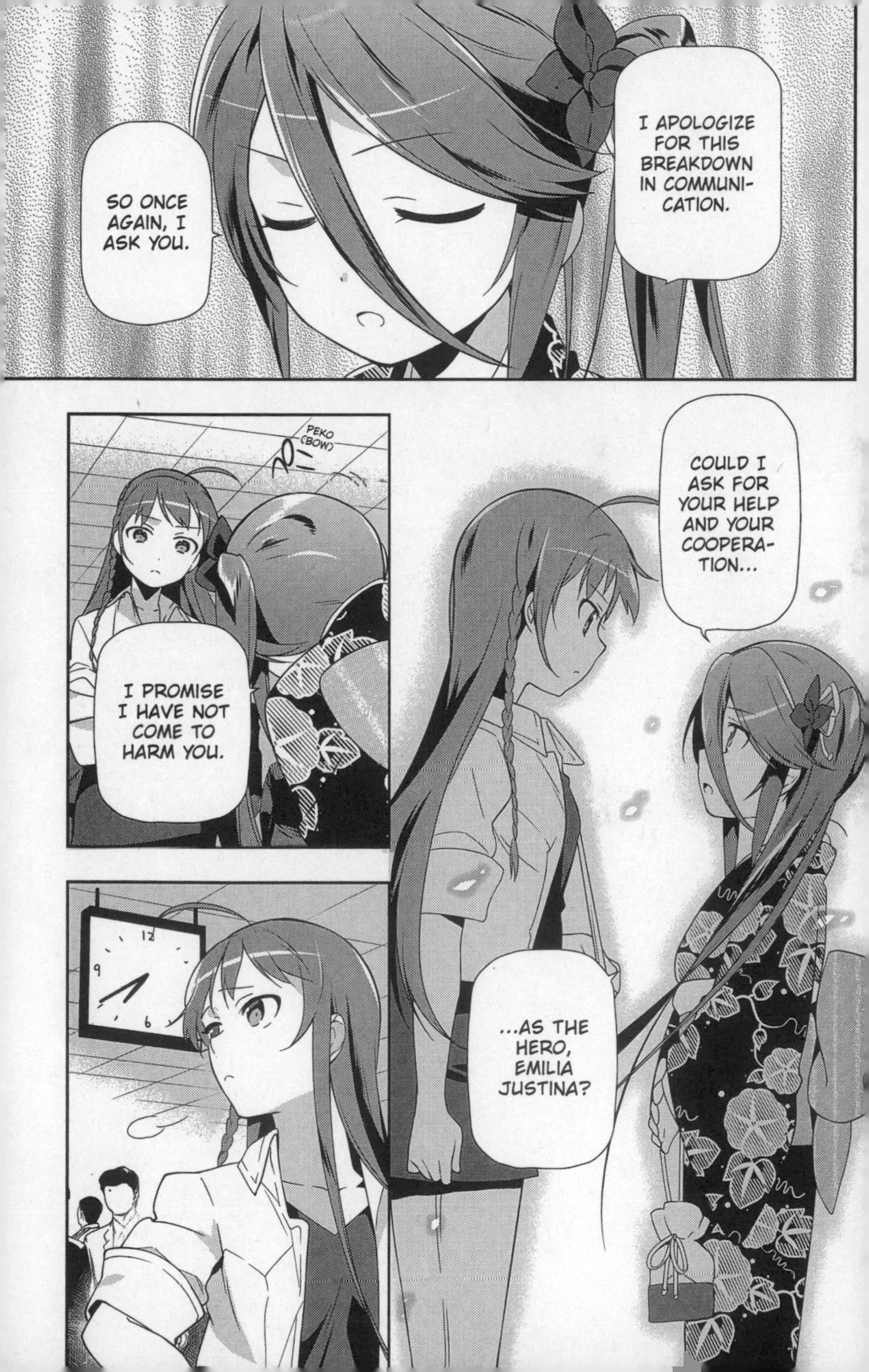
I APOLOGIZE FOR THIS BREAKDOWN IN COMMUNICATION.
SO ONCE AGAIN, I ASK YOU.
COULD I ASK FOR YOUR HELP AND YOUR COOPERATION...
...AS THE HERO, EMILIA JUSTINA?
PEKO (BOW)
I PROMISE I HAVE NOT COME TO HARM YOU.

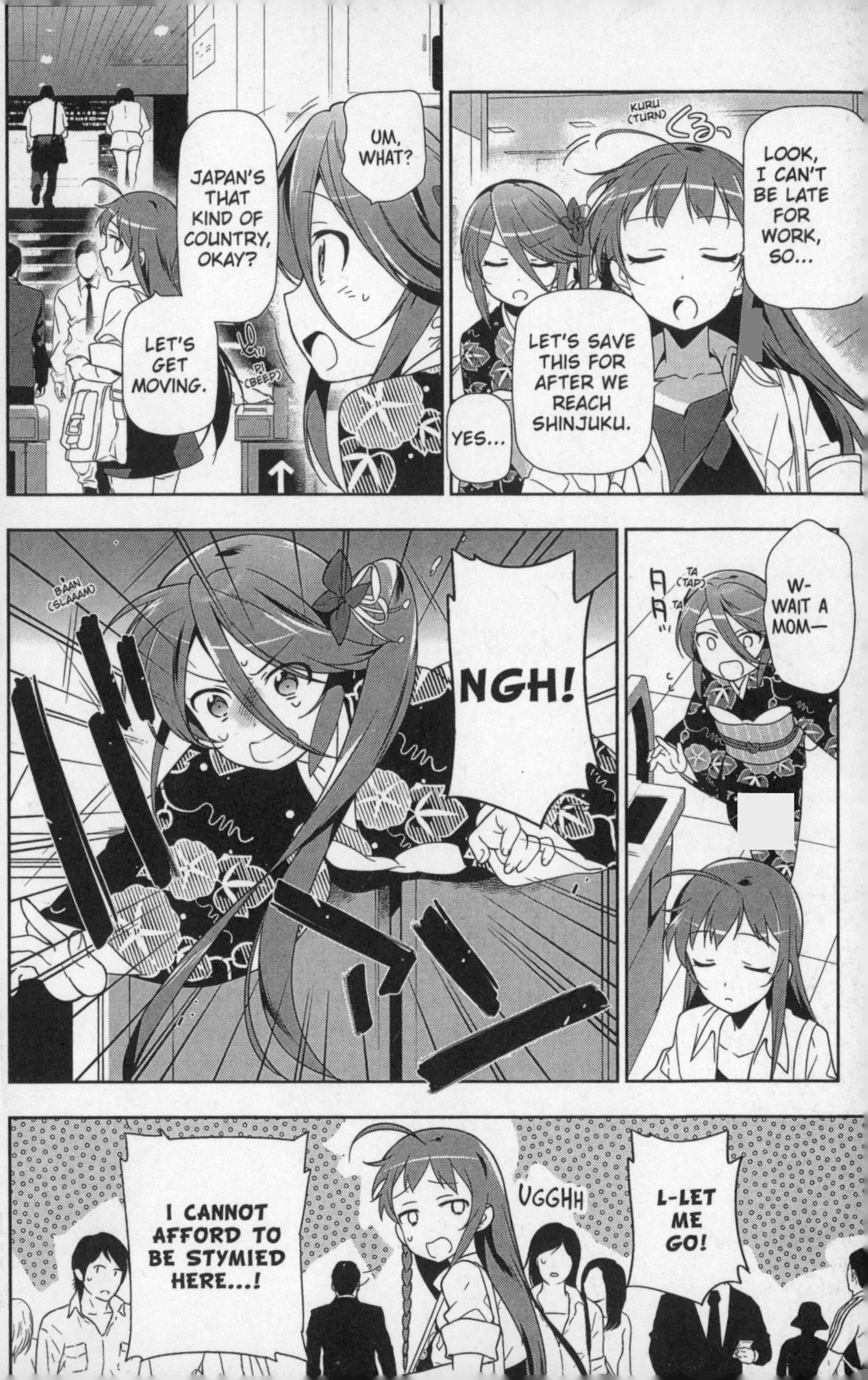
KURU (TURN)
LOOK, I CAN'T BE LATE FOR WORK, SO...
LET'S SAVE THIS FOR AFTER WE REACH SHINJUKU.
YES...
UM, WHAT?
JAPAN'S THAT KIND OF COUNTRY, OKAY?
PI (BEEP)
LET'S GET MOVING.
W- WAIT A MOM—
TA (TAP) TA
BAAN (SLAAAM)
NGH!
L-LET ME GO!
UGGHH
I CANNOT AFFORD TO BE STYMIED HERE...!

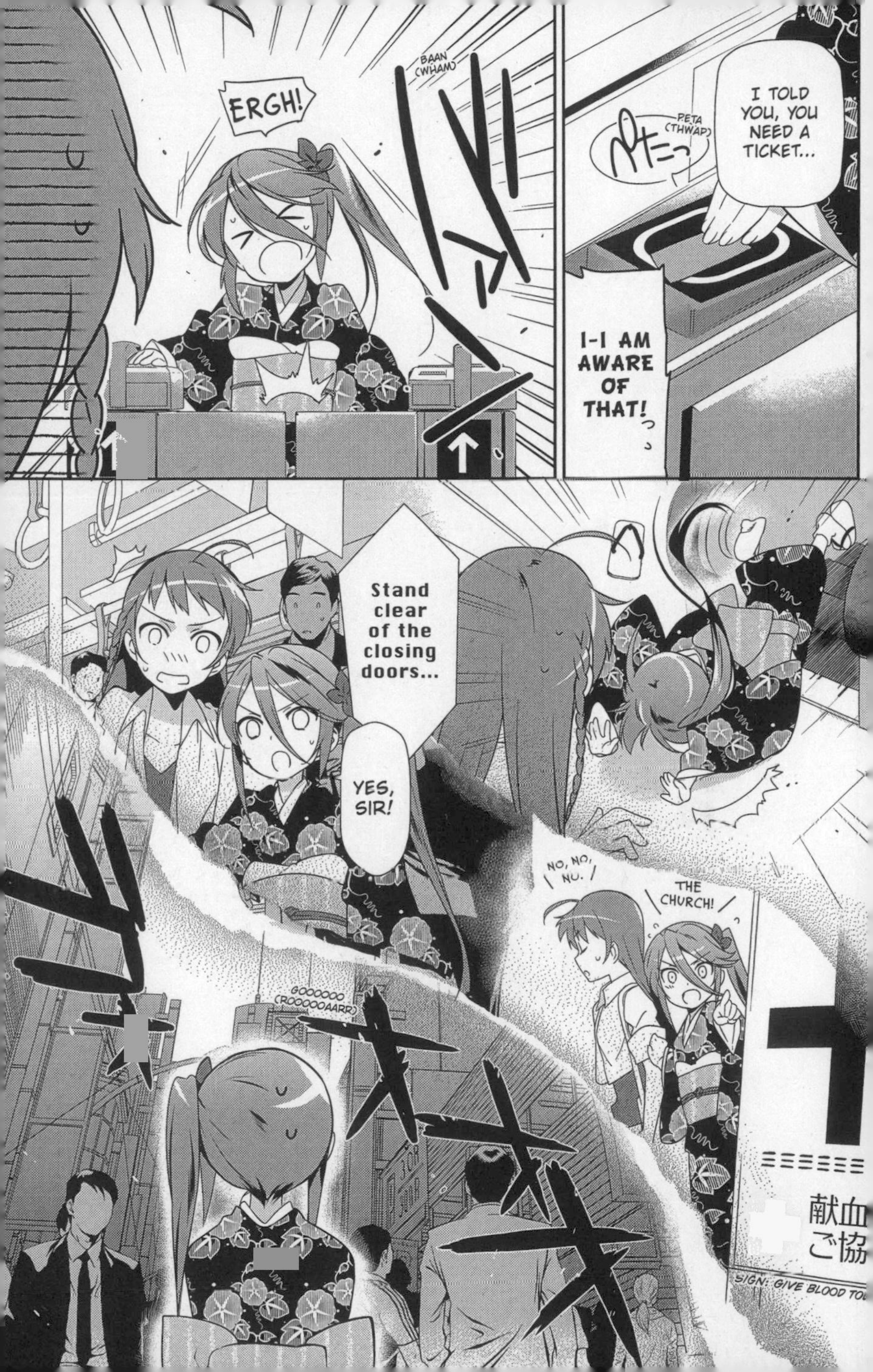
I TOLD YOU, YOU NEED A TICKET...
PETA (THWAP)
I-I AM AWARE OF THAT!
BAAN (WHAM)
ERGH!
Stand clear of the closing doors...
YES, SIR!
NO, NO, NO.
THE CHURCH!
GOOOOOO (ROOOOOAARR)
献血
ご協
SIGN: GIVE BLOOD TO

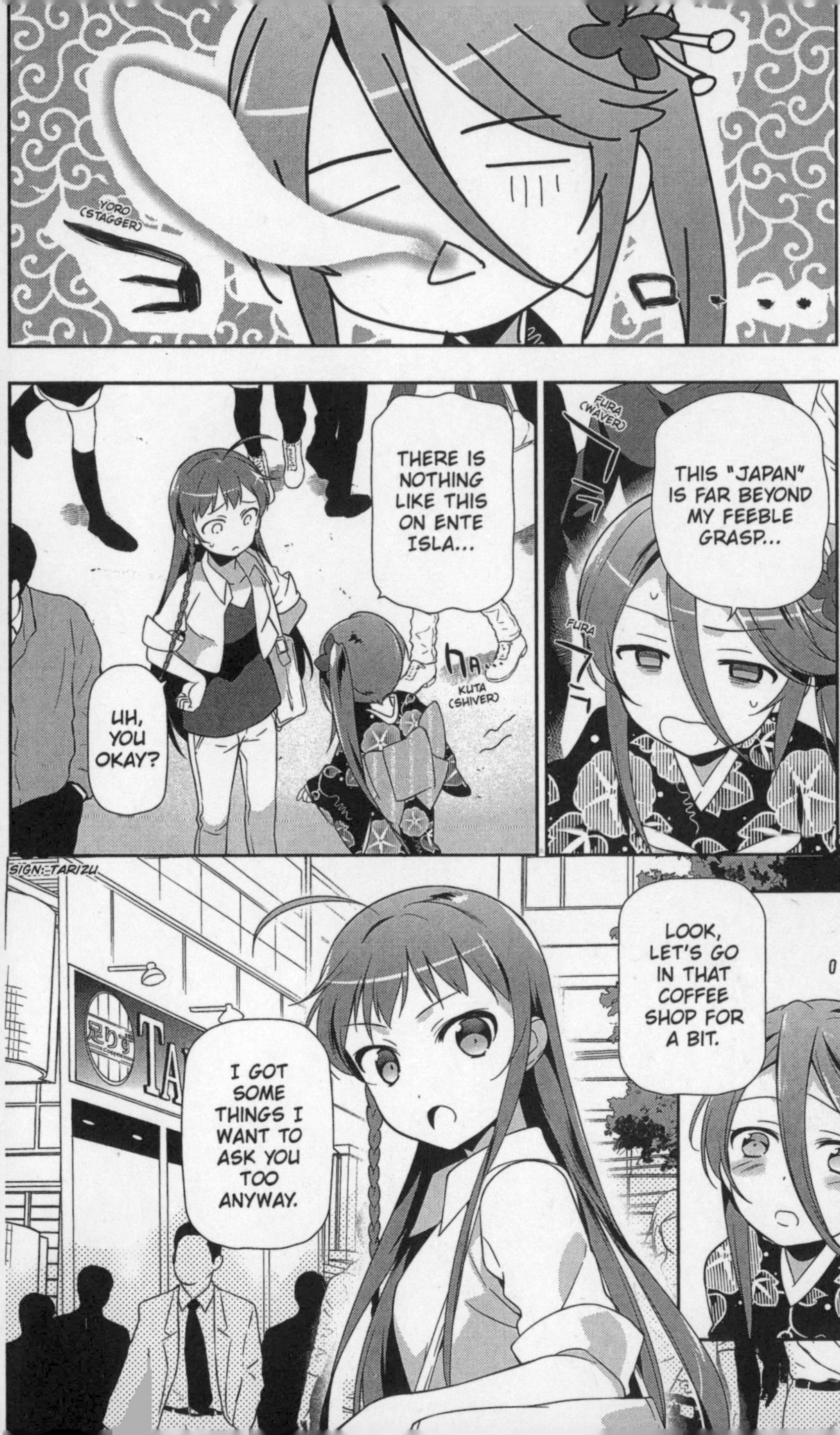
YORO (STAGGER)
FURA (WAVER)
THIS "JAPAN" IS FAR BEYOND MY FEEBLE GRASP...
FURA
THERE IS NOTHING LIKE THIS ON ENTE ISLA...
KUTA (SHIVER)
UH, YOU OKAY?
SIGN: TARIZU
LOOK, LET'S GO IN THAT COFFEE SHOP FOR A BIT.
I GOT SOME THINGS I WANT TO ASK YOU TOO ANYWAY.

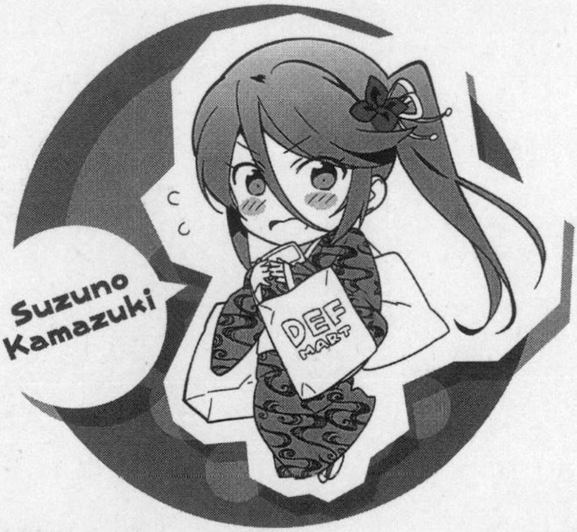
Suzuno Kamazuki
DEF MART

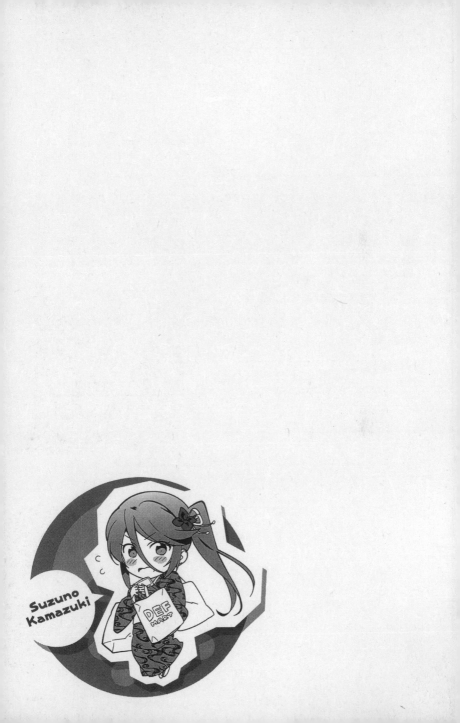

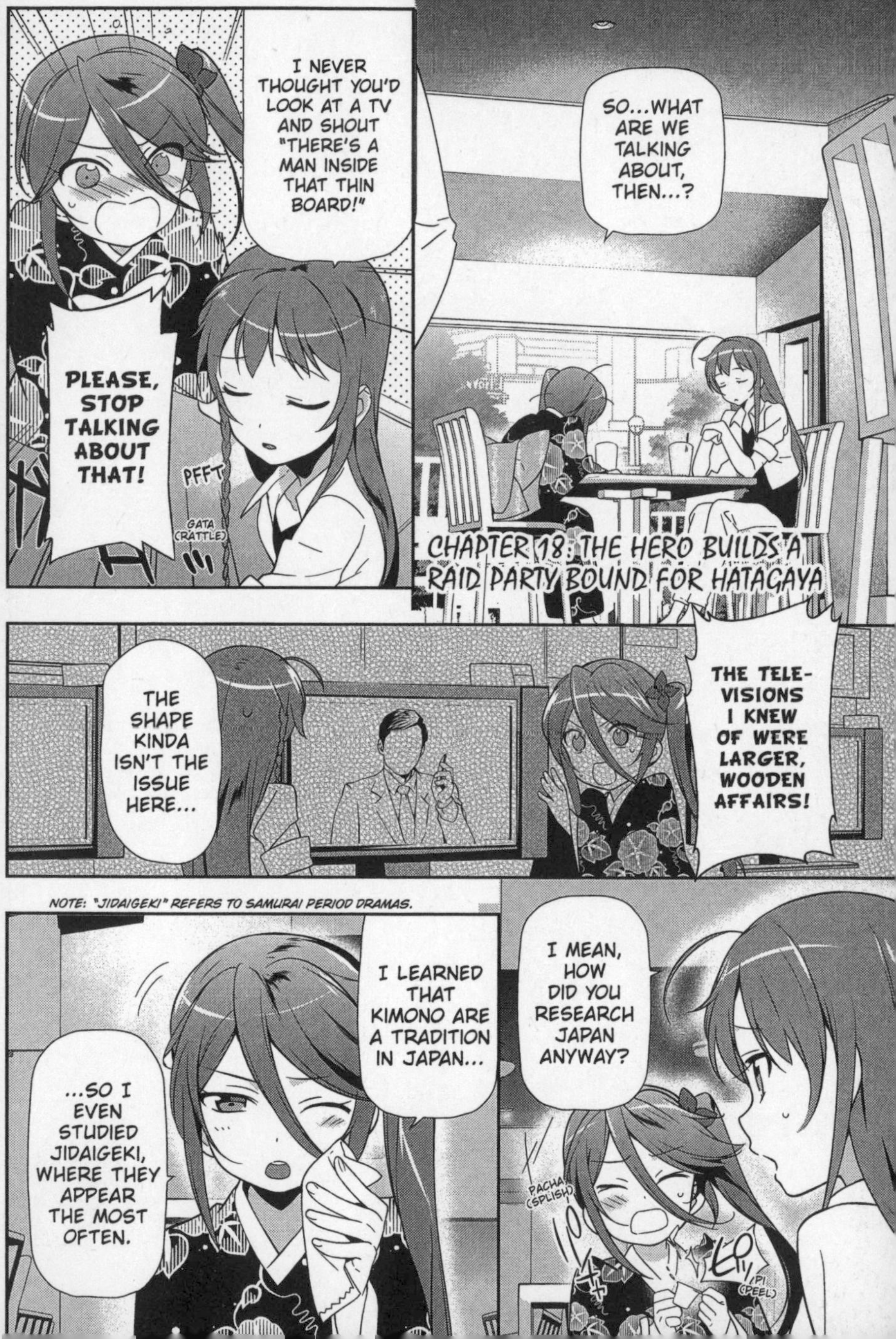
SO...WHAT ARE WE TALKING ABOUT, THEN...?
CHAPTER 18: THE HERO BUILDS A RAID PARTY BOUND FOR HATAGAYA
I NEVER THOUGHT YOU'D LOOK AT A TV AND SHOUT "THERE'S A MAN INSIDE THAT THIN BOARD!"
PLEASE, STOP TALKING ABOUT THAT!
PFFT
GATA (RATTLE)
THE TELE-VISIONS I KNEW OF WERE LARGER, WOODEN AFFAIRS!
THE SHAPE KINDA ISN'T THE ISSUE HERE...
I MEAN, HOW DID YOU RESEARCH JAPAN ANYWAY?
PI (PEEL)
PACHA (SPLISH)
I LEARNED THAT KIMONO ARE A TRADITION IN JAPAN...
...SO I EVEN STUDIED JIDAIGEKI, WHERE THEY APPEAR THE MOST OFTEN.

NOTE: "JIDAIGEKI" REFERS TO SAMURAI PERIOD DRAMAS.

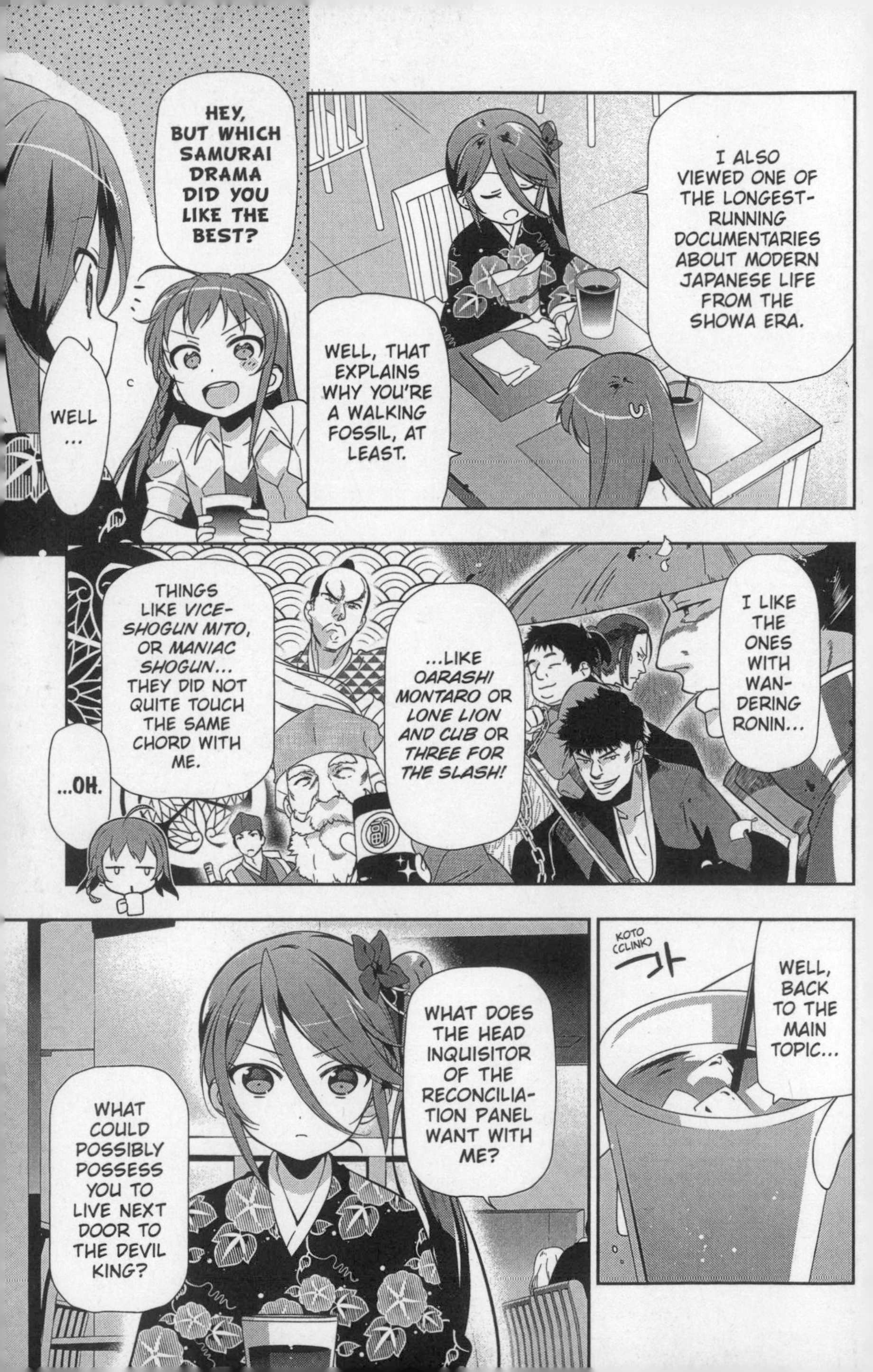
I ALSO VIEWED ONE OF THE LONGEST-RUNNING DOCUMENTARIES ABOUT MODERN JAPANESE LIFE FROM THE SHOWA ERA.
WELL, THAT EXPLAINS WHY YOU'RE A WALKING FOSSIL, AT LEAST.
HEY, BUT WHICH SAMURAI DRAMA DID YOU LIKE THE BEST?
WELL ...
I LIKE THE ONES WITH WAN-DERING RONIN...
...LIKE *OARASHI MONTARO* OR *LONE LION AND CUB* OR *THREE FOR THE SLASH!*
THINGS LIKE *VICE-SHOGUN MITO*, OR *MANIAC SHOGUN*... THEY DID NOT QUITE TOUCH THE SAME CHORD WITH ME.
...OH.
KOTO (CLINK)
コト
WELL, BACK TO THE MAIN TOPIC...
WHAT DOES THE HEAD INQUISITOR OF THE RECONCILIA-TION PANEL WANT WITH ME?
WHAT COULD POSSIBLY POSSESS YOU TO LIVE NEXT DOOR TO THE DEVIL KING?

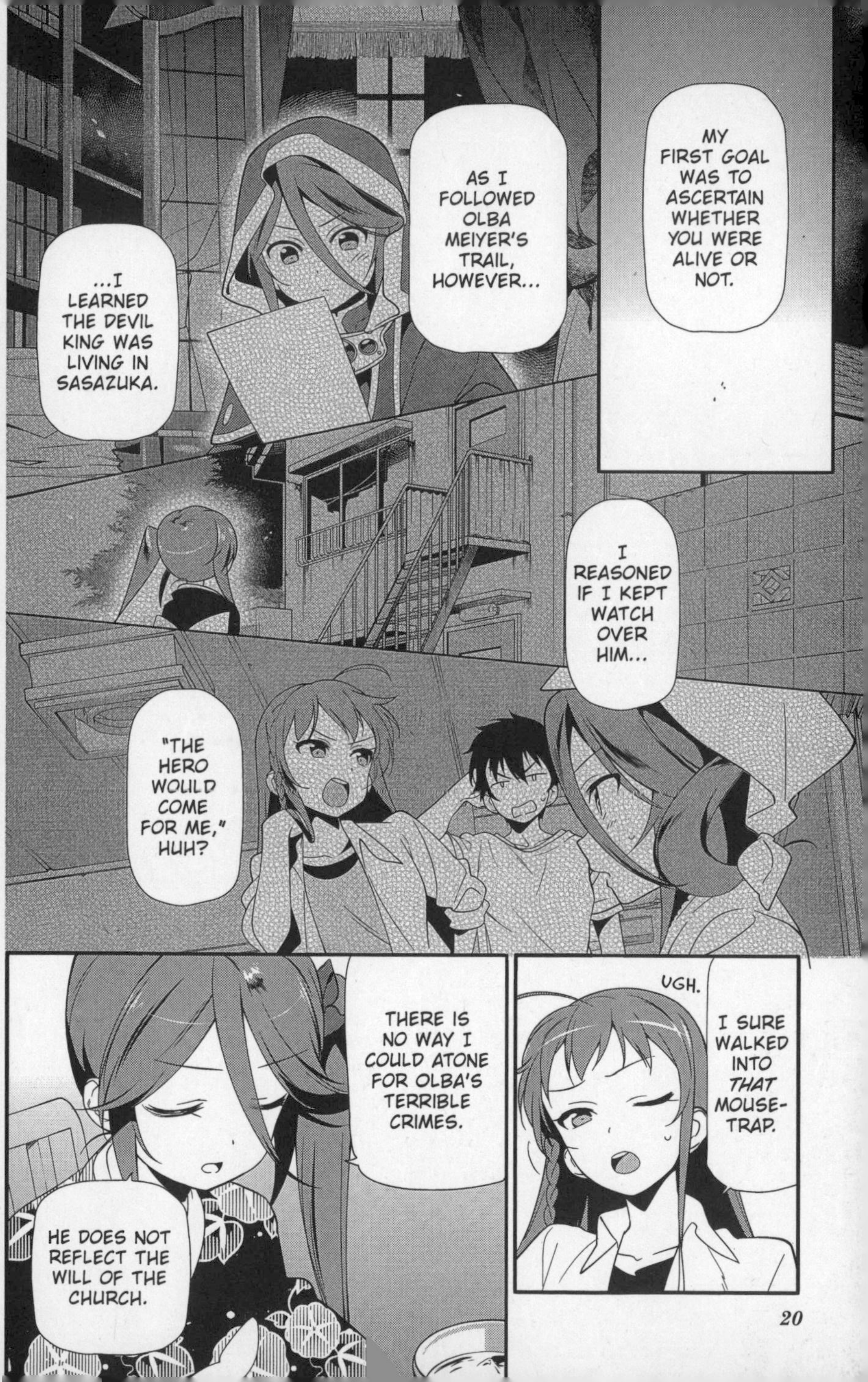
MY FIRST GOAL WAS TO ASCERTAIN WHETHER YOU WERE ALIVE OR NOT.
AS I FOLLOWED OLBA MEIYER'S TRAIL, HOWEVER...
...I LEARNED THE DEVIL KING WAS LIVING IN SASAZUKA.
I REASONED IF I KEPT WATCH OVER HIM...
"THE HERO WOULD COME FOR ME," HUH?
UGH.
I SURE WALKED INTO *THAT* MOUSE-TRAP.
THERE IS NO WAY I COULD ATONE FOR OLBA'S TERRIBLE CRIMES.
HE DOES NOT REFLECT THE WILL OF THE CHURCH.

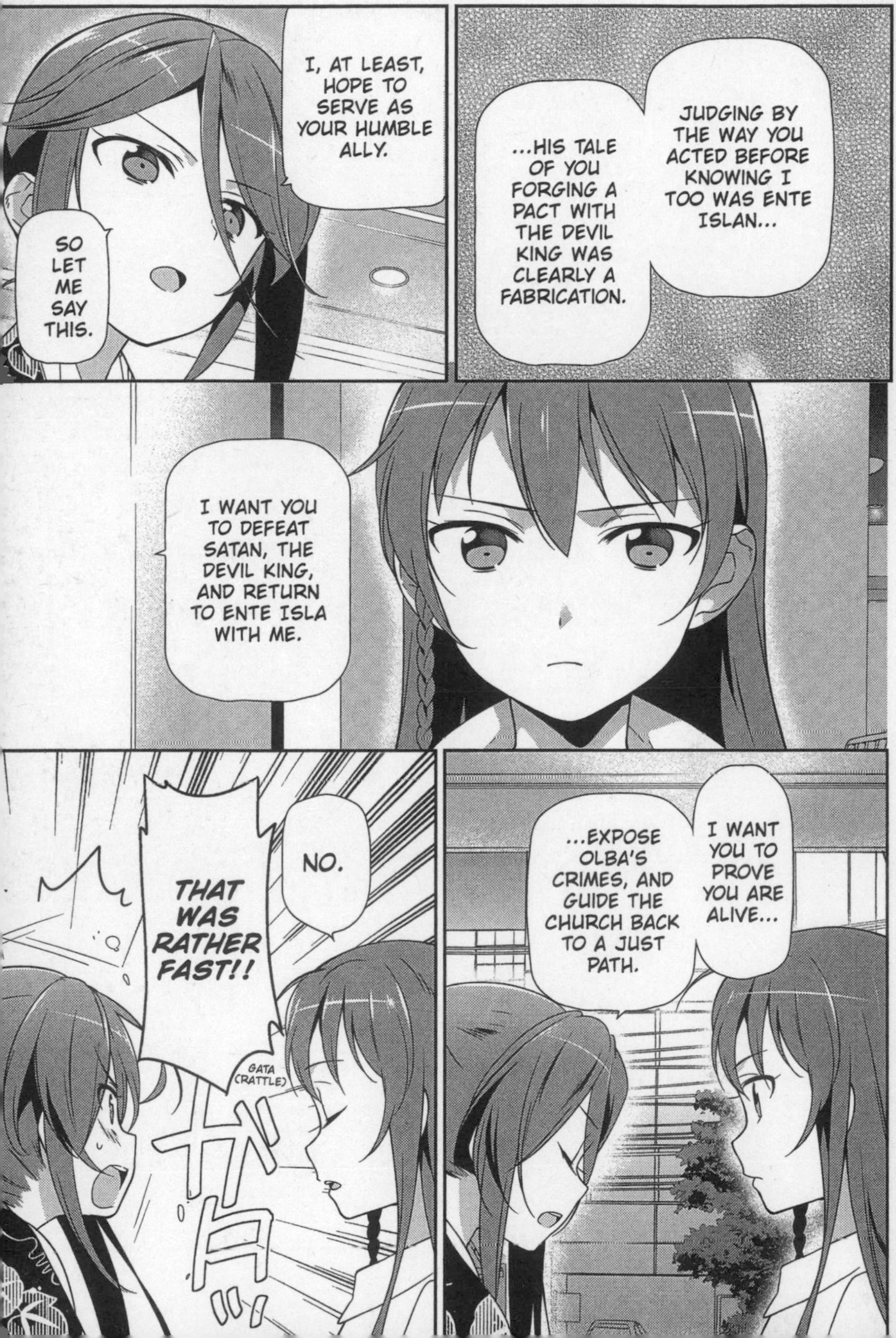
JUDGING BY THE WAY YOU ACTED BEFORE KNOWING I TOO WAS ENTE ISLAN...
...HIS TALE OF YOU FORGING A PACT WITH THE DEVIL KING WAS CLEARLY A FABRICATION.
I, AT LEAST, HOPE TO SERVE AS YOUR HUMBLE ALLY.
SO LET ME SAY THIS.
I WANT YOU TO DEFEAT SATAN, THE DEVIL KING, AND RETURN TO ENTE ISLA WITH ME.
I WANT YOU TO PROVE YOU ARE ALIVE...
...EXPOSE OLBA'S CRIMES, AND GUIDE THE CHURCH BACK TO A JUST PATH.
NO.
THAT WAS RATHER FAST!!
GATA (RATTLE)

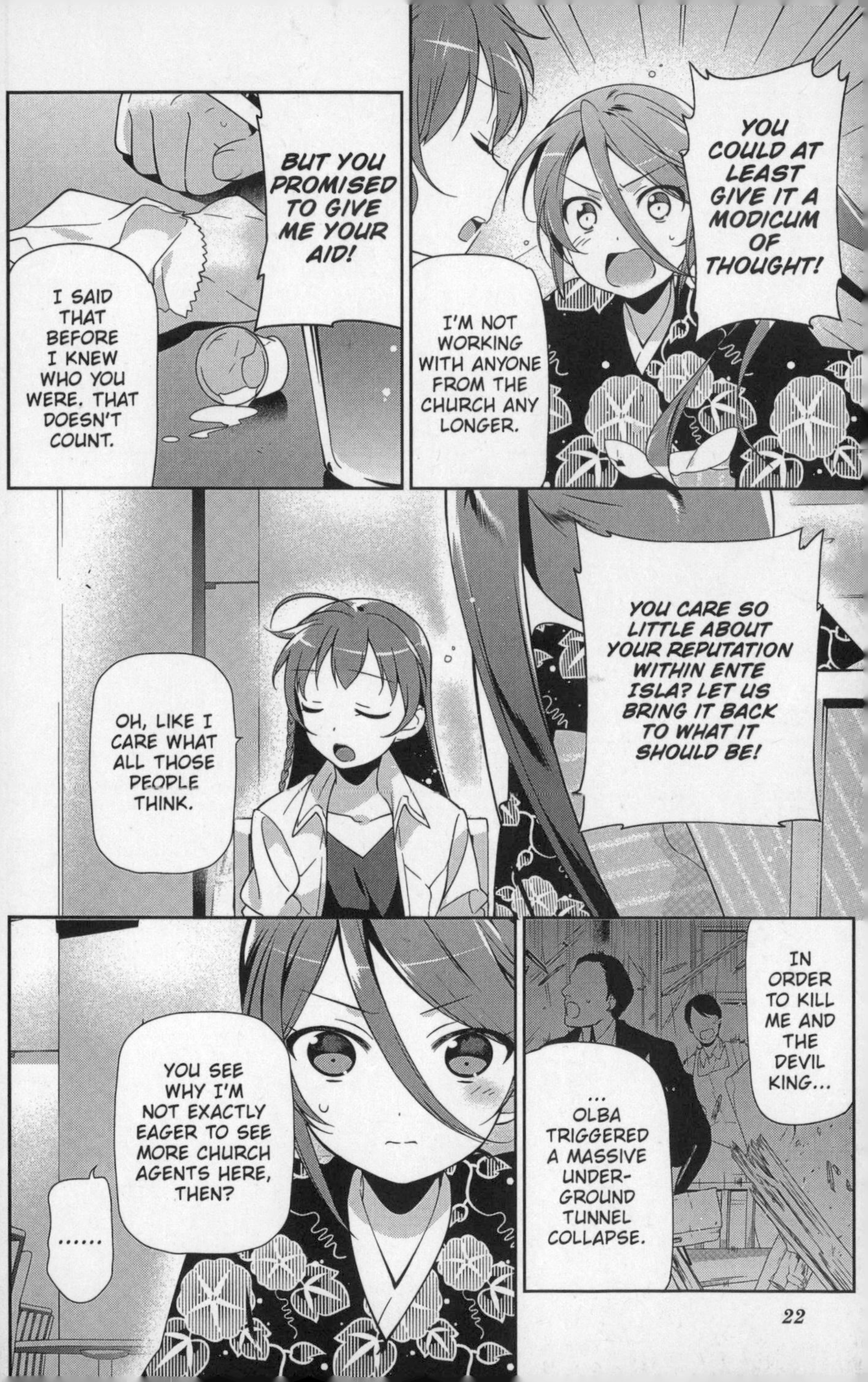
YOU COULD AT LEAST GIVE IT A MODICUM OF THOUGHT!
I'M NOT WORKING WITH ANYONE FROM THE CHURCH ANY LONGER.
BUT YOU PROMISED TO GIVE ME YOUR AID!
I SAID THAT BEFORE I KNEW WHO YOU WERE. THAT DOESN'T COUNT.
YOU CARE SO LITTLE ABOUT YOUR REPUTATION WITHIN ENTE ISLA? LET US BRING IT BACK TO WHAT IT SHOULD BE!
OH, LIKE I CARE WHAT ALL THOSE PEOPLE THINK.
IN ORDER TO KILL ME AND THE DEVIL KING...
...OLBA TRIGGERED A MASSIVE UNDER-GROUND TUNNEL COLLAPSE.
YOU SEE WHY I'M NOT EXACTLY EAGER TO SEE MORE CHURCH AGENTS HERE, THEN?
......

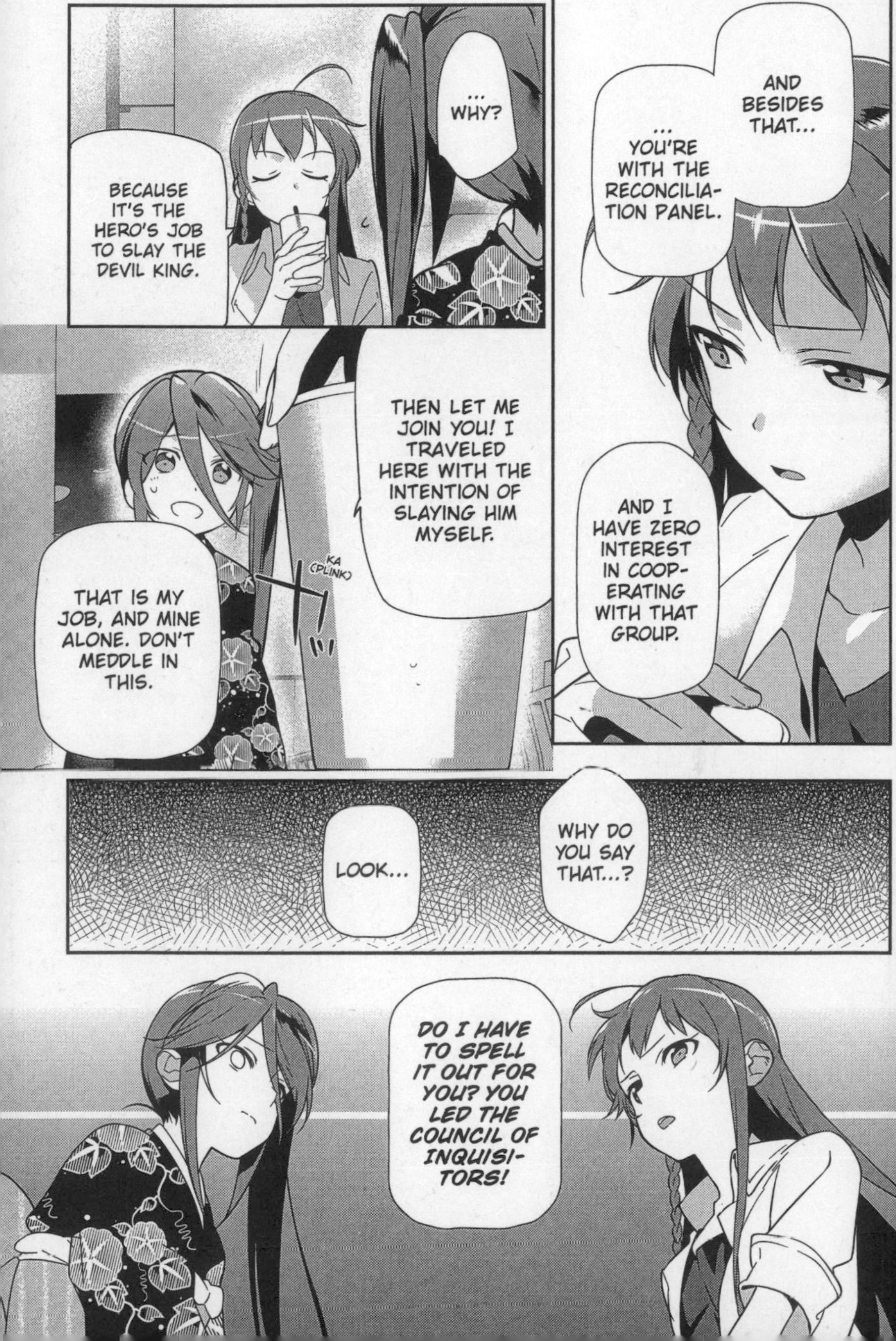
AND BESIDES THAT...
...YOU'RE WITH THE RECONCILIATION PANEL.
AND I HAVE ZERO INTEREST IN COOPERATING WITH THAT GROUP.
...WHY?
BECAUSE IT'S THE HERO'S JOB TO SLAY THE DEVIL KING.
THEN LET ME JOIN YOU! I TRAVELED HERE WITH THE INTENTION OF SLAYING HIM MYSELF.
KA (PLINK)
THAT IS MY JOB, AND MINE ALONE. DON'T MEDDLE IN THIS.
WHY DO YOU SAY THAT...?
LOOK...
*DO I HAVE TO SPELL IT OUT FOR YOU? YOU LED THE COUNCIL OF INQUISITORS!*

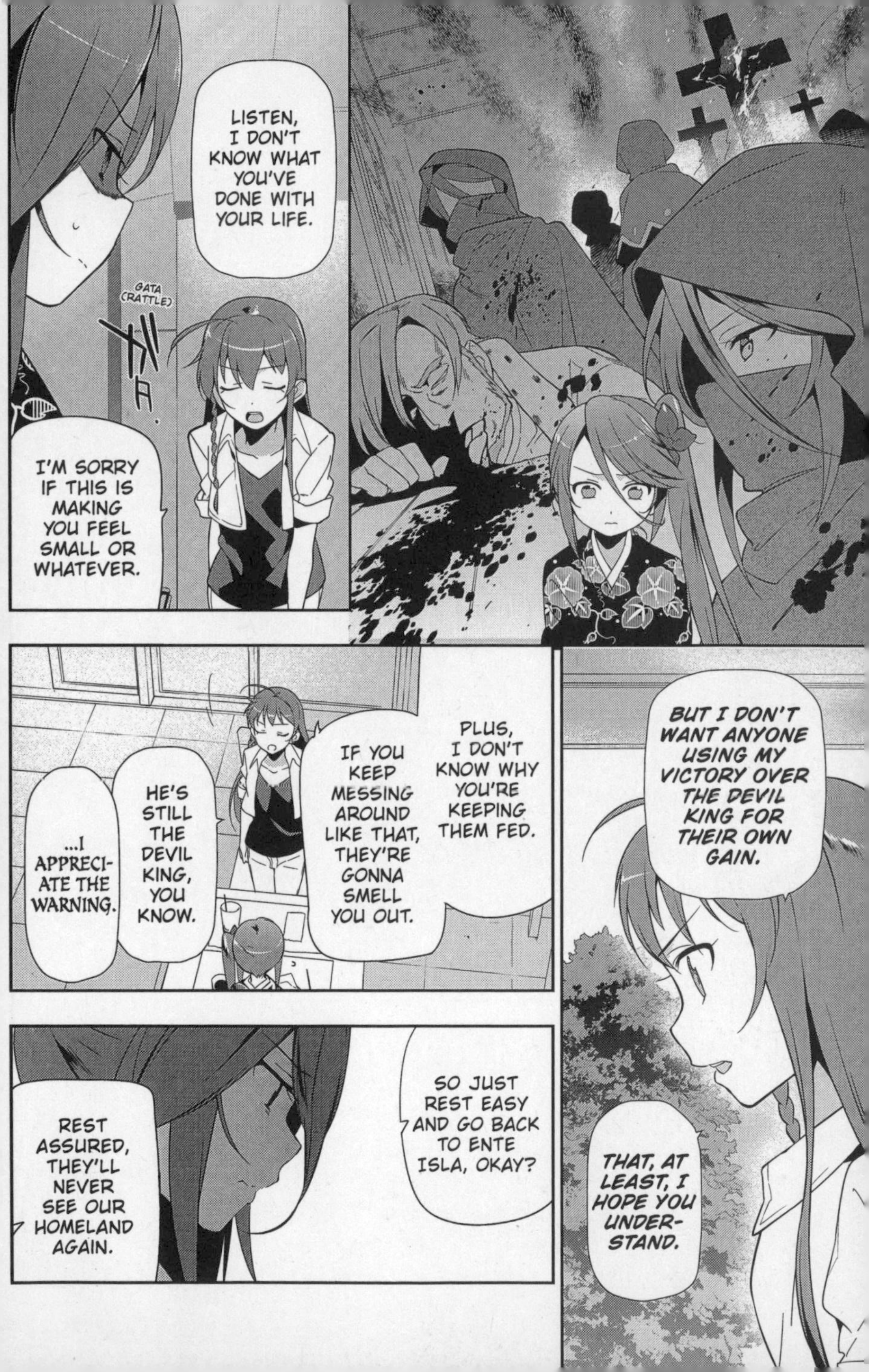
LISTEN, I DON'T KNOW WHAT YOU'VE DONE WITH YOUR LIFE.
GATA (RATTLE)
I'M SORRY IF THIS IS MAKING YOU FEEL SMALL OR WHATEVER.
BUT I DON'T WANT ANYONE USING MY VICTORY OVER THE DEVIL KING FOR THEIR OWN GAIN.
THAT, AT LEAST, I HOPE YOU UNDERSTAND.
PLUS, I DON'T KNOW WHY YOU'RE KEEPING THEM FED.
IF YOU KEEP MESSING AROUND LIKE THAT, THEY'RE GONNA SMELL YOU OUT.
HE'S STILL THE DEVIL KING, YOU KNOW.
...I APPRECI-ATE THE WARNING.
SO JUST REST EASY AND GO BACK TO ENTE ISLA, OKAY?
REST ASSURED, THEY'LL NEVER SEE OUR HOMELAND AGAIN.

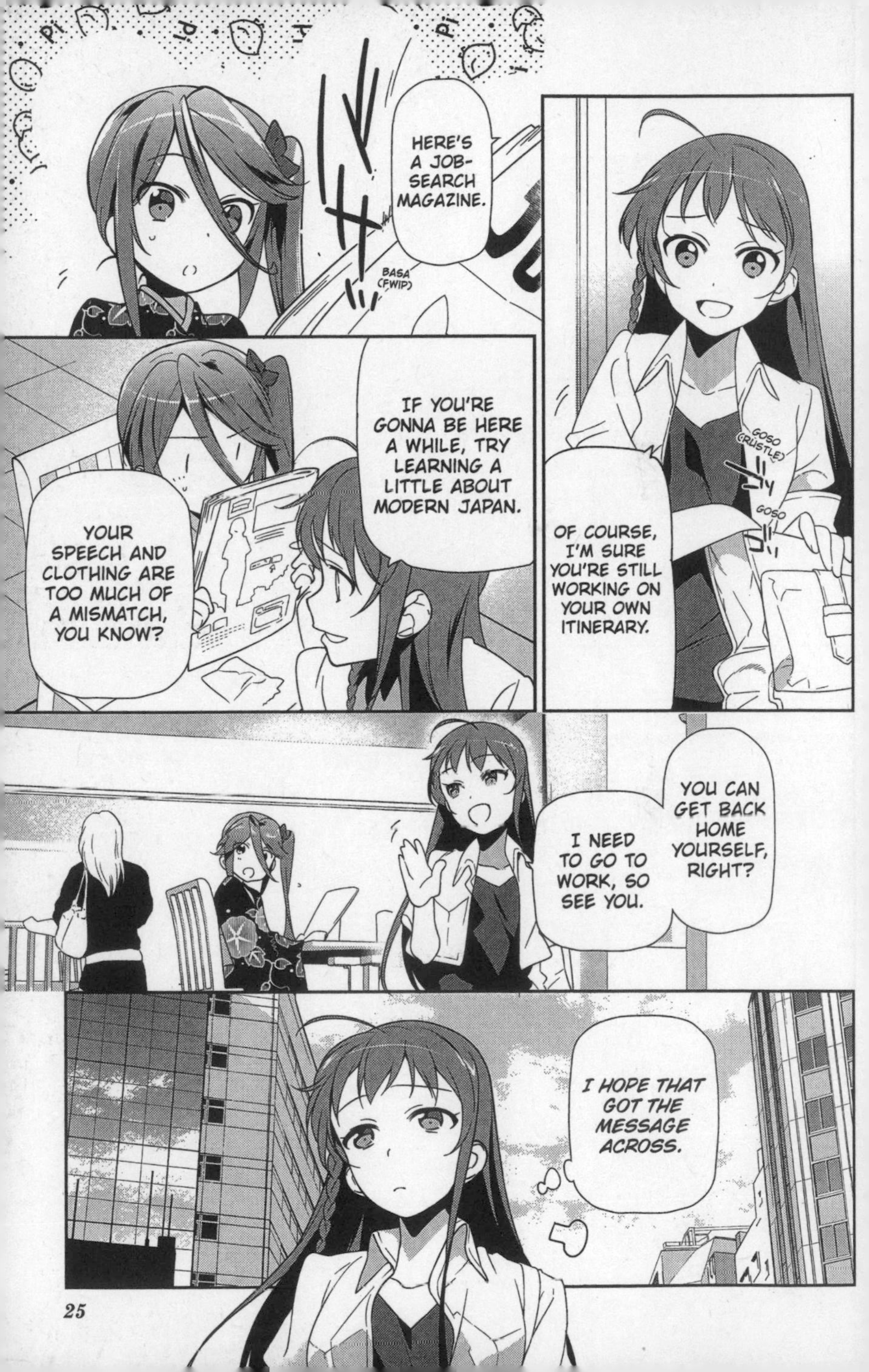
GOSO (RUSTLE)
GOSO
OF COURSE, I'M SURE YOU'RE STILL WORKING ON YOUR OWN ITINERARY.
Pi
Pi
Pi
Pi
HERE'S A JOB-SEARCH MAGAZINE.
BASA (FWIP)
IF YOU'RE GONNA BE HERE A WHILE, TRY LEARNING A LITTLE ABOUT MODERN JAPAN.
YOUR SPEECH AND CLOTHING ARE TOO MUCH OF A MISMATCH, YOU KNOW?
YOU CAN GET BACK HOME YOURSELF, RIGHT?
I NEED TO GO TO WORK, SO SEE YOU.
I HOPE THAT GOT THE MESSAGE ACROSS.

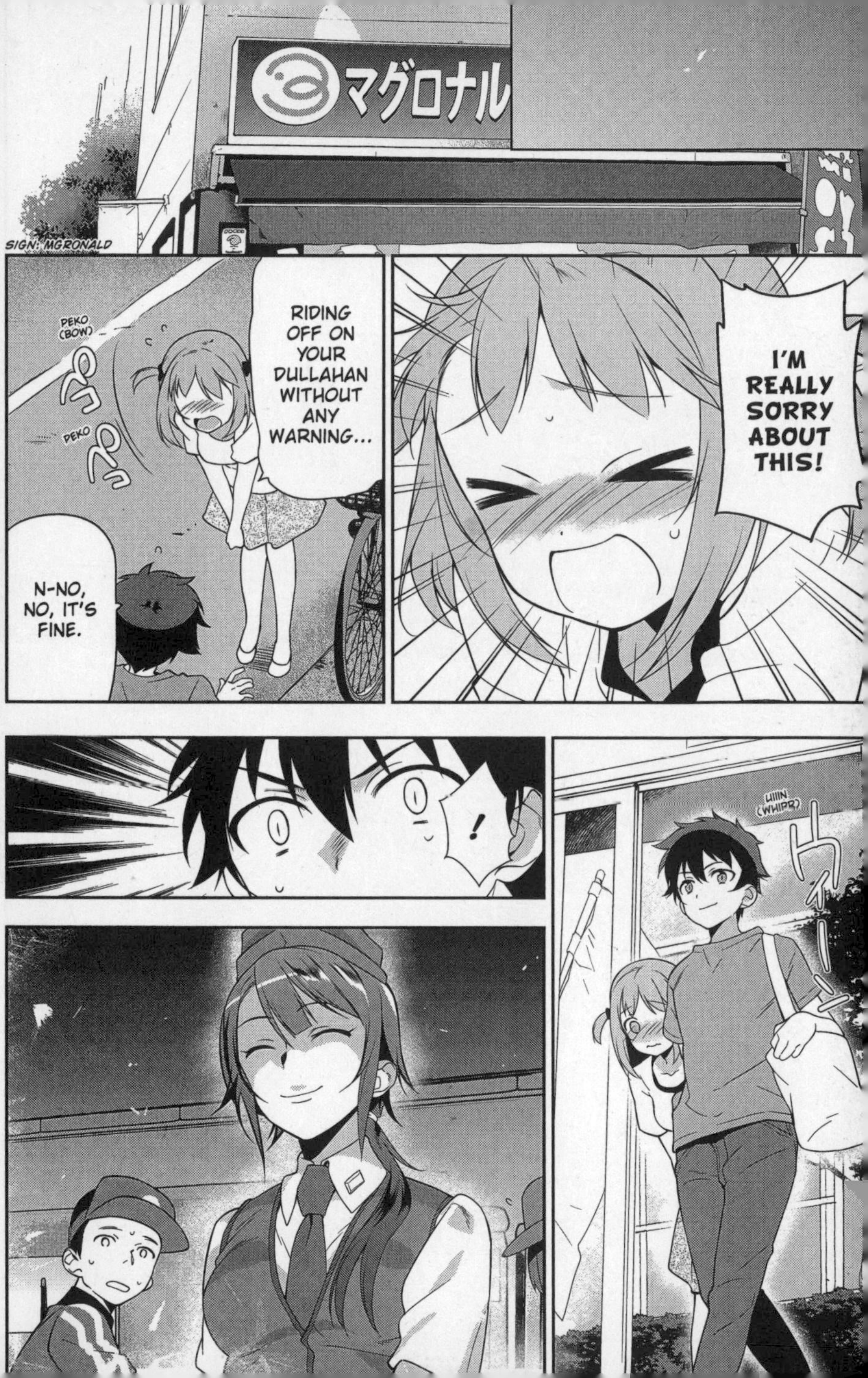
マグロナル
SIGN: MGRONALD
I'M REALLY SORRY ABOUT THIS!
PEKO (BOW)
RIDING OFF ON YOUR DULLAHAN WITHOUT ANY WARNING...
PEKO
N-NO, NO, IT'S FINE.
HIIIN (WHIRR)
!

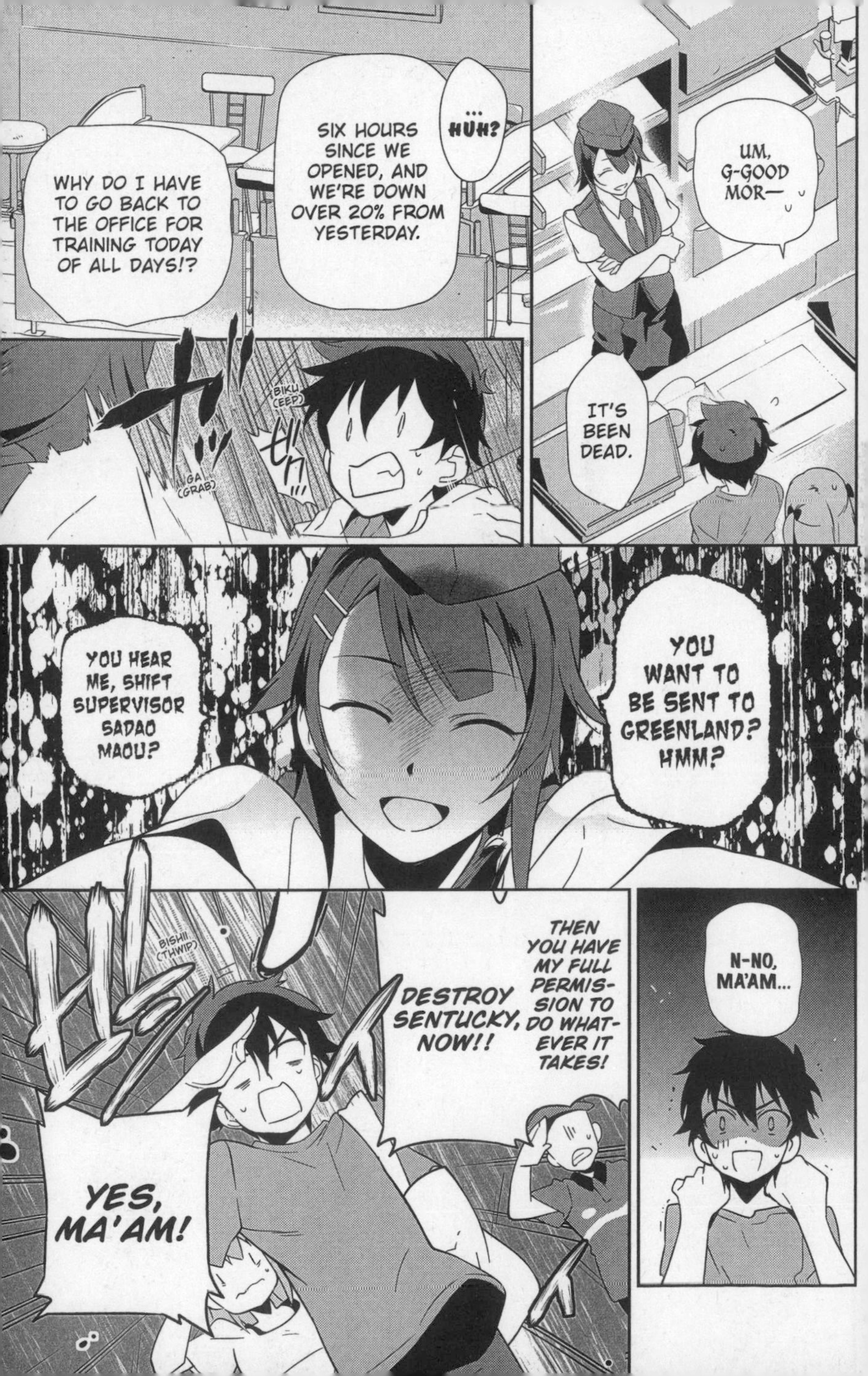

UM, G-GOOD MOR—
IT'S BEEN DEAD.
...HUH?
SIX HOURS SINCE WE OPENED, AND WE'RE DOWN OVER 20% FROM YESTERDAY.
WHY DO I HAVE TO GO BACK TO THE OFFICE FOR TRAINING TODAY OF ALL DAYS!?
BIKU (EEP)
GA (GRAB)
YOU WANT TO BE SENT TO GREENLAND? HMM?
YOU HEAR ME, SHIFT SUPERVISOR SADAO MAOU?
N-NO, MA'AM...
THEN YOU HAVE MY FULL PERMIS-SION TO DO WHAT-EVER IT TAKES!
DESTROY SENTUCKY, NOW!!
BISHI! (THWIP)
YES, MA'AM!

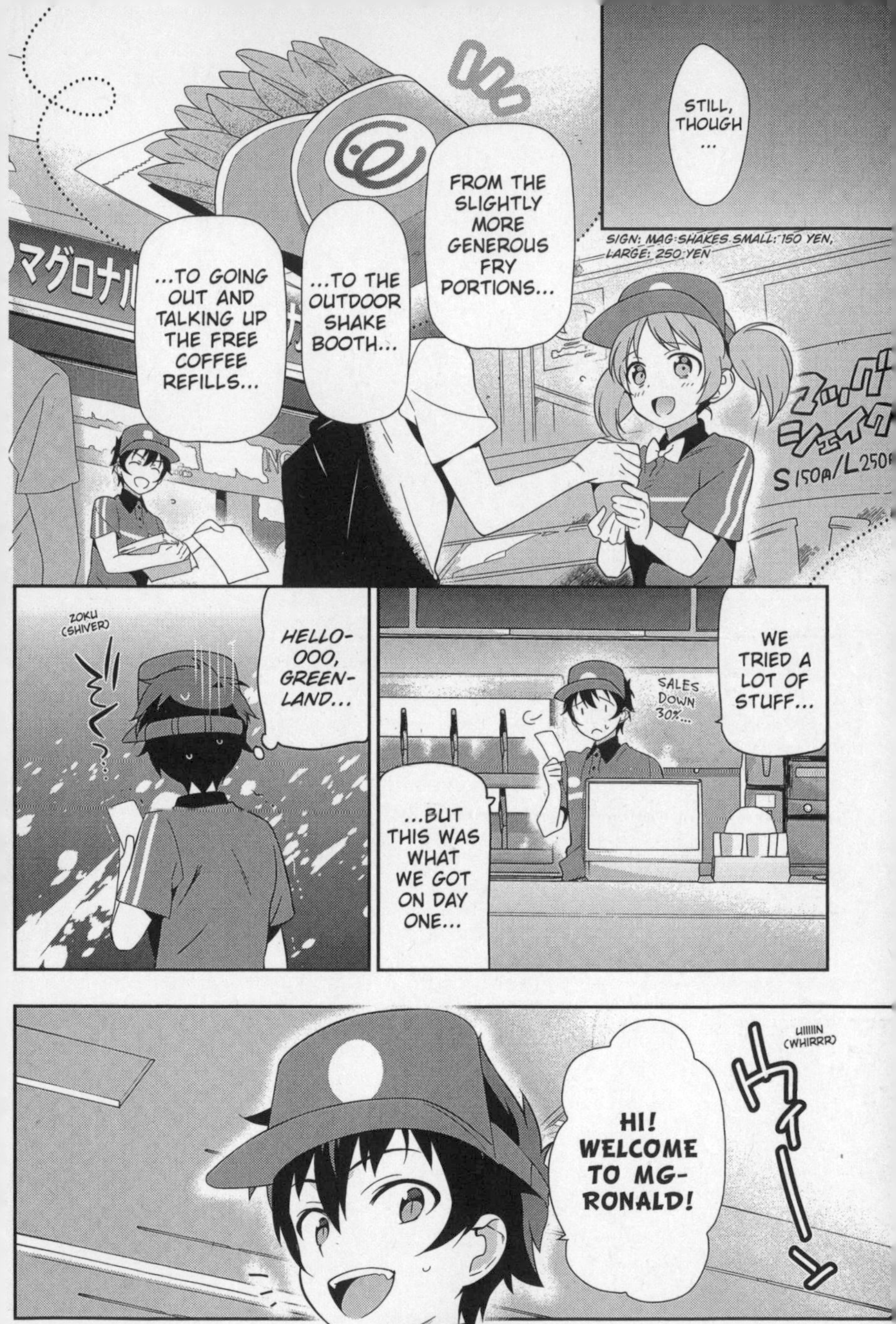
STILL, THOUGH...
FROM THE SLIGHTLY MORE GENEROUS FRY PORTIONS...
...TO THE OUTDOOR SHAKE BOOTH...
...TO GOING OUT AND TALKING UP THE FREE COFFEE REFILLS...
SIGN: MAG SHAKES SMALL: 150 YEN, LARGE: 250 YEN
WE TRIED A LOT OF STUFF...
SALES DOWN 30%...
...BUT THIS WAS WHAT WE GOT ON DAY ONE...
ZOKU (SHIVER)
HELLO-OOO, GREEN-LAND...
UIIIIN (WHIRRR)
HI! WELCOME TO MG-RONALD!

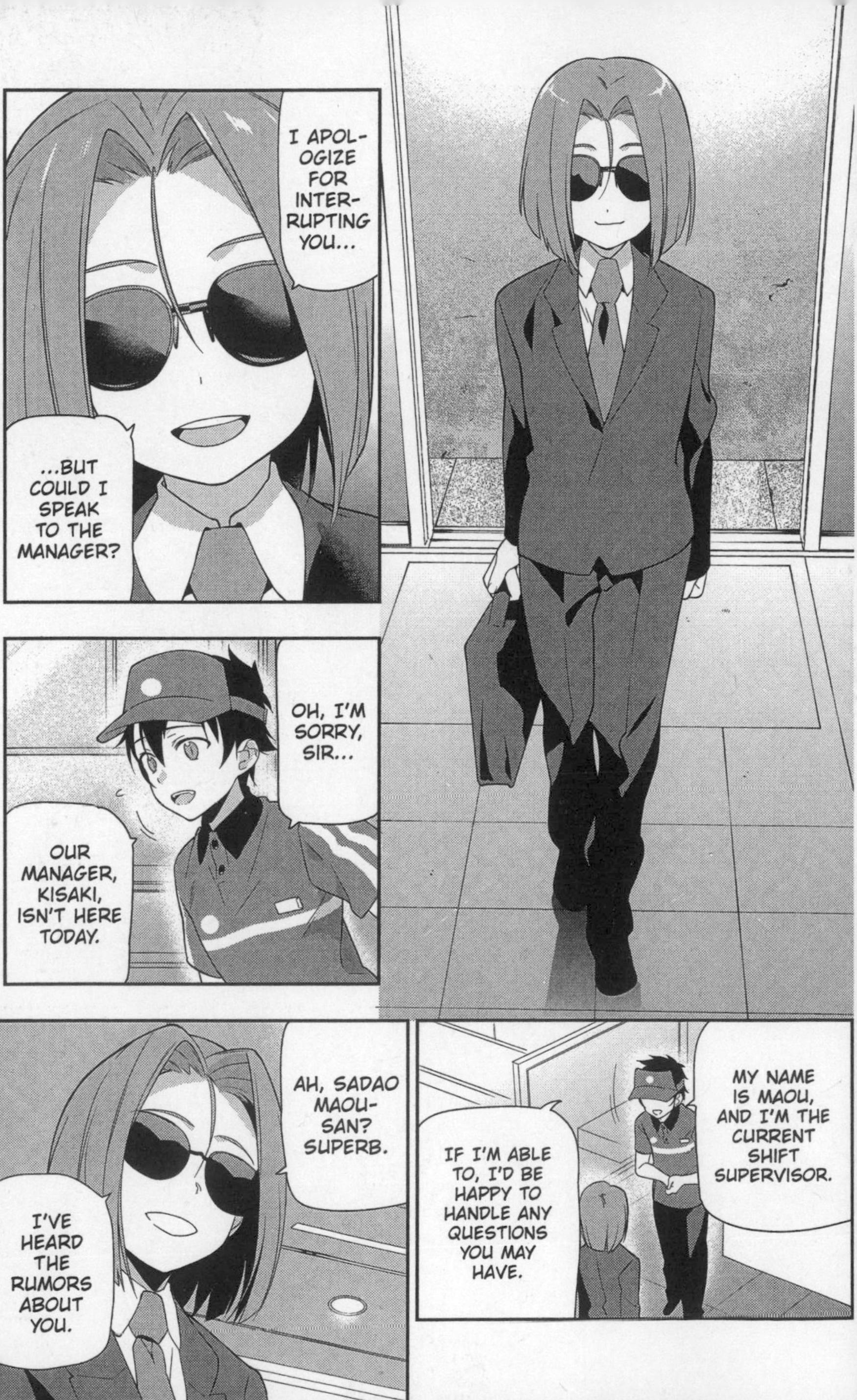
I APOLOGIZE FOR INTERRUPTING YOU...
...BUT COULD I SPEAK TO THE MANAGER?
OH, I'M SORRY, SIR...
OUR MANAGER, KISAKI, ISN'T HERE TODAY.
MY NAME IS MAOU, AND I'M THE CURRENT SHIFT SUPERVISOR.
IF I'M ABLE TO, I'D BE HAPPY TO HANDLE ANY QUESTIONS YOU MAY HAVE.
AH, SADAO MAOU-SAN? SUPERB.
I'VE HEARD THE RUMORS ABOUT YOU.

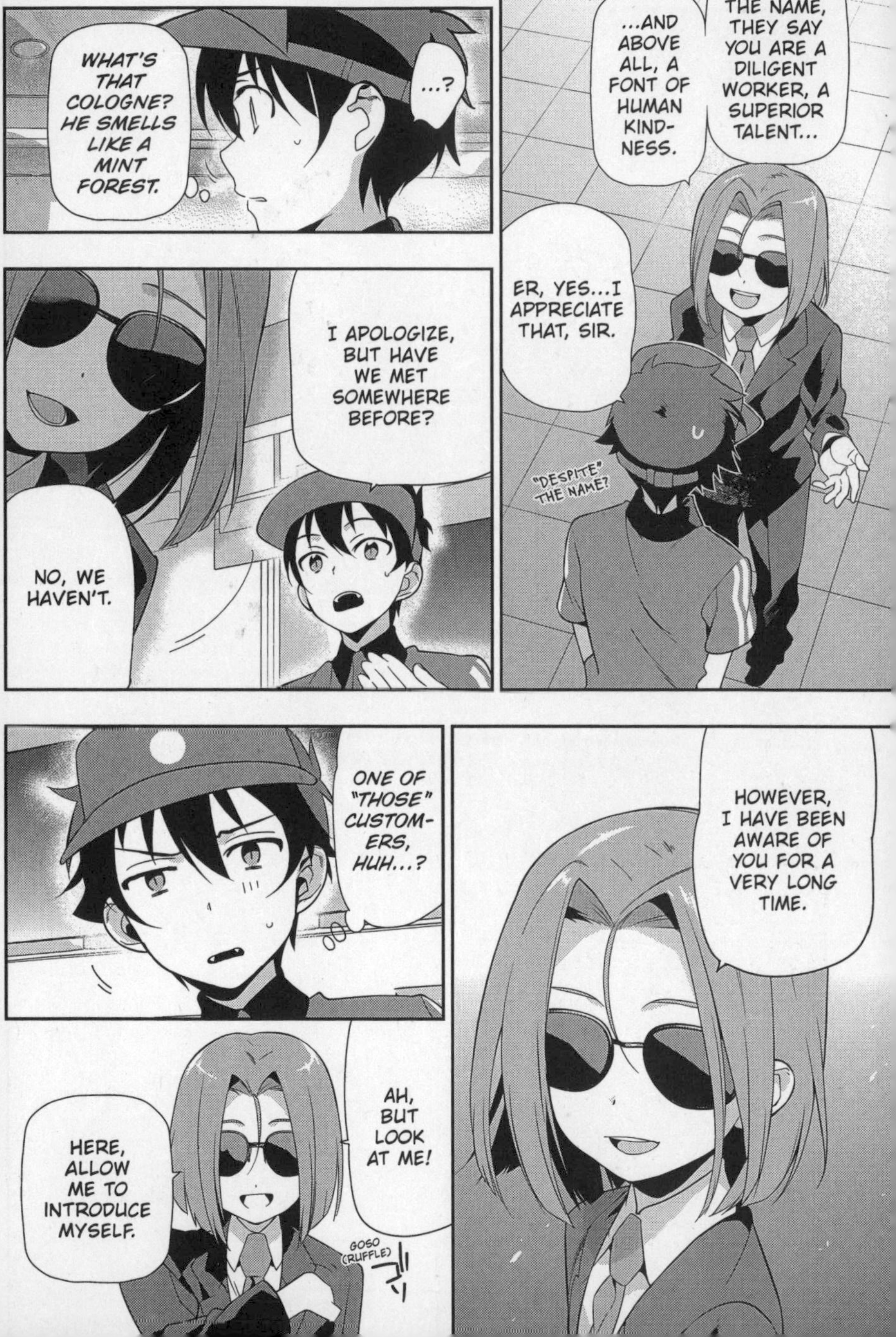
DESPITE THE NAME, THEY SAY YOU ARE A DILIGENT WORKER, A SUPERIOR TALENT...
...AND ABOVE ALL, A FONT OF HUMAN KIND-NESS.
ER, YES...I APPRECIATE THAT, SIR.
"DESPITE" THE NAME?
...?
WHAT'S THAT COLOGNE? HE SMELLS LIKE A MINT FOREST.
I APOLOGIZE, BUT HAVE WE MET SOMEWHERE BEFORE?
NO, WE HAVEN'T.
HOWEVER, I HAVE BEEN AWARE OF YOU FOR A VERY LONG TIME.
ONE OF "THOSE" CUSTOM-ERS, HUH...?
AH, BUT LOOK AT ME!
HERE, ALLOW ME TO INTRODUCE MYSELF.
GOSO (RUFFLE)

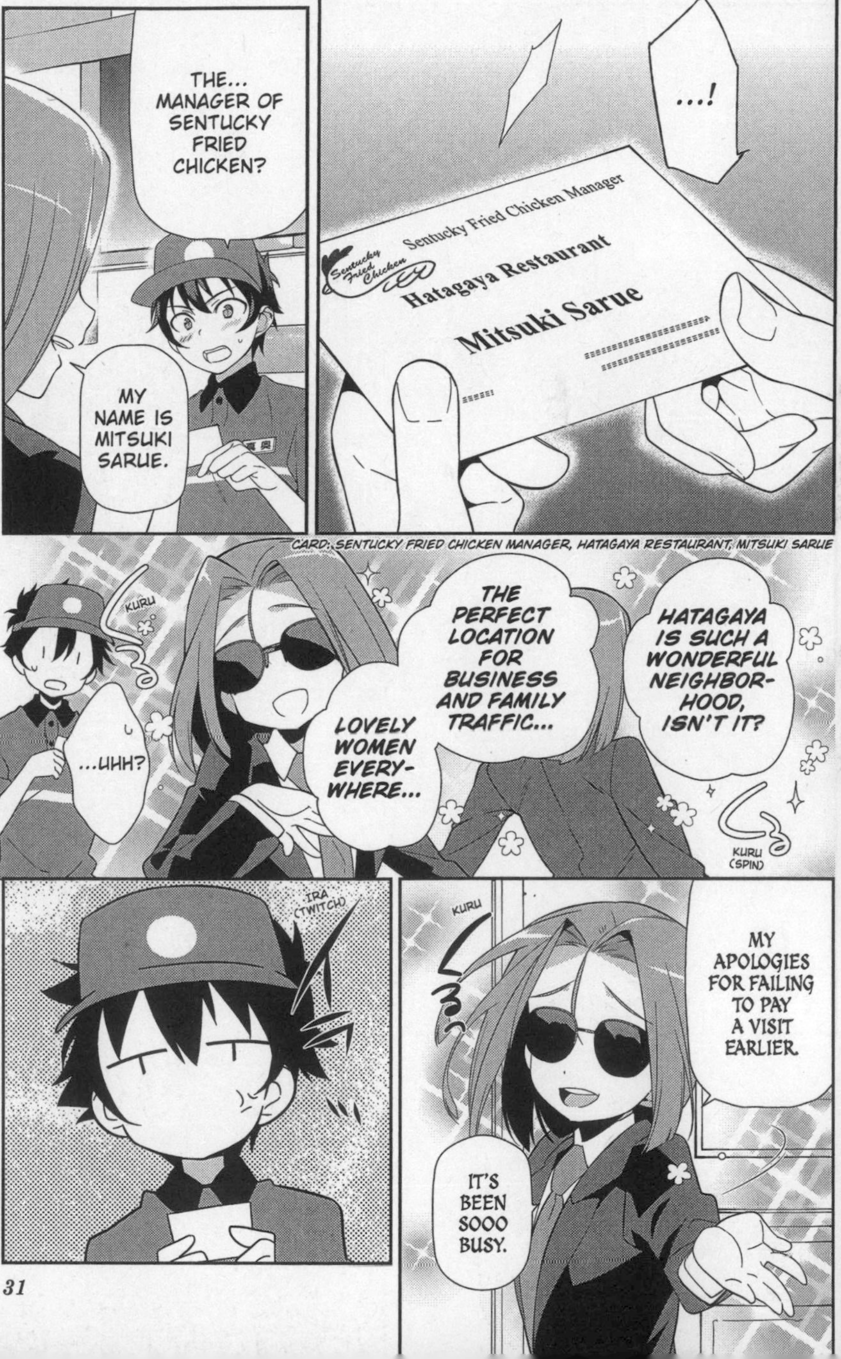
...!
Sentucky Fried Chicken
Sentucky Fried Chicken Manager
Hatagaya Restaurant
Mitsuki Sarue
THE... MANAGER OF SENTUCKY FRIED CHICKEN?
MY NAME IS MITSUKI SARUE.
CARD: SENTUCKY FRIED CHICKEN MANAGER, HATAGAYA RESTAURANT, MITSUKI SARUE
HATAGAYA IS SUCH A WONDERFUL NEIGHBOR-HOOD, ISN'T IT?
THE PERFECT LOCATION FOR BUSINESS AND FAMILY TRAFFIC...
LOVELY WOMEN EVERY-WHERE...
KURU (SPIN)
KURU
...UHH?
MY APOLOGIES FOR FAILING TO PAY A VISIT EARLIER.
IT'S BEEN SOOO BUSY.
KURU
IRA (TWITCH)

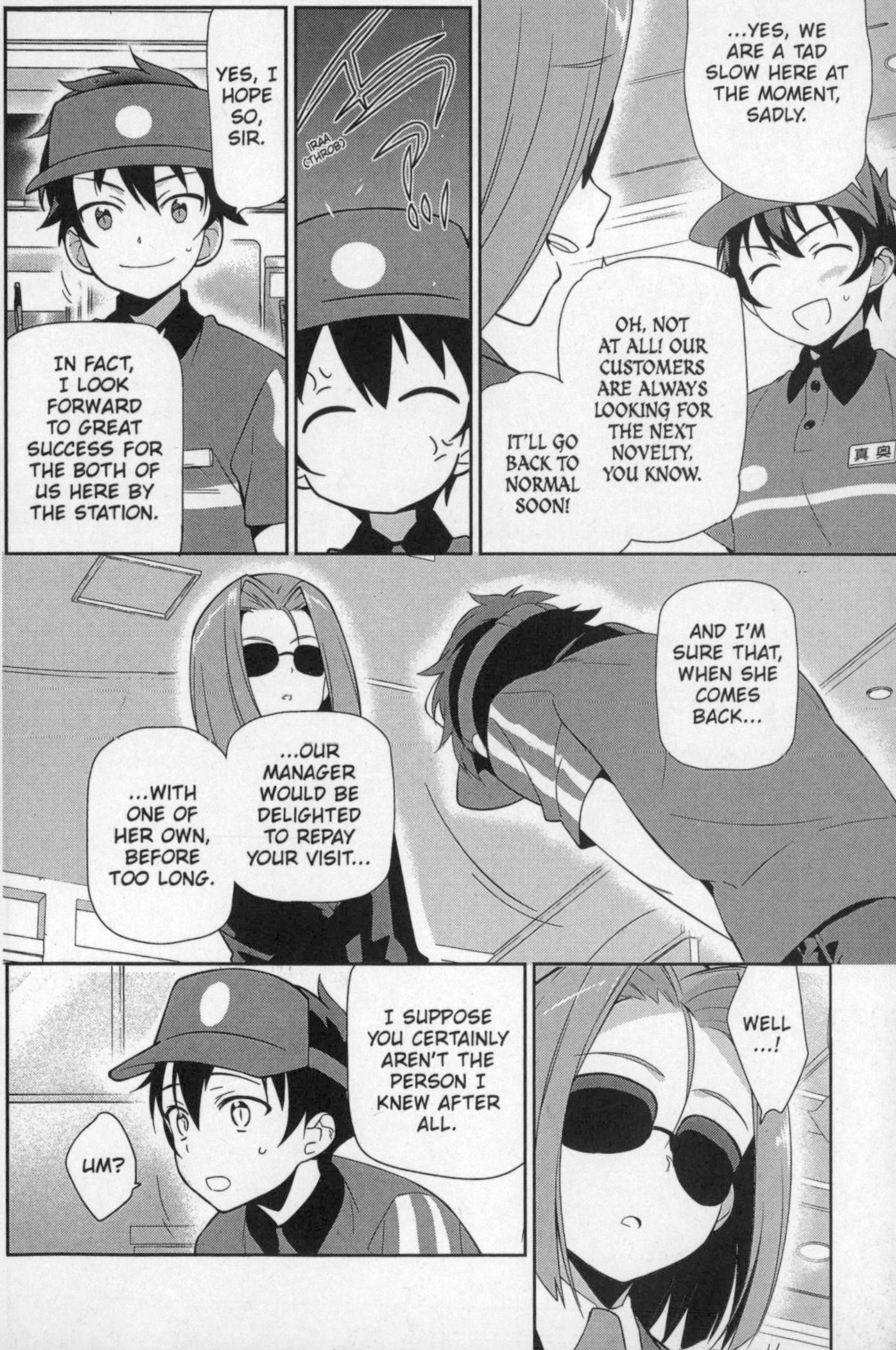
...YES, WE ARE A TAD SLOW HERE AT THE MOMENT, SADLY.
OH, NOT AT ALL! OUR CUSTOMERS ARE ALWAYS LOOKING FOR THE NEXT NOVELTY, YOU KNOW.
IT'LL GO BACK TO NORMAL SOON!
真奥
IRAA (THROB)
YES, I HOPE SO, SIR.
IN FACT, I LOOK FORWARD TO GREAT SUCCESS FOR THE BOTH OF US HERE BY THE STATION.
AND I'M SURE THAT, WHEN SHE COMES BACK...
...OUR MANAGER WOULD BE DELIGHTED TO REPAY YOUR VISIT...
...WITH ONE OF HER OWN, BEFORE TOO LONG.
WELL ...!
I SUPPOSE YOU CERTAINLY AREN'T THE PERSON I KNEW AFTER ALL.
UM?

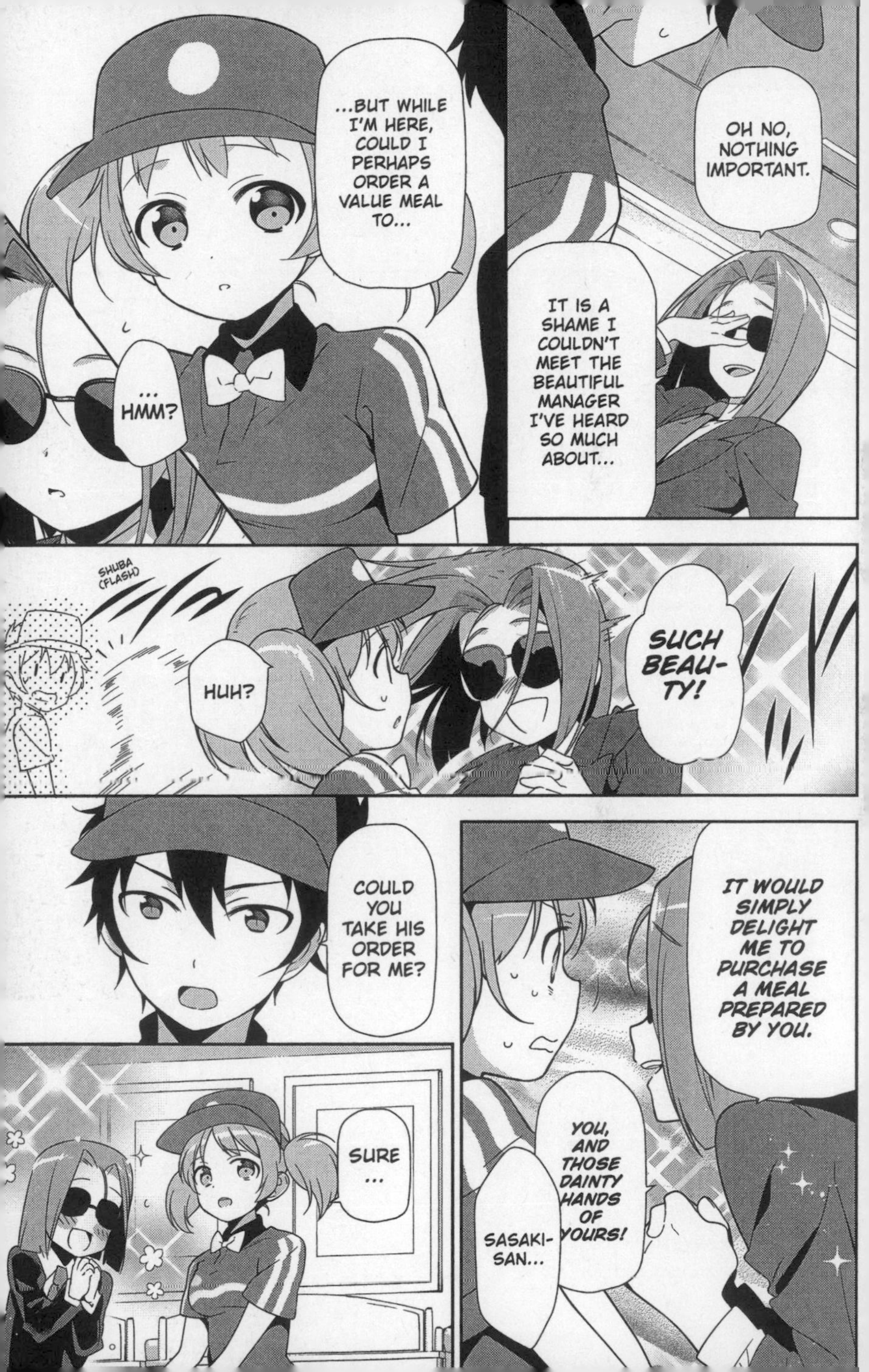
OH NO, NOTHING IMPORTANT.
IT IS A SHAME I COULDN'T MEET THE BEAUTIFUL MANAGER I'VE HEARD SO MUCH ABOUT...
...BUT WHILE I'M HERE, COULD I PERHAPS ORDER A VALUE MEAL TO...
... HMM?
SUCH BEAU-TY!
HUH?
SHUBA (FLASH)
IT WOULD SIMPLY DELIGHT ME TO PURCHASE A MEAL PREPARED BY YOU.
YOU, AND THOSE DAINTY HANDS OF YOURS!
SASAKI-SAN...
COULD YOU TAKE HIS ORDER FOR ME?
SURE...

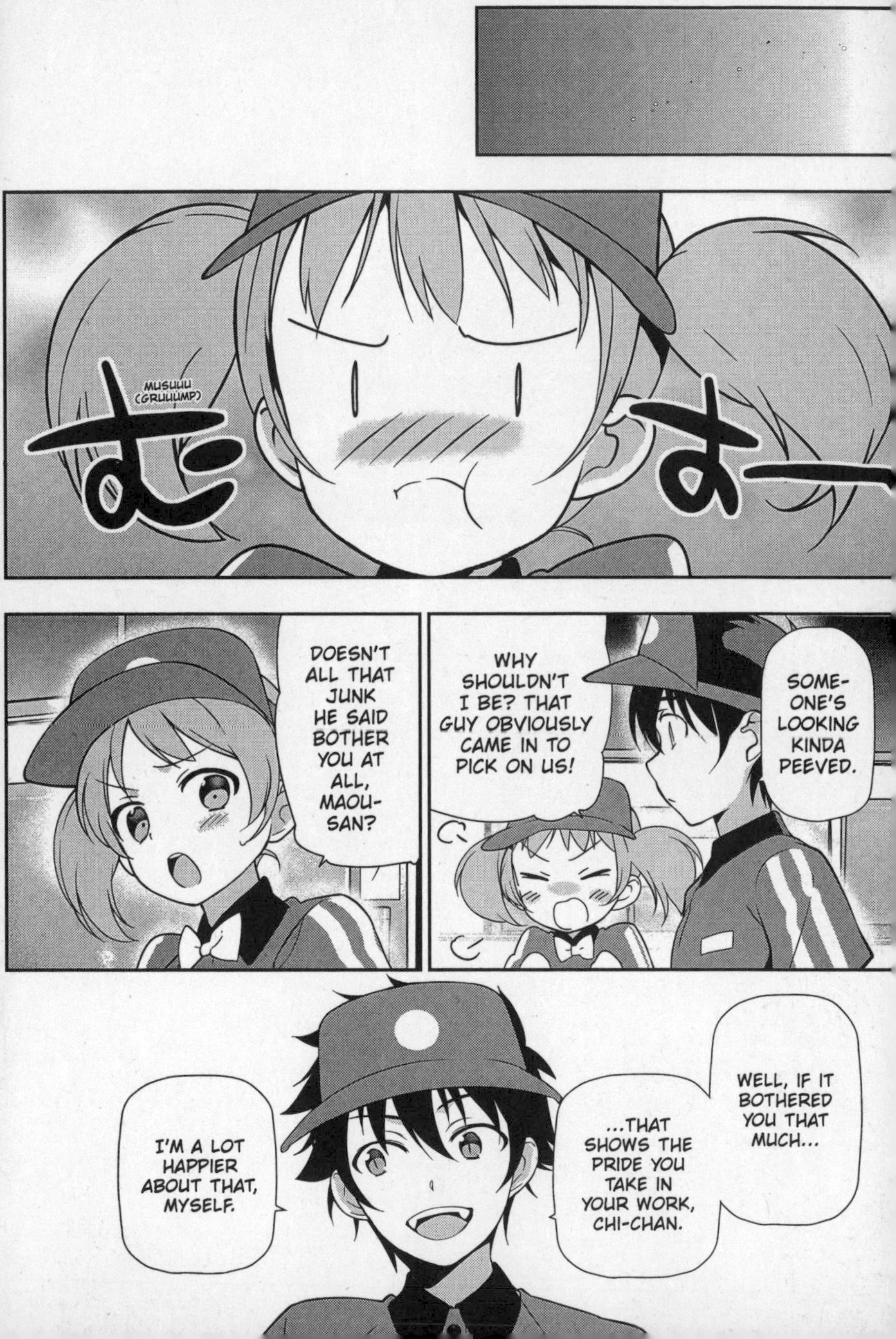
MUSUUU (GRUUUMP)
SOME-ONE'S LOOKING KINDA PEEVED.
WHY SHOULDN'T I BE? THAT GUY OBVIOUSLY CAME IN TO PICK ON US!
DOESN'T ALL THAT JUNK HE SAID BOTHER YOU AT ALL, MAOU-SAN?
WELL, IF IT BOTHERED YOU THAT MUCH...
...THAT SHOWS THE PRIDE YOU TAKE IN YOUR WORK, CHI-CHAN.
I'M A LOT HAPPIER ABOUT THAT, MYSELF.

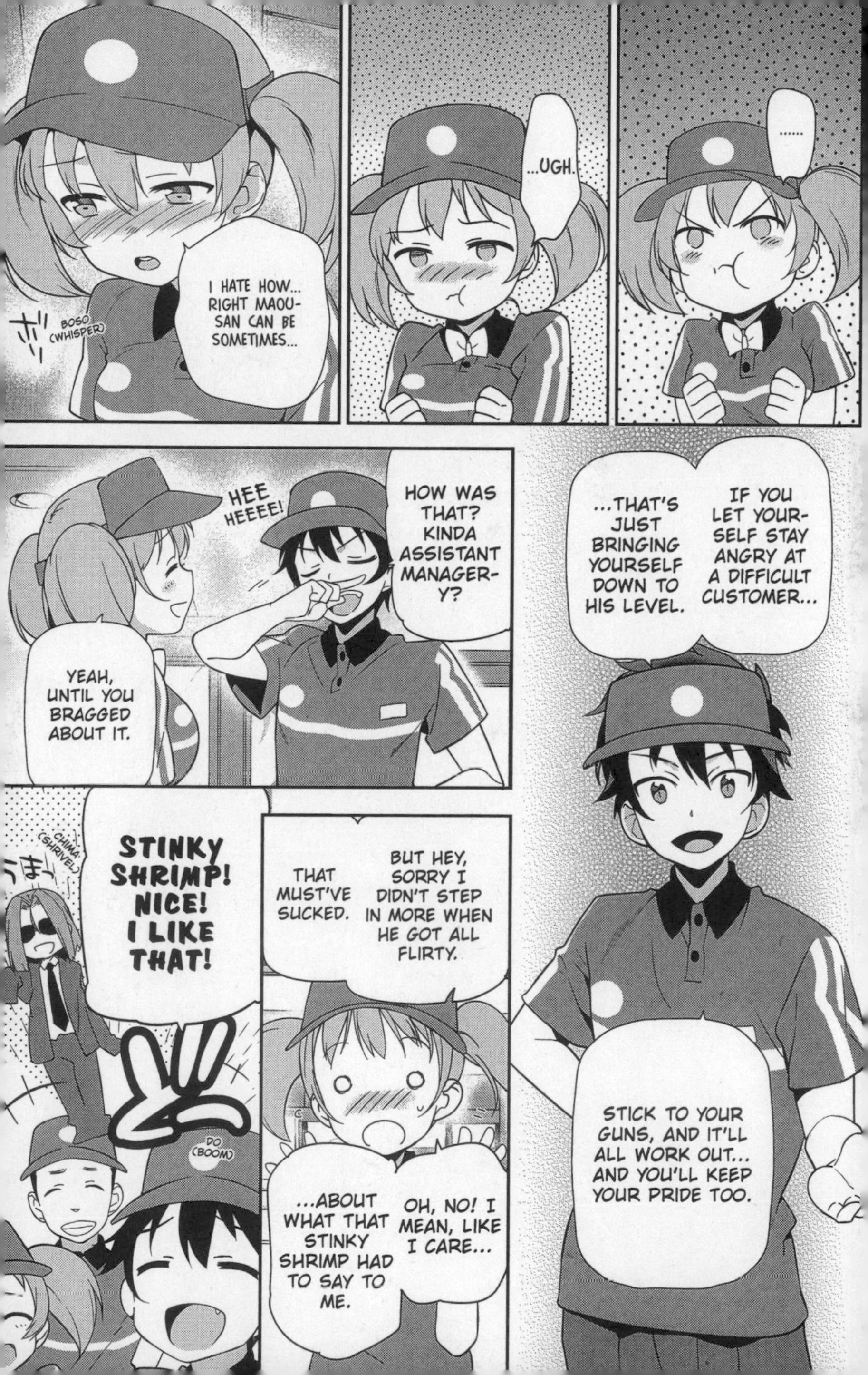
......
...UGH.
I HATE HOW... RIGHT MAOU-SAN CAN BE SOMETIMES...
BOSO (WHISPER)
IF YOU LET YOURSELF STAY ANGRY AT A DIFFICULT CUSTOMER...
...THAT'S JUST BRINGING YOURSELF DOWN TO HIS LEVEL.
STICK TO YOUR GUNS, AND IT'LL ALL WORK OUT... AND YOU'LL KEEP YOUR PRIDE TOO.
HOW WAS THAT? KINDA ASSISTANT MANAGER-Y?
HEE HEEEE!
YEAH, UNTIL YOU BRAGGED ABOUT IT.
BUT HEY, SORRY I DIDN'T STEP IN MORE WHEN HE GOT ALL FLIRTY.
THAT MUST'VE SUCKED.
OH, NO! I MEAN, LIKE I CARE...
...ABOUT WHAT THAT STINKY SHRIMP HAD TO SAY TO ME.
DO (BOOM)
STINKY SHRIMP! NICE! I LIKE THAT!
CHIMA (SHRIVEL)

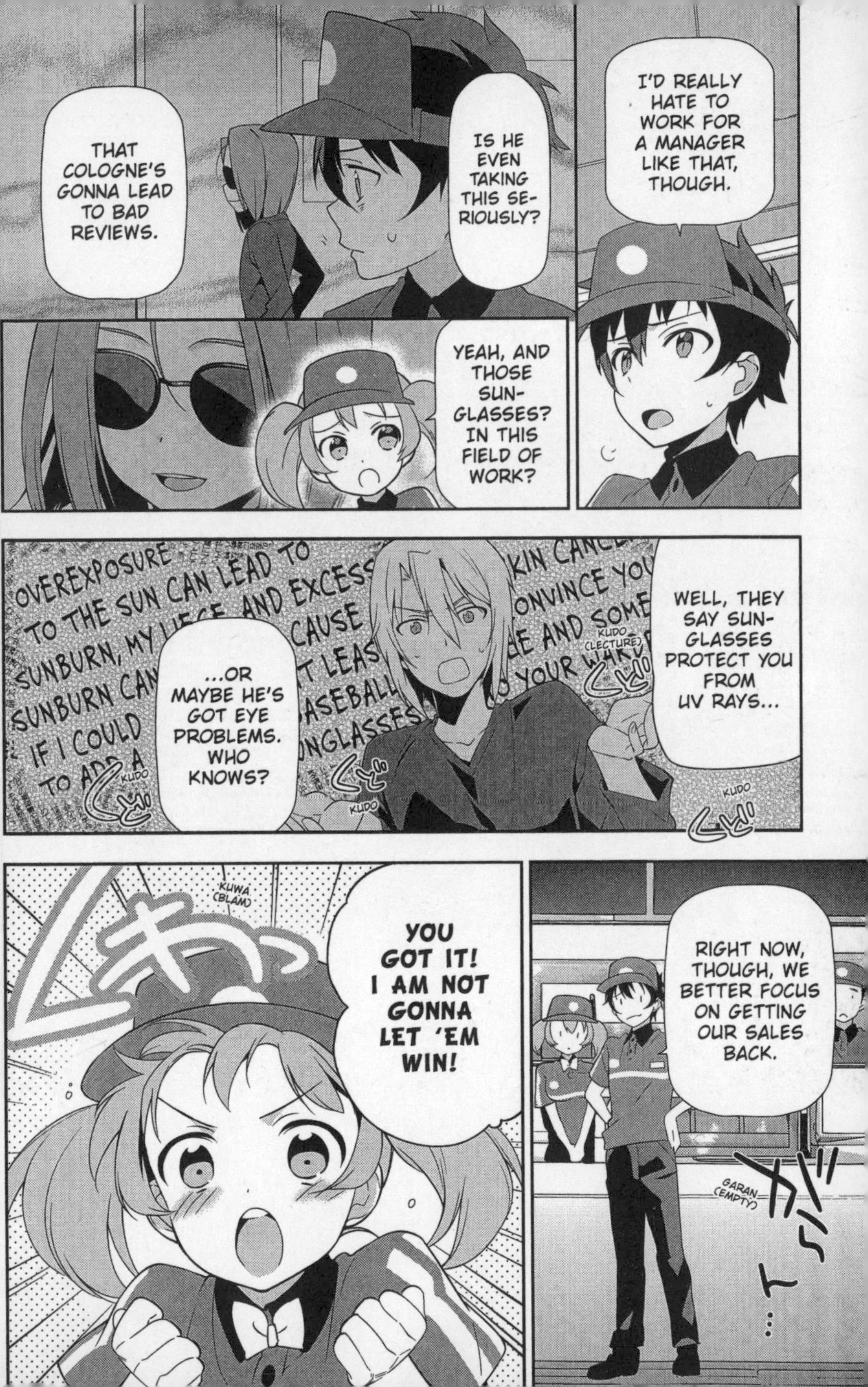
I'D REALLY HATE TO WORK FOR A MANAGER LIKE THAT, THOUGH.
IS HE EVEN TAKING THIS SE-RIOUSLY?
THAT COLOGNE'S GONNA LEAD TO BAD REVIEWS.
YEAH, AND THOSE SUN-GLASSES? IN THIS FIELD OF WORK?
KUDO
WELL, THEY SAY SUN-GLASSES PROTECT YOU FROM UV RAYS...
KUDO (LECTURE)
OVEREXPOSURE TO THE SUN CAN LEAD TO SUNBURN, MY LIEGE AND EXCESS
KUDO
KUDO
...OR MAYBE HE'S GOT EYE PROBLEMS. WHO KNOWS?
RIGHT NOW, THOUGH, WE BETTER FOCUS ON GETTING OUR SALES BACK.
GARAN (EMPTY)
KUWA (BLAM)
YOU GOT IT! I AM NOT GONNA LET 'EM WIN!

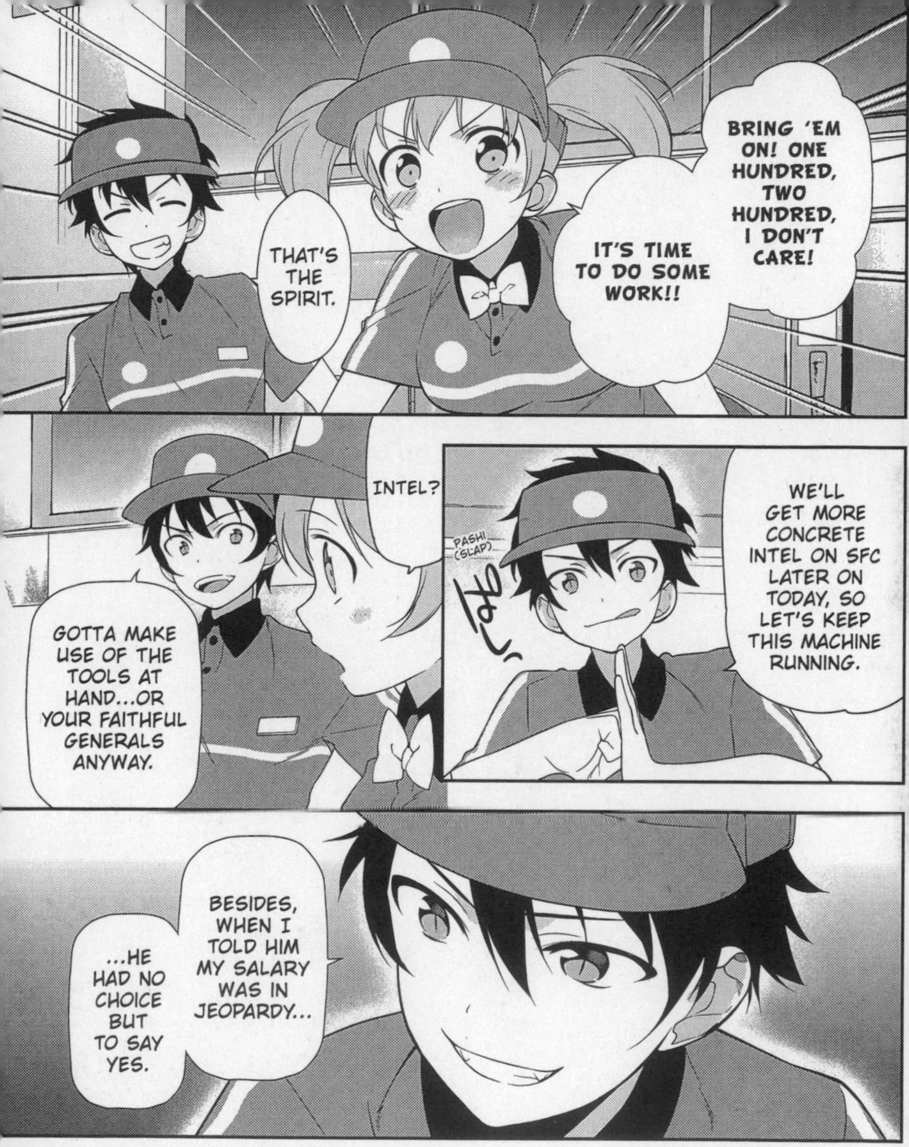
BRING 'EM ON! ONE HUNDRED, TWO HUNDRED, I DON'T CARE!
IT'S TIME TO DO SOME WORK!!
THAT'S THE SPIRIT.
PASHI (SLAP)
WE'LL GET MORE CONCRETE INTEL ON SFC LATER ON TODAY, SO LET'S KEEP THIS MACHINE RUNNING.
INTEL?
GOTTA MAKE USE OF THE TOOLS AT HAND...OR YOUR FAITHFUL GENERALS ANYWAY.
BESIDES, WHEN I TOLD HIM MY SALARY WAS IN JEOPARDY...
...HE HAD NO CHOICE BUT TO SAY YES.

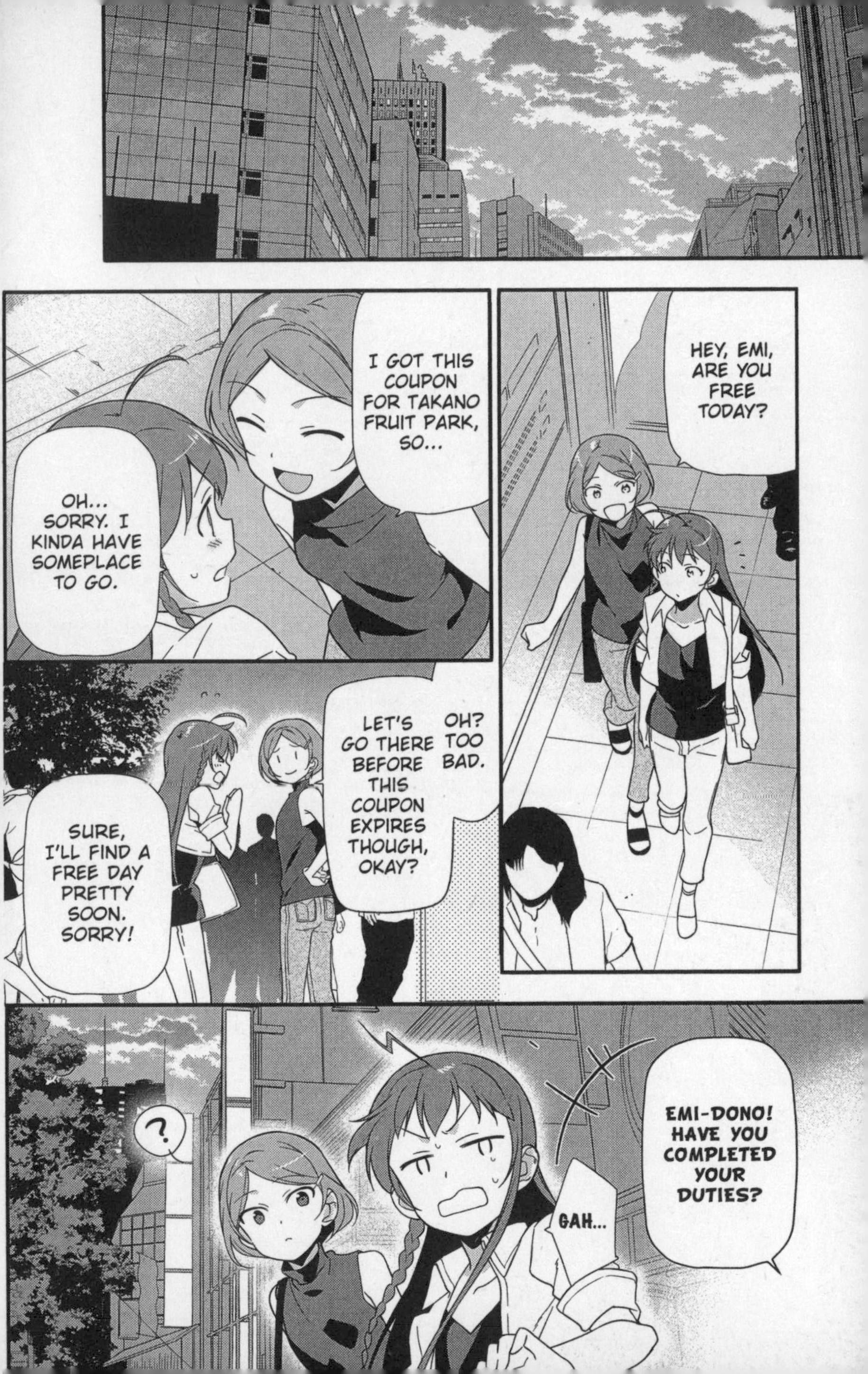
HEY, EMI, ARE YOU FREE TODAY?
I GOT THIS COUPON FOR TAKANO FRUIT PARK, SO...
OH... SORRY. I KINDA HAVE SOMEPLACE TO GO.
OH? TOO BAD.
LET'S GO THERE BEFORE THIS COUPON EXPIRES THOUGH, OKAY?
SURE, I'LL FIND A FREE DAY PRETTY SOON. SORRY!
EMI-DONO! HAVE YOU COMPLETED YOUR DUTIES?
GAH...
?

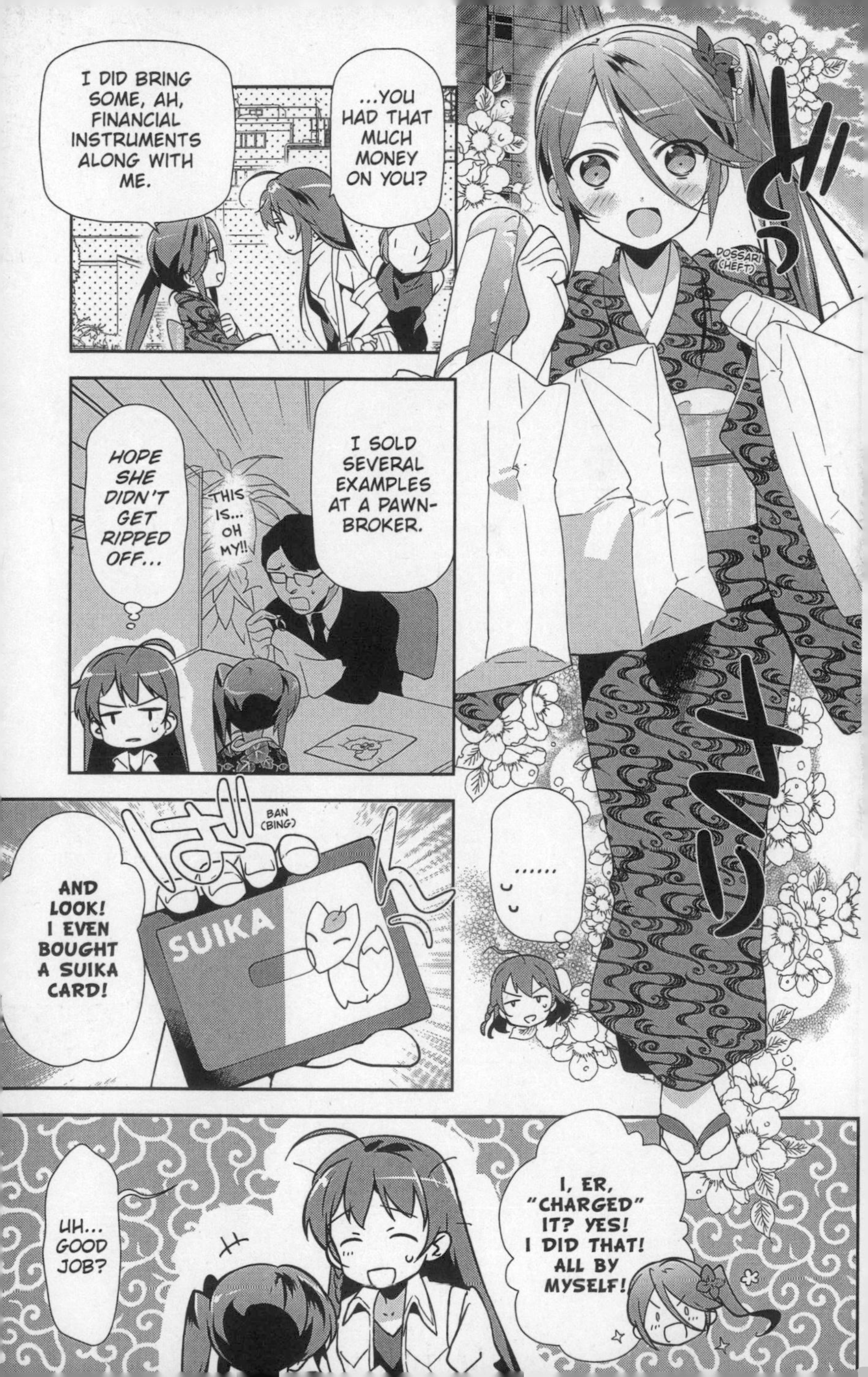
DOSSARI (HEFT)
......
...YOU HAD THAT MUCH MONEY ON YOU?
I DID BRING SOME, AH, FINANCIAL INSTRUMENTS ALONG WITH ME.
I SOLD SEVERAL EXAMPLES AT A PAWN-BROKER.
THIS IS... OH MY!!
HOPE SHE DIDN'T GET RIPPED OFF...
BAN (BING)
SUIKA
AND LOOK! I EVEN BOUGHT A SUIKA CARD!
I, ER, "CHARGED" IT? YES! I DID THAT! ALL BY MYSELF!
UH... GOOD JOB?

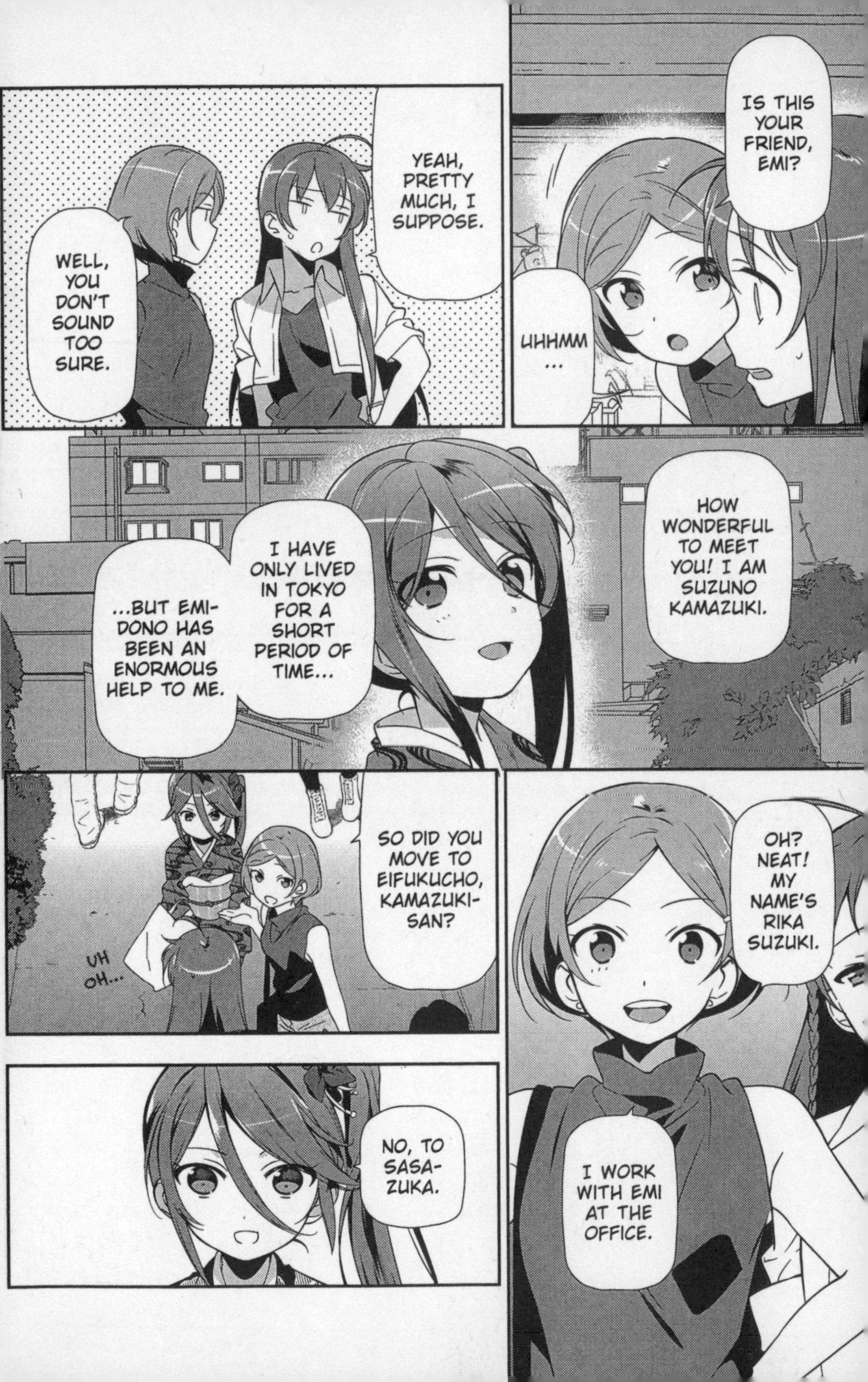
IS THIS YOUR FRIEND, EMI?
UHHMM ...
YEAH, PRETTY MUCH, I SUPPOSE.
WELL, YOU DON'T SOUND TOO SURE.
HOW WONDERFUL TO MEET YOU! I AM SUZUNO KAMAZUKI.
I HAVE ONLY LIVED IN TOKYO FOR A SHORT PERIOD OF TIME...
...BUT EMI-DONO HAS BEEN AN ENORMOUS HELP TO ME.
OH? NEAT! MY NAME'S RIKA SUZUKI.
I WORK WITH EMI AT THE OFFICE.
SO DID YOU MOVE TO EIFUKUCHO, KAMAZUKI-SAN?
UH OH...
NO, TO SASAZUKA.

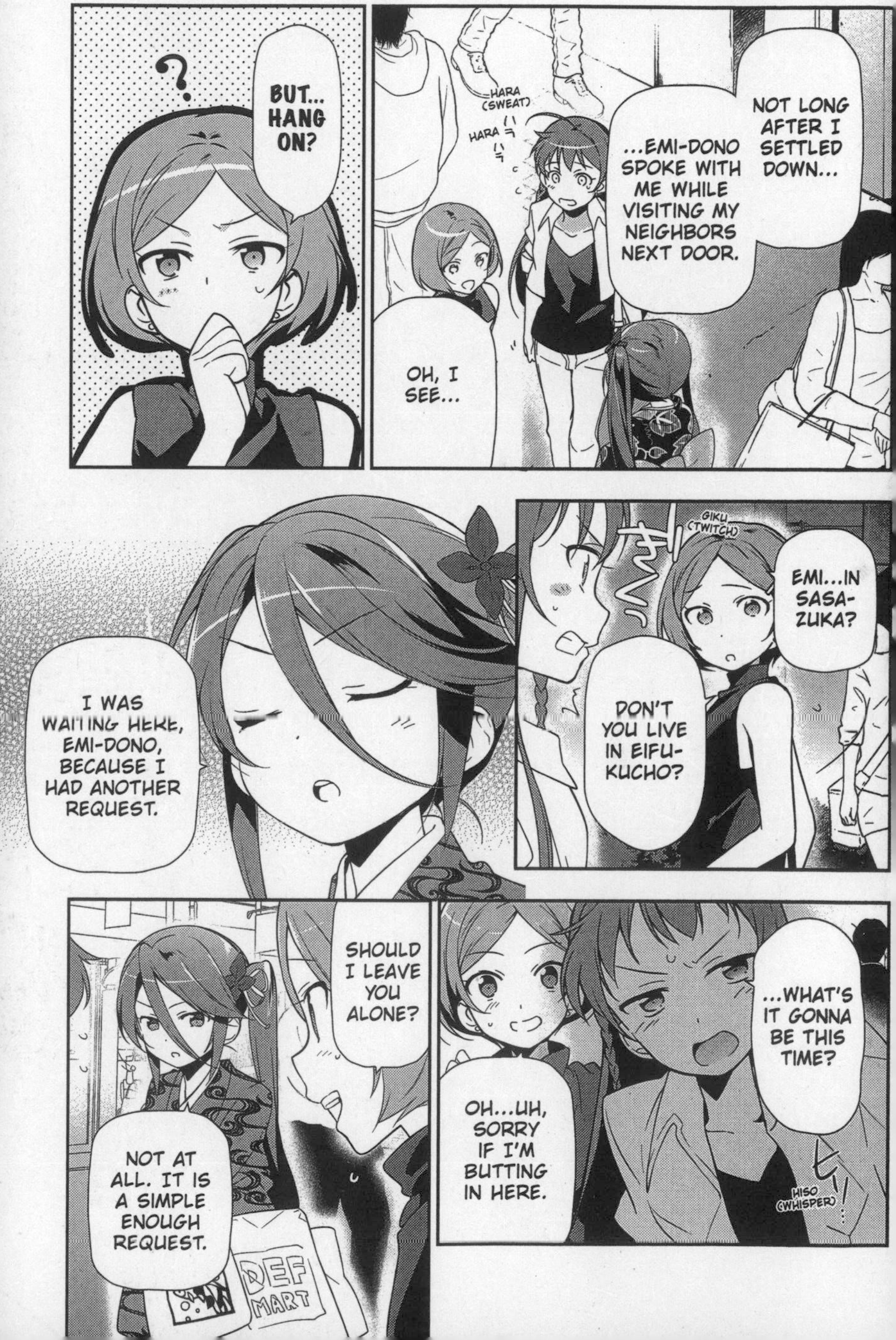
NOT LONG AFTER I SETTLED DOWN...
...EMI-DONO SPOKE WITH ME WHILE VISITING MY NEIGHBORS NEXT DOOR.
HARA (SWEAT)
HARA
OH, I SEE...
BUT... HANG ON?
GIKU (TWITCH)
EMI...IN SASA-ZUKA?
DON'T YOU LIVE IN EIFU-KUCHO?
I WAS WAITING HERE, EMI-DONO, BECAUSE I HAD ANOTHER REQUEST.
...WHAT'S IT GONNA BE THIS TIME?
HISO (WHISPER)
OH...UH, SORRY IF I'M BUTTING IN HERE.
SHOULD I LEAVE YOU ALONE?
NOT AT ALL. IT IS A SIMPLE ENOUGH REQUEST.
DEF MART

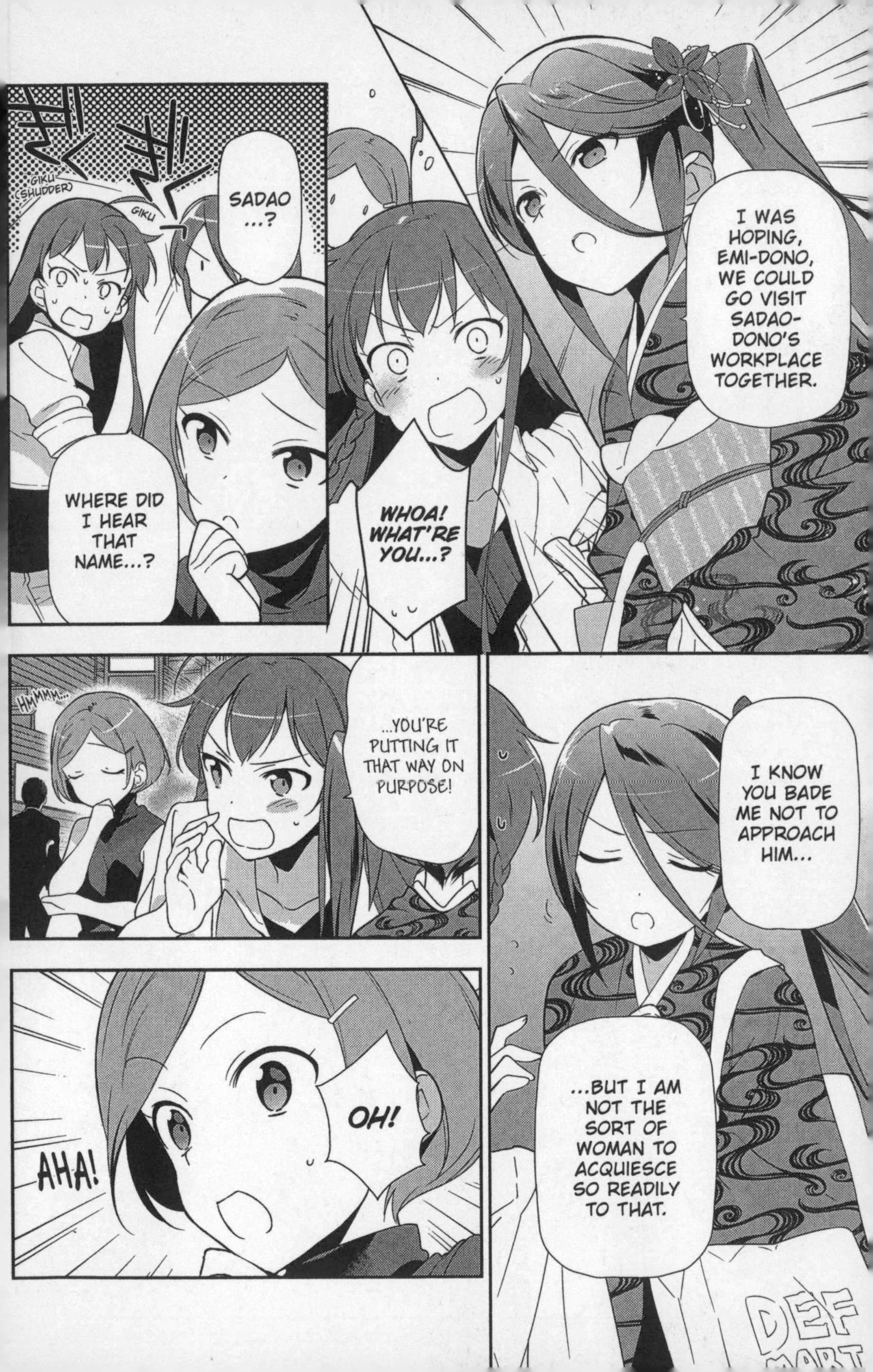
I WAS HOPING, EMI-DONO, WE COULD GO VISIT SADAO-DONO'S WORKPLACE TOGETHER.
WHOA! WHAT'RE YOU...?
SADAO ...?
GIKU (SHUDDER)
GIKU
WHERE DID I HEAR THAT NAME...?
I KNOW YOU BADE ME NOT TO APPROACH HIM...
...BUT I AM NOT THE SORT OF WOMAN TO ACQUIESCE SO READILY TO THAT.
DEF MART
HMMMM...
...YOU'RE PUTTING IT THAT WAY ON PURPOSE!
OH!
AHA!

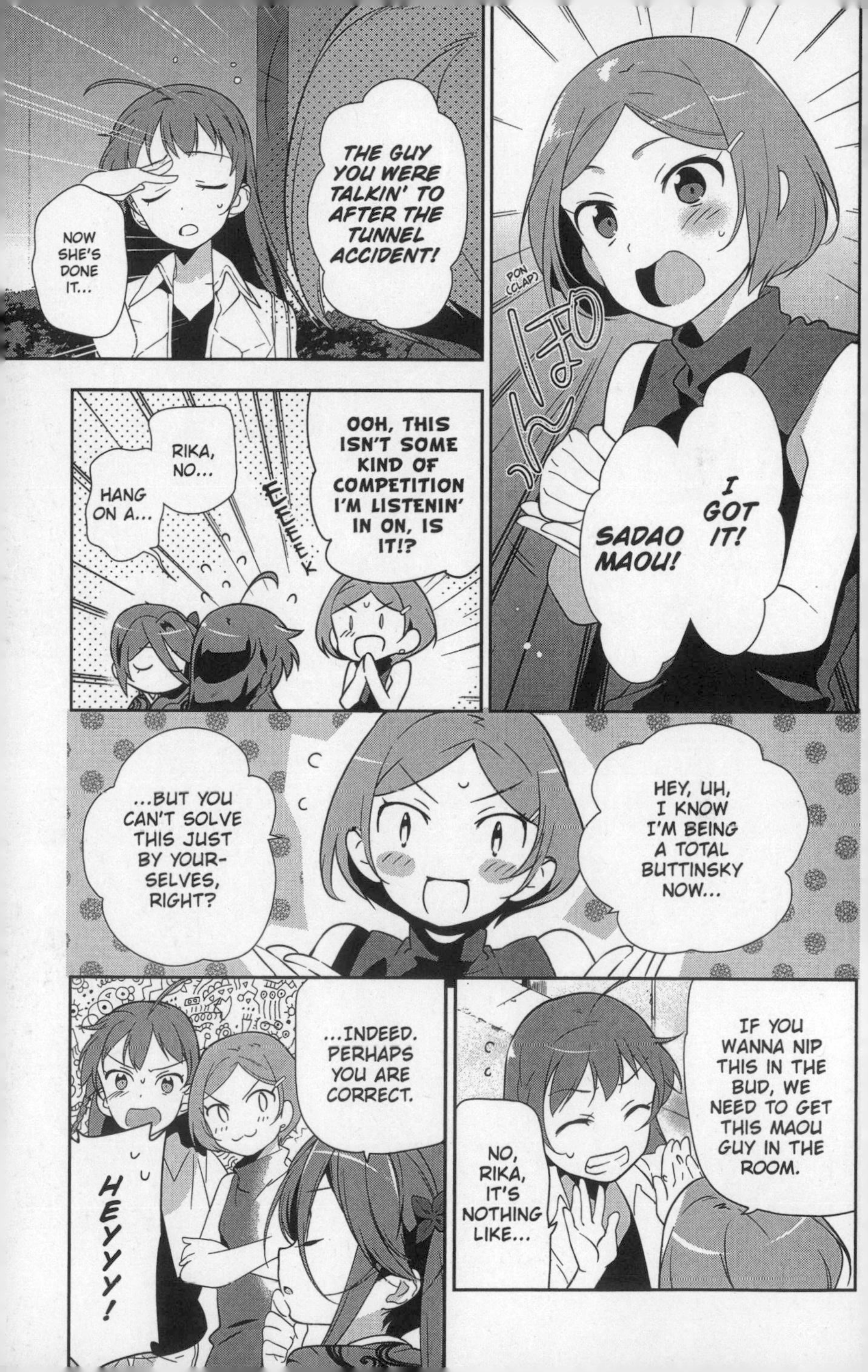
PON (CLAP)
I GOT IT!
SADAO MAOU!
THE GUY YOU WERE TALKIN' TO AFTER THE TUNNEL ACCIDENT!
NOW SHE'S DONE IT...
OOH, THIS ISN'T SOME KIND OF COMPETITION I'M LISTENIN' IN ON, IS IT!?
EEEEK
RIKA, NO...
HANG ON A...
HEY, UH, I KNOW I'M BEING A TOTAL BUTTINSKY NOW...
...BUT YOU CAN'T SOLVE THIS JUST BY YOUR-SELVES, RIGHT?
IF YOU WANNA NIP THIS IN THE BUD, WE NEED TO GET THIS MAOU GUY IN THE ROOM.
NO, RIKA, IT'S NOTHING LIKE...
...INDEED. PERHAPS YOU ARE CORRECT.
HEYYY!

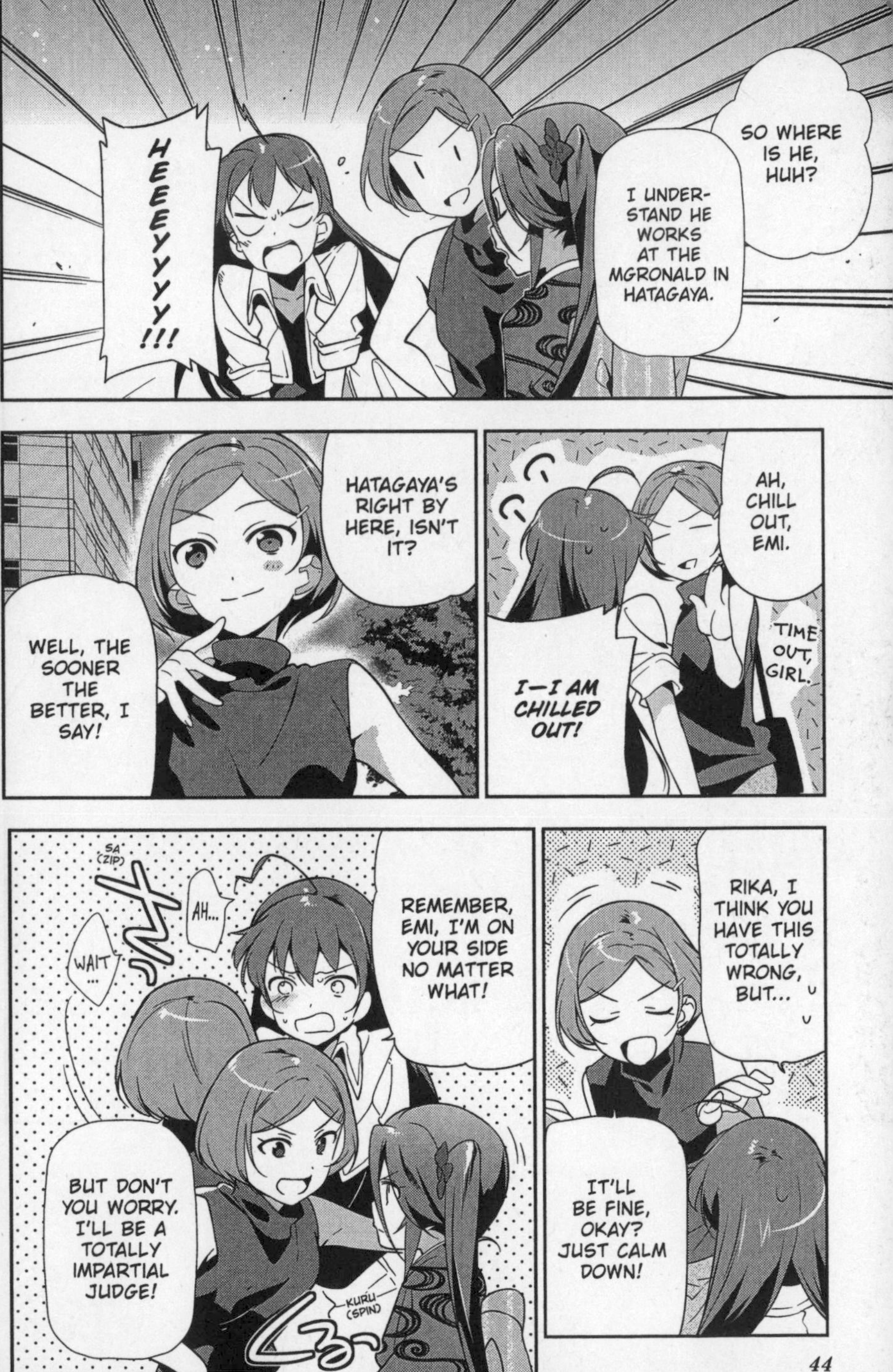
SO WHERE IS HE, HUH?
I UNDER-STAND HE WORKS AT THE MGRONALD IN HATAGAYA.
HEEEYYYY!!!
AH, CHILL OUT, EMI.
TIME OUT, GIRL.
I—I AM CHILLED OUT!
HATAGAYA'S RIGHT BY HERE, ISN'T IT?
WELL, THE SOONER THE BETTER, I SAY!
RIKA, I THINK YOU HAVE THIS TOTALLY WRONG, BUT...
IT'LL BE FINE, OKAY? JUST CALM DOWN!
REMEMBER, EMI, I'M ON YOUR SIDE NO MATTER WHAT!
AH...
SA (ZIP)
WAIT...
BUT DON'T YOU WORRY. I'LL BE A TOTALLY IMPARTIAL JUDGE!
KURU (SPIN)

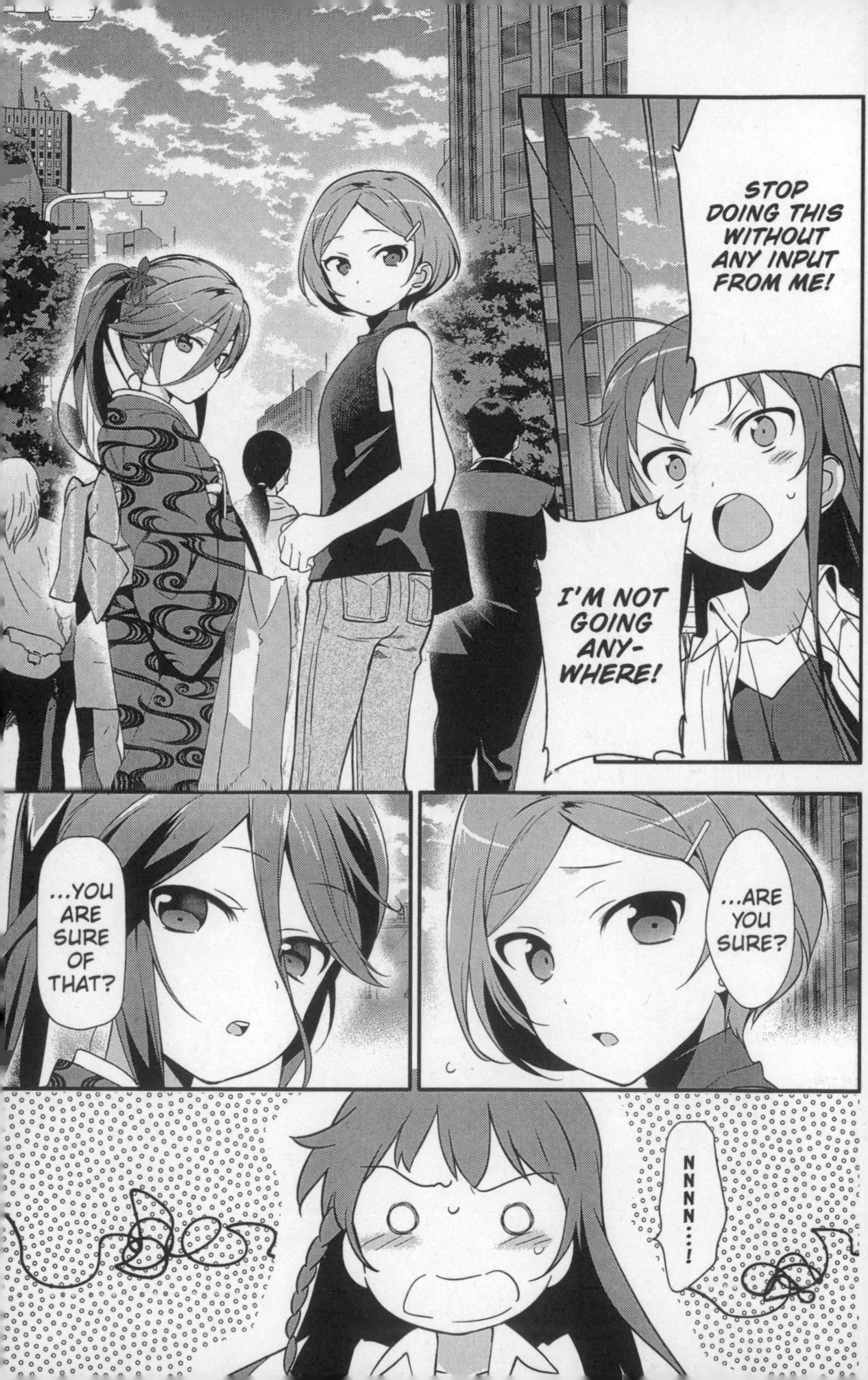
STOP DOING THIS WITHOUT ANY INPUT FROM ME!
I'M NOT GOING ANY-WHERE!
...ARE YOU SURE?
...YOU ARE SURE OF THAT?
NNNN...!

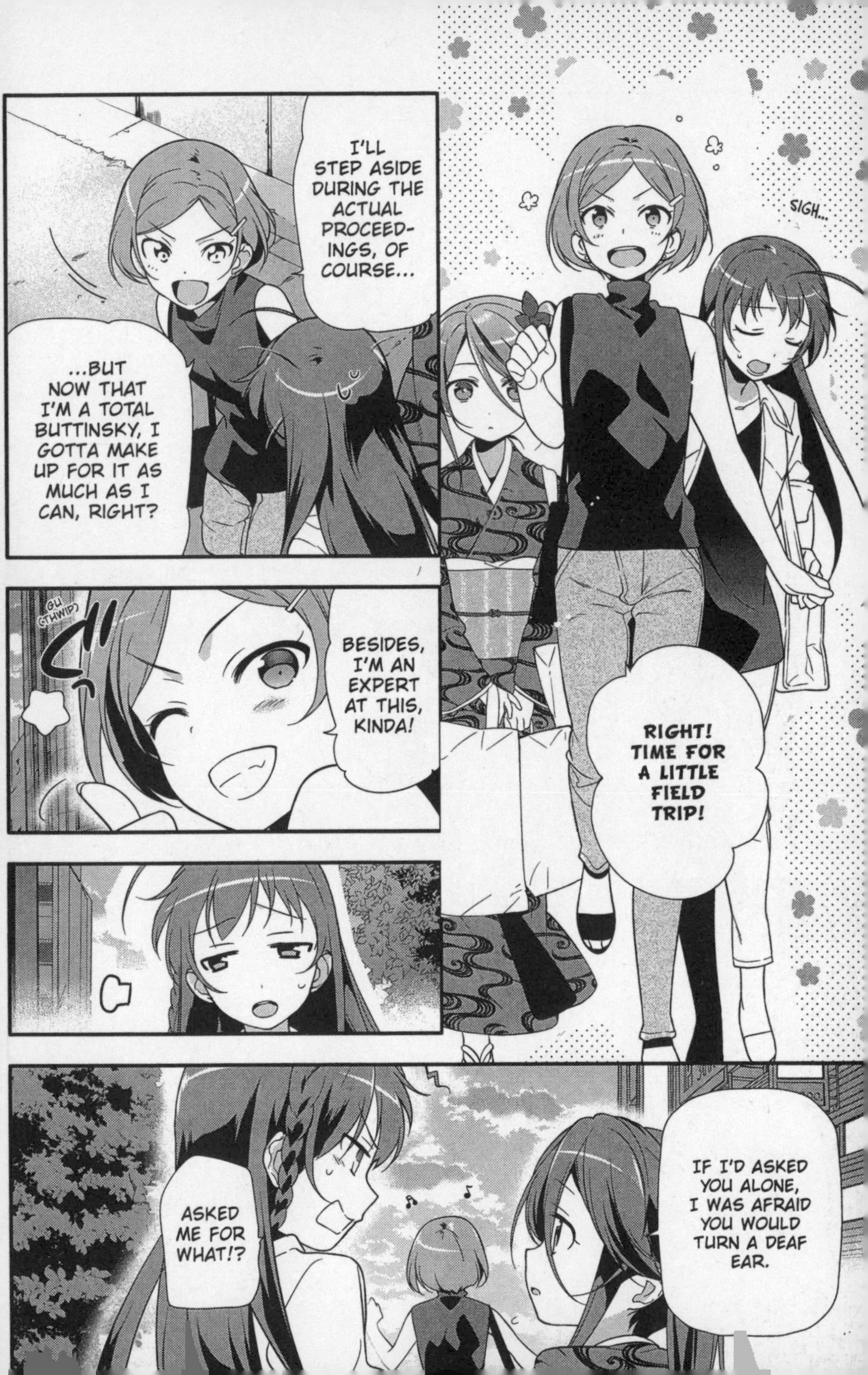
SIGH...
RIGHT! TIME FOR A LITTLE FIELD TRIP!
I'LL STEP ASIDE DURING THE ACTUAL PROCEED-INGS, OF COURSE...
...BUT NOW THAT I'M A TOTAL BUTTINSKY, I GOTTA MAKE UP FOR IT AS MUCH AS I CAN, RIGHT?
BESIDES, I'M AN EXPERT AT THIS, KINDA!
GU (THWIP)
IF I'D ASKED YOU ALONE, I WAS AFRAID YOU WOULD TURN A DEAF EAR.
ASKED ME FOR WHAT!?

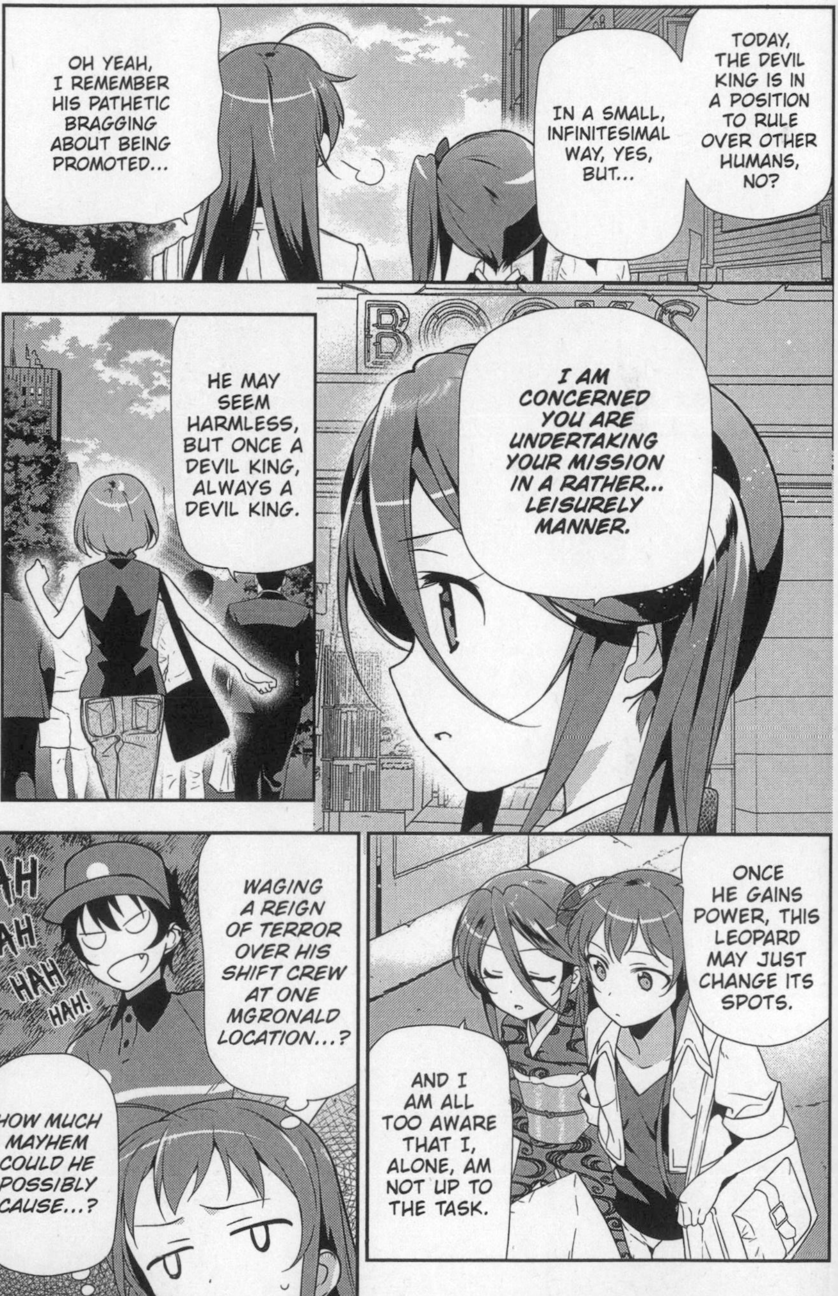
TODAY, THE DEVIL KING IS IN A POSITION TO RULE OVER OTHER HUMANS, NO?
IN A SMALL, INFINITESIMAL WAY, YES, BUT...
OH YEAH, I REMEMBER HIS PATHETIC BRAGGING ABOUT BEING PROMOTED...
I AM CONCERNED YOU ARE UNDERTAKING YOUR MISSION IN A RATHER... LEISURELY MANNER.
HE MAY SEEM HARMLESS, BUT ONCE A DEVIL KING, ALWAYS A DEVIL KING.
ONCE HE GAINS POWER, THIS LEOPARD MAY JUST CHANGE ITS SPOTS.
AND I AM ALL TOO AWARE THAT I, ALONE, AM NOT UP TO THE TASK.
WAGING A REIGN OF TERROR OVER HIS SHIFT CREW AT ONE MGRONALD LOCATION...?
BAH HAH HAH HAH!
HOW MUCH MAYHEM COULD HE POSSIBLY CAUSE...?

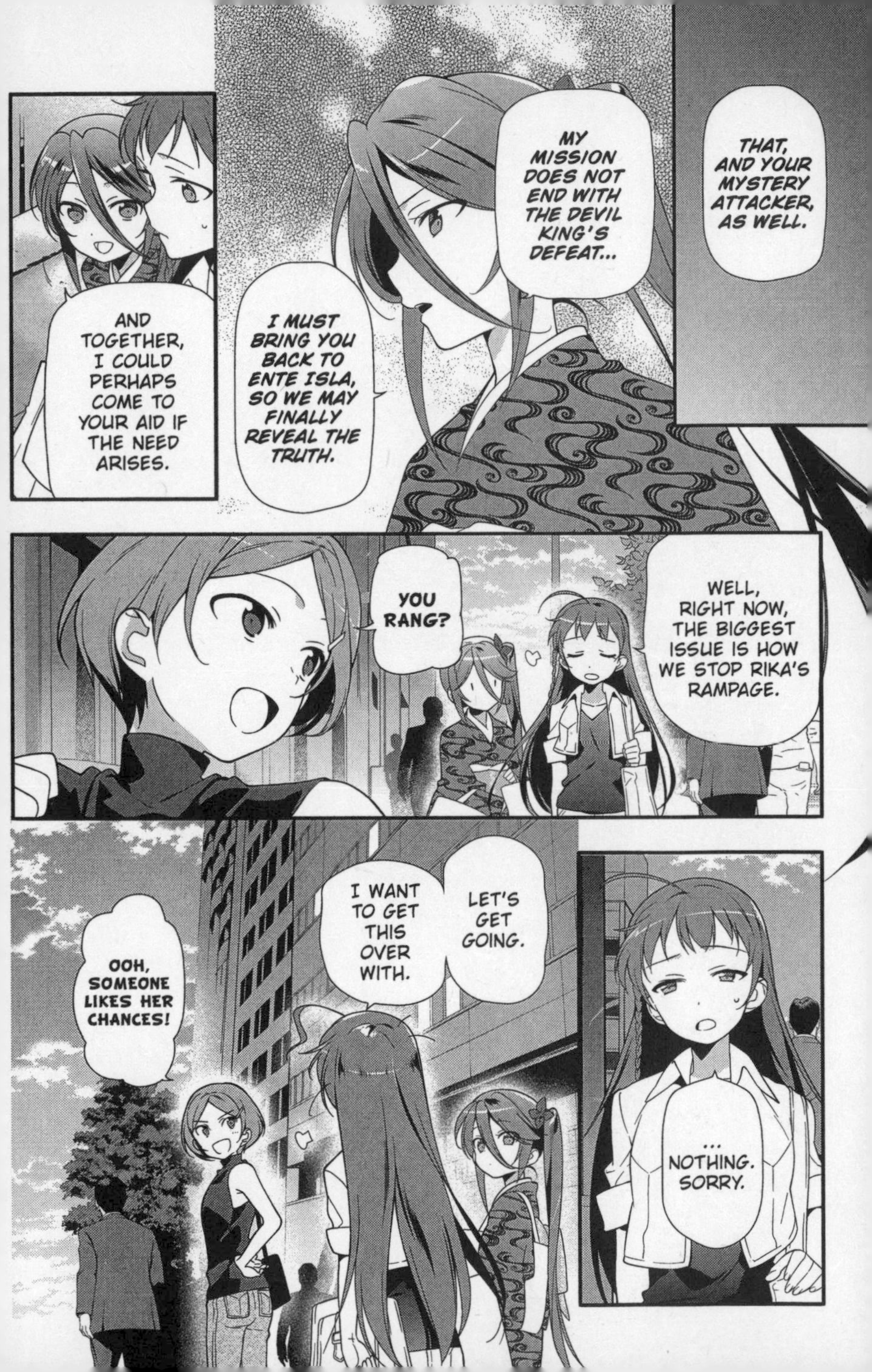
THAT, AND YOUR MYSTERY ATTACKER, AS WELL.
MY MISSION DOES NOT END WITH THE DEVIL KING'S DEFEAT...
I MUST BRING YOU BACK TO ENTE ISLA, SO WE MAY FINALLY REVEAL THE TRUTH.
AND TOGETHER, I COULD PERHAPS COME TO YOUR AID IF THE NEED ARISES.
WELL, RIGHT NOW, THE BIGGEST ISSUE IS HOW WE STOP RIKA'S RAMPAGE.
YOU RANG?
... NOTHING. SORRY.
LET'S GET GOING.
I WANT TO GET THIS OVER WITH.
OOH, SOMEONE LIKES HER CHANCES!

Mitsuki
Sarue

SIGN: TAMURA LADIES' CLEANING

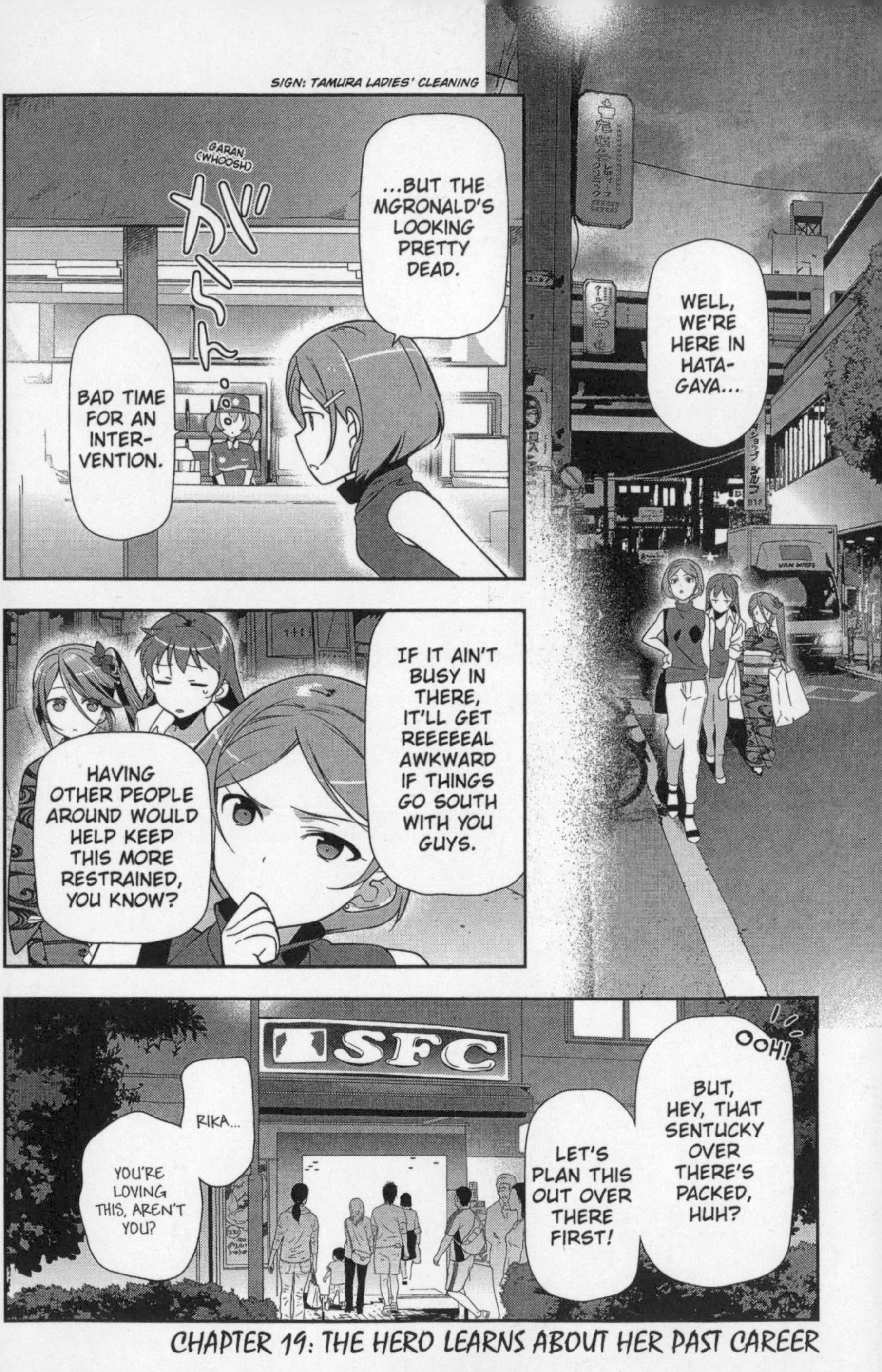

WELL, WE'RE HERE IN HATA-GAYA...
...BUT THE MGRONALD'S LOOKING PRETTY DEAD.
GARAN (WHOOSH)
BAD TIME FOR AN INTER-VENTION.
IF IT AIN'T BUSY IN THERE, IT'LL GET REEEEEAL AWKWARD IF THINGS GO SOUTH WITH YOU GUYS.
HAVING OTHER PEOPLE AROUND WOULD HELP KEEP THIS MORE RESTRAINED, YOU KNOW?
OOH!
BUT, HEY, THAT SENTUCKY OVER THERE'S PACKED, HUH?
LET'S PLAN THIS OUT OVER THERE FIRST!
SFC
RIKA...
YOU'RE LOVING THIS, AREN'T YOU?


CHAPTER 19: THE HERO LEARNS ABOUT HER PAST CAREER

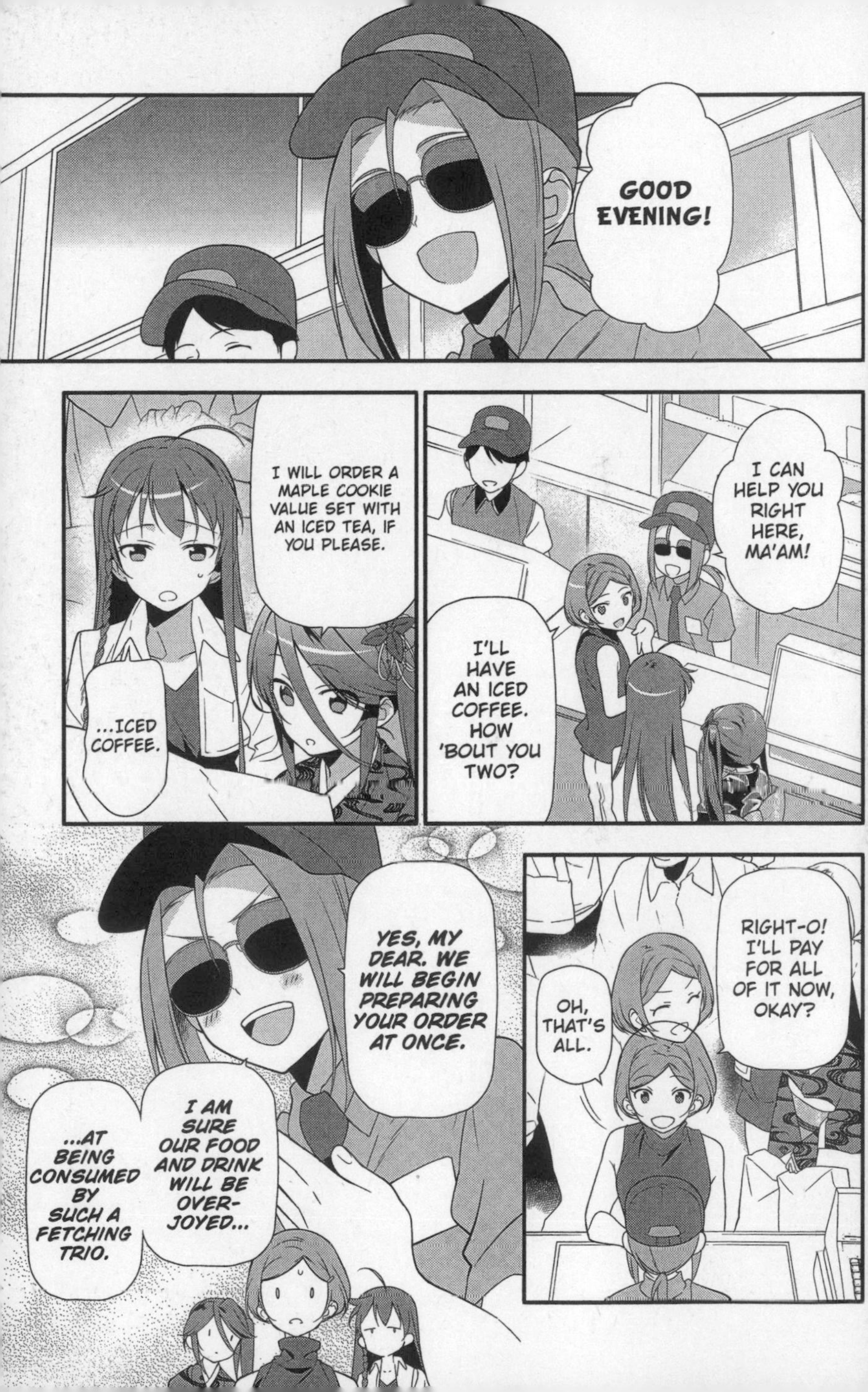
GOOD EVENING!
I CAN HELP YOU RIGHT HERE, MA'AM!
I'LL HAVE AN ICED COFFEE. HOW 'BOUT YOU TWO?
I WILL ORDER A MAPLE COOKIE VALUE SET WITH AN ICED TEA, IF YOU PLEASE.
...ICED COFFEE.
RIGHT-O! I'LL PAY FOR ALL OF IT NOW, OKAY?
OH, THAT'S ALL.
YES, MY DEAR. WE WILL BEGIN PREPARING YOUR ORDER AT ONCE.
I AM SURE OUR FOOD AND DRINK WILL BE OVER-JOYED...
...AT BEING CONSUMED BY SUCH A FETCHING TRIO.

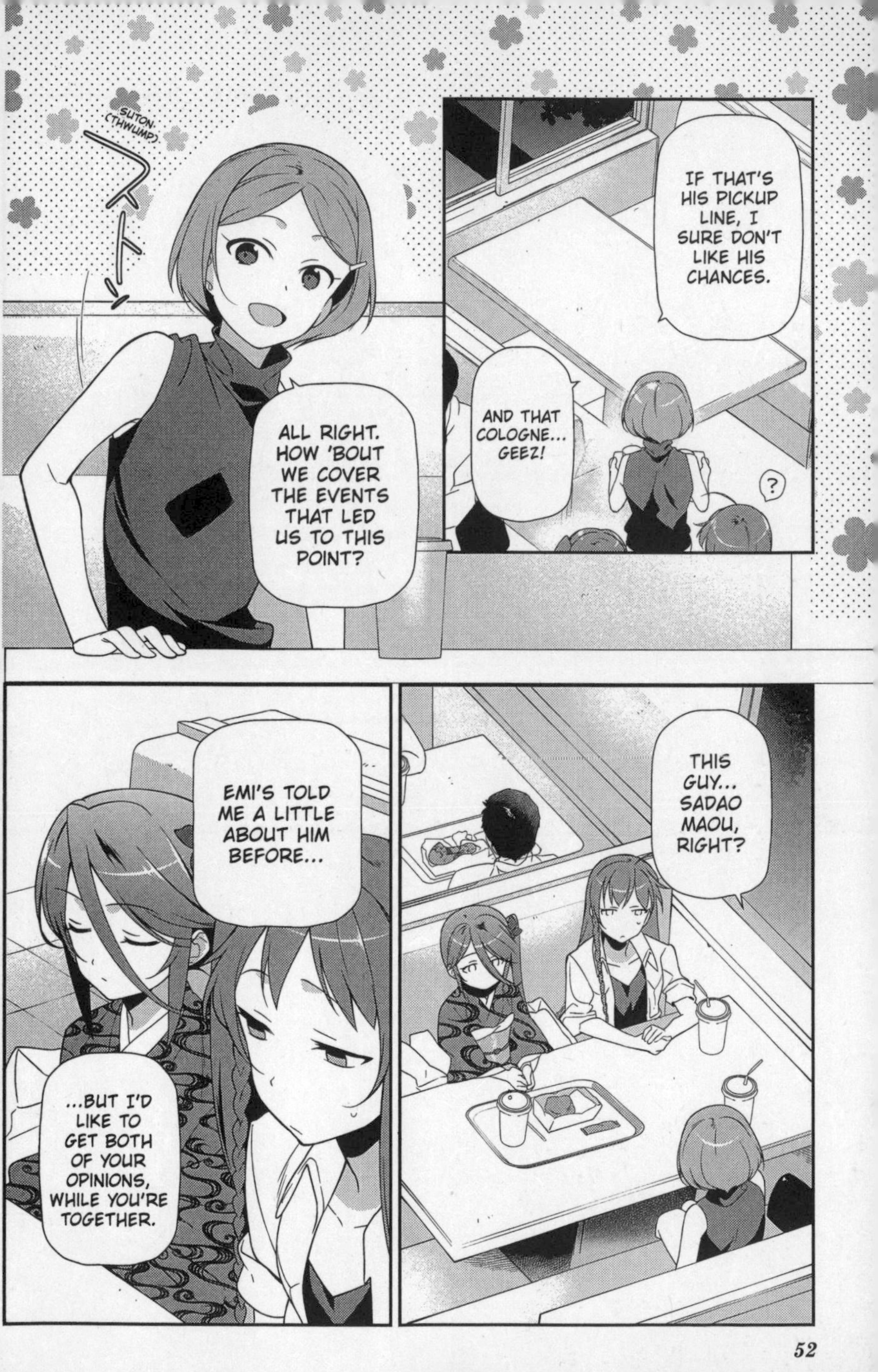
IF THAT'S HIS PICKUP LINE, I SURE DON'T LIKE HIS CHANCES.
AND THAT COLOGNE... GEEZ!
?
SUTON (THWUMP)
ALL RIGHT. HOW 'BOUT WE COVER THE EVENTS THAT LED US TO THIS POINT?
THIS GUY... SADAO MAOU, RIGHT?
EMI'S TOLD ME A LITTLE ABOUT HIM BEFORE...
...BUT I'D LIKE TO GET BOTH OF YOUR OPINIONS, WHILE YOU'RE TOGETHER.

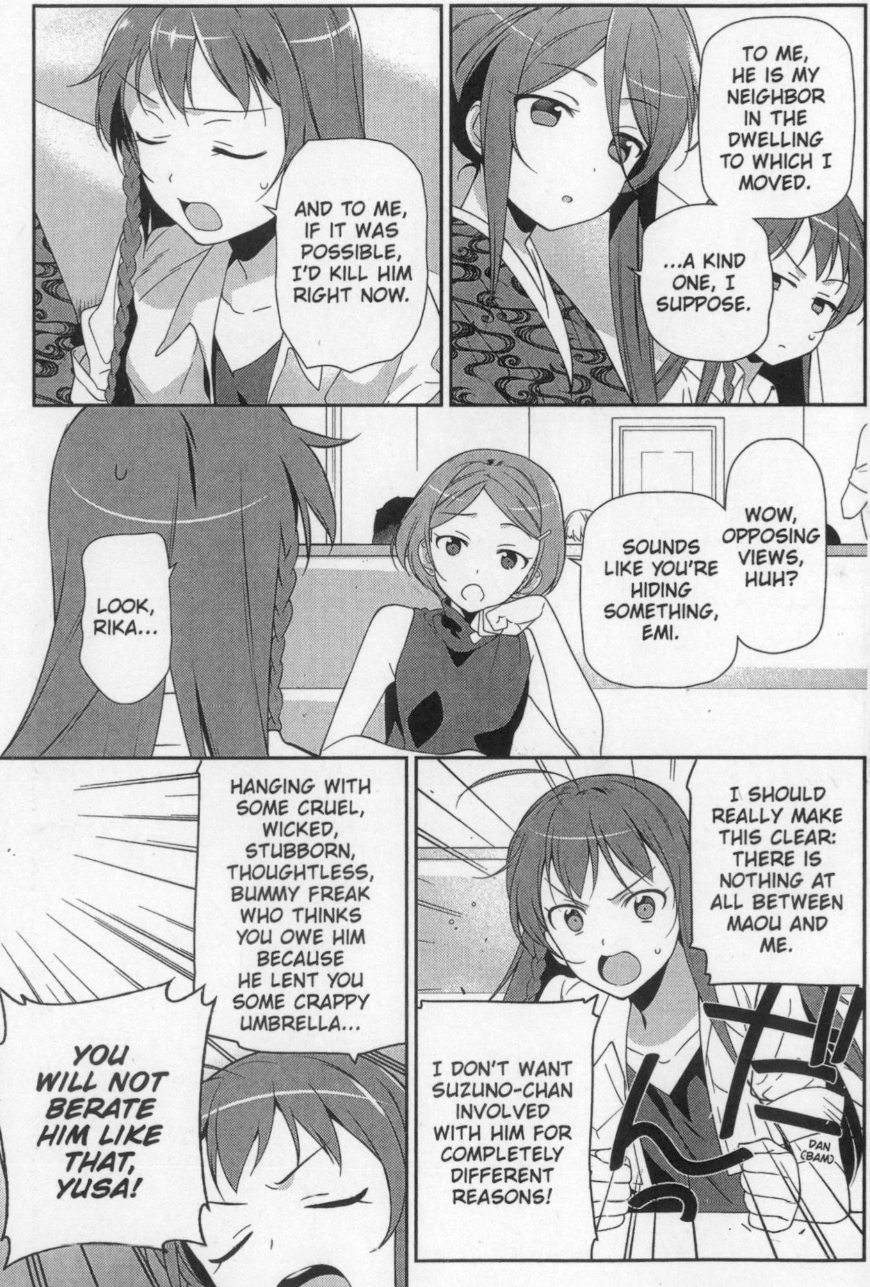
TO ME, HE IS MY NEIGHBOR IN THE DWELLING TO WHICH I MOVED.
...A KIND ONE, I SUPPOSE.
AND TO ME, IF IT WAS POSSIBLE, I'D KILL HIM RIGHT NOW.
WOW, OPPOSING VIEWS, HUH?
SOUNDS LIKE YOU'RE HIDING SOMETHING, EMI.
LOOK, RIKA...
I SHOULD REALLY MAKE THIS CLEAR: THERE IS NOTHING AT ALL BETWEEN MAOU AND ME.
I DON'T WANT SUZUNO-CHAN INVOLVED WITH HIM FOR COMPLETELY DIFFERENT REASONS!
DAN (BAM)
HANGING WITH SOME CRUEL, WICKED, STUBBORN, THOUGHTLESS, BUMMY FREAK WHO THINKS YOU OWE HIM BECAUSE HE LENT YOU SOME CRAPPY UMBRELLA...
YOU WILL NOT BERATE HIM LIKE THAT, YUSA!

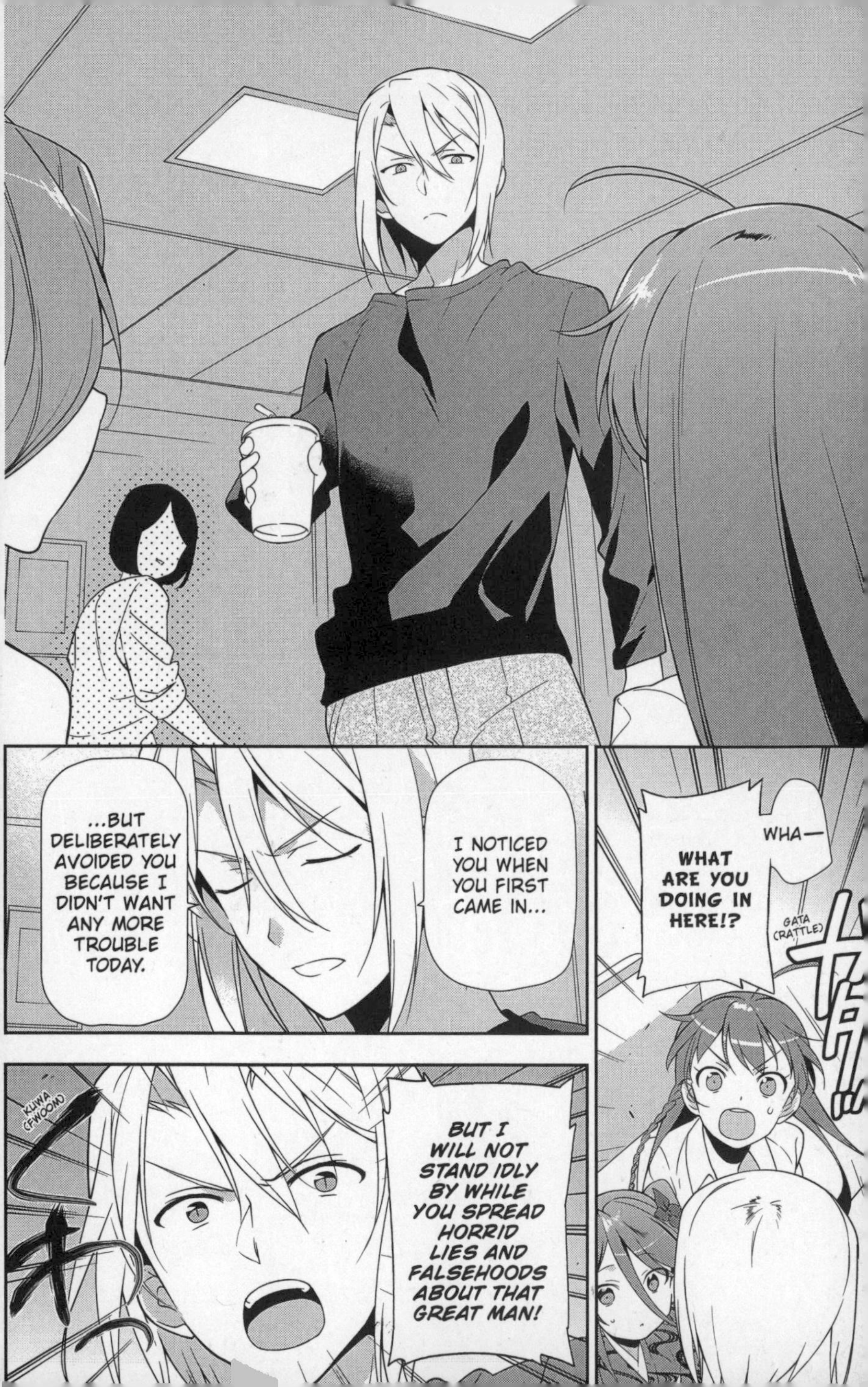
WHA—
WHAT ARE YOU DOING IN HERE!?
GATA (RATTLE)
I NOTICED YOU WHEN YOU FIRST CAME IN...
...BUT DELIBERATELY AVOIDED YOU BECAUSE I DIDN'T WANT ANY MORE TROUBLE TODAY.
BUT I WILL NOT STAND IDLY BY WHILE YOU SPREAD HORRID LIES AND FALSEHOODS ABOUT THAT GREAT MAN!
KUWA (FWOOM)

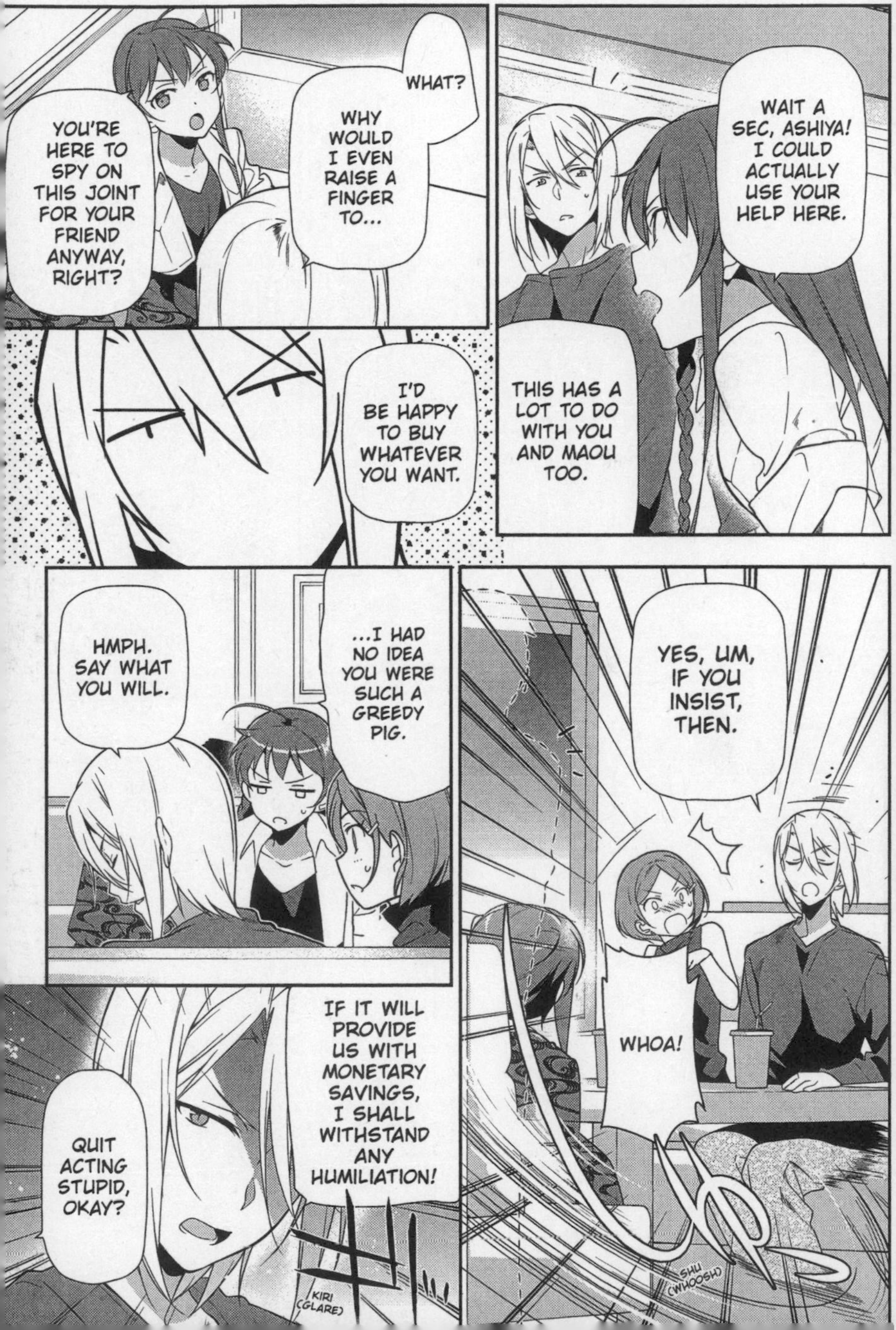
WAIT A SEC, ASHIYA! I COULD ACTUALLY USE YOUR HELP HERE.
THIS HAS A LOT TO DO WITH YOU AND MAOU TOO.
WHAT?
WHY WOULD I EVEN RAISE A FINGER TO...
YOU'RE HERE TO SPY ON THIS JOINT FOR YOUR FRIEND ANYWAY, RIGHT?
I'D BE HAPPY TO BUY WHATEVER YOU WANT.
YES, UM, IF YOU INSIST, THEN.
WHOA!
SHU (WHOOSH)
...I HAD NO IDEA YOU WERE SUCH A GREEDY PIG.
HMPH. SAY WHAT YOU WILL.
IF IT WILL PROVIDE US WITH MONETARY SAVINGS, I SHALL WITHSTAND ANY HUMILIATION!
QUIT ACTING STUPID, OKAY?
KIRI (GLARE)

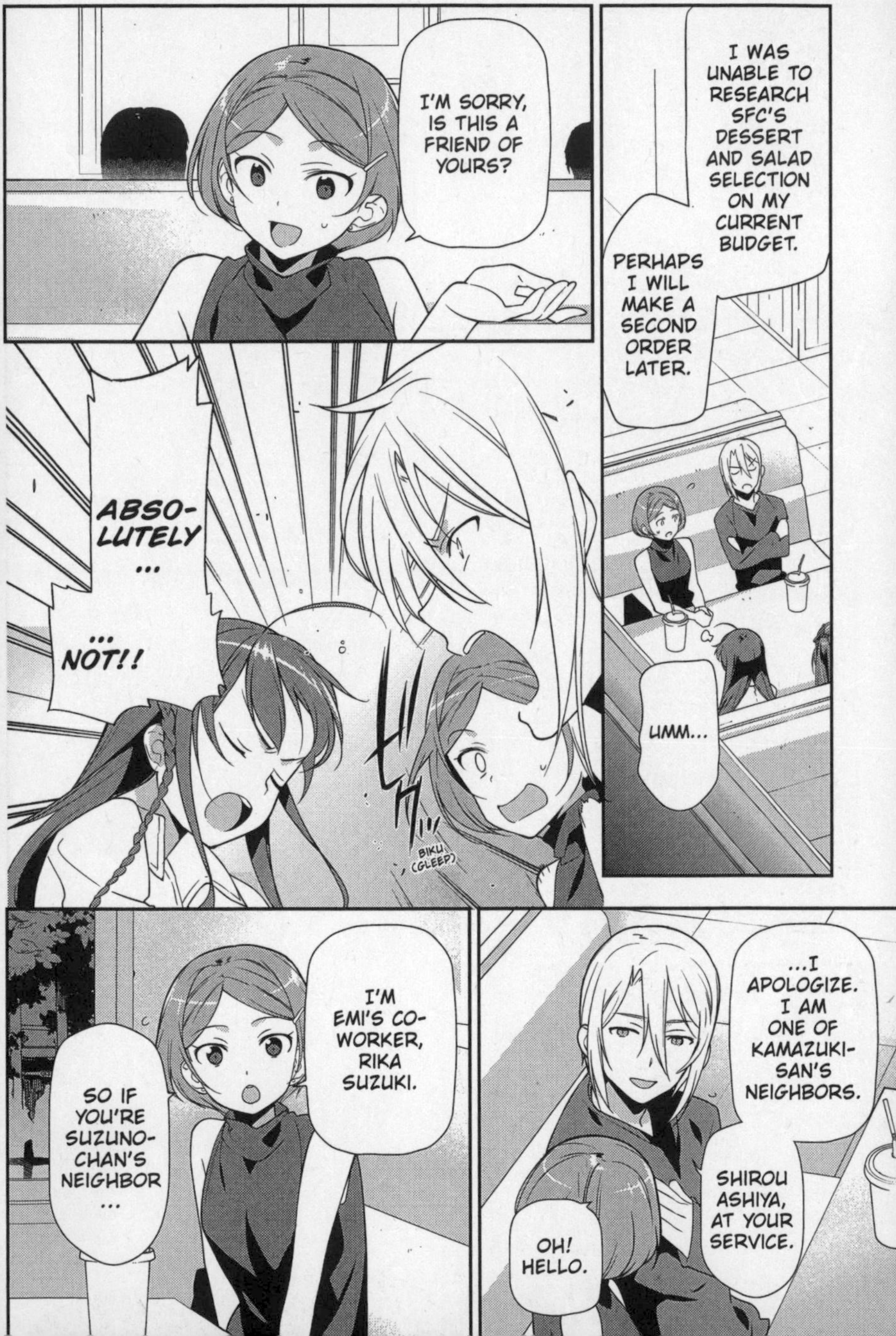
I WAS UNABLE TO RESEARCH SFC'S DESSERT AND SALAD SELECTION ON MY CURRENT BUDGET.
PERHAPS I WILL MAKE A SECOND ORDER LATER.
UMM...
I'M SORRY, IS THIS A FRIEND OF YOURS?
ABSO-LUTELY ...
... NOT!!
BIKU (GLEEP)
...I APOLOGIZE. I AM ONE OF KAMAZUKI-SAN'S NEIGHBORS.
SHIROU ASHIYA, AT YOUR SERVICE.
OH! HELLO.
I'M EMI'S CO-WORKER, RIKA SUZUKI.
SO IF YOU'RE SUZUNO-CHAN'S NEIGHBOR ...

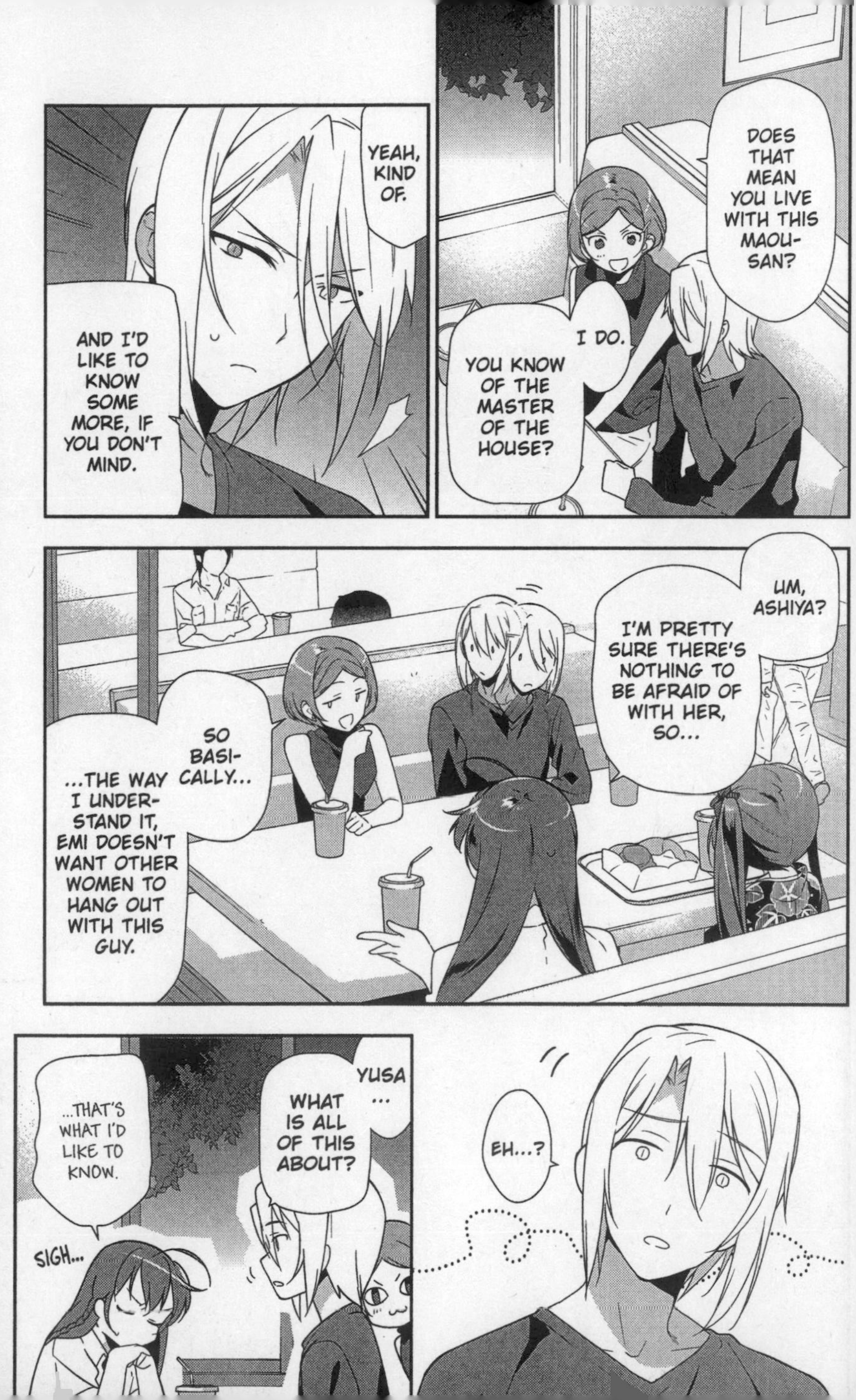
DOES THAT MEAN YOU LIVE WITH THIS MAOU-SAN?
I DO.
YOU KNOW OF THE MASTER OF THE HOUSE?
YEAH, KIND OF.
AND I'D LIKE TO KNOW SOME MORE, IF YOU DON'T MIND.
UM, ASHIYA?
I'M PRETTY SURE THERE'S NOTHING TO BE AFRAID OF WITH HER, SO...
SO BASI-CALLY...
...THE WAY I UNDER-STAND IT, EMI DOESN'T WANT OTHER WOMEN TO HANG OUT WITH THIS GUY.
EH...?
YUSA...
WHAT IS ALL OF THIS ABOUT?
...THAT'S WHAT I'D LIKE TO KNOW.
SIGH...

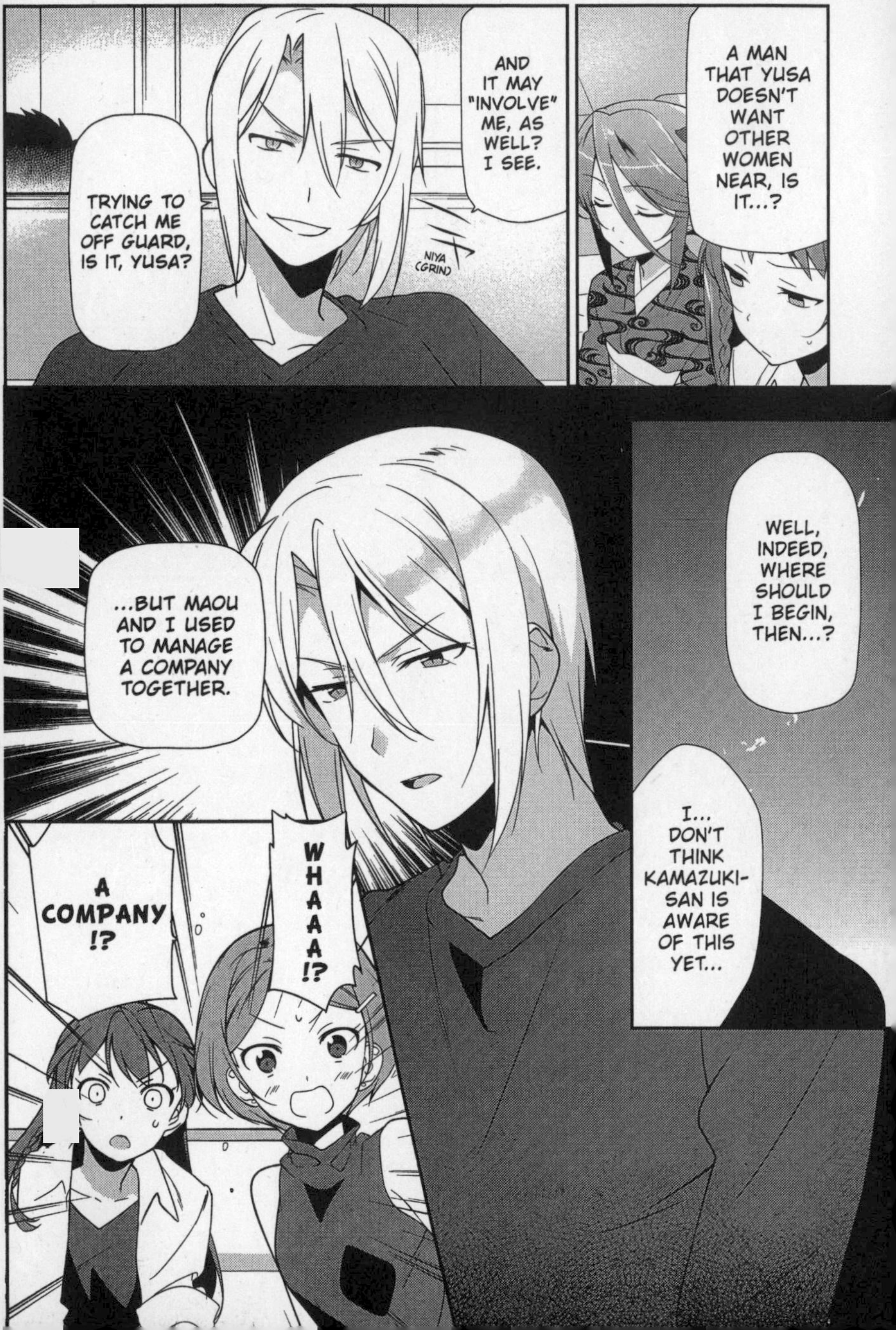
A MAN THAT YUSA DOESN'T WANT OTHER WOMEN NEAR, IS IT...?
AND IT MAY "INVOLVE" ME, AS WELL? I SEE.
TRYING TO CATCH ME OFF GUARD, IS IT, YUSA?
NIYA (GRIND)
WELL, INDEED, WHERE SHOULD I BEGIN, THEN...?
...BUT MAOU AND I USED TO MANAGE A COMPANY TOGETHER.
I... DON'T THINK KAMAZUKI-SAN IS AWARE OF THIS YET...
WHAAAA!?
A COMPANY!?

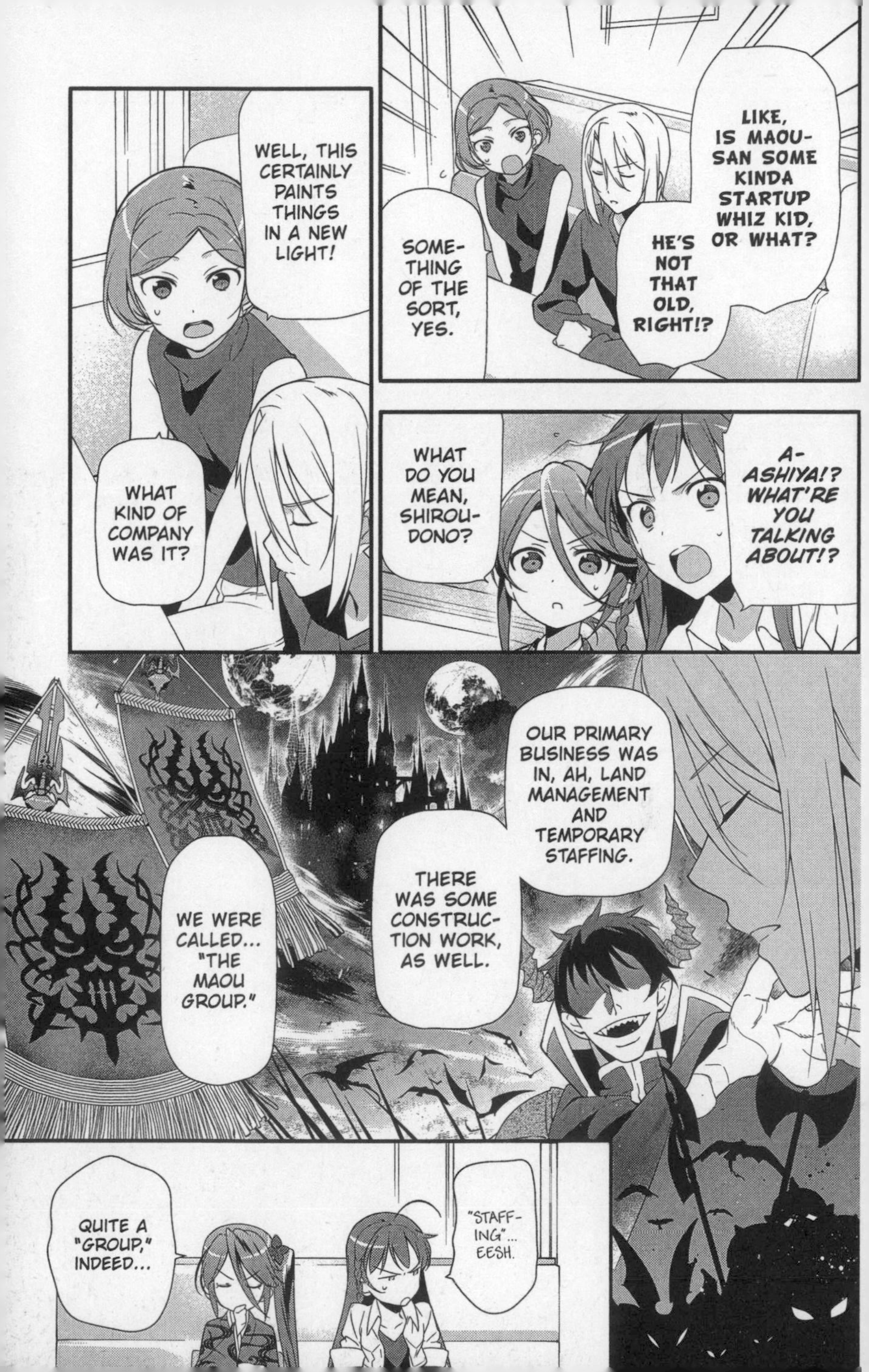
LIKE, IS MAOU-SAN SOME KINDA STARTUP WHIZ KID, OR WHAT?
HE'S NOT THAT OLD, RIGHT!?
SOME-THING OF THE SORT, YES.
A-ASHIYA!? WHAT'RE YOU TALKING ABOUT!?
WHAT DO YOU MEAN, SHIROU-DONO?
WELL, THIS CERTAINLY PAINTS THINGS IN A NEW LIGHT!
WHAT KIND OF COMPANY WAS IT?
OUR PRIMARY BUSINESS WAS IN, AH, LAND MANAGEMENT AND TEMPORARY STAFFING.
THERE WAS SOME CONSTRUC-TION WORK, AS WELL.
WE WERE CALLED... "THE MAOU GROUP."
"STAFF-ING"... EESH.
QUITE A "GROUP," INDEED...

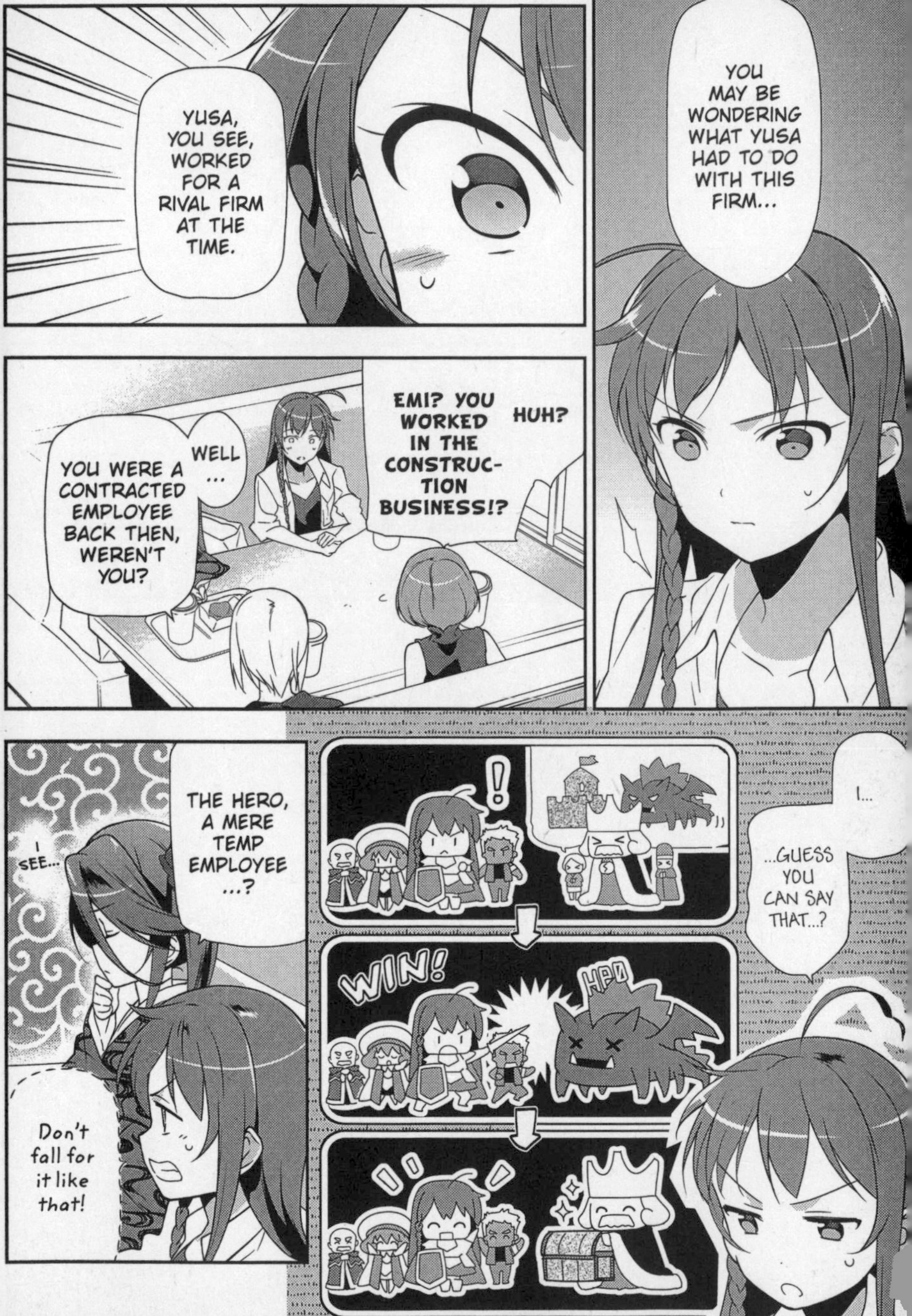
YOU MAY BE WONDERING WHAT YUSA HAD TO DO WITH THIS FIRM...
YUSA, YOU SEE, WORKED FOR A RIVAL FIRM AT THE TIME.
HUH?
EMI? YOU WORKED IN THE CONSTRUCTION BUSINESS!?
WELL...
YOU WERE A CONTRACTED EMPLOYEE BACK THEN, WEREN'T YOU?
I...
...GUESS YOU CAN SAY THAT...?
!
WIN!
HP0
THE HERO, A MERE TEMP EMPLOYEE...?
I SEE...
Don't fall for it like that!

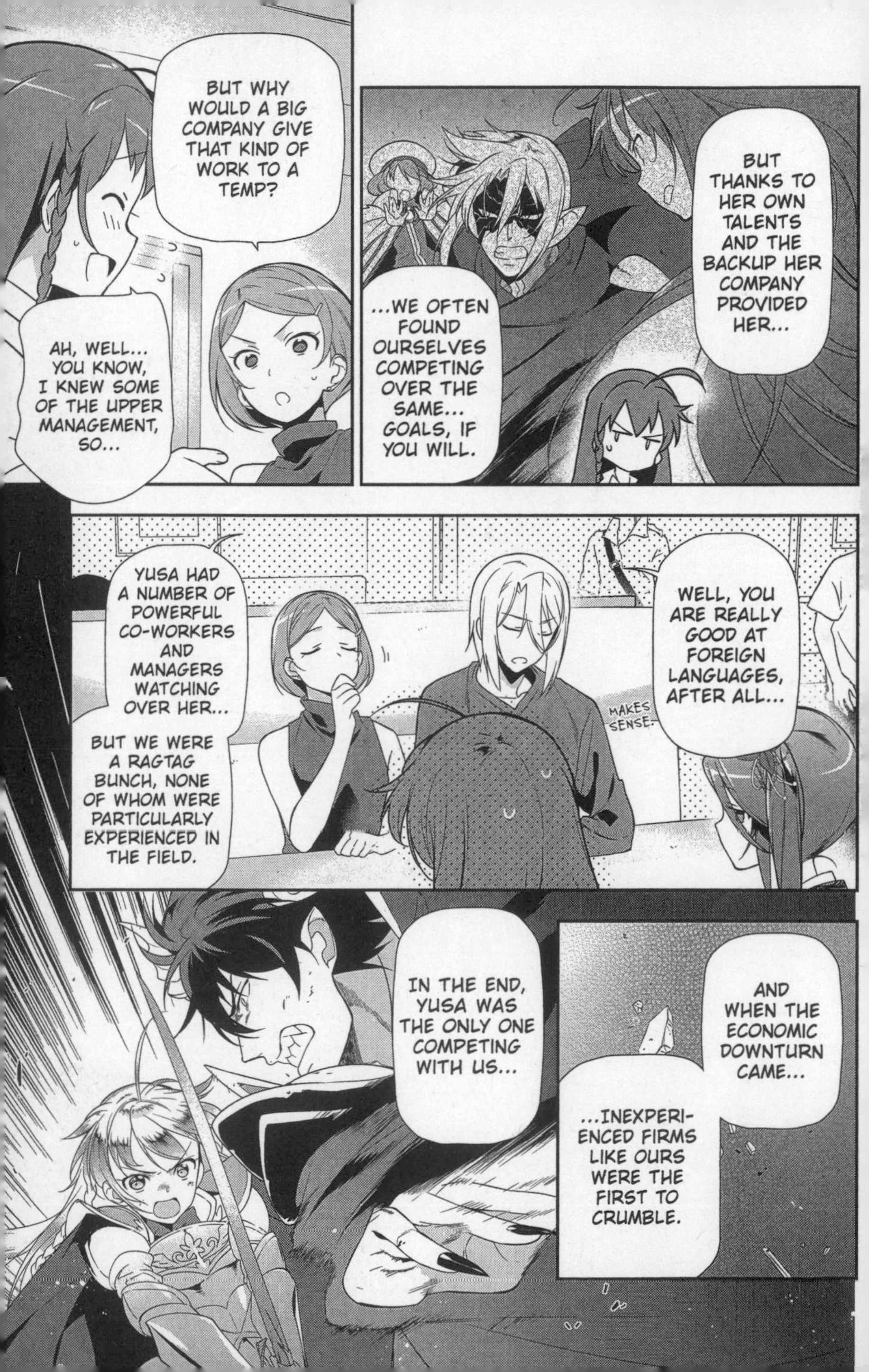
BUT THANKS TO HER OWN TALENTS AND THE BACKUP HER COMPANY PROVIDED HER...
...WE OFTEN FOUND OURSELVES COMPETING OVER THE SAME... GOALS, IF YOU WILL.
BUT WHY WOULD A BIG COMPANY GIVE THAT KIND OF WORK TO A TEMP?
AH, WELL... YOU KNOW, I KNEW SOME OF THE UPPER MANAGEMENT, SO...
WELL, YOU ARE REALLY GOOD AT FOREIGN LANGUAGES, AFTER ALL...
MAKES SENSE.
YUSA HAD A NUMBER OF POWERFUL CO-WORKERS AND MANAGERS WATCHING OVER HER...
BUT WE WERE A RAGTAG BUNCH, NONE OF WHOM WERE PARTICULARLY EXPERIENCED IN THE FIELD.
AND WHEN THE ECONOMIC DOWNTURN CAME...
...INEXPERIENCED FIRMS LIKE OURS WERE THE FIRST TO CRUMBLE.
IN THE END, YUSA WAS THE ONLY ONE COMPETING WITH US...

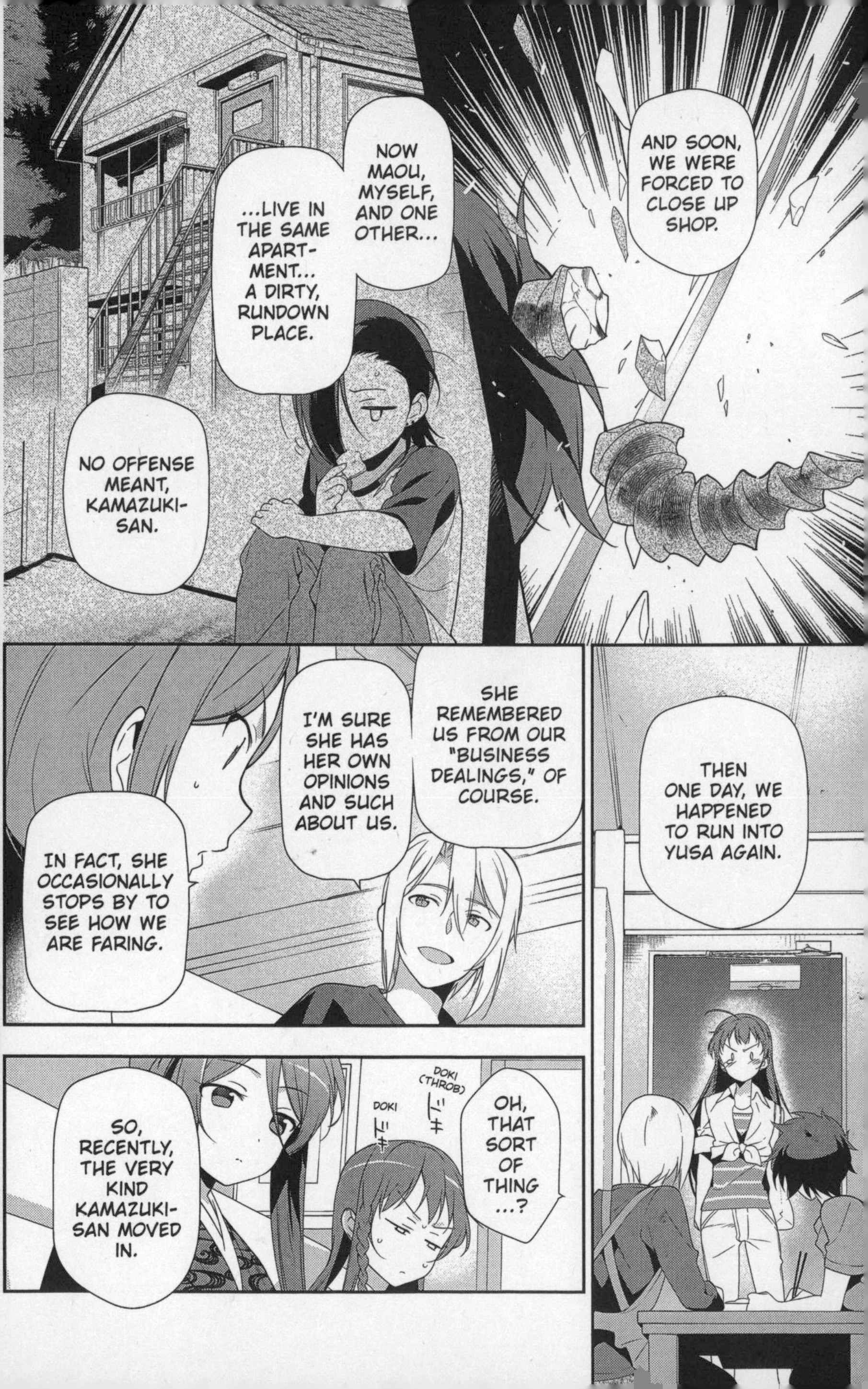
AND SOON, WE WERE FORCED TO CLOSE UP SHOP.
NOW MAOU, MYSELF, AND ONE OTHER...
...LIVE IN THE SAME APARTMENT... A DIRTY, RUNDOWN PLACE.
NO OFFENSE MEANT, KAMAZUKI-SAN.
THEN ONE DAY, WE HAPPENED TO RUN INTO YUSA AGAIN.
SHE REMEMBERED US FROM OUR "BUSINESS DEALINGS," OF COURSE.
I'M SURE SHE HAS HER OWN OPINIONS AND SUCH ABOUT US.
IN FACT, SHE OCCASIONALLY STOPS BY TO SEE HOW WE ARE FARING.
OH, THAT SORT OF THING ...?
DOKI (THROB)
DOKI
SO, RECENTLY, THE VERY KIND KAMAZUKI-SAN MOVED IN.

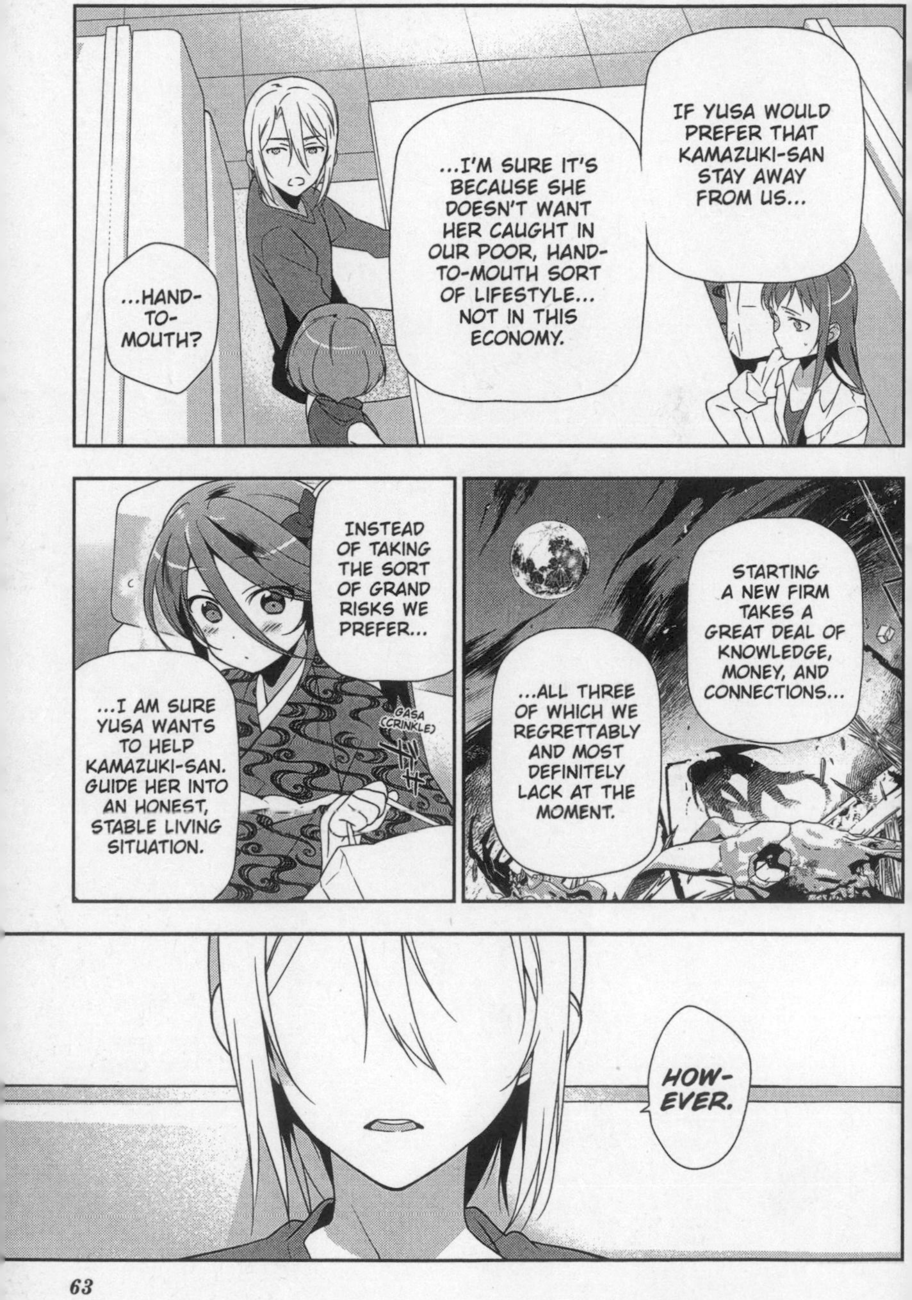
IF YUSA WOULD PREFER THAT KAMAZUKI-SAN STAY AWAY FROM US...
...I'M SURE IT'S BECAUSE SHE DOESN'T WANT HER CAUGHT IN OUR POOR, HAND-TO-MOUTH SORT OF LIFESTYLE... NOT IN THIS ECONOMY.
...HAND-TO-MOUTH?
STARTING A NEW FIRM TAKES A GREAT DEAL OF KNOWLEDGE, MONEY, AND CONNECTIONS...
...ALL THREE OF WHICH WE REGRETTABLY AND MOST DEFINITELY LACK AT THE MOMENT.
INSTEAD OF TAKING THE SORT OF GRAND RISKS WE PREFER...
GASA (CRINKLE)
...I AM SURE YUSA WANTS TO HELP KAMAZUKI-SAN. GUIDE HER INTO AN HONEST, STABLE LIVING SITUATION.
HOW-EVER.

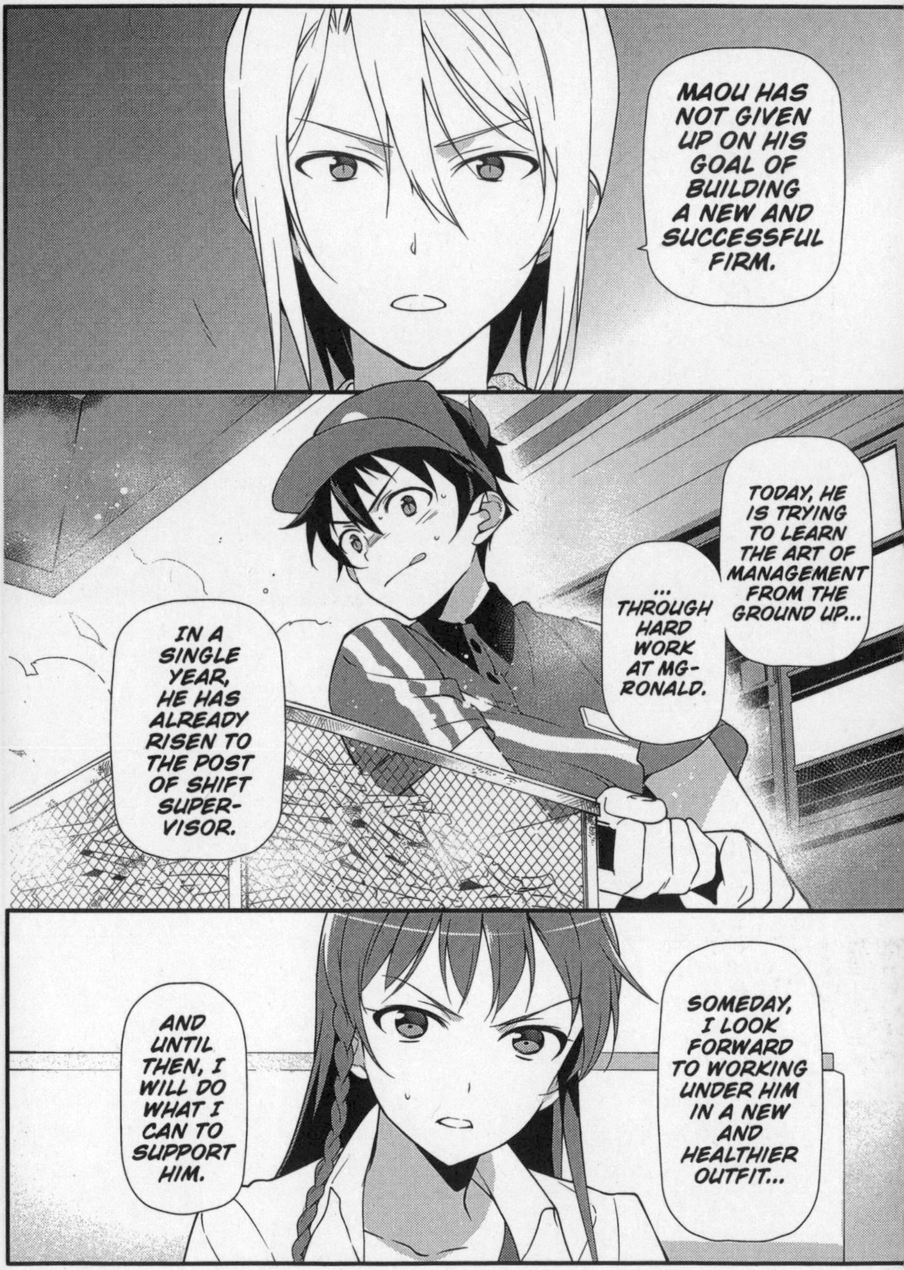
MAOU HAS NOT GIVEN UP ON HIS GOAL OF BUILDING A NEW AND SUCCESSFUL FIRM.
TODAY, HE IS TRYING TO LEARN THE ART OF MANAGEMENT FROM THE GROUND UP...
...THROUGH HARD WORK AT MG-RONALD.
IN A SINGLE YEAR, HE HAS ALREADY RISEN TO THE POST OF SHIFT SUPER-VISOR.
SOMEDAY, I LOOK FORWARD TO WORKING UNDER HIM IN A NEW AND HEALTHIER OUTFIT...
AND UNTIL THEN, I WILL DO WHAT I CAN TO SUPPORT HIM.

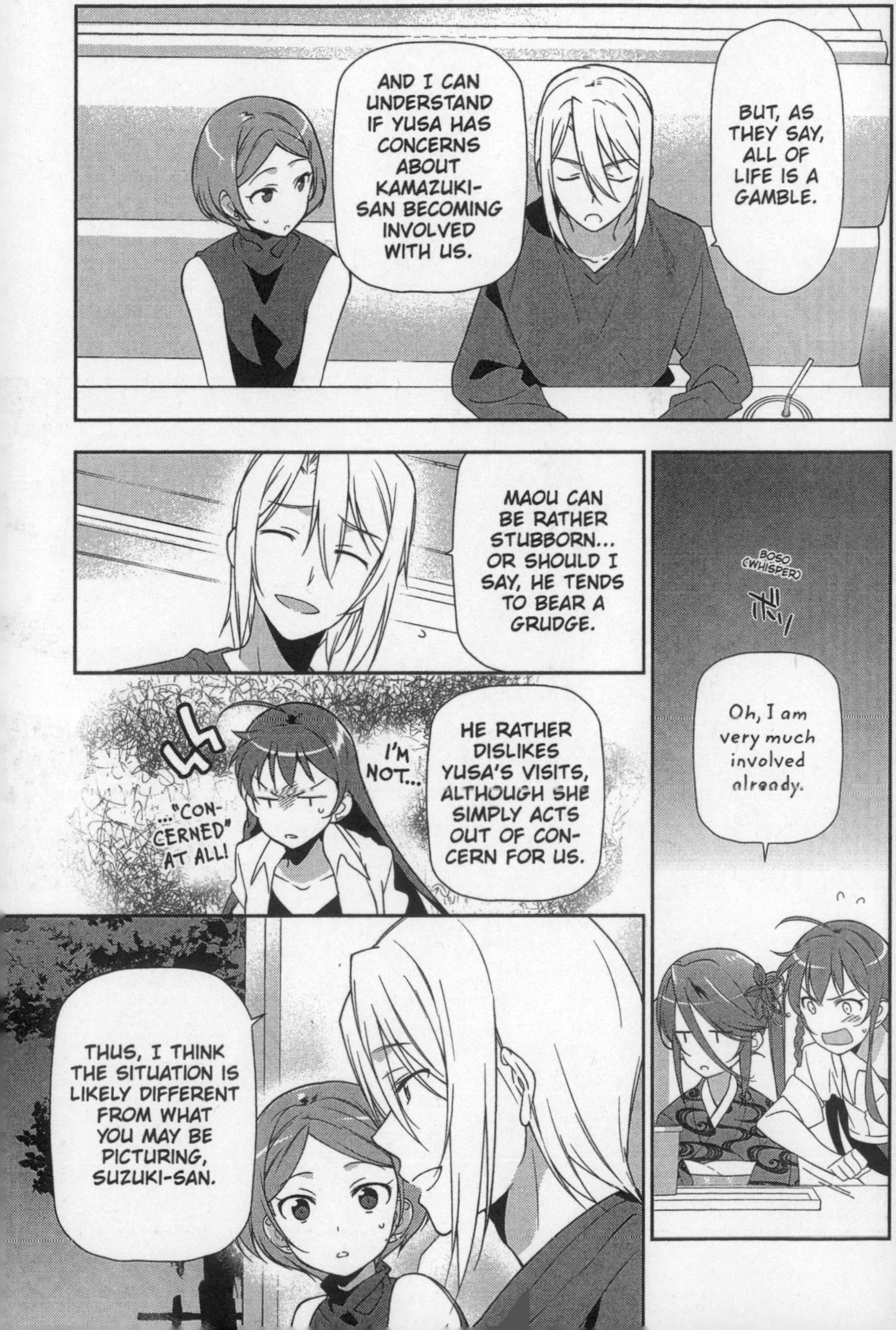
BUT, AS THEY SAY, ALL OF LIFE IS A GAMBLE.
AND I CAN UNDERSTAND IF YUSA HAS CONCERNS ABOUT KAMAZUKI-SAN BECOMING INVOLVED WITH US.
BOSO (WHISPER)
ボソッ
Oh, I am very much involved already.
MAOU CAN BE RATHER STUBBORN... OR SHOULD I SAY, HE TENDS TO BEAR A GRUDGE.
HE RATHER DISLIKES YUSA'S VISITS, ALTHOUGH SHE SIMPLY ACTS OUT OF CONCERN FOR US.
I'M NOT...
..."CONCERNED" AT ALL!
THUS, I THINK THE SITUATION IS LIKELY DIFFERENT FROM WHAT YOU MAY BE PICTURING, SUZUKI-SAN.

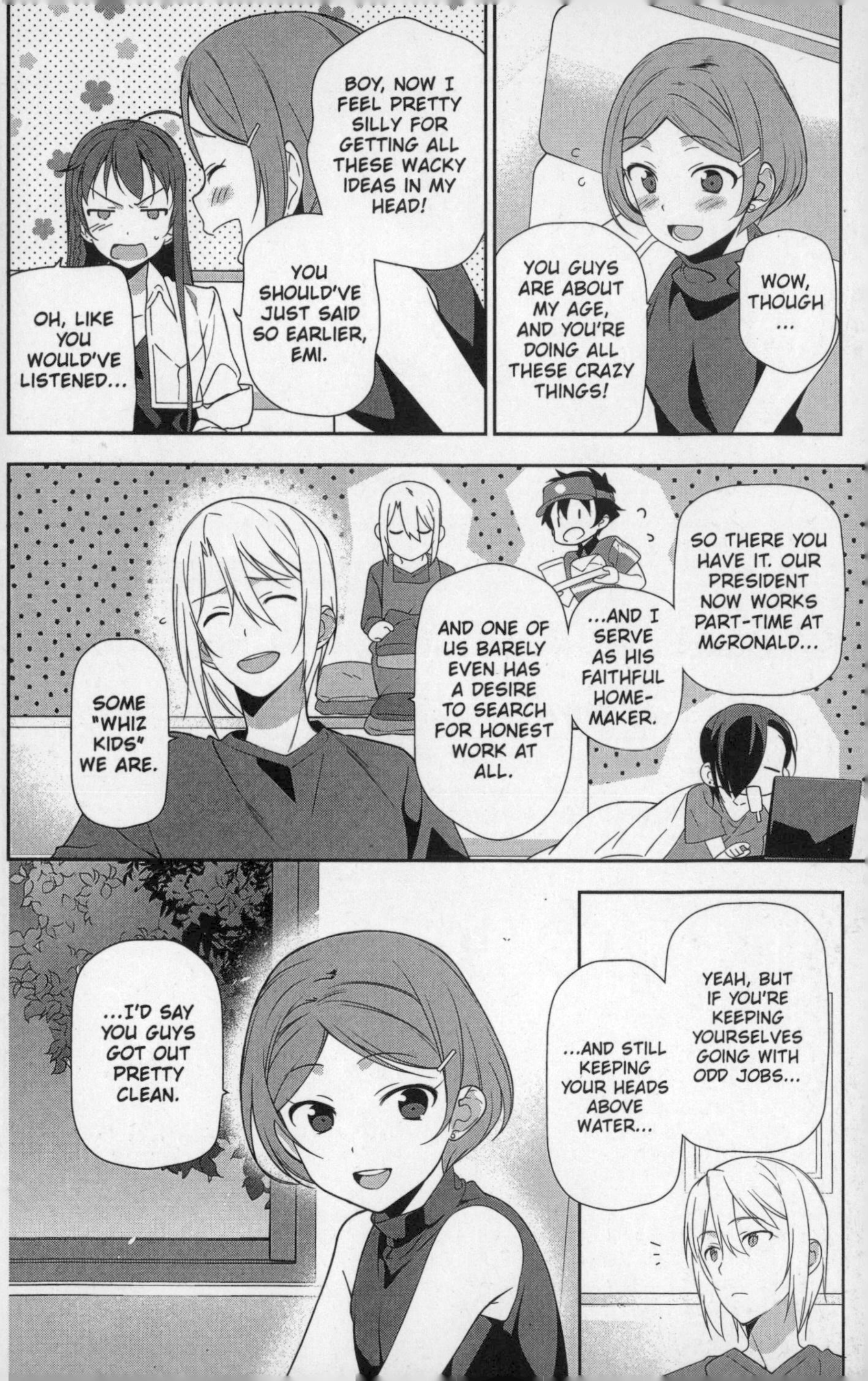
WOW, THOUGH ...
YOU GUYS ARE ABOUT MY AGE, AND YOU'RE DOING ALL THESE CRAZY THINGS!
BOY, NOW I FEEL PRETTY SILLY FOR GETTING ALL THESE WACKY IDEAS IN MY HEAD!
YOU SHOULD'VE JUST SAID SO EARLIER, EMI.
OH, LIKE YOU WOULD'VE LISTENED...
SO THERE YOU HAVE IT. OUR PRESIDENT NOW WORKS PART-TIME AT MGRONALD...
...AND I SERVE AS HIS FAITHFUL HOME-MAKER.
AND ONE OF US BARELY EVEN HAS A DESIRE TO SEARCH FOR HONEST WORK AT ALL.
SOME "WHIZ KIDS" WE ARE.
YEAH, BUT IF YOU'RE KEEPING YOURSELVES GOING WITH ODD JOBS...
...AND STILL KEEPING YOUR HEADS ABOVE WATER...
...I'D SAY YOU GUYS GOT OUT PRETTY CLEAN.

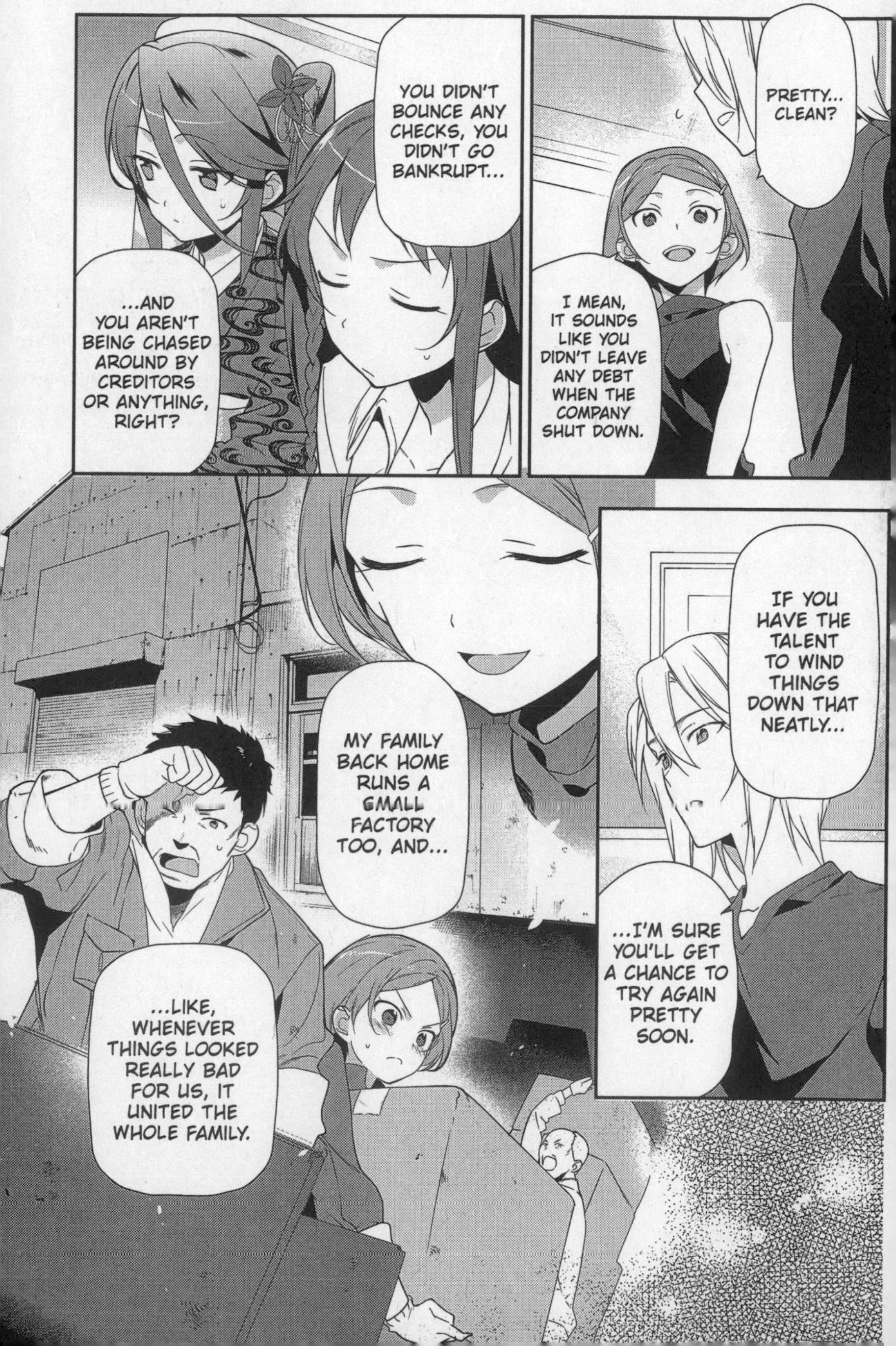
PRETTY... CLEAN?
I MEAN, IT SOUNDS LIKE YOU DIDN'T LEAVE ANY DEBT WHEN THE COMPANY SHUT DOWN.
YOU DIDN'T BOUNCE ANY CHECKS, YOU DIDN'T GO BANKRUPT...
...AND YOU AREN'T BEING CHASED AROUND BY CREDITORS OR ANYTHING, RIGHT?
IF YOU HAVE THE TALENT TO WIND THINGS DOWN THAT NEATLY...
...I'M SURE YOU'LL GET A CHANCE TO TRY AGAIN PRETTY SOON.
MY FAMILY BACK HOME RUNS A SMALL FACTORY TOO, AND...
...LIKE, WHENEVER THINGS LOOKED REALLY BAD FOR US, IT UNITED THE WHOLE FAMILY.

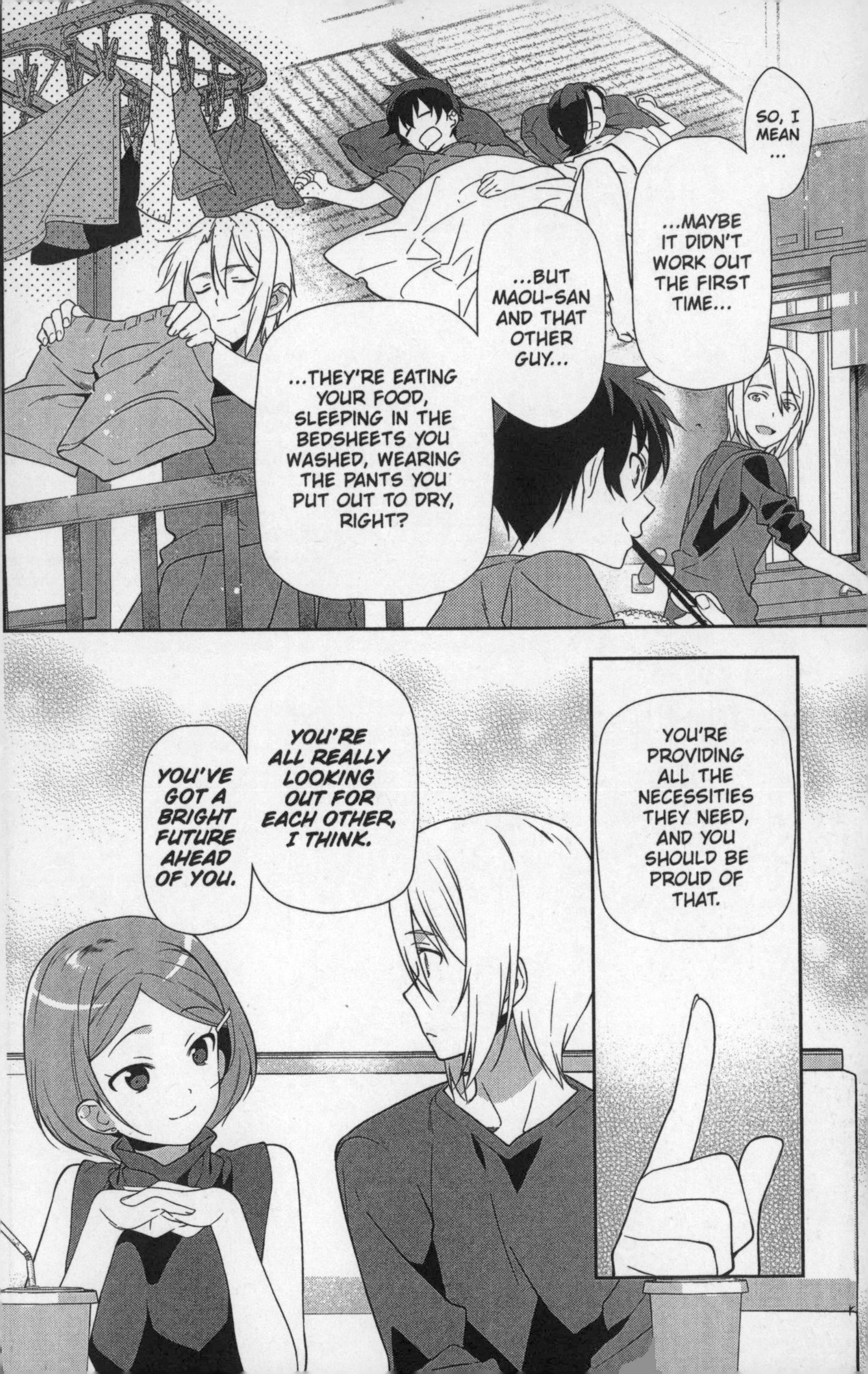
SO, I MEAN ...
...MAYBE IT DIDN'T WORK OUT THE FIRST TIME...
...BUT MAOU-SAN AND THAT OTHER GUY...
...THEY'RE EATING YOUR FOOD, SLEEPING IN THE BEDSHEETS YOU WASHED, WEARING THE PANTS YOU PUT OUT TO DRY, RIGHT?
YOU'RE PROVIDING ALL THE NECESSITIES THEY NEED, AND YOU SHOULD BE PROUD OF THAT.
YOU'RE ALL REALLY LOOKING OUT FOR EACH OTHER, I THINK.
YOU'VE GOT A BRIGHT FUTURE AHEAD OF YOU.

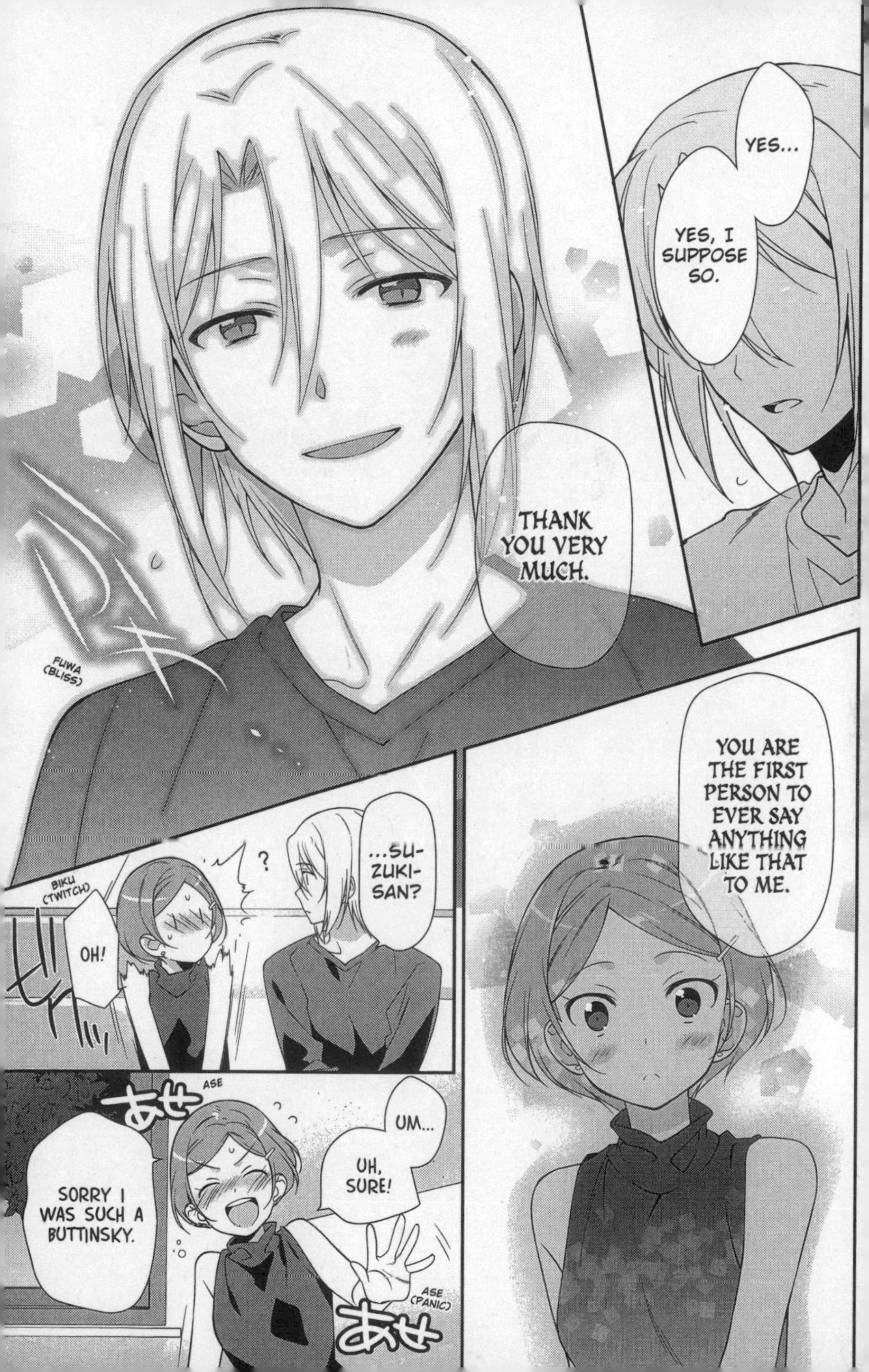

YES...
YES, I SUPPOSE SO.
THANK YOU VERY MUCH.
FUWA (BLISS)
YOU ARE THE FIRST PERSON TO EVER SAY ANYTHING LIKE THAT TO ME.
...SU-ZUKI-SAN?
?
BIKU (TWITCH)
OH!
ASE
UM...
UH, SURE!
SORRY I WAS SUCH A BUTTINSKY.
ASE (PANIC)

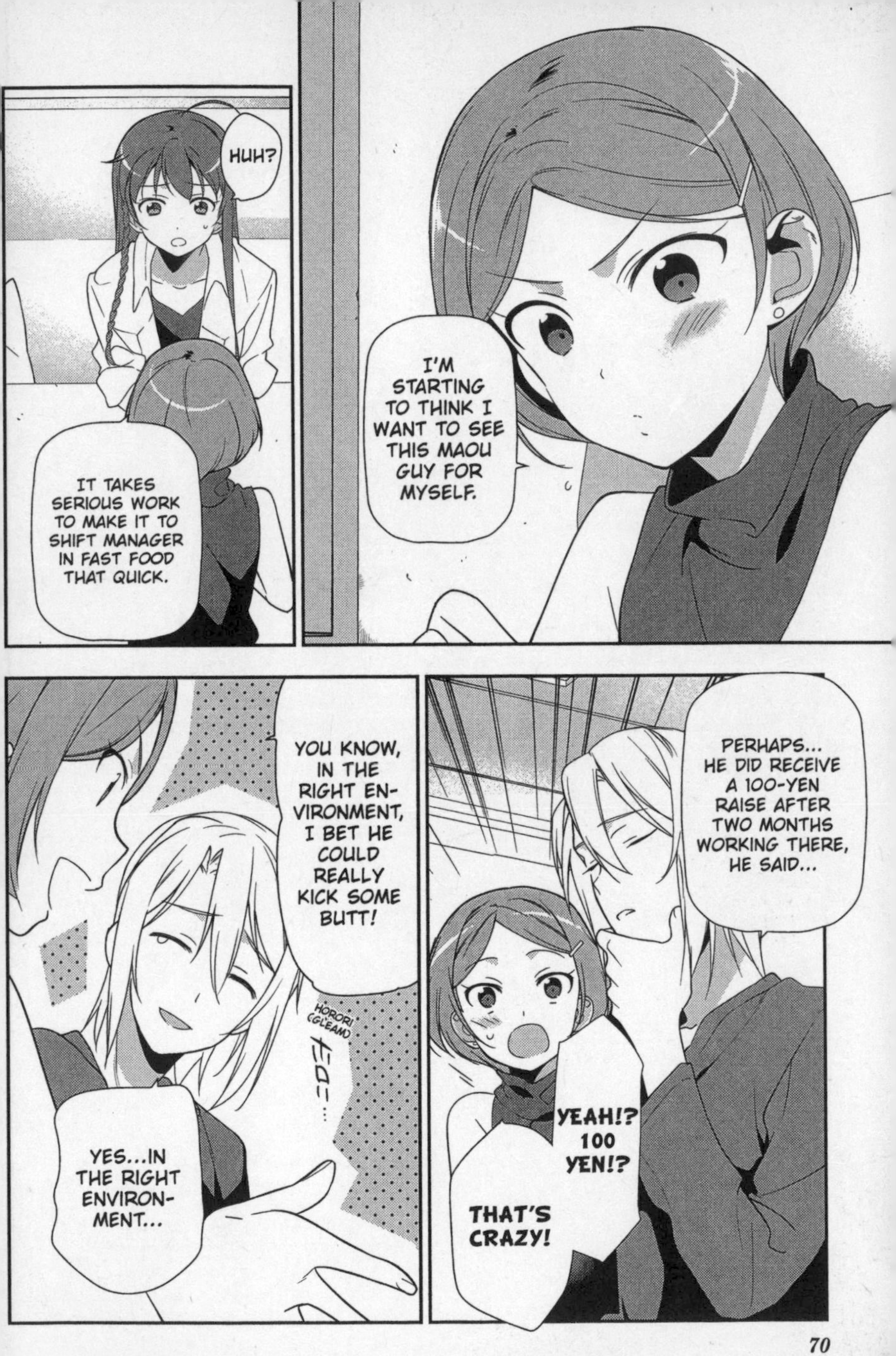
I'M STARTING TO THINK I WANT TO SEE THIS MAOU GUY FOR MYSELF.
HUH?
IT TAKES SERIOUS WORK TO MAKE IT TO SHIFT MANAGER IN FAST FOOD THAT QUICK.
PERHAPS... HE DID RECEIVE A 100-YEN RAISE AFTER TWO MONTHS WORKING THERE, HE SAID...
YEAH!? 100 YEN!?
THAT'S CRAZY!
YOU KNOW, IN THE RIGHT EN-VIRONMENT, I BET HE COULD REALLY KICK SOME BUTT!
HORORI (GLEAM)
YES...IN THE RIGHT ENVIRON-MENT...

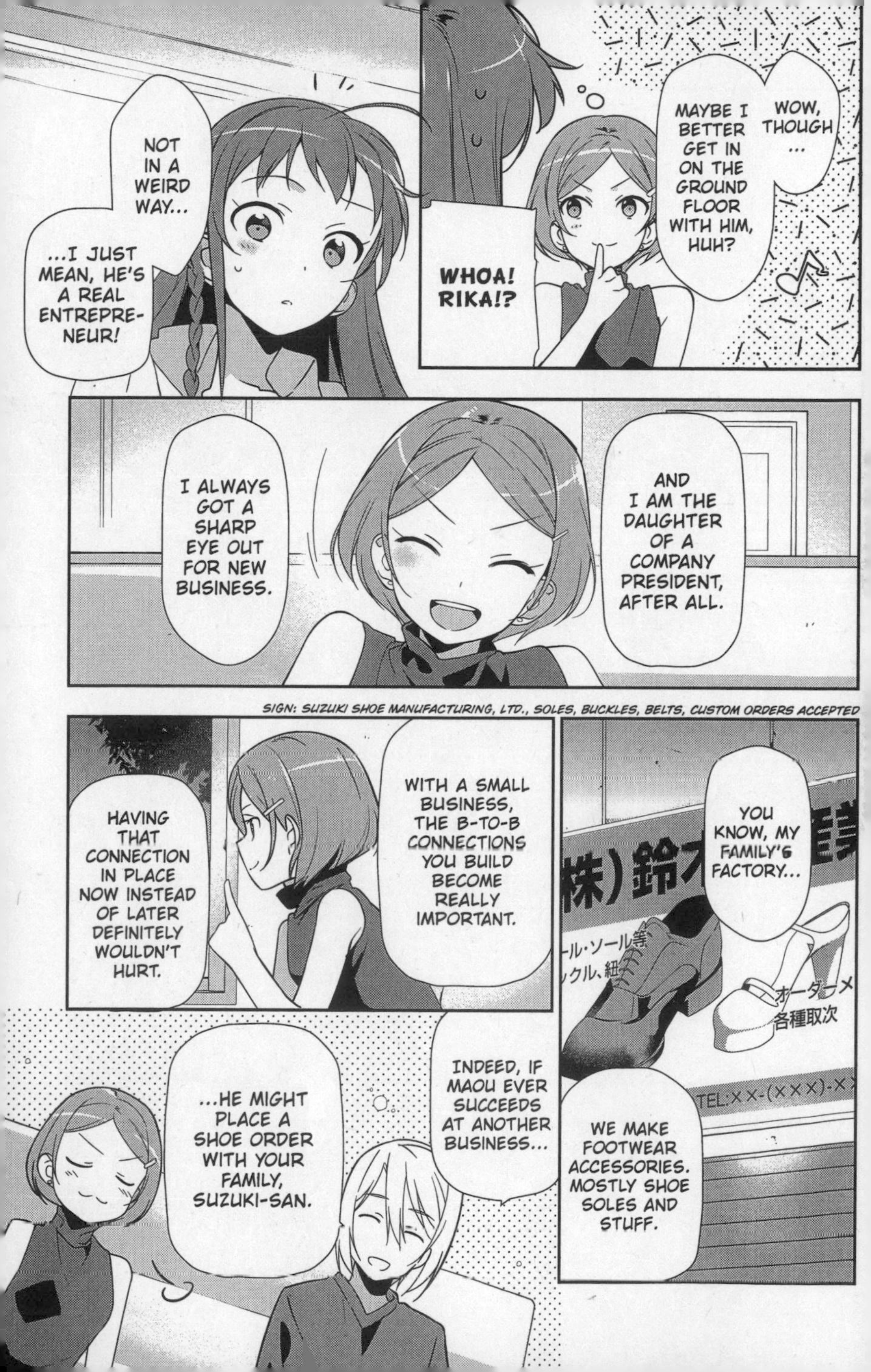
WOW, THOUGH...
MAYBE I BETTER GET IN ON THE GROUND FLOOR WITH HIM, HUH?
WHOA! RIKA!?
NOT IN A WEIRD WAY...
...I JUST MEAN, HE'S A REAL ENTREPRENEUR!
AND I AM THE DAUGHTER OF A COMPANY PRESIDENT, AFTER ALL.
I ALWAYS GOT A SHARP EYE OUT FOR NEW BUSINESS.
SIGN: SUZUKI SHOE MANUFACTURING, LTD., SOLES, BUCKLES, BELTS, CUSTOM ORDERS ACCEPTED
YOU KNOW, MY FAMILY'S FACTORY...
各種取次
TEL:××-(×××)-××
WE MAKE FOOTWEAR ACCESSORIES. MOSTLY SHOE SOLES AND STUFF.
WITH A SMALL BUSINESS, THE B-TO-B CONNECTIONS YOU BUILD BECOME REALLY IMPORTANT.
HAVING THAT CONNECTION IN PLACE NOW INSTEAD OF LATER DEFINITELY WOULDN'T HURT.
INDEED, IF MAOU EVER SUCCEEDS AT ANOTHER BUSINESS...
...HE MIGHT PLACE A SHOE ORDER WITH YOUR FAMILY, SUZUKI-SAN.

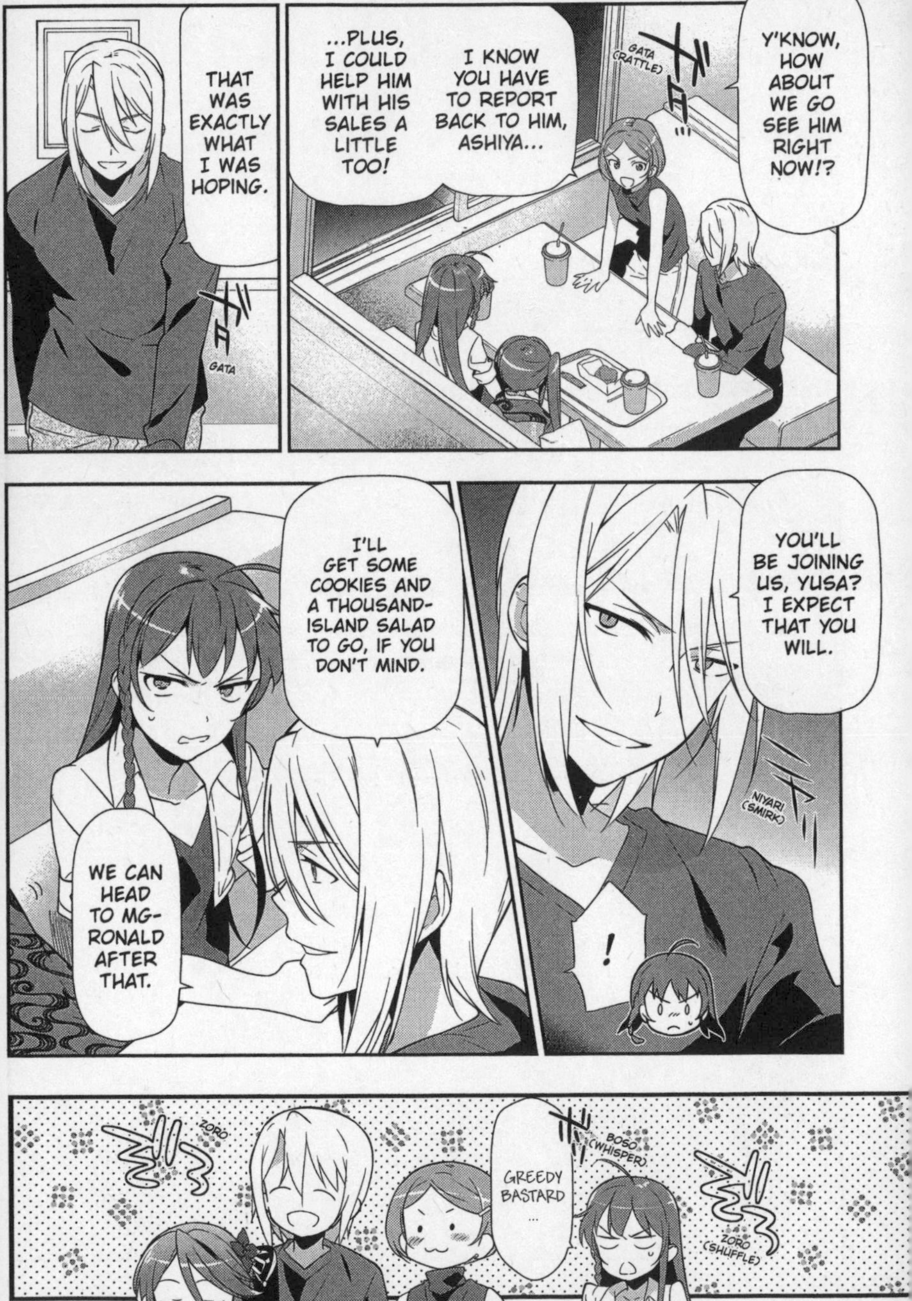
Y'KNOW, HOW ABOUT WE GO SEE HIM RIGHT NOW!?
GATA (RATTLE)
I KNOW YOU HAVE TO REPORT BACK TO HIM, ASHIYA...
...PLUS, I COULD HELP HIM WITH HIS SALES A LITTLE TOO!
THAT WAS EXACTLY WHAT I WAS HOPING.
GATA
YOU'LL BE JOINING US, YUSA? I EXPECT THAT YOU WILL.
NIYARI (SMIRK)
!
I'LL GET SOME COOKIES AND A THOUSAND-ISLAND SALAD TO GO, IF YOU DON'T MIND.
WE CAN HEAD TO MG-RONALD AFTER THAT.
ZORO (SHUFFLE)
BOSO (WHISPER)
GREEDY BASTARD ...
ZORO

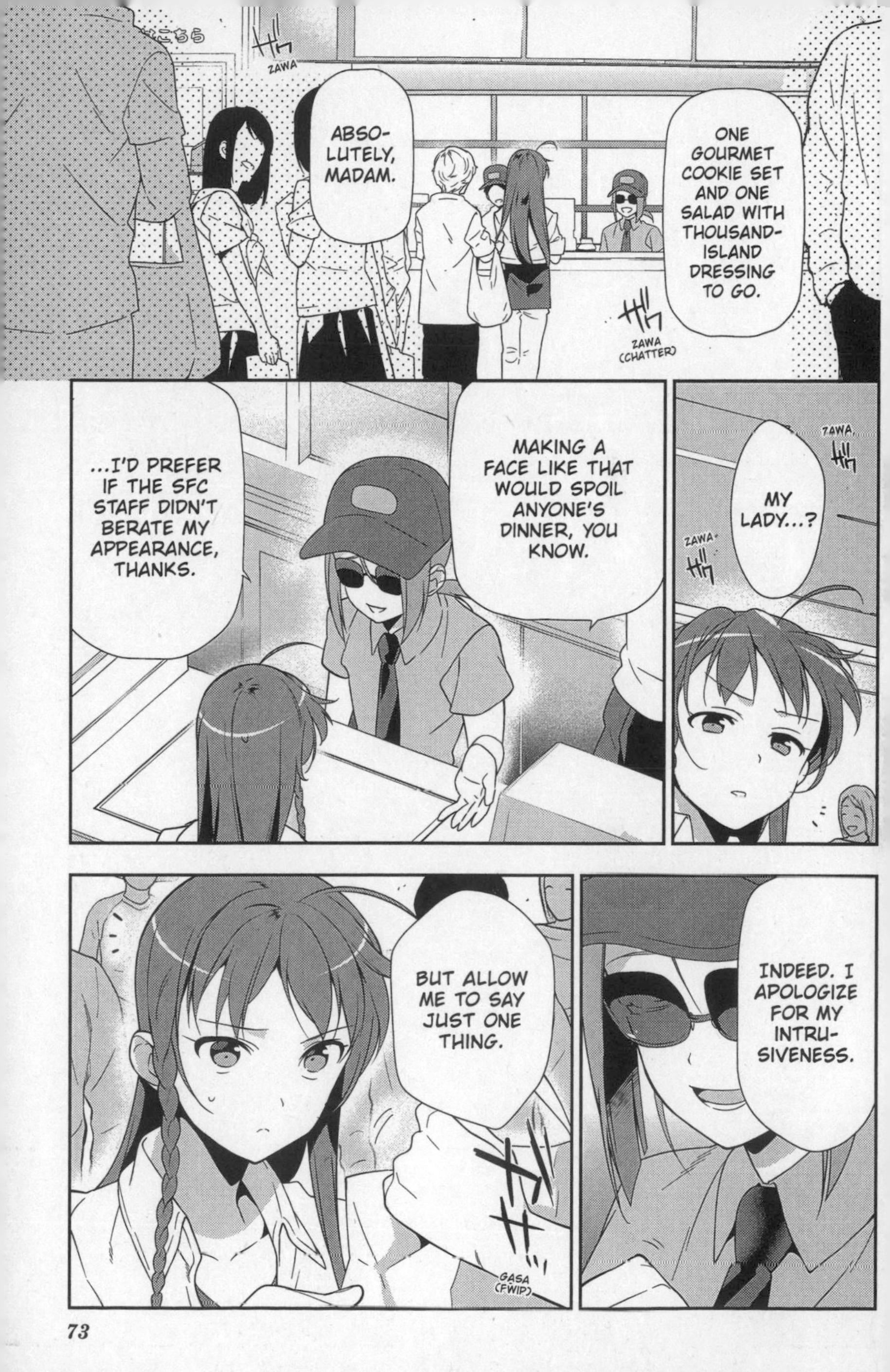
ONE GOURMET COOKIE SET AND ONE SALAD WITH THOUSAND-ISLAND DRESSING TO GO.
ZAWA (CHATTER)
ABSO-LUTELY, MADAM.
ZAWA
ZAWA
MY LADY...?
ZAWA
MAKING A FACE LIKE THAT WOULD SPOIL ANYONE'S DINNER, YOU KNOW.
...I'D PREFER IF THE SFC STAFF DIDN'T BERATE MY APPEARANCE, THANKS.
INDEED. I APOLOGIZE FOR MY INTRU-SIVENESS.
BUT ALLOW ME TO SAY JUST ONE THING.
GASA (FWIP)

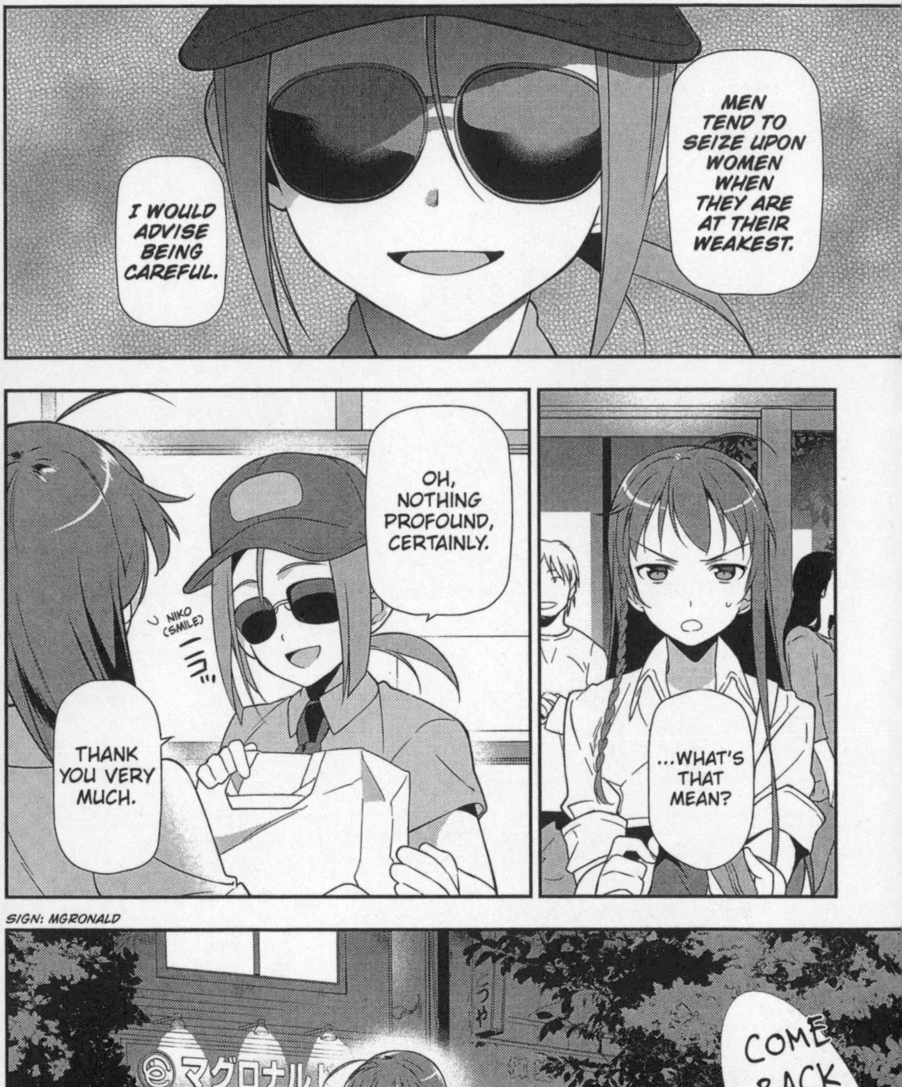
MEN TEND TO SEIZE UPON WOMEN WHEN THEY ARE AT THEIR WEAKEST.
I WOULD ADVISE BEING CAREFUL.
...WHAT'S THAT MEAN?
OH, NOTHING PROFOUND, CERTAINLY.
NIKO (SMILE)
ニコッ
THANK YOU VERY MUCH.

SIGN: MGRONALD

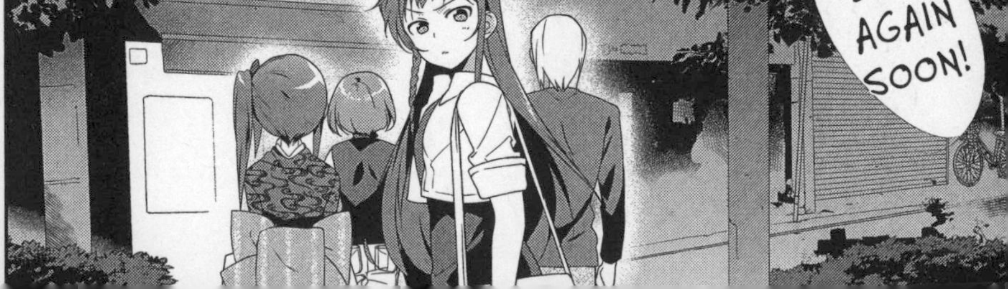
COME BACK AGAIN SOON!
マグロナルド

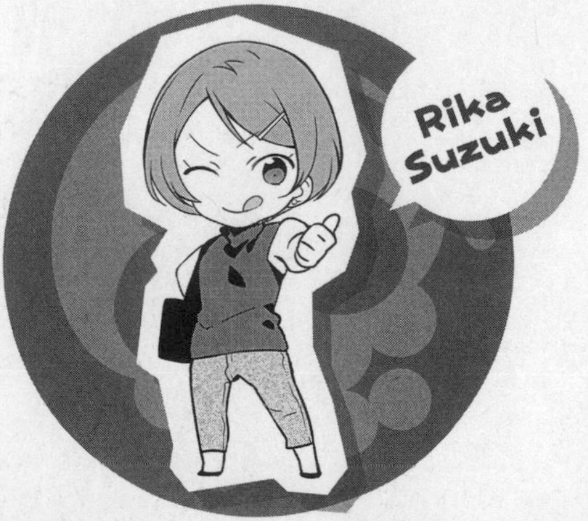
Rika
Suzuki

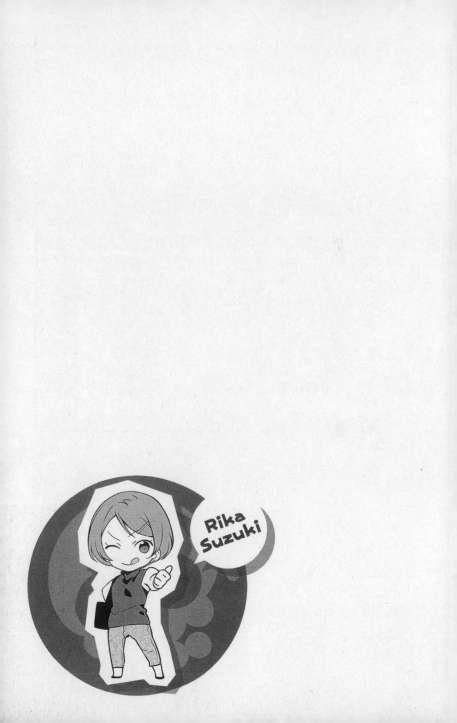

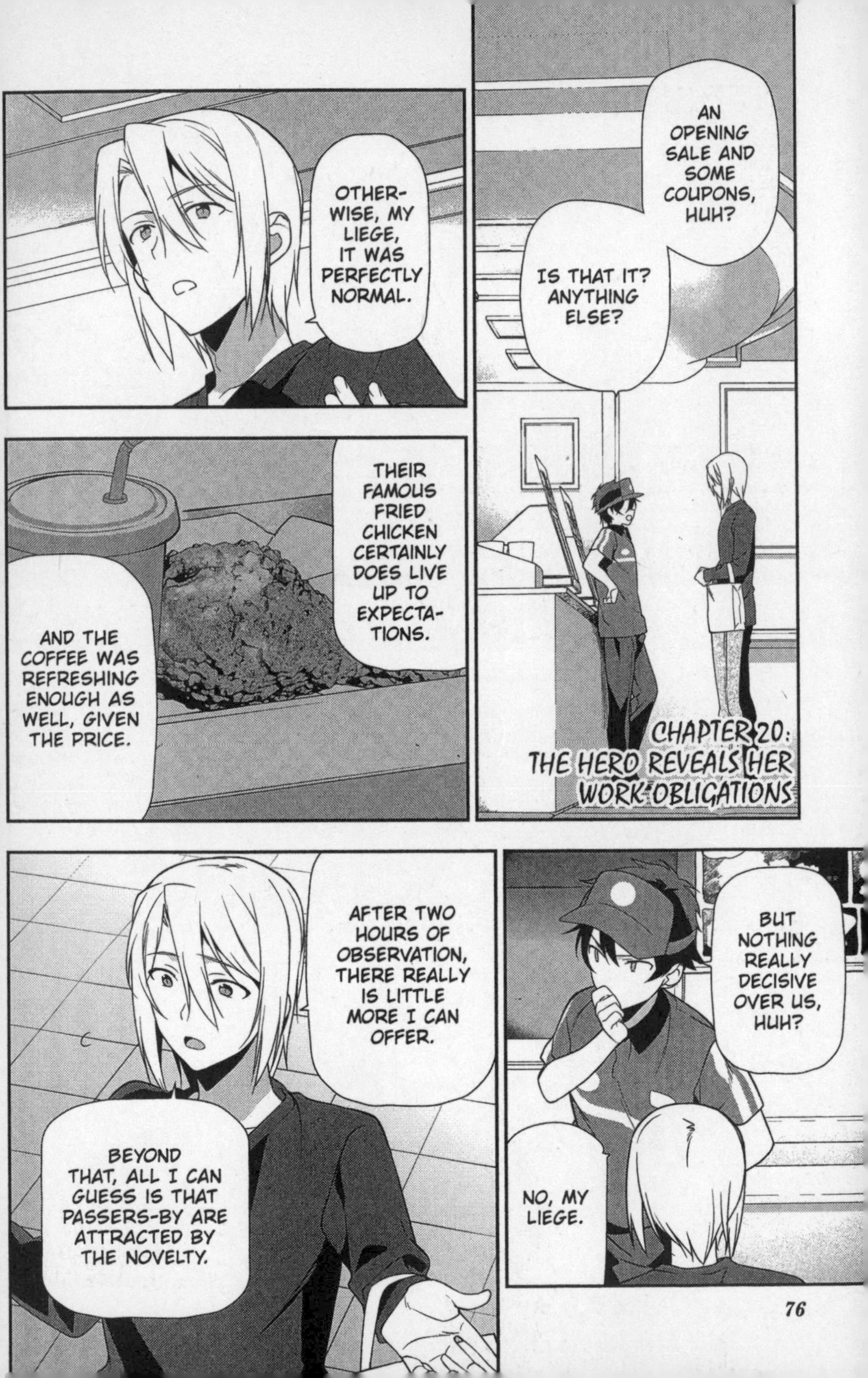
AN OPENING SALE AND SOME COUPONS, HUH?
IS THAT IT? ANYTHING ELSE?
CHAPTER 20: THE HERO REVEALS HER WORK OBLIGATIONS
OTHER-WISE, MY LIEGE, IT WAS PERFECTLY NORMAL.
THEIR FAMOUS FRIED CHICKEN CERTAINLY DOES LIVE UP TO EXPECTA-TIONS.
AND THE COFFEE WAS REFRESHING ENOUGH AS WELL, GIVEN THE PRICE.
BUT NOTHING REALLY DECISIVE OVER US, HUH?
NO, MY LIEGE.
AFTER TWO HOURS OF OBSERVATION, THERE REALLY IS LITTLE MORE I CAN OFFER.
BEYOND THAT, ALL I CAN GUESS IS THAT PASSERS-BY ARE ATTRACTED BY THE NOVELTY.

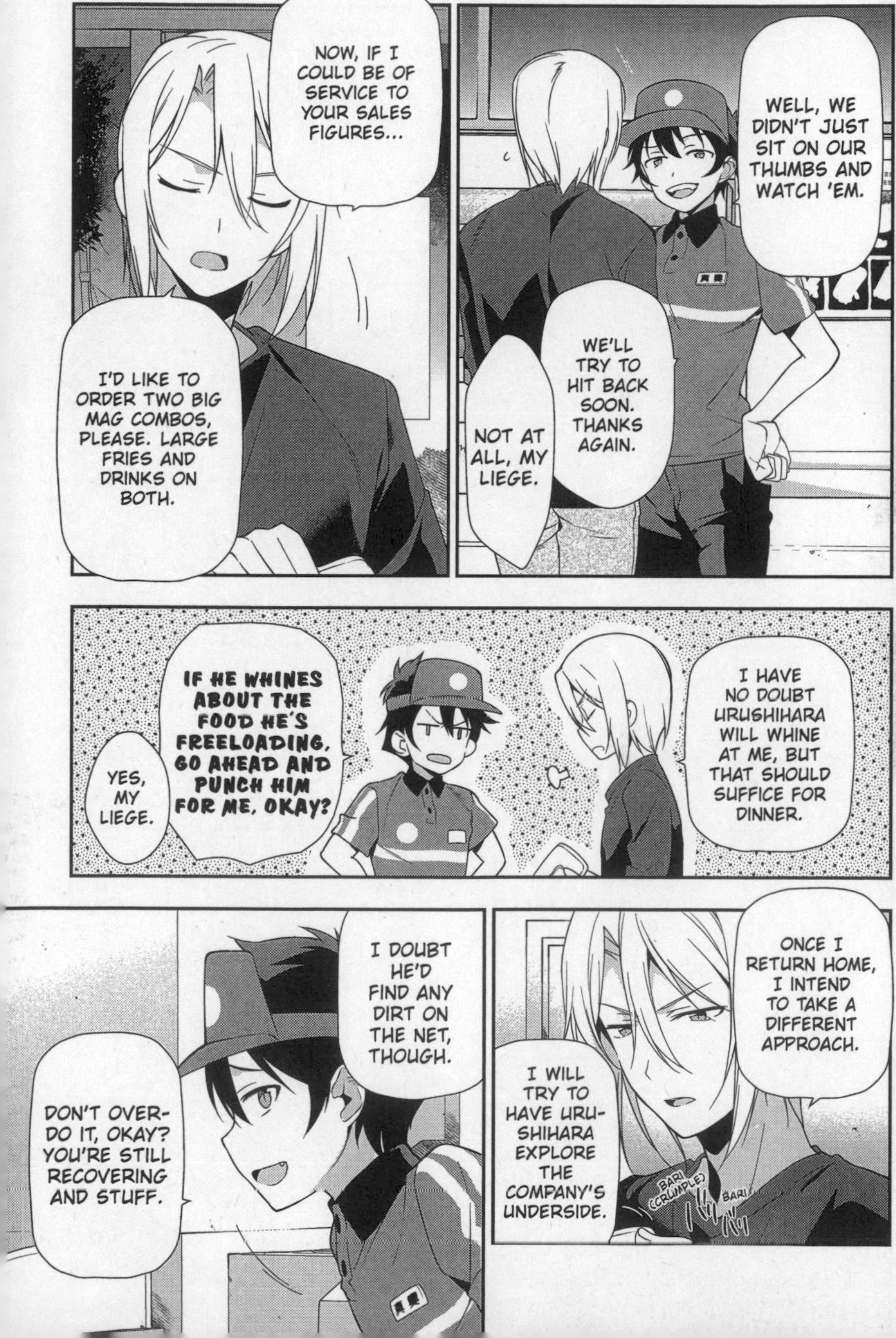
WELL, WE DIDN'T JUST SIT ON OUR THUMBS AND WATCH 'EM.
WE'LL TRY TO HIT BACK SOON. THANKS AGAIN.
NOT AT ALL, MY LIEGE.
NOW, IF I COULD BE OF SERVICE TO YOUR SALES FIGURES...
I'D LIKE TO ORDER TWO BIG MAG COMBOS, PLEASE. LARGE FRIES AND DRINKS ON BOTH.
I HAVE NO DOUBT URUSHIHARA WILL WHINE AT ME, BUT THAT SHOULD SUFFICE FOR DINNER.
IF HE WHINES ABOUT THE FOOD HE'S FREELOADING, GO AHEAD AND PUNCH HIM FOR ME, OKAY?
YES, MY LIEGE.
ONCE I RETURN HOME, I INTEND TO TAKE A DIFFERENT APPROACH.
I WILL TRY TO HAVE URUSHIHARA EXPLORE THE COMPANY'S UNDERSIDE.
BARI (CRUMPLE)
BARI
I DOUBT HE'D FIND ANY DIRT ON THE NET, THOUGH.
DON'T OVERDO IT, OKAY? YOU'RE STILL RECOVERING AND STUFF.

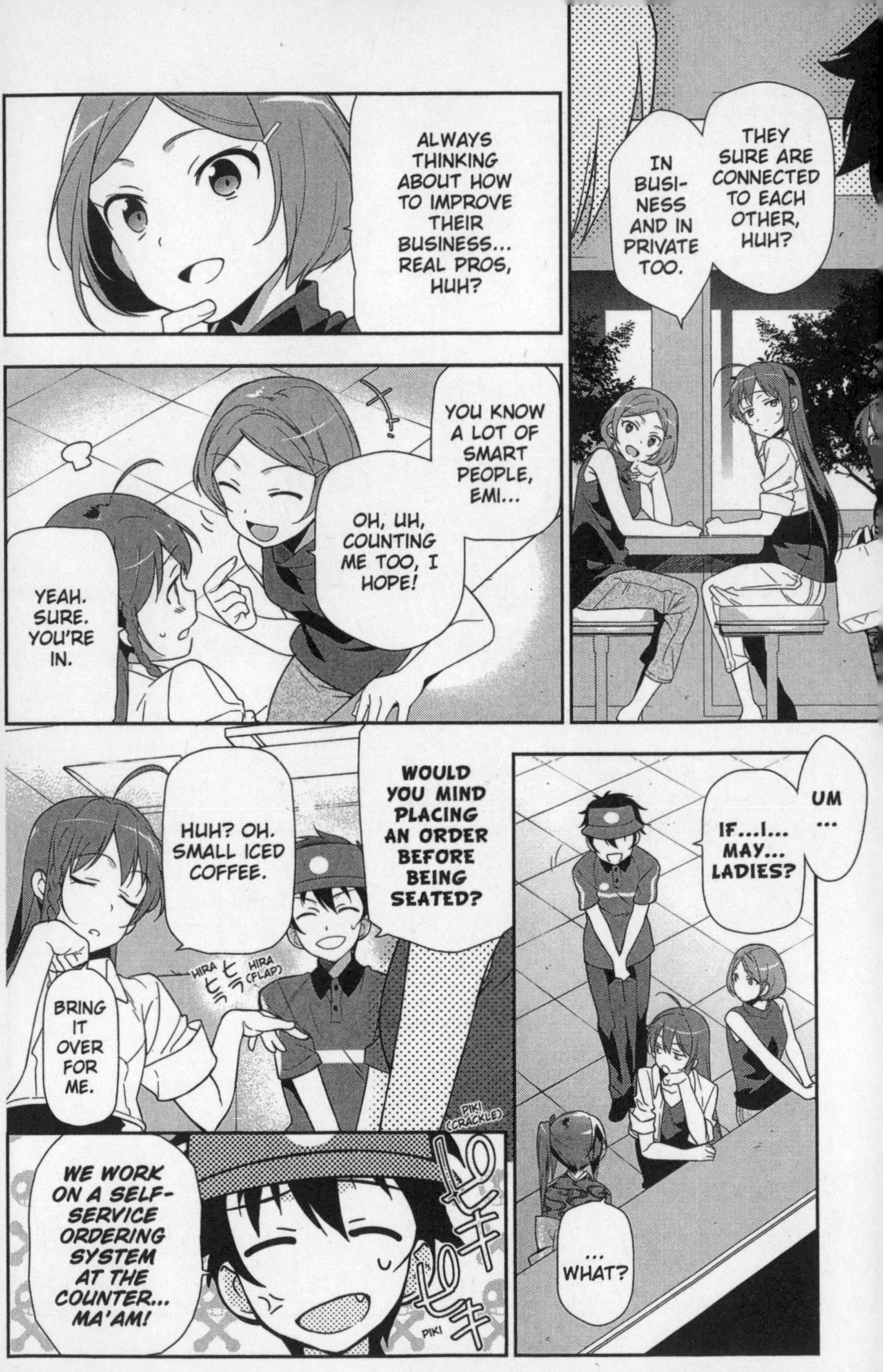
THEY SURE ARE CONNECTED TO EACH OTHER, HUH?
IN BUSINESS AND IN PRIVATE TOO.
ALWAYS THINKING ABOUT HOW TO IMPROVE THEIR BUSINESS... REAL PROS, HUH?
YOU KNOW A LOT OF SMART PEOPLE, EMI...
OH, UH, COUNTING ME TOO, I HOPE!
YEAH. SURE. YOU'RE IN.
UM ...
IF...I... MAY... LADIES?
... WHAT?
WOULD YOU MIND PLACING AN ORDER BEFORE BEING SEATED?
HUH? OH. SMALL ICED COFFEE.
HIRA HIRA (FLAP)
BRING IT OVER FOR ME.
PIKI (CRACKLE)
WE WORK ON A SELF-SERVICE ORDERING SYSTEM AT THE COUNTER... MA'AM!
PIKI

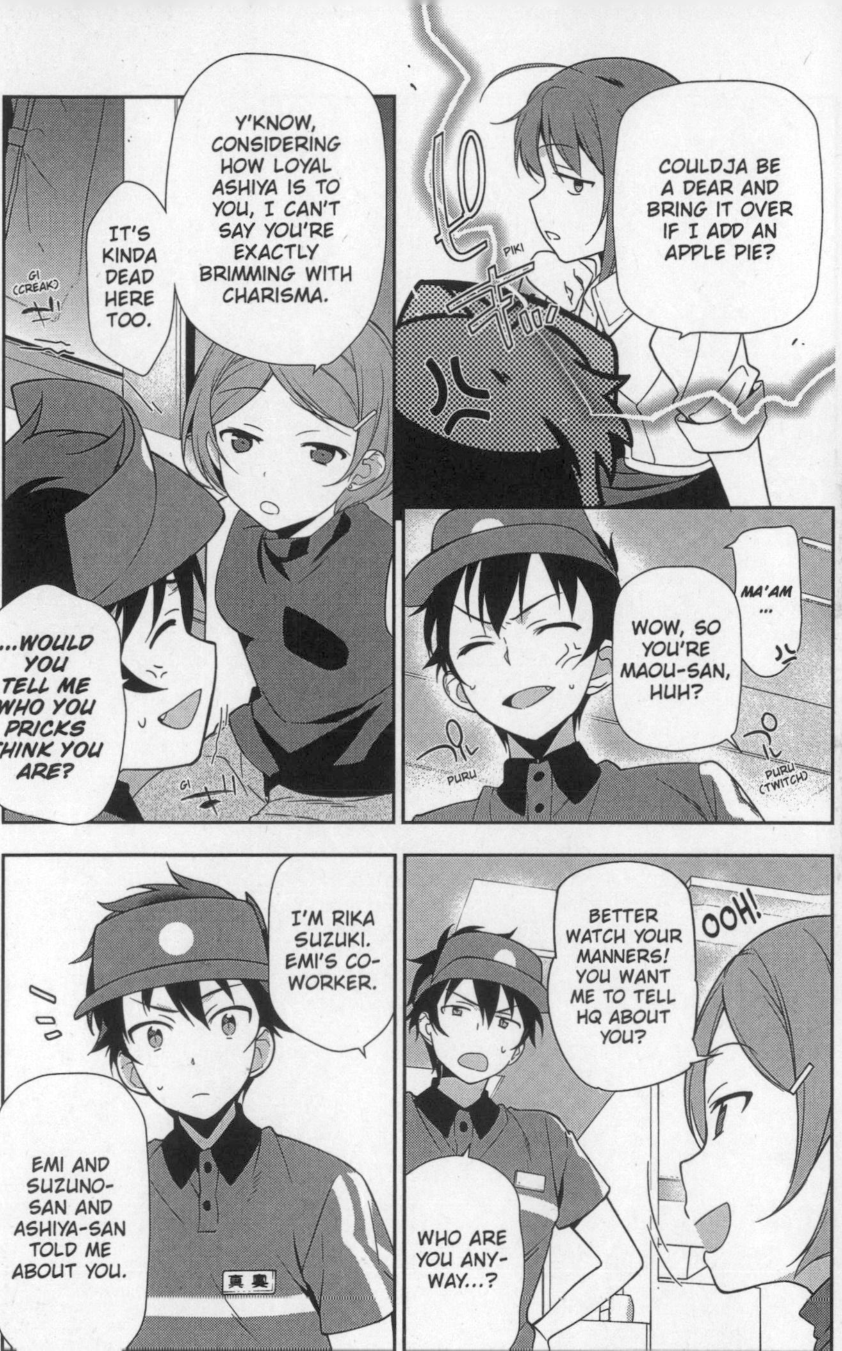
COULDJA BE A DEAR AND BRING IT OVER IF I ADD AN APPLE PIE?
PIKI
MA'AM...
WOW, SO YOU'RE MAOU-SAN, HUH?
PURU (TWITCH)
PURU
Y'KNOW, CONSIDERING HOW LOYAL ASHIYA IS TO YOU, I CAN'T SAY YOU'RE EXACTLY BRIMMING WITH CHARISMA.
IT'S KINDA DEAD HERE TOO.
GI (CREAK)
...WOULD YOU TELL ME WHO YOU PRICKS THINK YOU ARE?
GI
OOH!
BETTER WATCH YOUR MANNERS! YOU WANT ME TO TELL HQ ABOUT YOU?
WHO ARE YOU ANY-WAY...?
I'M RIKA SUZUKI. EMI'S CO-WORKER.
EMI AND SUZUNO-SAN AND ASHIYA-SAN TOLD ME ABOUT YOU.
真奥

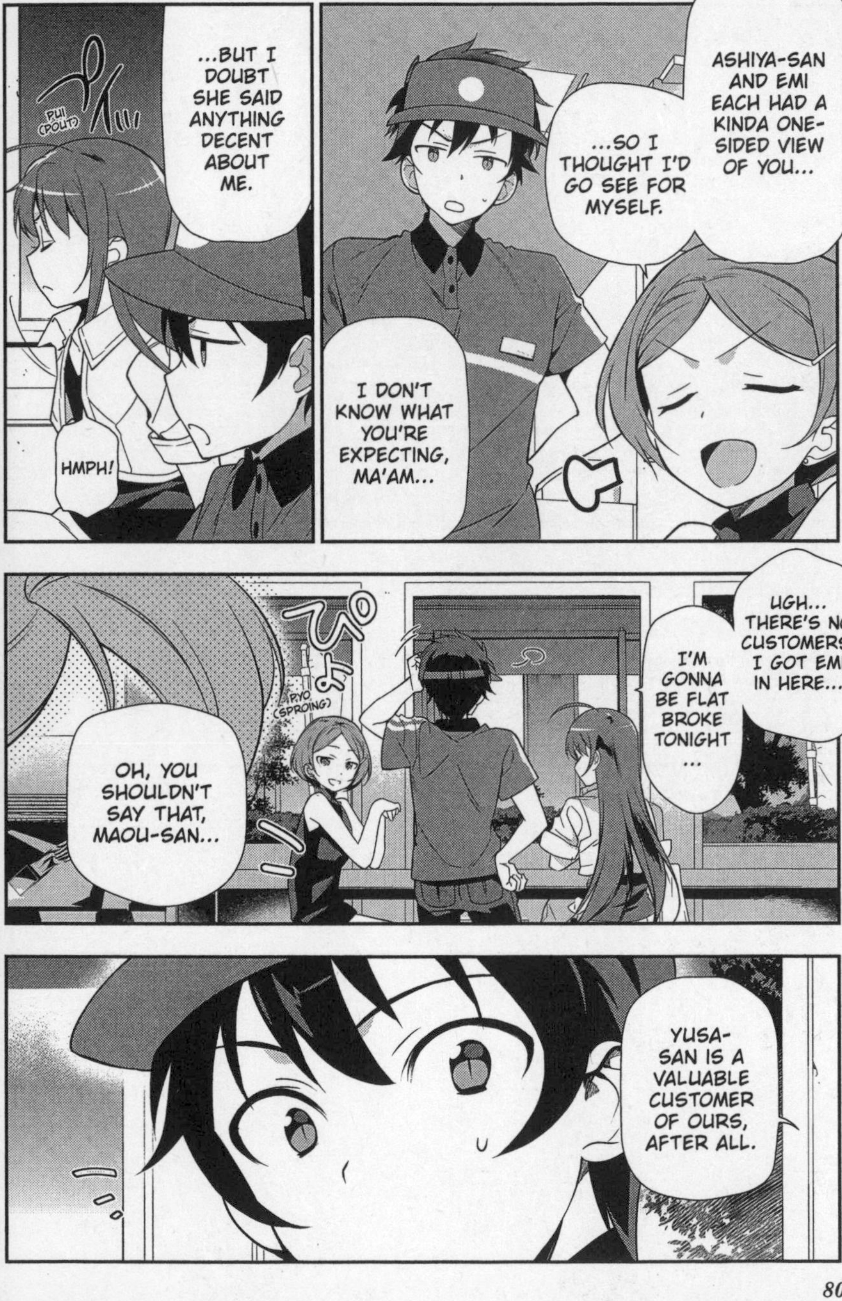
ASHIYA-SAN AND EMI EACH HAD A KINDA ONE-SIDED VIEW OF YOU...
...SO I THOUGHT I'D GO SEE FOR MYSELF.
I DON'T KNOW WHAT YOU'RE EXPECTING, MA'AM...
...BUT I DOUBT SHE SAID ANYTHING DECENT ABOUT ME.
PUI (POUT)
HMPH!
UGH... THERE'S NO CUSTOMERS, I GOT EMI IN HERE...
I'M GONNA BE FLAT BROKE TONIGHT ...
PYO (SPROING)
OH, YOU SHOULDN'T SAY THAT, MAOU-SAN...
YUSA-SAN IS A VALUABLE CUSTOMER OF OURS, AFTER ALL.

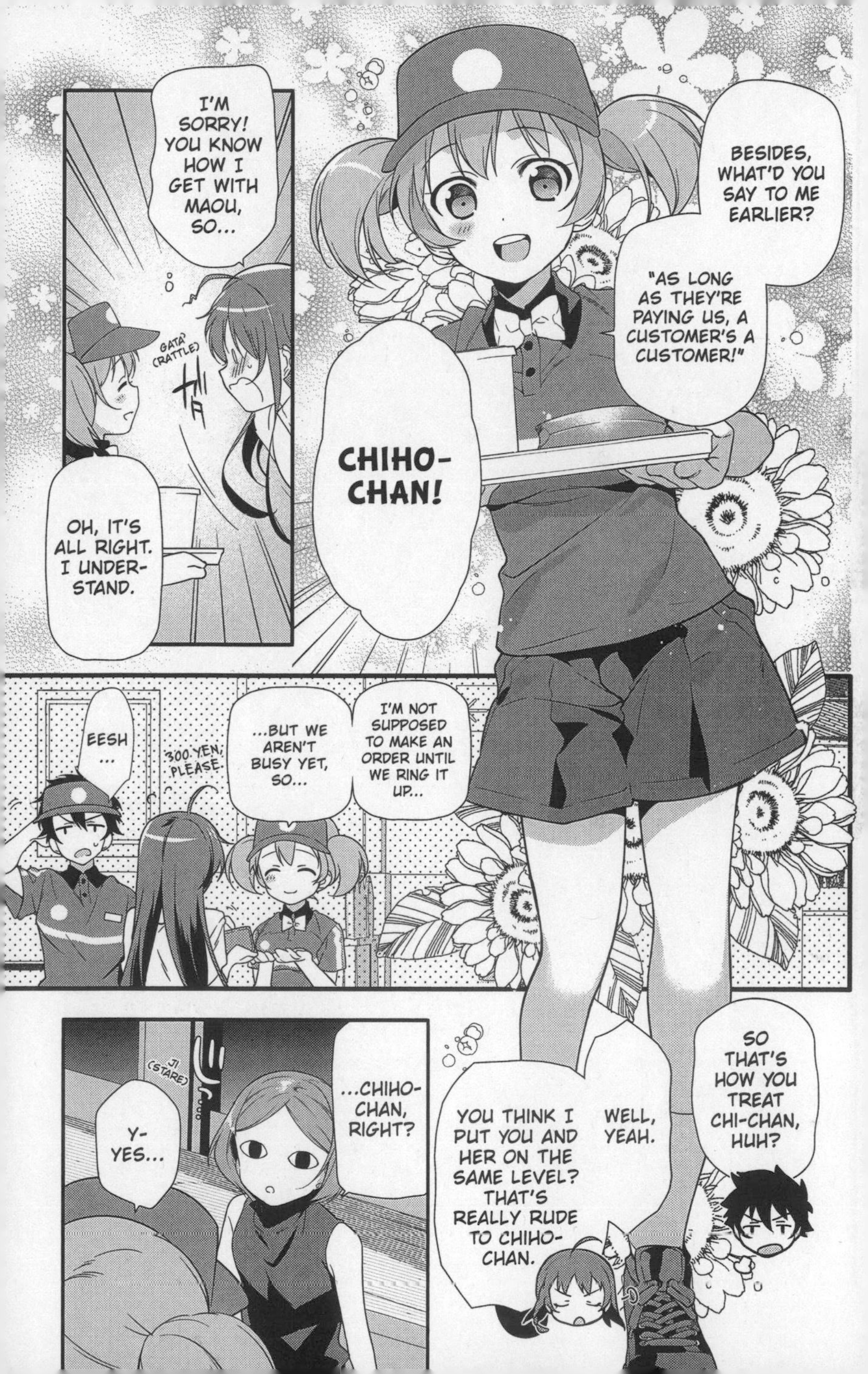
BESIDES, WHAT'D YOU SAY TO ME EARLIER?
"AS LONG AS THEY'RE PAYING US, A CUSTOMER'S A CUSTOMER!"
CHIHO-CHAN!
I'M SORRY! YOU KNOW HOW I GET WITH MAOU, SO...
GATA (RATTLE)
OH, IT'S ALL RIGHT. I UNDER-STAND.
I'M NOT SUPPOSED TO MAKE AN ORDER UNTIL WE RING IT UP...
...BUT WE AREN'T BUSY YET, SO...
300 YEN, PLEASE.
EESH...
SO THAT'S HOW YOU TREAT CHI-CHAN, HUH?
WELL, YEAH.
YOU THINK I PUT YOU AND HER ON THE SAME LEVEL? THAT'S REALLY RUDE TO CHIHO-CHAN.
...CHIHO-CHAN, RIGHT?
JI (STARE)
Y-YES...

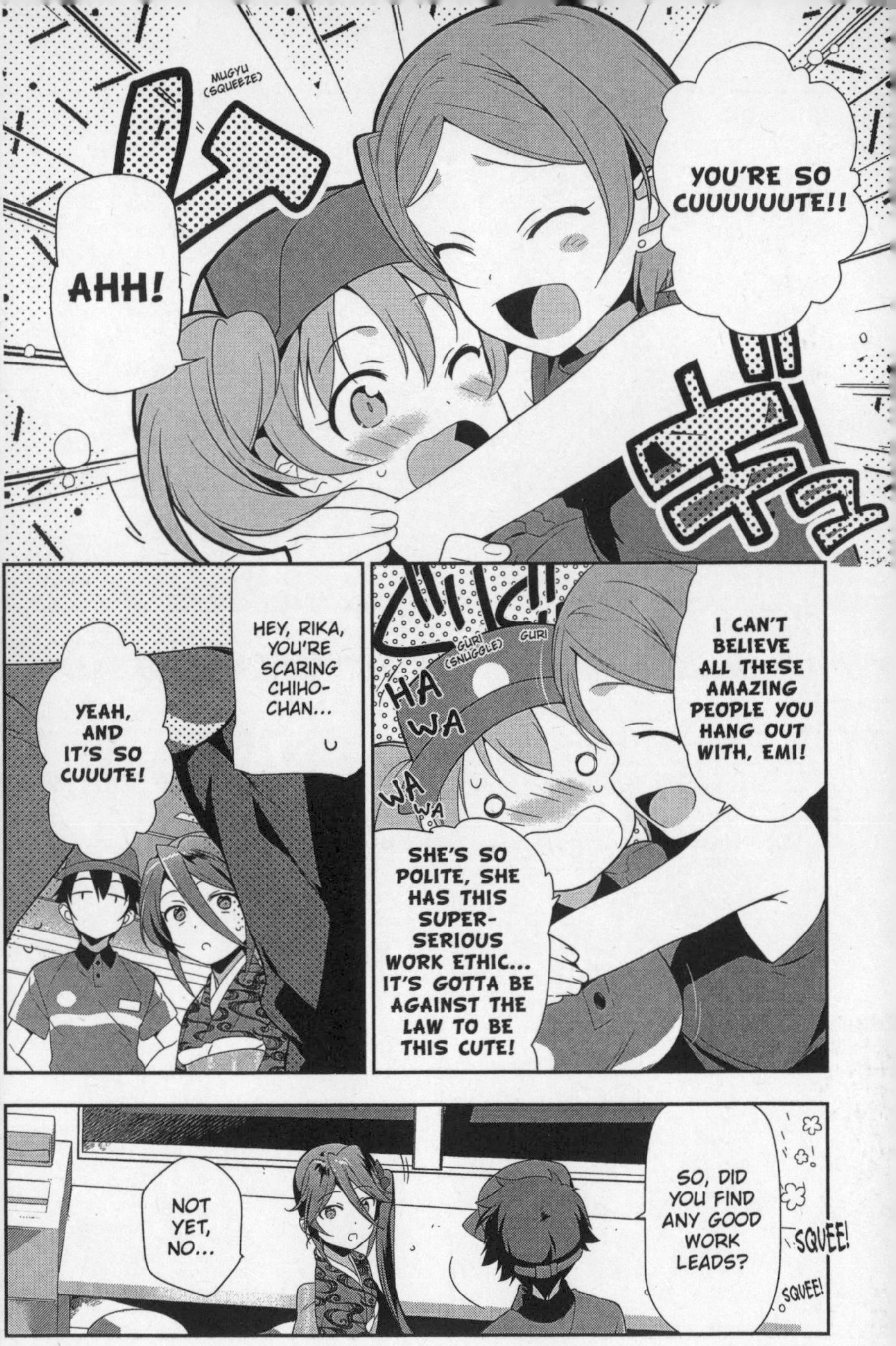
YOU'RE SO CUUUUUUTE!!
MUGYU (SQUEEZE)
AHH!
I CAN'T BELIEVE ALL THESE AMAZING PEOPLE YOU HANG OUT WITH, EMI!
GURI (SNUGGLE) GURI
HA WA
WA WA
SHE'S SO POLITE, SHE HAS THIS SUPER-SERIOUS WORK ETHIC... IT'S GOTTA BE AGAINST THE LAW TO BE THIS CUTE!
HEY, RIKA, YOU'RE SCARING CHIHO-CHAN...
YEAH, AND IT'S SO CUUUTE!
SO, DID YOU FIND ANY GOOD WORK LEADS?
SQUEE!
SQUEE!
NOT YET, NO...

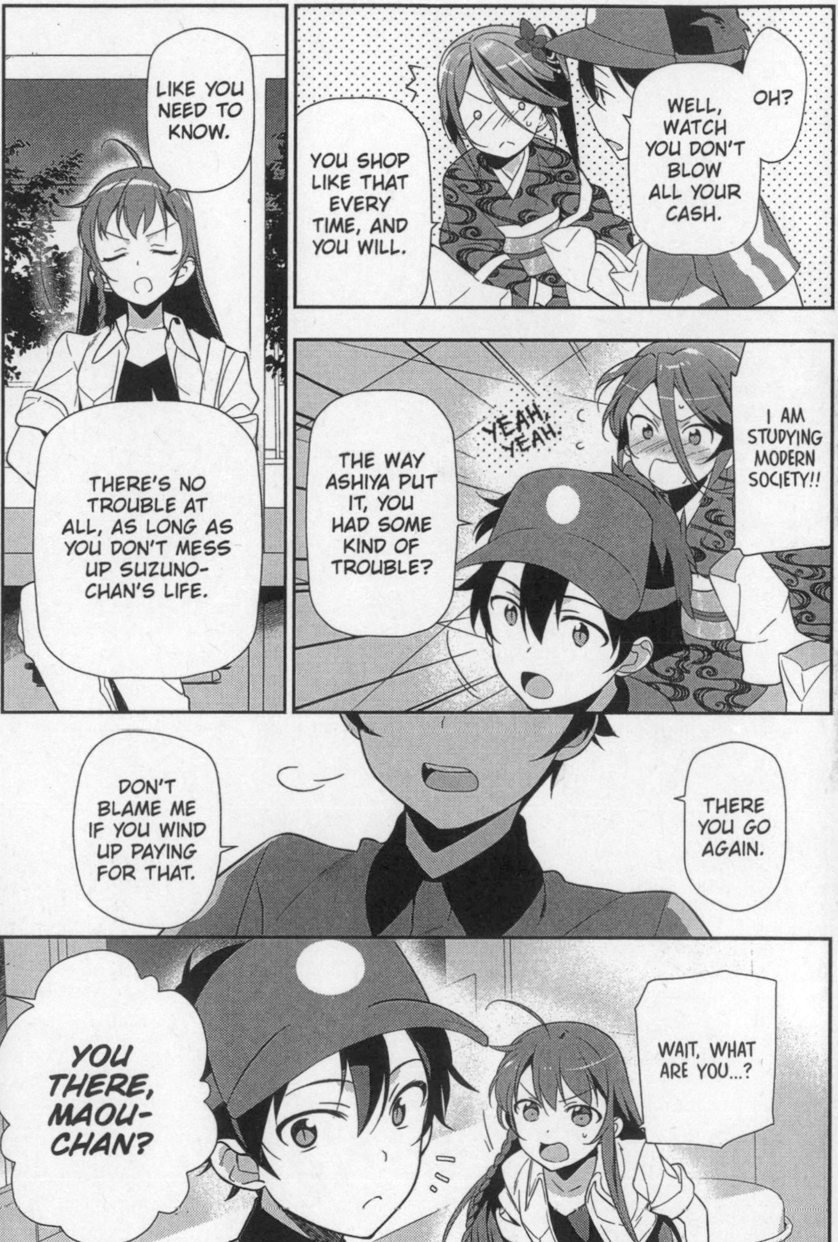
OH?
WELL, WATCH YOU DON'T BLOW ALL YOUR CASH.
YOU SHOP LIKE THAT EVERY TIME, AND YOU WILL.
I AM STUDYING MODERN SOCIETY!!
YEAH, YEAH.
THE WAY ASHIYA PUT IT, YOU HAD SOME KIND OF TROUBLE?
LIKE YOU NEED TO KNOW.
THERE'S NO TROUBLE AT ALL, AS LONG AS YOU DON'T MESS UP SUZUNO-CHAN'S LIFE.
THERE YOU GO AGAIN.
DON'T BLAME ME IF YOU WIND UP PAYING FOR THAT.
WAIT, WHAT ARE YOU...?
YOU THERE, MAOU-CHAN?

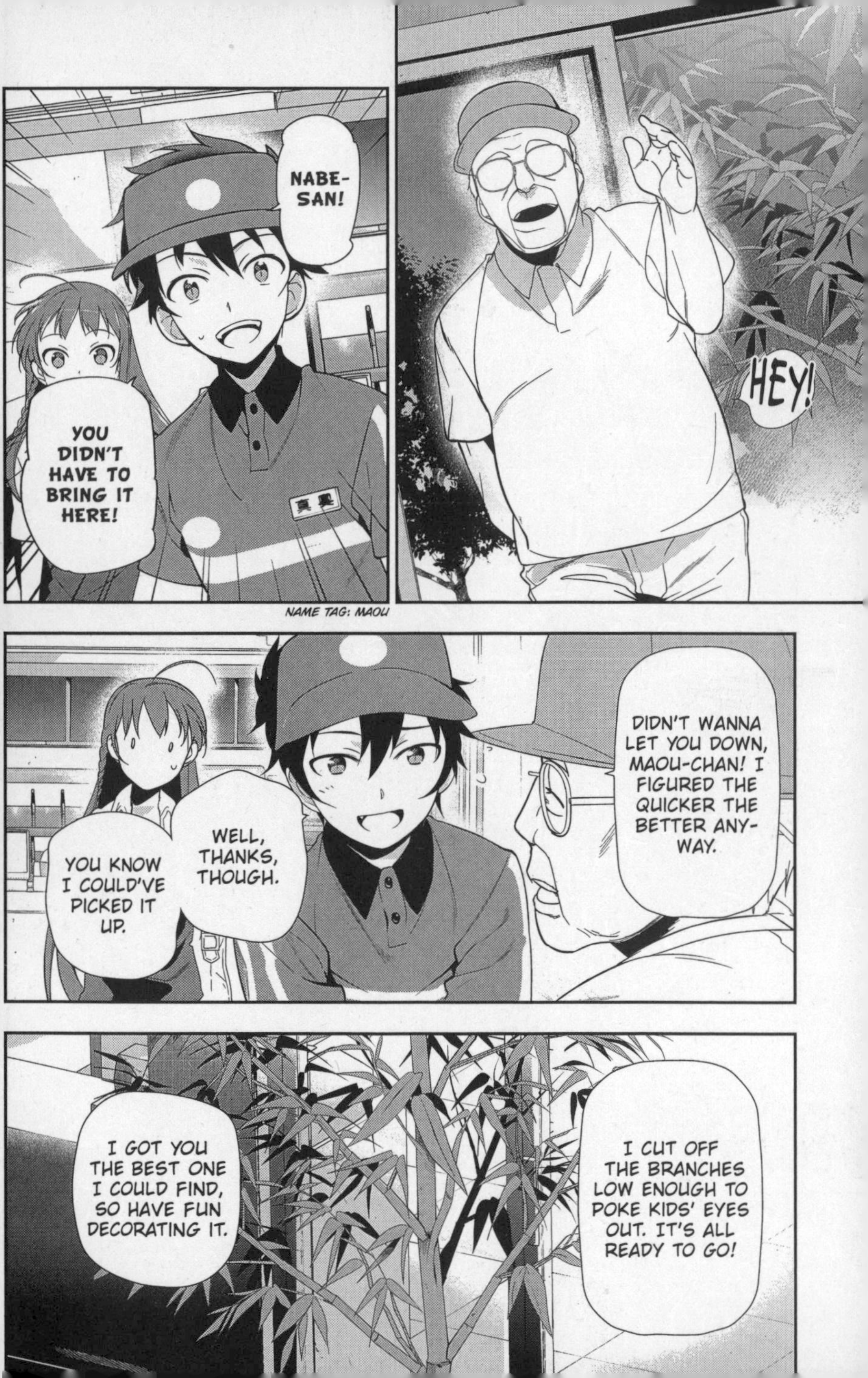
HEY!
NABE-SAN!
YOU DIDN'T HAVE TO BRING IT HERE!
DIDN'T WANNA LET YOU DOWN, MAOU-CHAN! I FIGURED THE QUICKER THE BETTER ANY-WAY.
WELL, THANKS, THOUGH.
YOU KNOW I COULD'VE PICKED IT UP.
I CUT OFF THE BRANCHES LOW ENOUGH TO POKE KIDS' EYES OUT. IT'S ALL READY TO GO!
I GOT YOU THE BEST ONE I COULD FIND, SO HAVE FUN DECORATING IT.

NAME TAG: MAOU

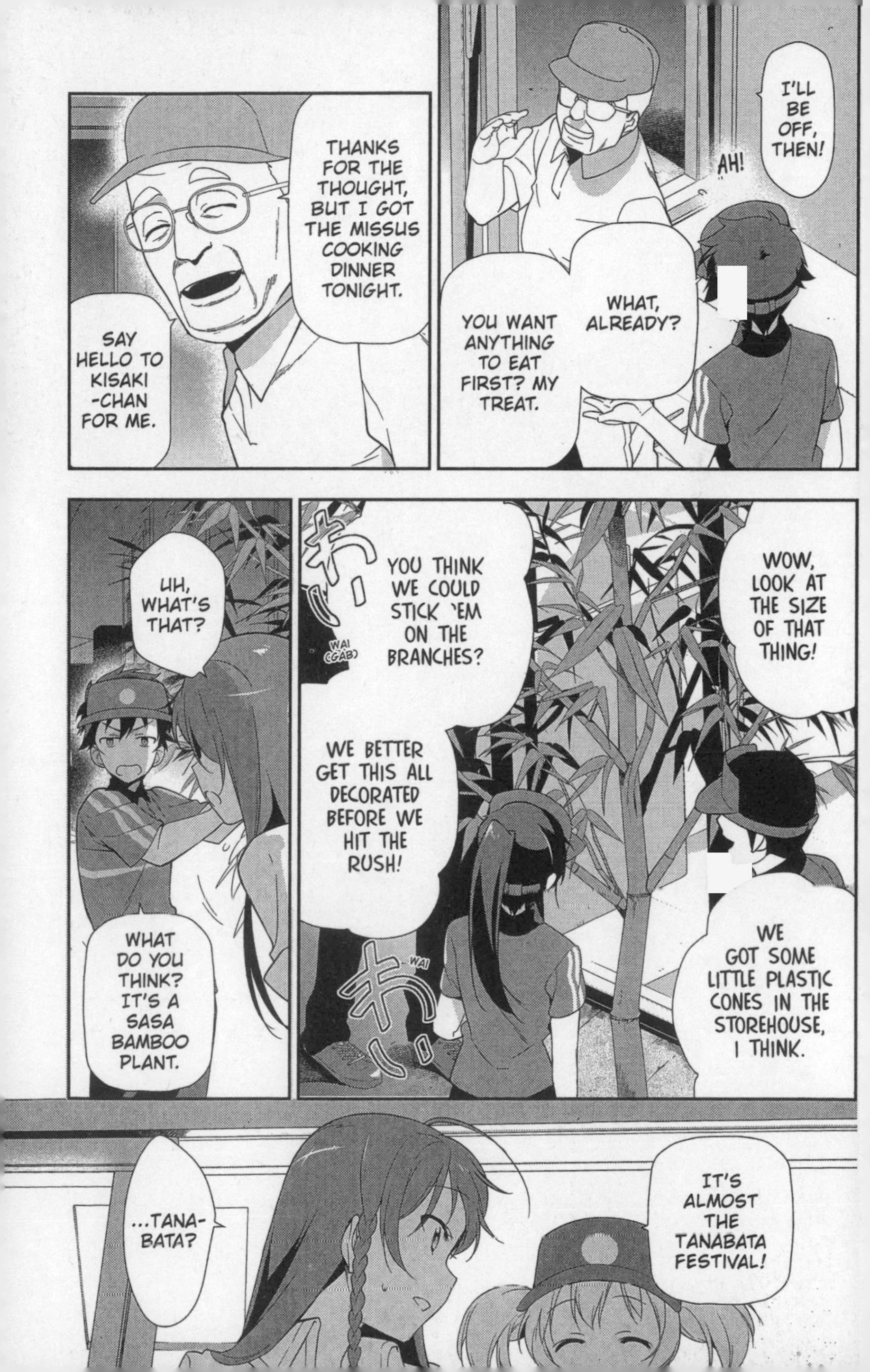
I'LL BE OFF, THEN!
AH!
WHAT, ALREADY?
YOU WANT ANYTHING TO EAT FIRST? MY TREAT.
THANKS FOR THE THOUGHT, BUT I GOT THE MISSUS COOKING DINNER TONIGHT.
SAY HELLO TO KISAKI-CHAN FOR ME.
WOW, LOOK AT THE SIZE OF THAT THING!
YOU THINK WE COULD STICK 'EM ON THE BRANCHES?
WAI (GAB)
WE BETTER GET THIS ALL DECORATED BEFORE WE HIT THE RUSH!
WE GOT SOME LITTLE PLASTIC CONES IN THE STOREHOUSE, I THINK.
WAI
UH, WHAT'S THAT?
WHAT DO YOU THINK? IT'S A SASA BAMBOO PLANT.
IT'S ALMOST THE TANABATA FESTIVAL!
...TANA-BATA?

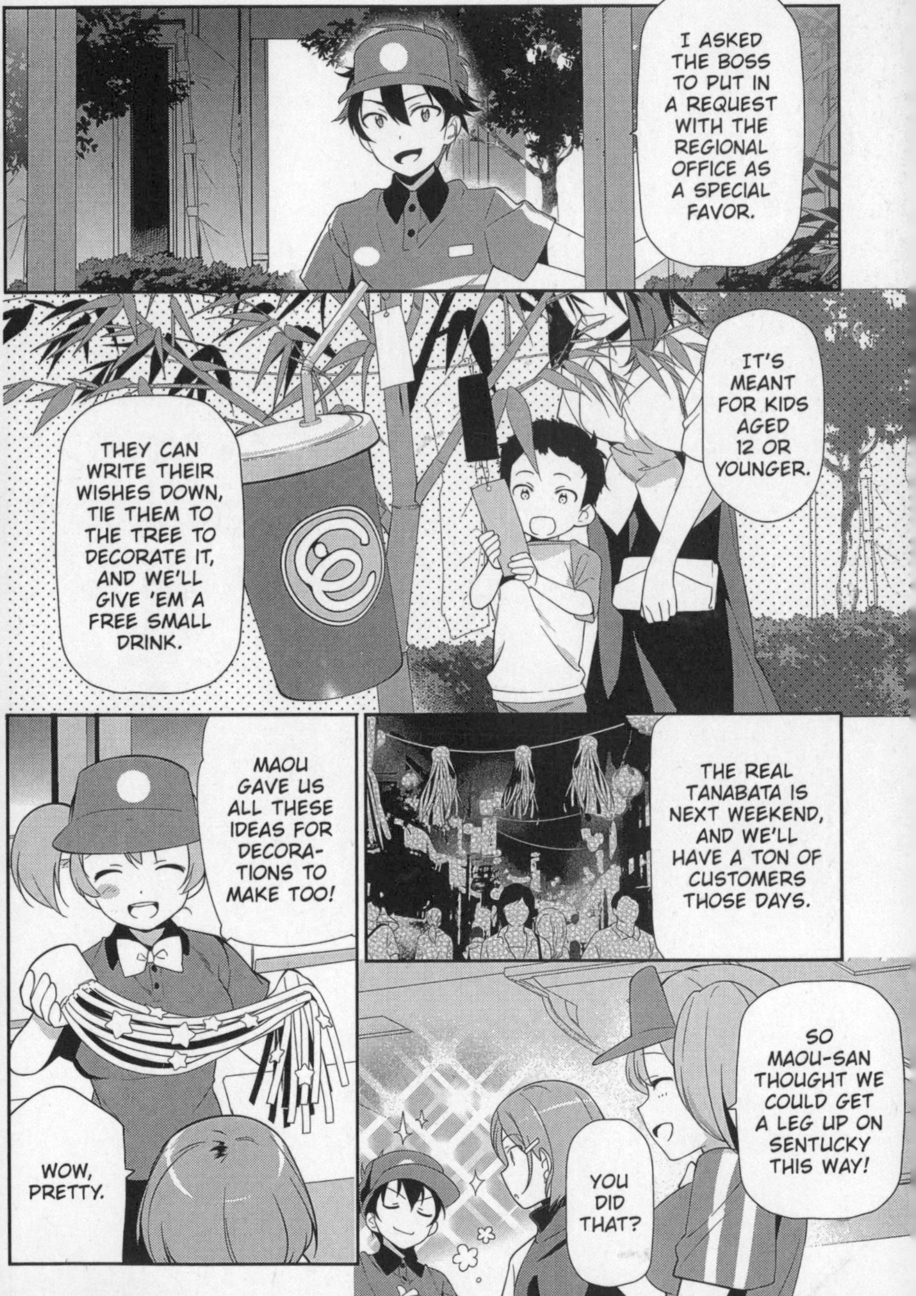
I ASKED THE BOSS TO PUT IN A REQUEST WITH THE REGIONAL OFFICE AS A SPECIAL FAVOR.
IT'S MEANT FOR KIDS AGED 12 OR YOUNGER.
THEY CAN WRITE THEIR WISHES DOWN, TIE THEM TO THE TREE TO DECORATE IT, AND WE'LL GIVE 'EM A FREE SMALL DRINK.
THE REAL TANABATA IS NEXT WEEKEND, AND WE'LL HAVE A TON OF CUSTOMERS THOSE DAYS.
SO MAOU-SAN THOUGHT WE COULD GET A LEG UP ON SENTUCKY THIS WAY!
YOU DID THAT?
MAOU GAVE US ALL THESE IDEAS FOR DECORA-TIONS TO MAKE TOO!
WOW, PRETTY.

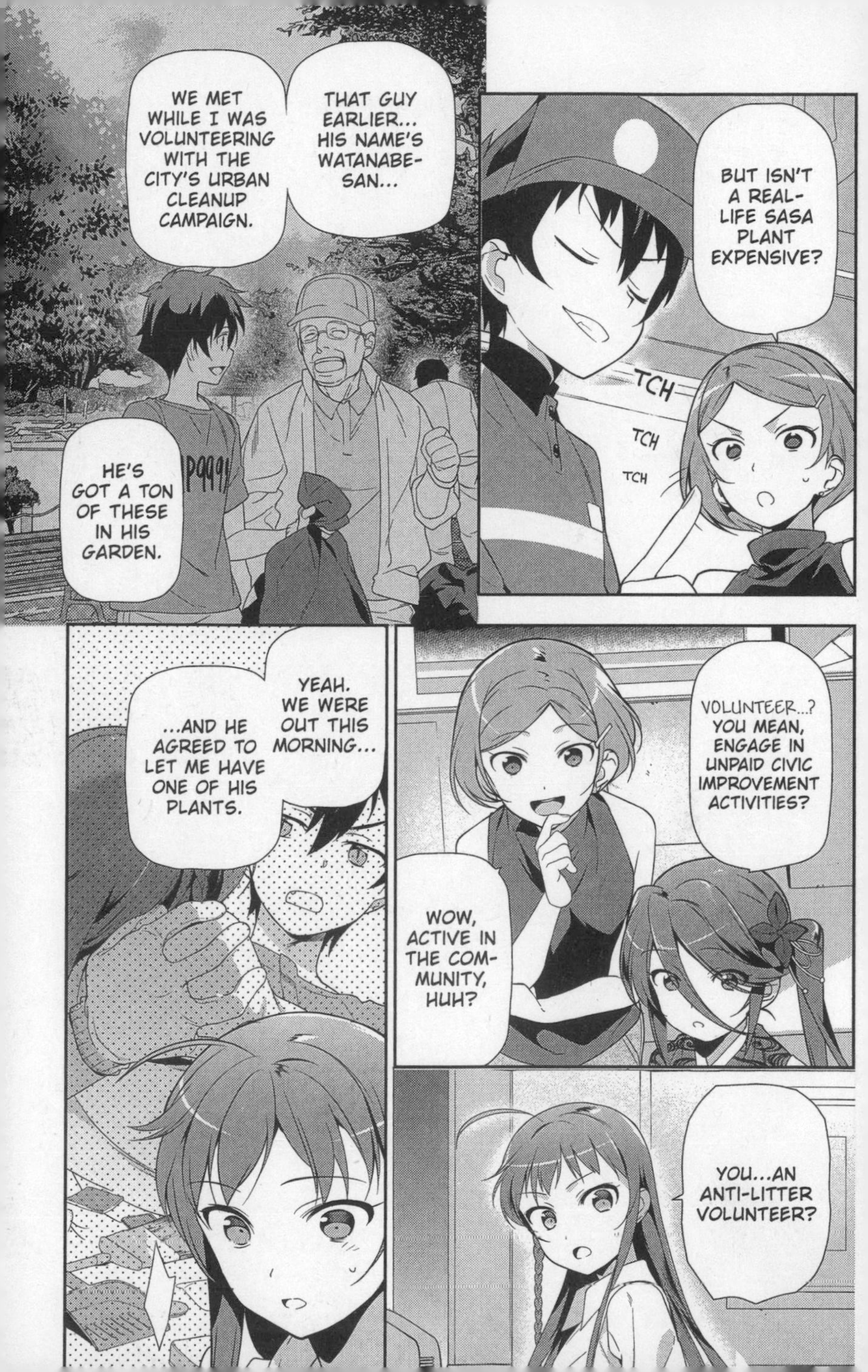
BUT ISN'T A REAL-LIFE SASA PLANT EXPENSIVE?
TCH
TCH
TCH
THAT GUY EARLIER... HIS NAME'S WATANABE-SAN...
WE MET WHILE I WAS VOLUNTEERING WITH THE CITY'S URBAN CLEANUP CAMPAIGN.
HE'S GOT A TON OF THESE IN HIS GARDEN.
VOLUNTEER...? YOU MEAN, ENGAGE IN UNPAID CIVIC IMPROVEMENT ACTIVITIES?
WOW, ACTIVE IN THE COM-MUNITY, HUH?
YOU...AN ANTI-LITTER VOLUNTEER?
YEAH. WE WERE OUT THIS MORNING...
...AND HE AGREED TO LET ME HAVE ONE OF HIS PLANTS.

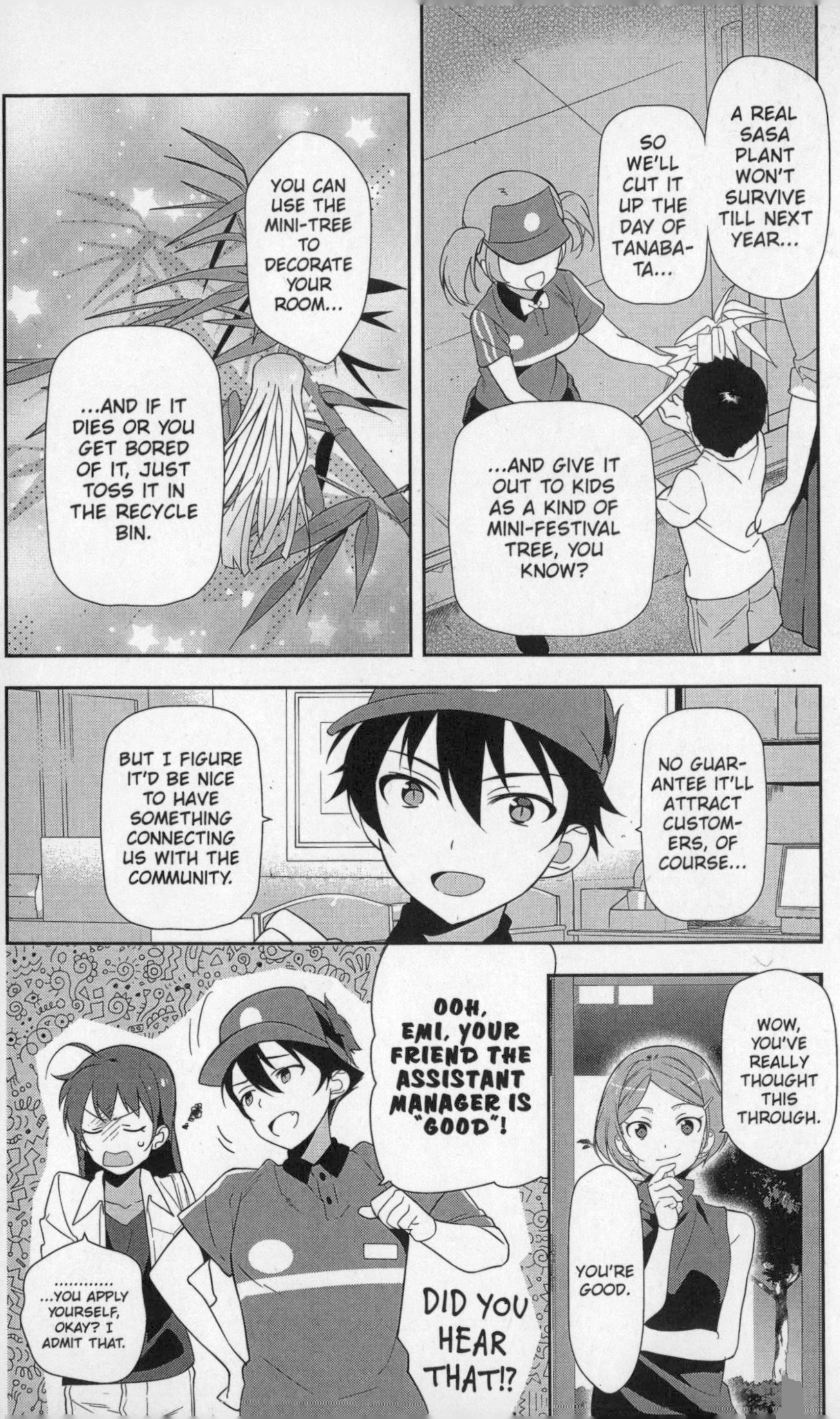
A REAL SASA PLANT WON'T SURVIVE TILL NEXT YEAR...
SO WE'LL CUT IT UP THE DAY OF TANABATA...
...AND GIVE IT OUT TO KIDS AS A KIND OF MINI-FESTIVAL TREE, YOU KNOW?
YOU CAN USE THE MINI-TREE TO DECORATE YOUR ROOM...
...AND IF IT DIES OR YOU GET BORED OF IT, JUST TOSS IT IN THE RECYCLE BIN.
NO GUARANTEE IT'LL ATTRACT CUSTOMERS, OF COURSE...
BUT I FIGURE IT'D BE NICE TO HAVE SOMETHING CONNECTING US WITH THE COMMUNITY.
WOW, YOU'VE REALLY THOUGHT THIS THROUGH.
YOU'RE GOOD.
OOH, EMI, YOUR FRIEND THE ASSISTANT MANAGER IS "GOOD"!
DID YOU HEAR THAT!?
............ ...YOU APPLY YOURSELF, OKAY? I ADMIT THAT.

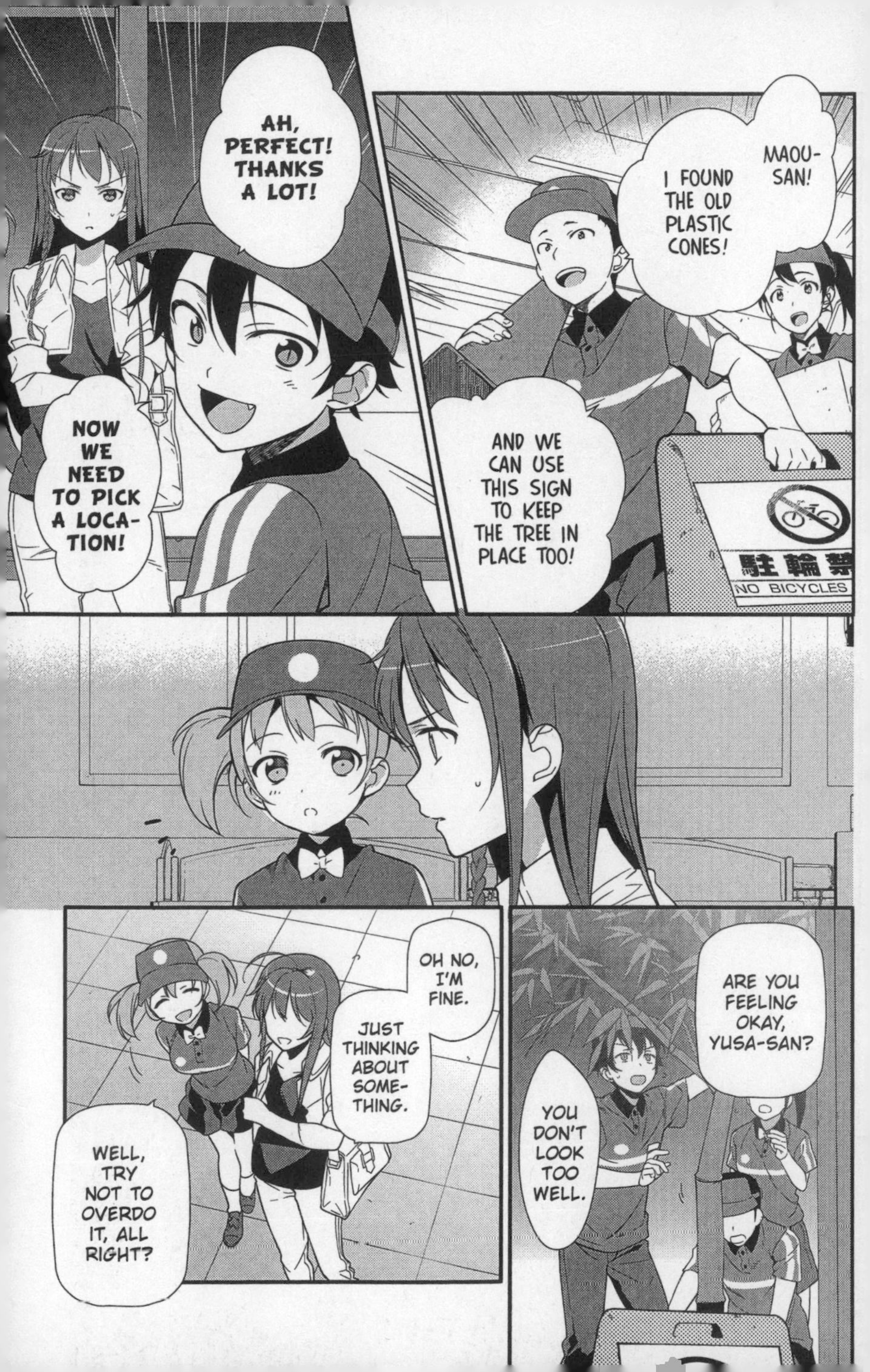
MAOU-SAN!
I FOUND THE OLD PLASTIC CONES!
AND WE CAN USE THIS SIGN TO KEEP THE TREE IN PLACE TOO!
駐輪禁
NO BICYCLES
AH, PERFECT! THANKS A LOT!
NOW WE NEED TO PICK A LOCATION!
ARE YOU FEELING OKAY, YUSA-SAN?
YOU DON'T LOOK TOO WELL.
OH NO, I'M FINE.
JUST THINKING ABOUT SOMETHING.
WELL, TRY NOT TO OVERDO IT, ALL RIGHT?

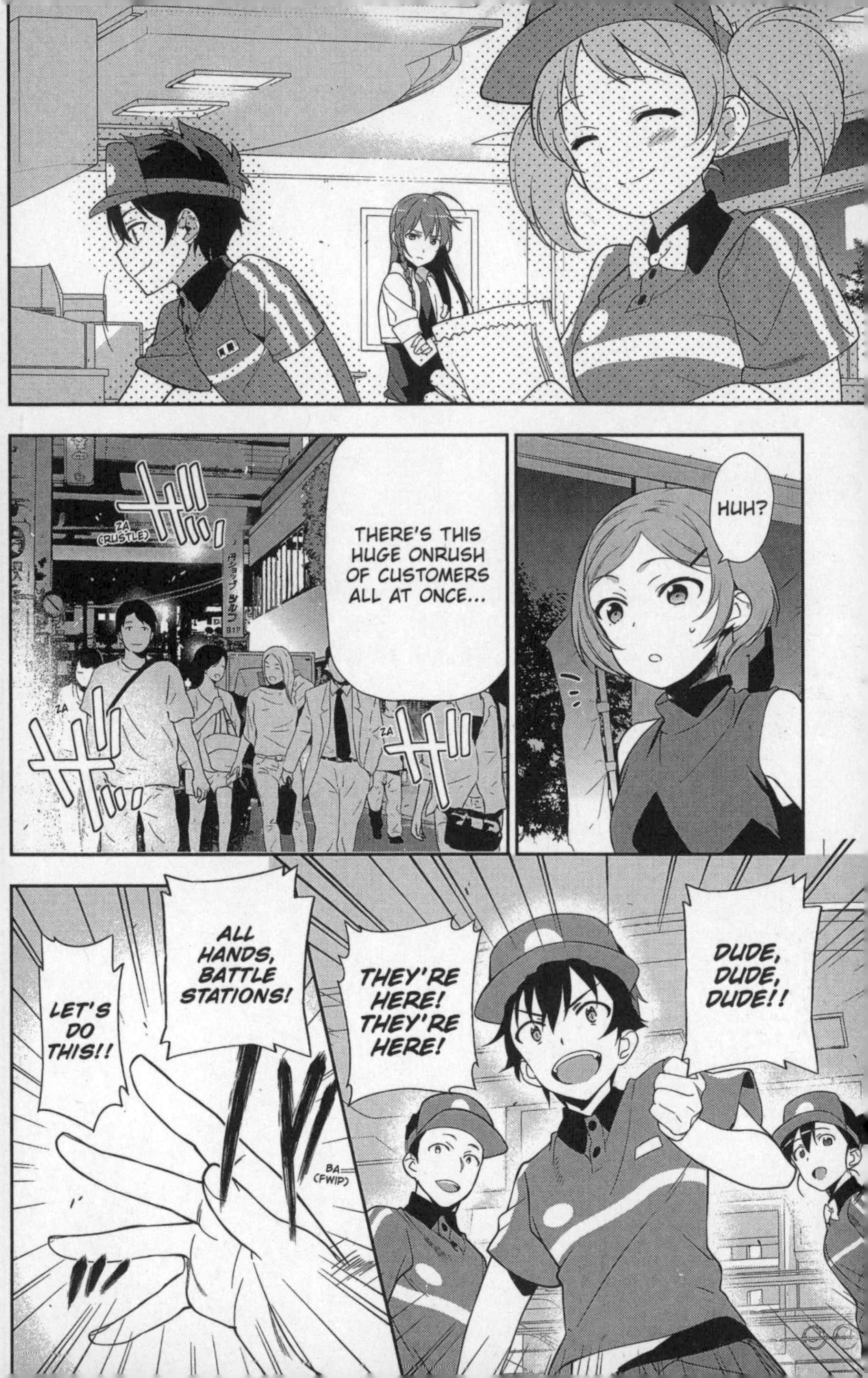
HUH?
THERE'S THIS HUGE ONRUSH OF CUSTOMERS ALL AT ONCE...
ZA (RUSTLE)
ZA
ZA
DUDE, DUDE, DUDE!!
THEY'RE HERE! THEY'RE HERE!
ALL HANDS, BATTLE STATIONS!
LET'S DO THIS!!
BA (FWIP)

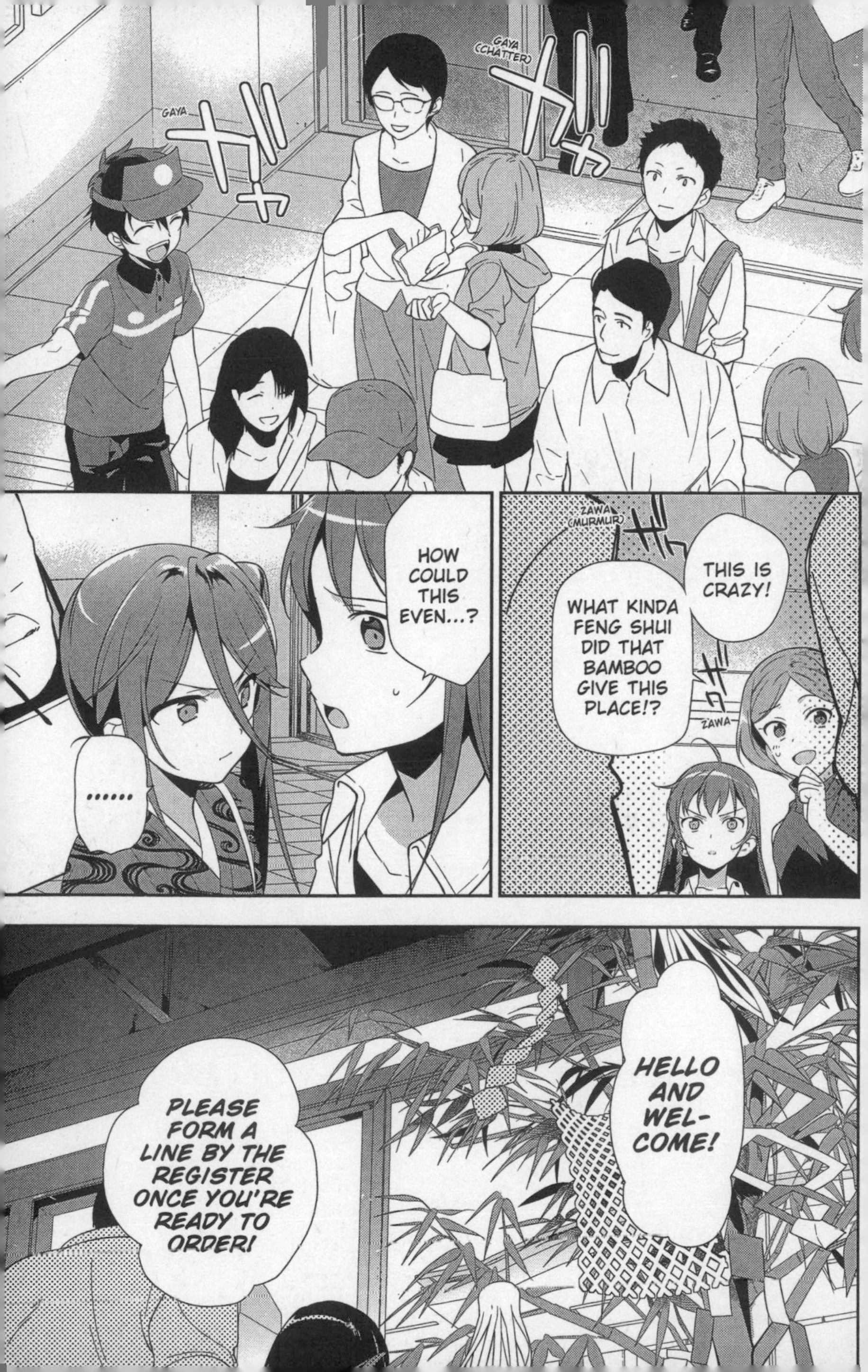
GAYA (CHATTER)
GAYA
ZAWA (MURMUR)
THIS IS CRAZY!
WHAT KINDA FENG SHUI DID THAT BAMBOO GIVE THIS PLACE!?
ZAWA
HOW COULD THIS EVEN...?
.......
HELLO AND WEL-COME!
PLEASE FORM A LINE BY THE REGISTER ONCE YOU'RE READY TO ORDER!

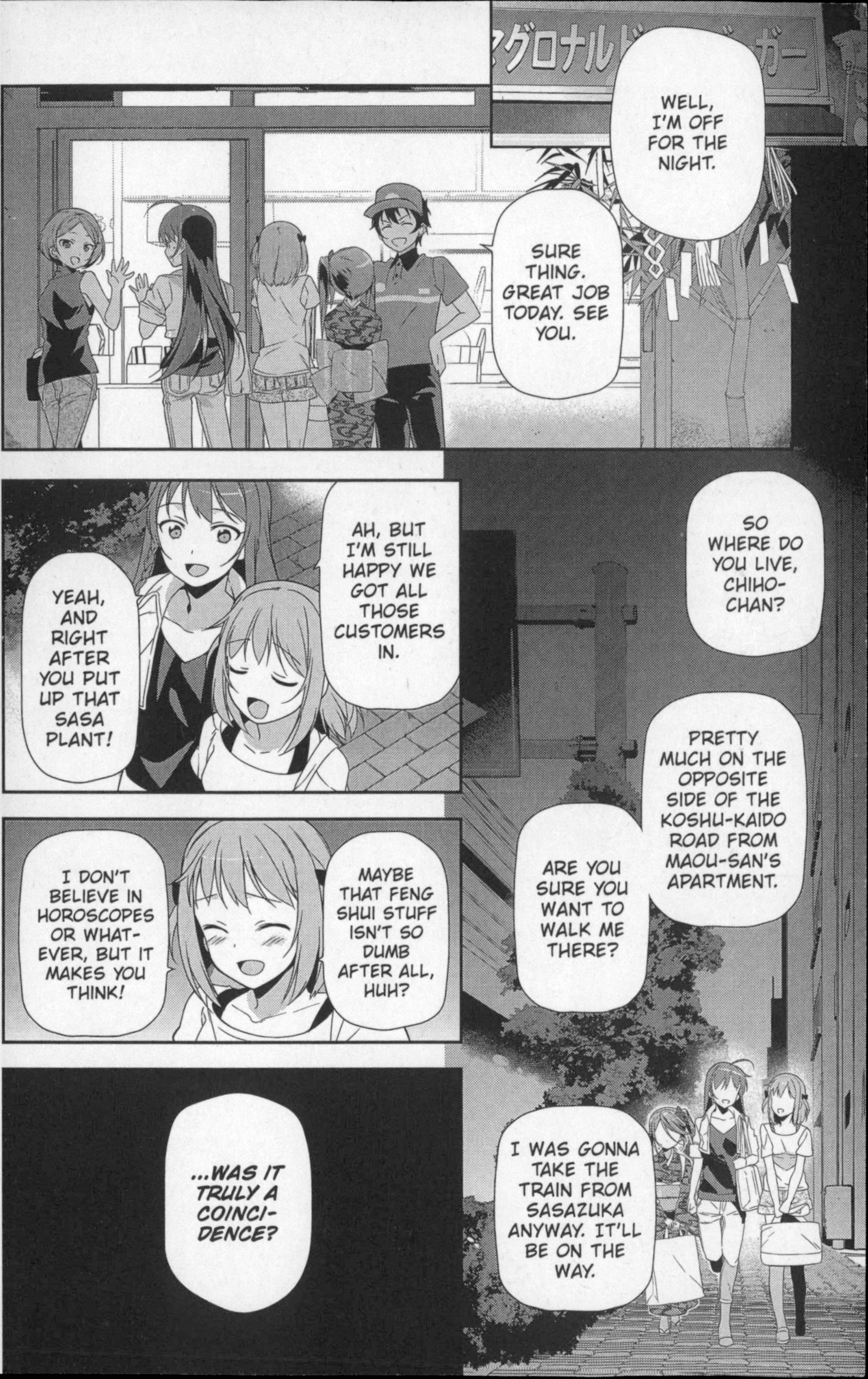
WELL, I'M OFF FOR THE NIGHT.
SURE THING. GREAT JOB TODAY. SEE YOU.
SO WHERE DO YOU LIVE, CHIHO-CHAN?
PRETTY MUCH ON THE OPPOSITE SIDE OF THE KOSHU-KAIDO ROAD FROM MAOU-SAN'S APARTMENT.
ARE YOU SURE YOU WANT TO WALK ME THERE?
I WAS GONNA TAKE THE TRAIN FROM SASAZUKA ANYWAY. IT'LL BE ON THE WAY.
AH, BUT I'M STILL HAPPY WE GOT ALL THOSE CUSTOMERS IN.
YEAH, AND RIGHT AFTER YOU PUT UP THAT SASA PLANT!
MAYBE THAT FENG SHUI STUFF ISN'T SO DUMB AFTER ALL, HUH?
I DON'T BELIEVE IN HOROSCOPES OR WHATEVER, BUT IT MAKES YOU THINK!
...WAS IT TRULY A COINCIDENCE?

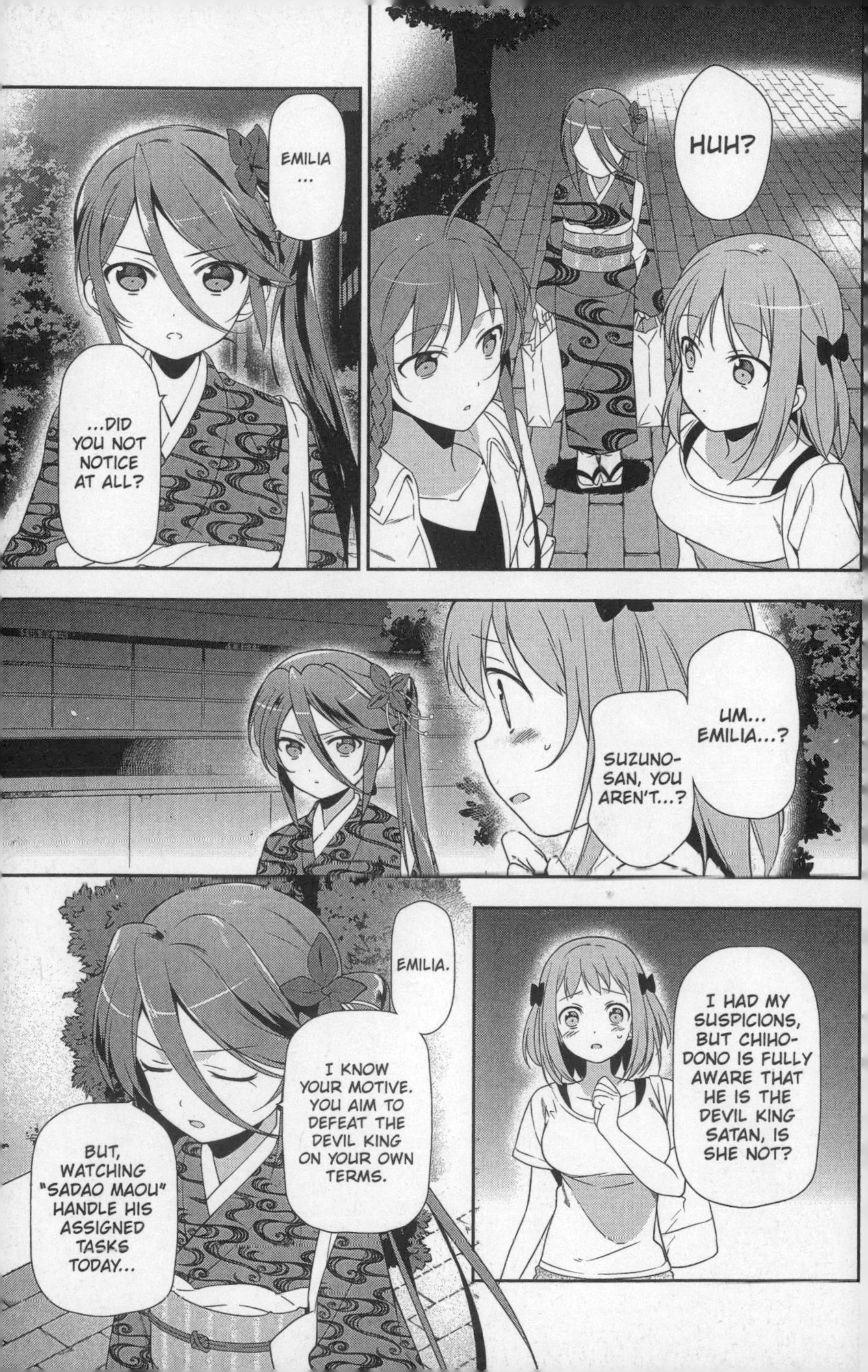
HUH?
EMILIA ...
...DID YOU NOT NOTICE AT ALL?
UM... EMILIA...?
SUZUNO-SAN, YOU AREN'T...?
I HAD MY SUSPICIONS, BUT CHIHO-DONO IS FULLY AWARE THAT HE IS THE DEVIL KING SATAN, IS SHE NOT?
EMILIA.
I KNOW YOUR MOTIVE. YOU AIM TO DEFEAT THE DEVIL KING ON YOUR OWN TERMS.
BUT, WATCHING "SADAO MAOU" HANDLE HIS ASSIGNED TASKS TODAY...

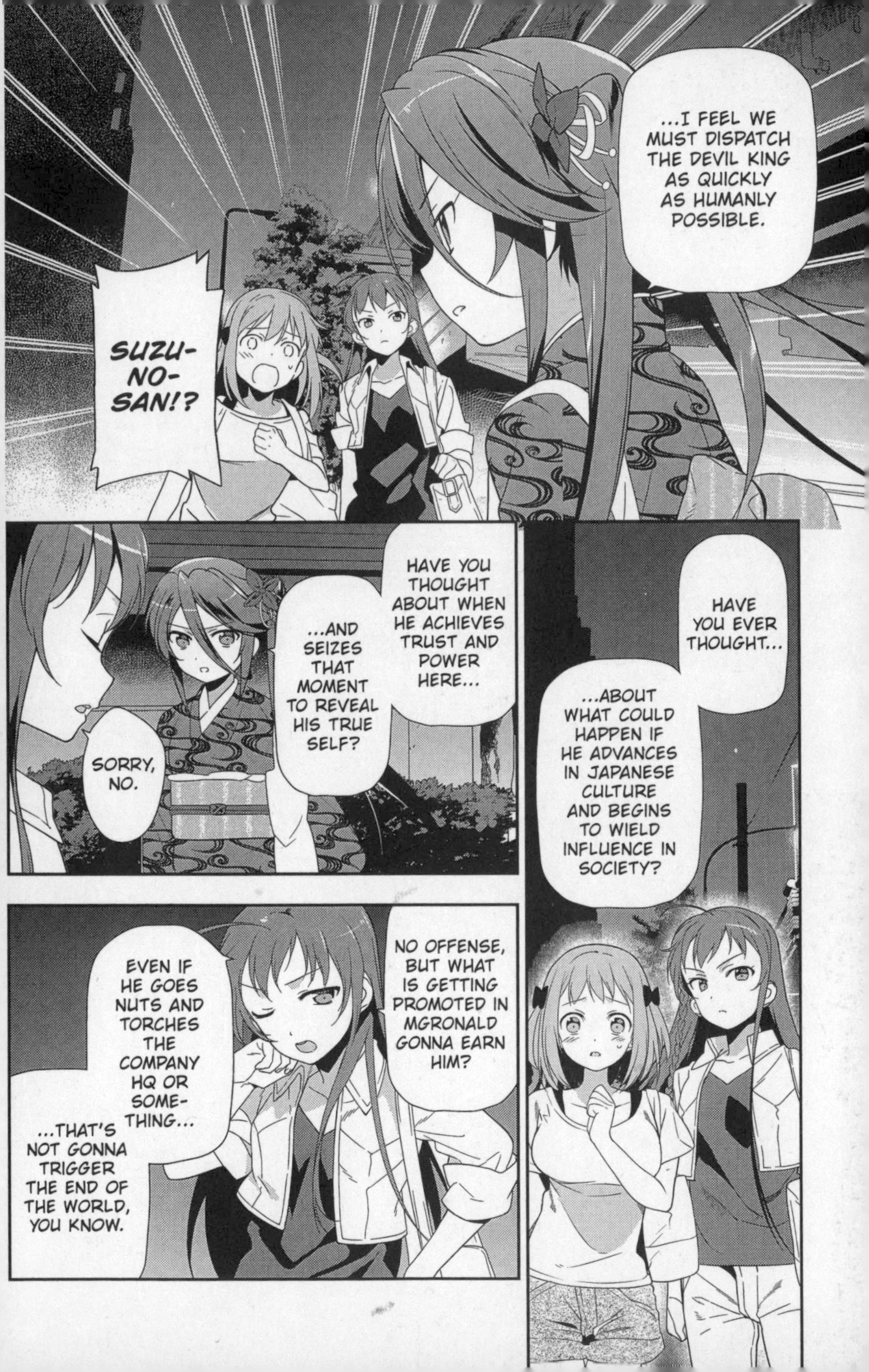
...I FEEL WE MUST DISPATCH THE DEVIL KING AS QUICKLY AS HUMANLY POSSIBLE.
SUZU-NO-SAN!?
HAVE YOU EVER THOUGHT...
...ABOUT WHAT COULD HAPPEN IF HE ADVANCES IN JAPANESE CULTURE AND BEGINS TO WIELD INFLUENCE IN SOCIETY?
HAVE YOU THOUGHT ABOUT WHEN HE ACHIEVES TRUST AND POWER HERE...
...AND SEIZES THAT MOMENT TO REVEAL HIS TRUE SELF?
SORRY, NO.
NO OFFENSE, BUT WHAT IS GETTING PROMOTED IN MGRONALD GONNA EARN HIM?
EVEN IF HE GOES NUTS AND TORCHES THE COMPANY HQ OR SOME-THING...
...THAT'S NOT GONNA TRIGGER THE END OF THE WORLD, YOU KNOW.

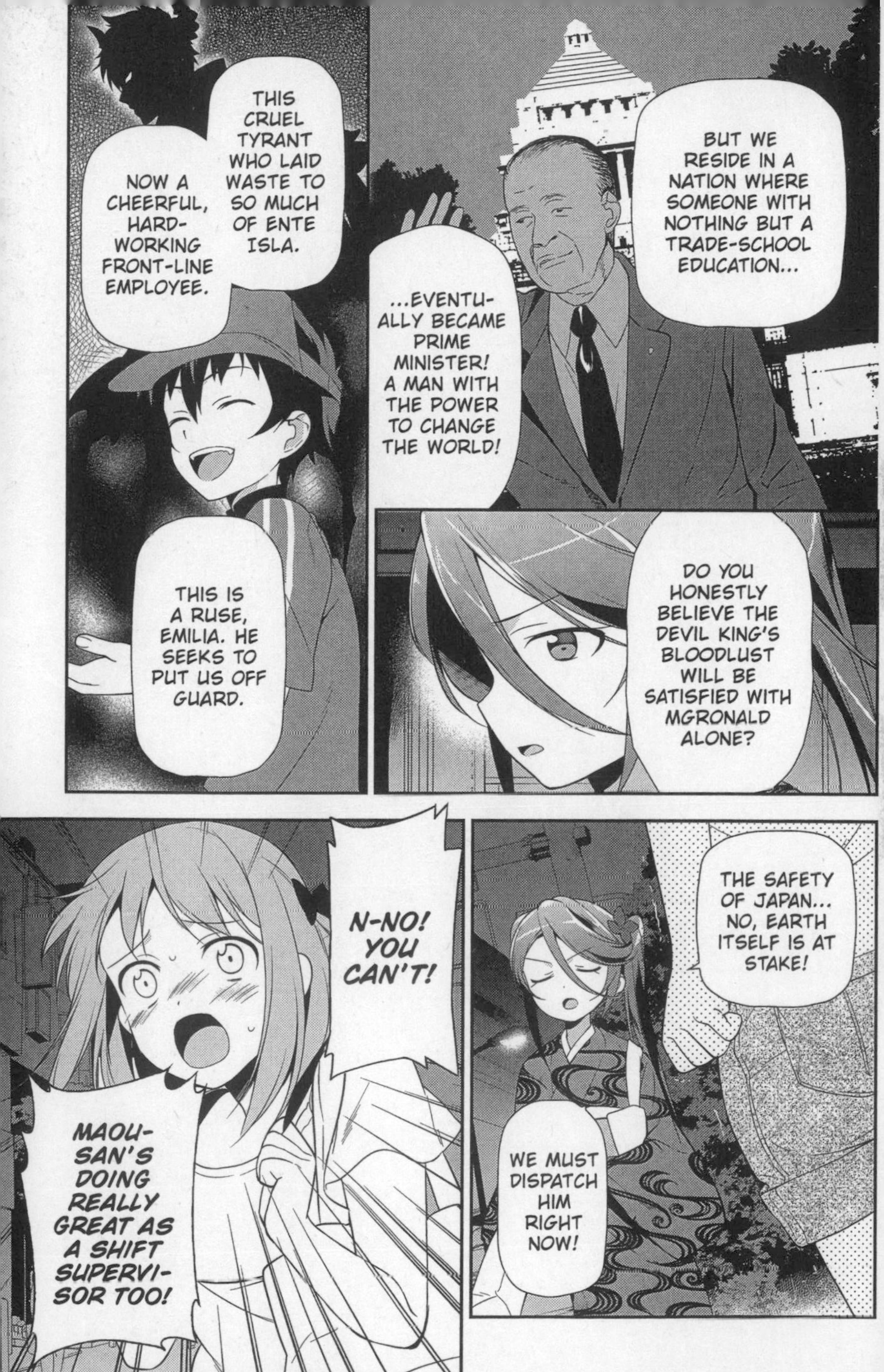
BUT WE RESIDE IN A NATION WHERE SOMEONE WITH NOTHING BUT A TRADE-SCHOOL EDUCATION...
...EVENTUALLY BECAME PRIME MINISTER! A MAN WITH THE POWER TO CHANGE THE WORLD!
DO YOU HONESTLY BELIEVE THE DEVIL KING'S BLOODLUST WILL BE SATISFIED WITH MGRONALD ALONE?
THIS CRUEL TYRANT WHO LAID WASTE TO SO MUCH OF ENTE ISLA.
NOW A CHEERFUL, HARD-WORKING FRONT-LINE EMPLOYEE.
THIS IS A RUSE, EMILIA. HE SEEKS TO PUT US OFF GUARD.
THE SAFETY OF JAPAN... NO, EARTH ITSELF IS AT STAKE!
WE MUST DISPATCH HIM RIGHT NOW!
N-NO! YOU CAN'T!
MAOU-SAN'S DOING REALLY GREAT AS A SHIFT SUPERVISOR TOO!

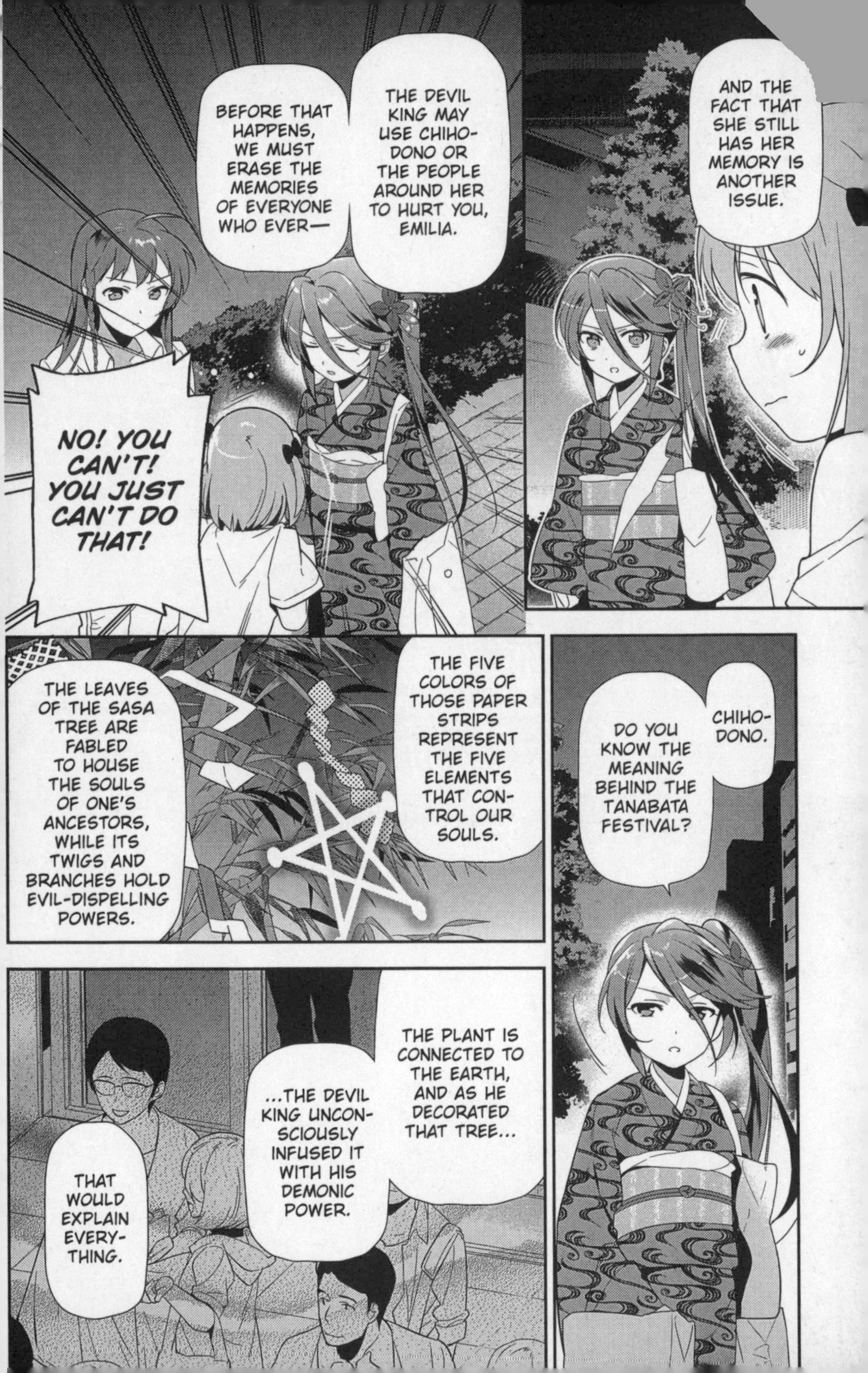
AND THE FACT THAT SHE STILL HAS HER MEMORY IS ANOTHER ISSUE.
THE DEVIL KING MAY USE CHIHO-DONO OR THE PEOPLE AROUND HER TO HURT YOU, EMILIA.
BEFORE THAT HAPPENS, WE MUST ERASE THE MEMORIES OF EVERYONE WHO EVER—
NO! YOU CAN'T! YOU JUST CAN'T DO THAT!
CHIHO-DONO.
DO YOU KNOW THE MEANING BEHIND THE TANABATA FESTIVAL?
THE FIVE COLORS OF THOSE PAPER STRIPS REPRESENT THE FIVE ELEMENTS THAT CONTROL OUR SOULS.
THE LEAVES OF THE SASA TREE ARE FABLED TO HOUSE THE SOULS OF ONE'S ANCESTORS, WHILE ITS TWIGS AND BRANCHES HOLD EVIL-DISPELLING POWERS.
THE PLANT IS CONNECTED TO THE EARTH, AND AS HE DECORATED THAT TREE...
...THE DEVIL KING UNCONSCIOUSLY INFUSED IT WITH HIS DEMONIC POWER.
THAT WOULD EXPLAIN EVERYTHING.

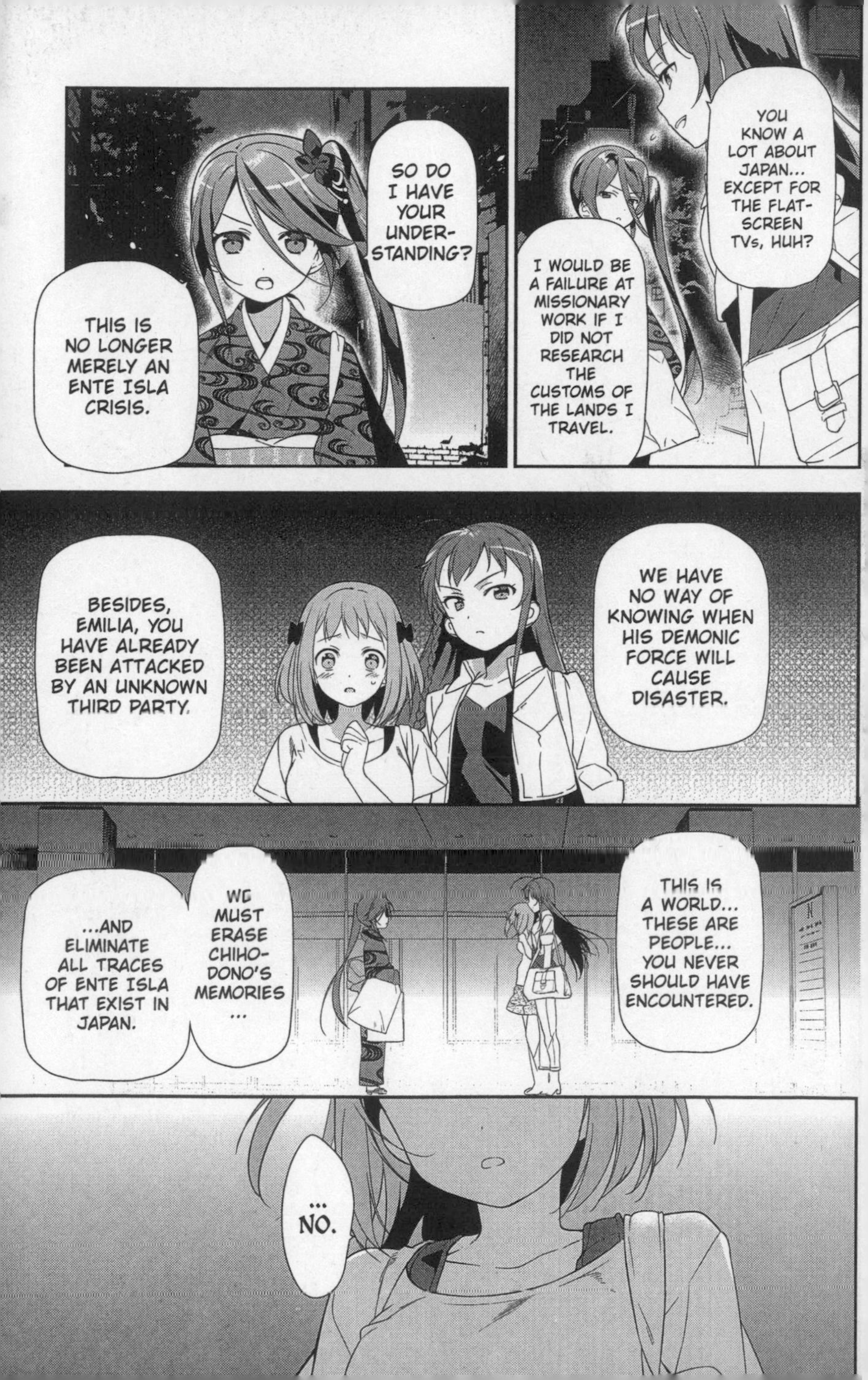
YOU KNOW A LOT ABOUT JAPAN... EXCEPT FOR THE FLAT-SCREEN TVs, HUH?
I WOULD BE A FAILURE AT MISSIONARY WORK IF I DID NOT RESEARCH THE CUSTOMS OF THE LANDS I TRAVEL.
SO DO I HAVE YOUR UNDERSTANDING?
THIS IS NO LONGER MERELY AN ENTE ISLA CRISIS.
WE HAVE NO WAY OF KNOWING WHEN HIS DEMONIC FORCE WILL CAUSE DISASTER.
BESIDES, EMILIA, YOU HAVE ALREADY BEEN ATTACKED BY AN UNKNOWN THIRD PARTY.
THIS IS A WORLD... THESE ARE PEOPLE... YOU NEVER SHOULD HAVE ENCOUNTERED.
WE MUST ERASE CHIHO-DONO'S MEMORIES...
...AND ELIMINATE ALL TRACES OF ENTE ISLA THAT EXIST IN JAPAN.
... NO.

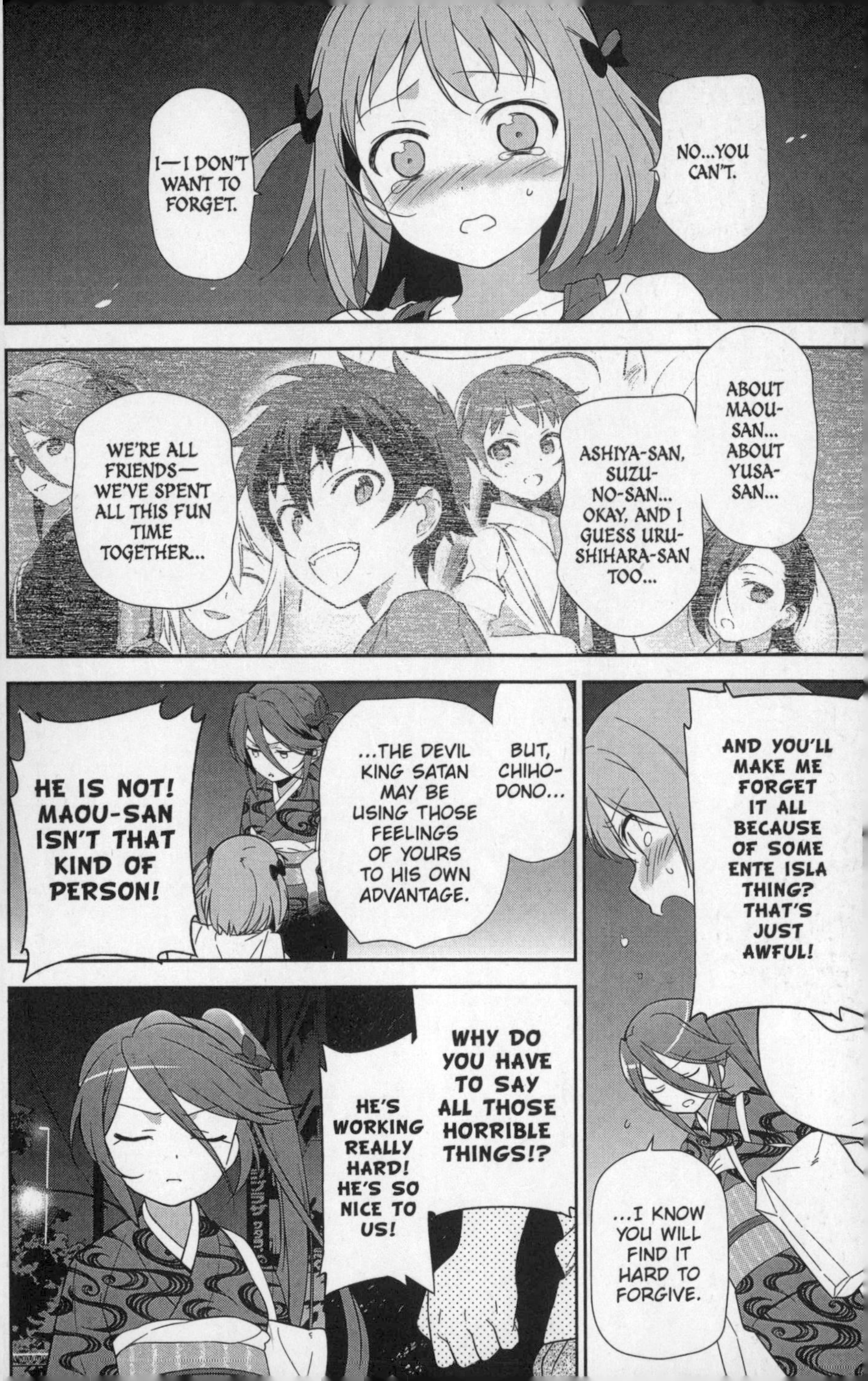
NO...YOU CAN'T.
I—I DON'T WANT TO FORGET.
ABOUT MAOU-SAN... ABOUT YUSA-SAN...
ASHIYA-SAN, SUZU-NO-SAN... OKAY, AND I GUESS URU-SHIHARA-SAN TOO...
WE'RE ALL FRIENDS—WE'VE SPENT ALL THIS FUN TIME TOGETHER...
AND YOU'LL MAKE ME FORGET IT ALL BECAUSE OF SOME ENTE ISLA THING? THAT'S JUST AWFUL!
...I KNOW YOU WILL FIND IT HARD TO FORGIVE.
BUT, CHIHO-DONO...
...THE DEVIL KING SATAN MAY BE USING THOSE FEELINGS OF YOURS TO HIS OWN ADVANTAGE.
HE IS NOT! MAOU-SAN ISN'T THAT KIND OF PERSON!
WHY DO YOU HAVE TO SAY ALL THOSE HORRIBLE THINGS!?
HE'S WORKING REALLY HARD! HE'S SO NICE TO US!

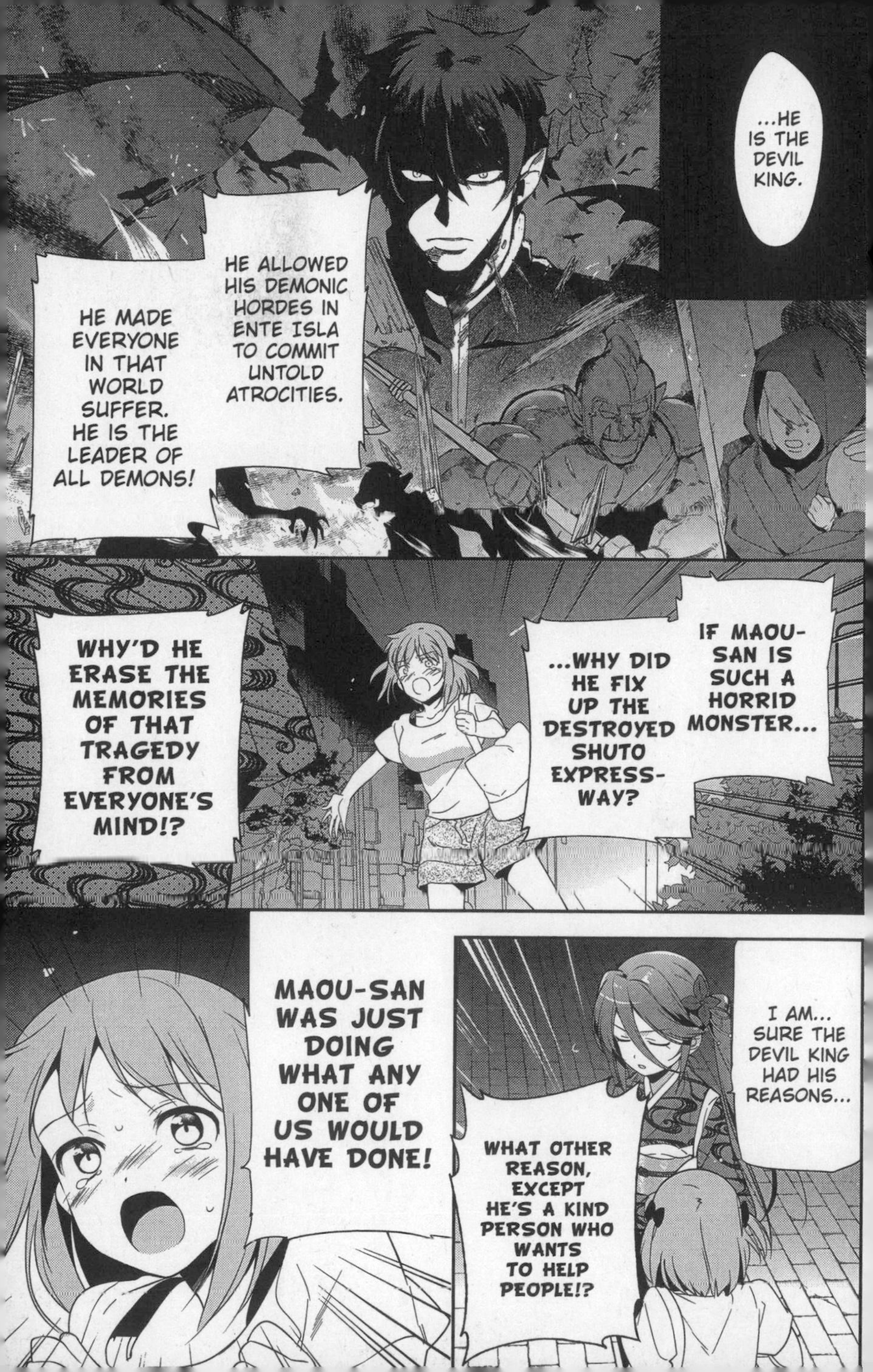
...HE IS THE DEVIL KING.
HE ALLOWED HIS DEMONIC HORDES IN ENTE ISLA TO COMMIT UNTOLD ATROCITIES.
HE MADE EVERYONE IN THAT WORLD SUFFER. HE IS THE LEADER OF ALL DEMONS!
IF MAOU-SAN IS SUCH A HORRID MONSTER...
...WHY DID HE FIX UP THE DESTROYED SHUTO EXPRESS-WAY?
WHY'D HE ERASE THE MEMORIES OF THAT TRAGEDY FROM EVERYONE'S MIND!?
I AM... SURE THE DEVIL KING HAD HIS REASONS...
WHAT OTHER REASON, EXCEPT HE'S A KIND PERSON WHO WANTS TO HELP PEOPLE!?
MAOU-SAN WAS JUST DOING WHAT ANY ONE OF US WOULD HAVE DONE!

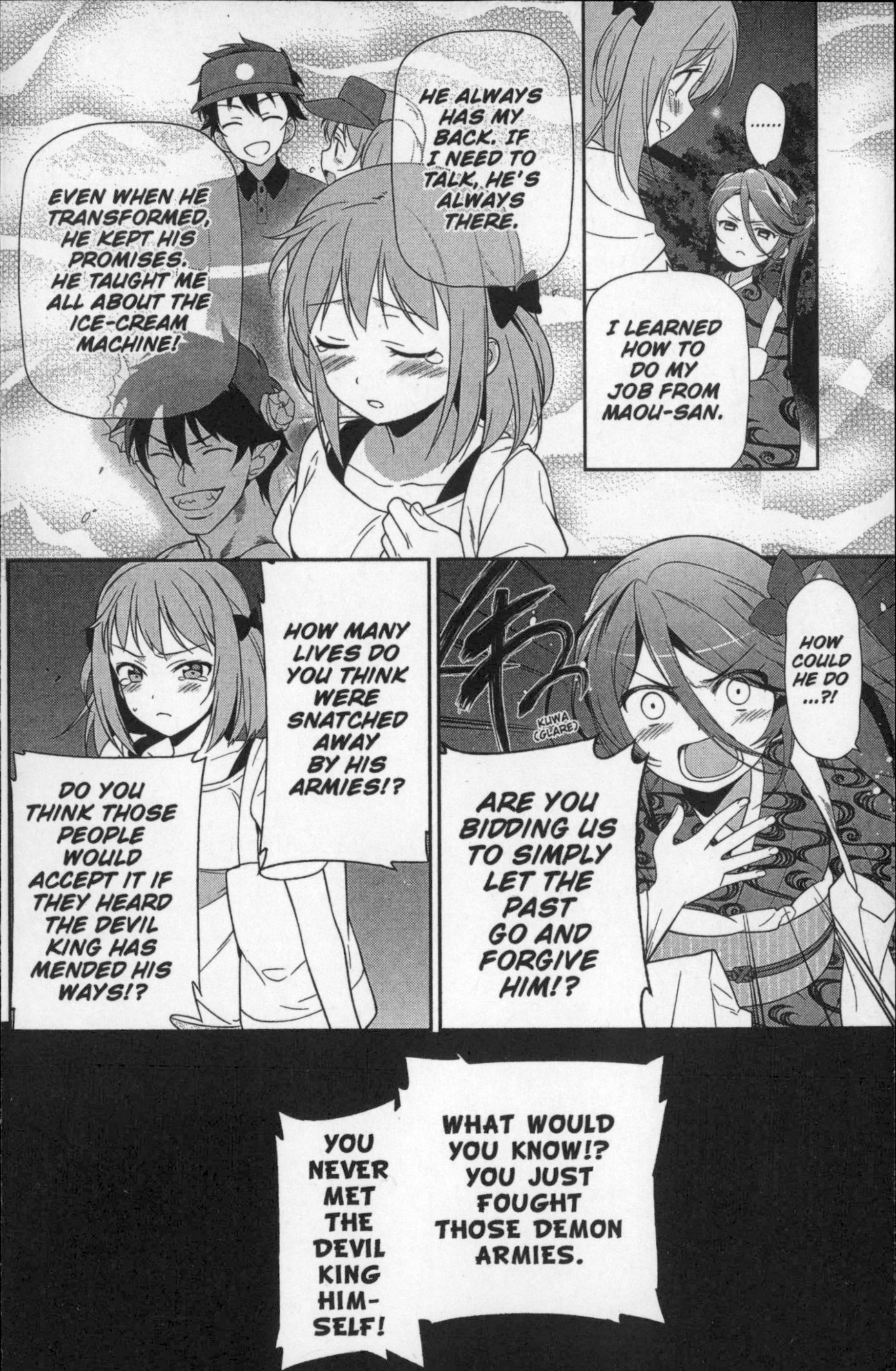
......
I LEARNED HOW TO DO MY JOB FROM MAOU-SAN.
HE ALWAYS HAS MY BACK. IF I NEED TO TALK, HE'S ALWAYS THERE.
EVEN WHEN HE TRANSFORMED, HE KEPT HIS PROMISES. HE TAUGHT ME ALL ABOUT THE ICE-CREAM MACHINE!
HOW COULD HE DO ...?!
KUWA (GLARE)
ARE YOU BIDDING US TO SIMPLY LET THE PAST GO AND FORGIVE HIM!?
HOW MANY LIVES DO YOU THINK WERE SNATCHED AWAY BY HIS ARMIES!?
DO YOU THINK THOSE PEOPLE WOULD ACCEPT IT IF THEY HEARD THE DEVIL KING HAS MENDED HIS WAYS!?
WHAT WOULD YOU KNOW!? YOU JUST FOUGHT THOSE DEMON ARMIES.
YOU NEVER MET THE DEVIL KING HIM-SELF!

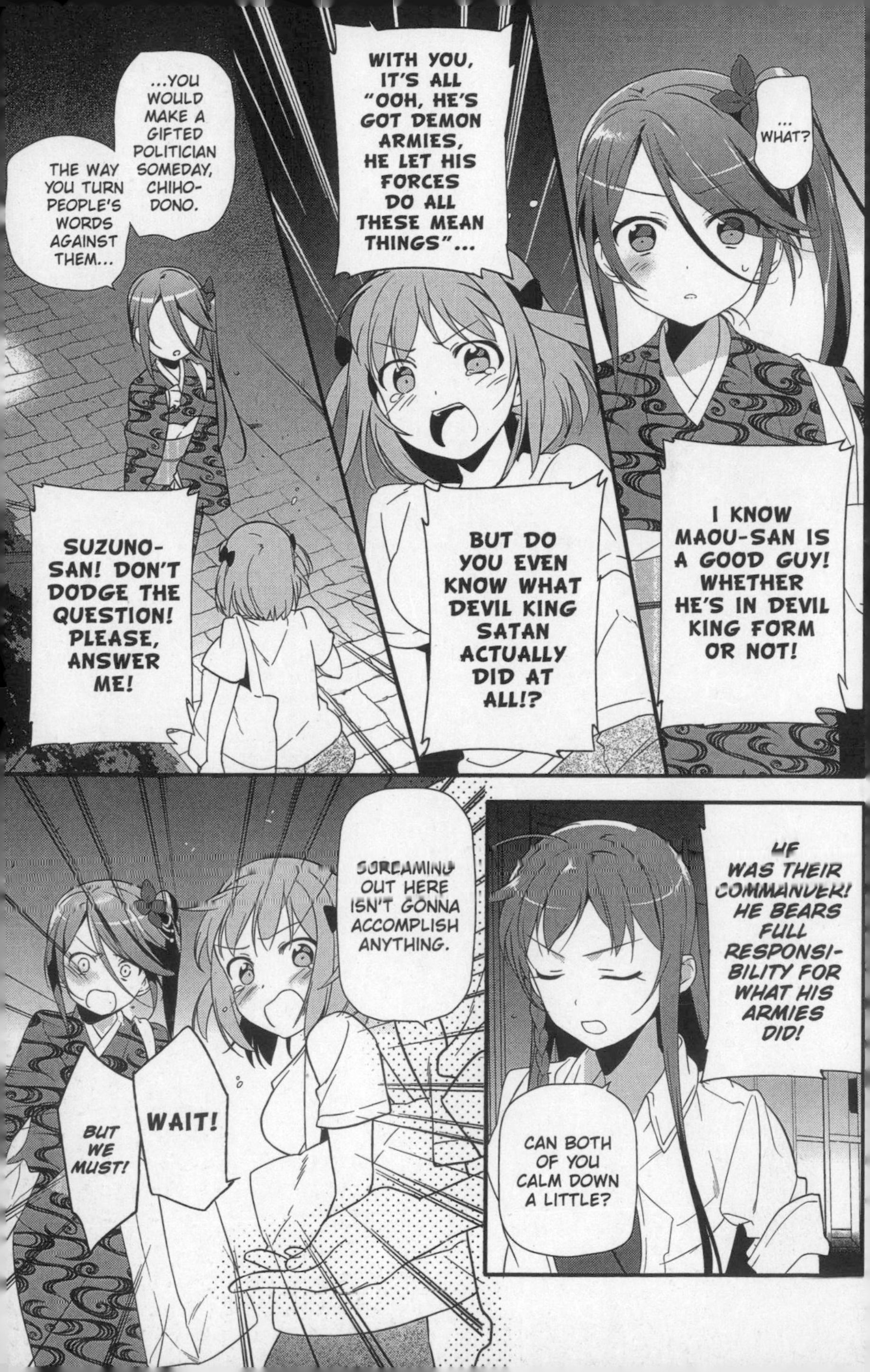
...WHAT?
I KNOW MAOU-SAN IS A GOOD GUY! WHETHER HE'S IN DEVIL KING FORM OR NOT!
WITH YOU, IT'S ALL "OOH, HE'S GOT DEMON ARMIES, HE LET HIS FORCES DO ALL THESE MEAN THINGS"...
BUT DO YOU EVEN KNOW WHAT DEVIL KING SATAN ACTUALLY DID AT ALL!?
THE WAY YOU TURN PEOPLE'S WORDS AGAINST THEM...
...YOU WOULD MAKE A GIFTED POLITICIAN SOMEDAY, CHIHO-DONO.
SUZUNO-SAN! DON'T DODGE THE QUESTION! PLEASE, ANSWER ME!
HE WAS THEIR COMMANDER! HE BEARS FULL RESPONSIBILITY FOR WHAT HIS ARMIES DID!
CAN BOTH OF YOU CALM DOWN A LITTLE?
SCREAMING OUT HERE ISN'T GONNA ACCOMPLISH ANYTHING.
WAIT!
BUT WE MUST!

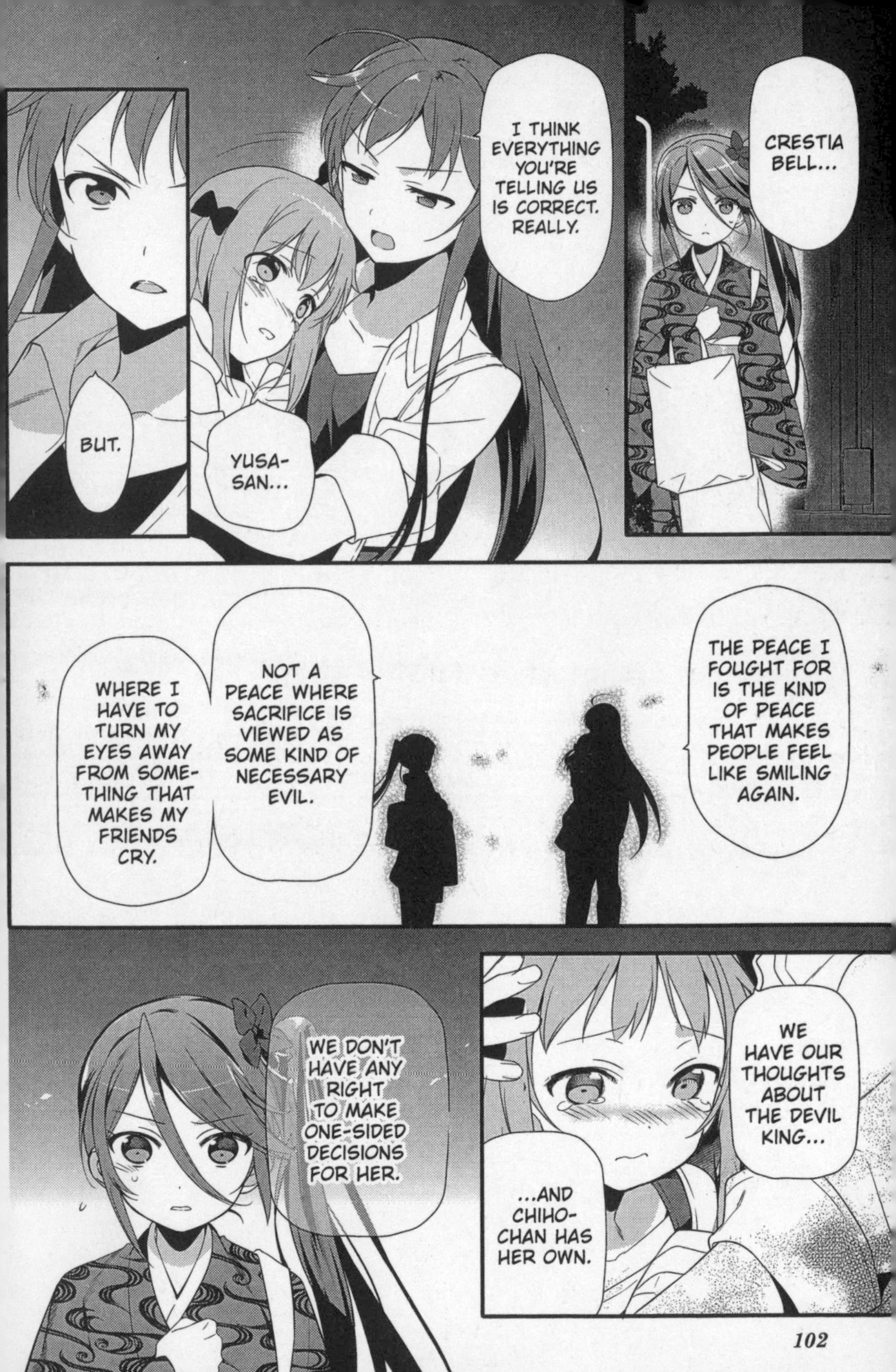
CRESTIA BELL...
I THINK EVERYTHING YOU'RE TELLING US IS CORRECT. REALLY.
YUSA-SAN...
BUT.
THE PEACE I FOUGHT FOR IS THE KIND OF PEACE THAT MAKES PEOPLE FEEL LIKE SMILING AGAIN.
NOT A PEACE WHERE SACRIFICE IS VIEWED AS SOME KIND OF NECESSARY EVIL.
WHERE I HAVE TO TURN MY EYES AWAY FROM SOMETHING THAT MAKES MY FRIENDS CRY.
WE HAVE OUR THOUGHTS ABOUT THE DEVIL KING...
...AND CHIHO-CHAN HAS HER OWN.
WE DON'T HAVE ANY RIGHT TO MAKE ONE-SIDED DECISIONS FOR HER.

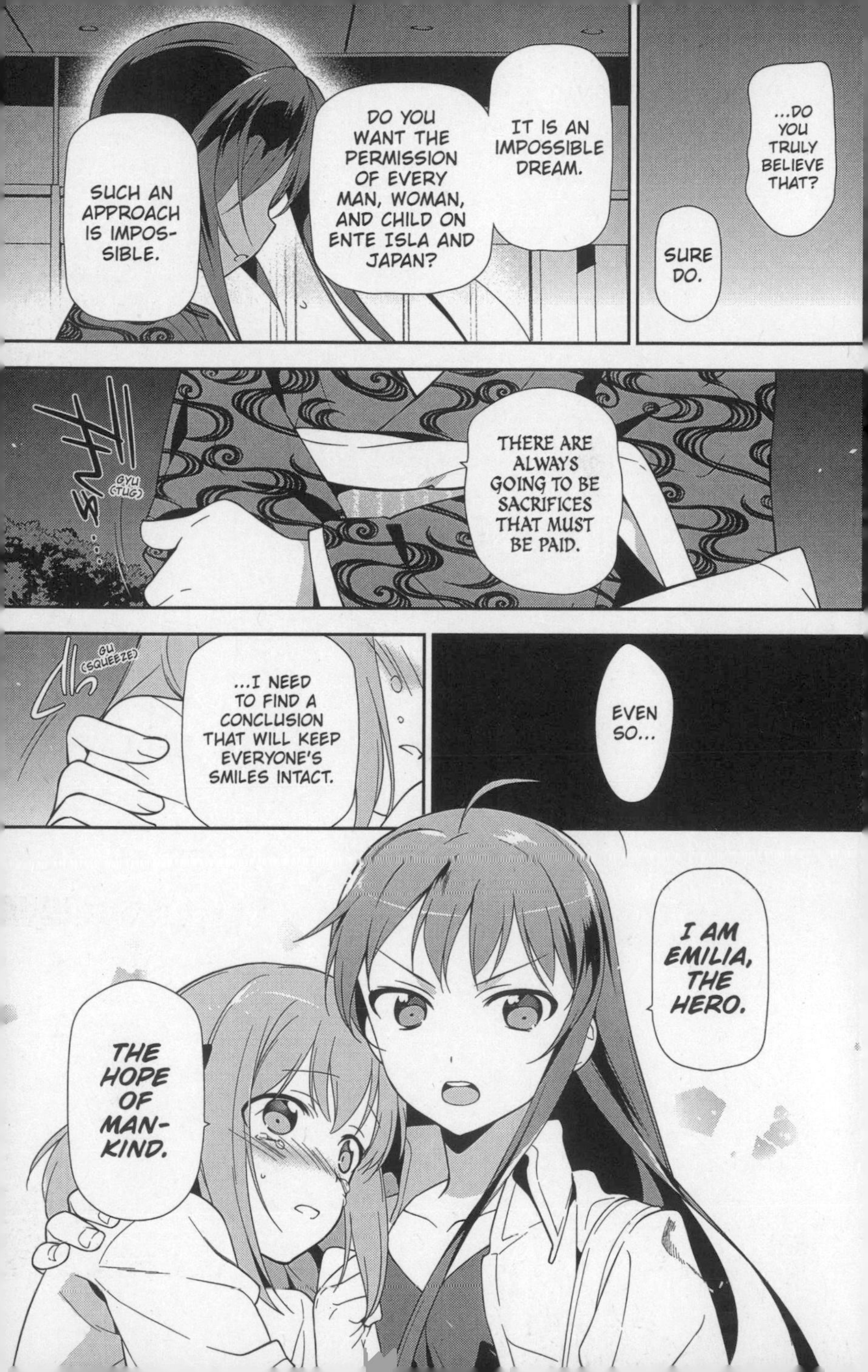
...DO YOU TRULY BELIEVE THAT?
SURE DO.
IT IS AN IMPOSSIBLE DREAM.
DO YOU WANT THE PERMISSION OF EVERY MAN, WOMAN, AND CHILD ON ENTE ISLA AND JAPAN?
SUCH AN APPROACH IS IMPOS-SIBLE.
THERE ARE ALWAYS GOING TO BE SACRIFICES THAT MUST BE PAID.
GYU (TUG)
EVEN SO...
...I NEED TO FIND A CONCLUSION THAT WILL KEEP EVERYONE'S SMILES INTACT.
GU (SQUEEZE)
I AM EMILIA, THE HERO.
THE HOPE OF MAN-KIND.

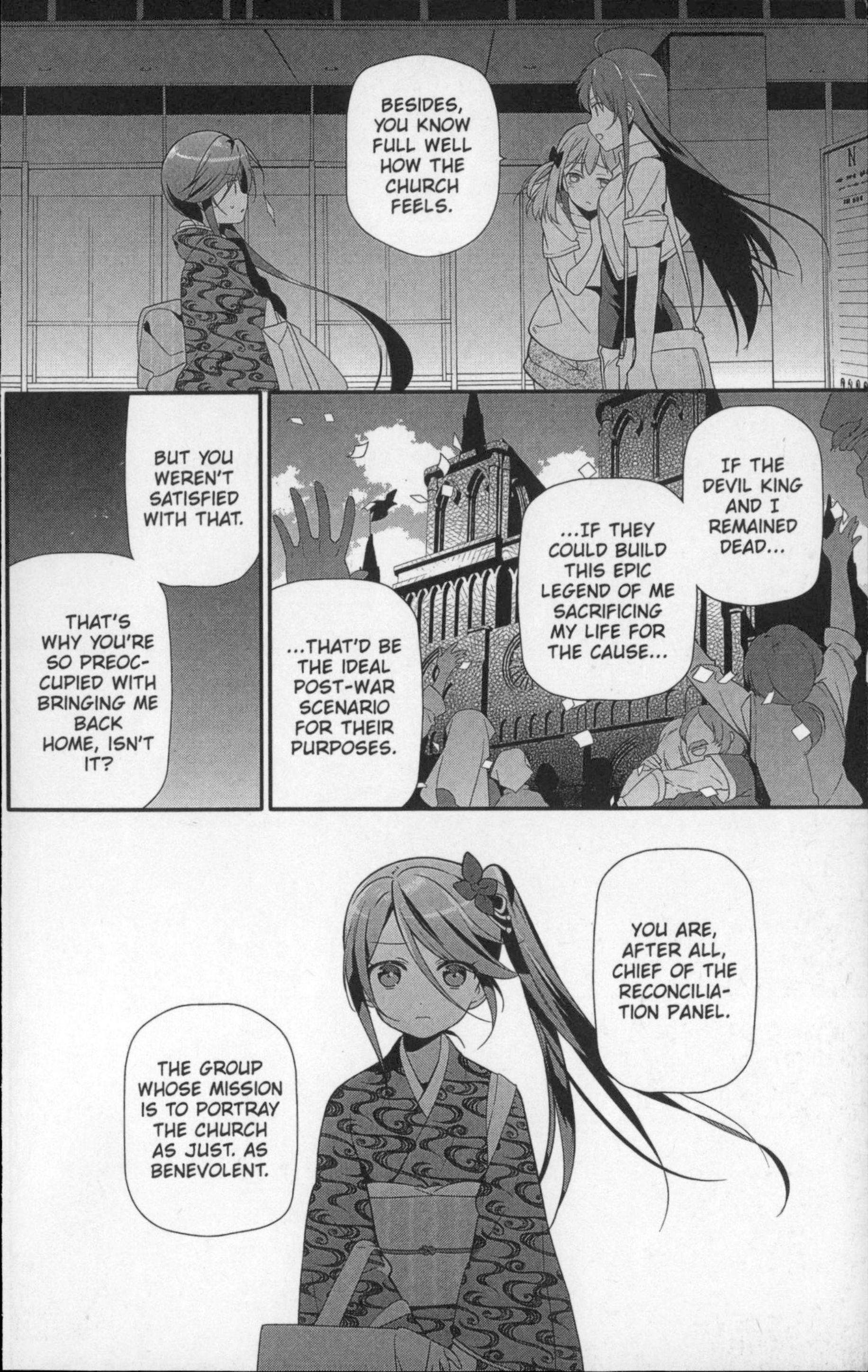
BESIDES, YOU KNOW FULL WELL HOW THE CHURCH FEELS.
IF THE DEVIL KING AND I REMAINED DEAD...
...IF THEY COULD BUILD THIS EPIC LEGEND OF ME SACRIFICING MY LIFE FOR THE CAUSE...
...THAT'D BE THE IDEAL POST-WAR SCENARIO FOR THEIR PURPOSES.
BUT YOU WEREN'T SATISFIED WITH THAT.
THAT'S WHY YOU'RE SO PREOC-CUPIED WITH BRINGING ME BACK HOME, ISN'T IT?
YOU ARE, AFTER ALL, CHIEF OF THE RECONCILIA-TION PANEL.
THE GROUP WHOSE MISSION IS TO PORTRAY THE CHURCH AS JUST. AS BENEVOLENT.

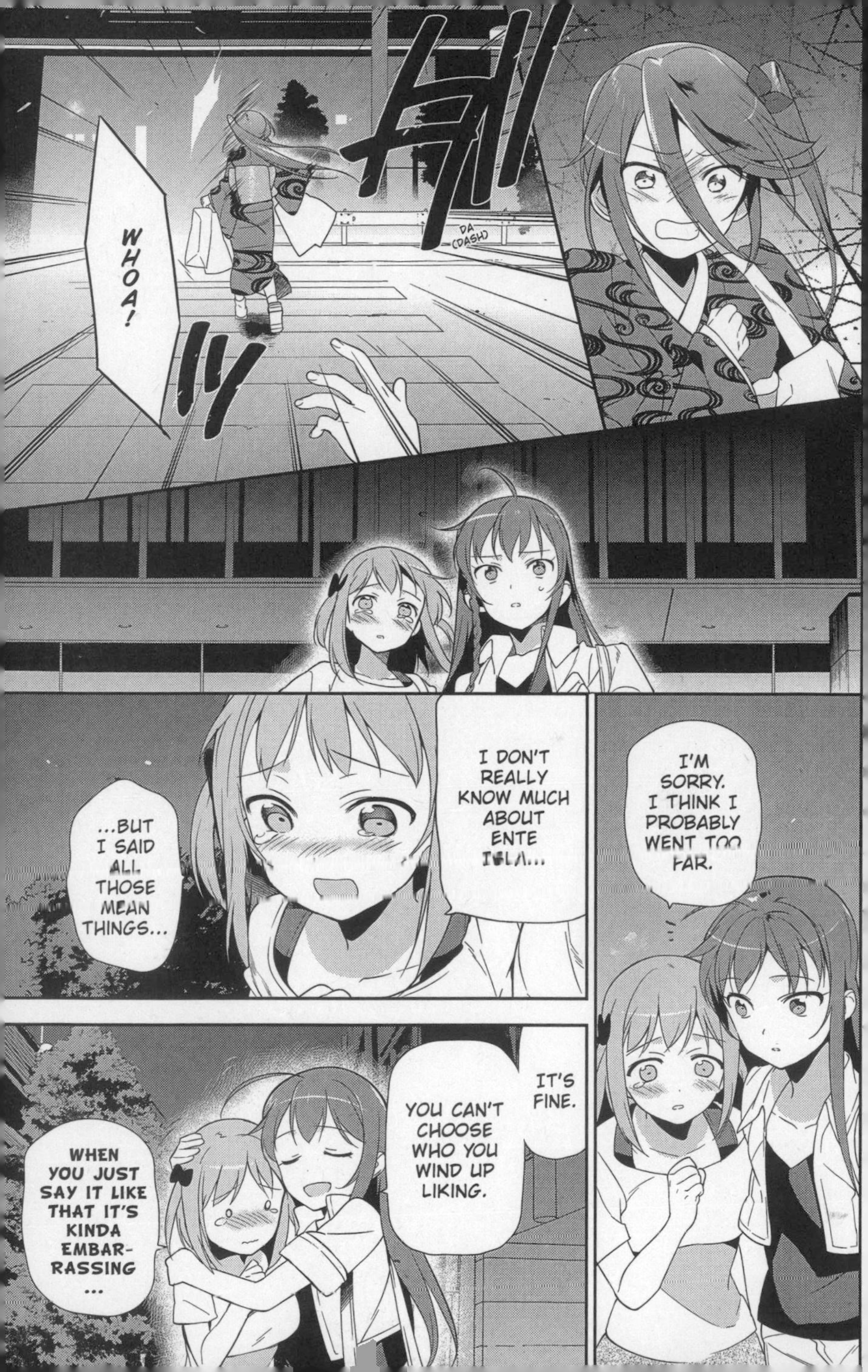
DA (DASH)
WHOA!
I'M SORRY. I THINK I PROBABLY WENT TOO FAR.
I DON'T REALLY KNOW MUCH ABOUT ENTE ISLA...
...BUT I SAID ALL THOSE MEAN THINGS...
IT'S FINE.
YOU CAN'T CHOOSE WHO YOU WIND UP LIKING.
WHEN YOU JUST SAY IT LIKE THAT IT'S KINDA EMBAR-RASSING...

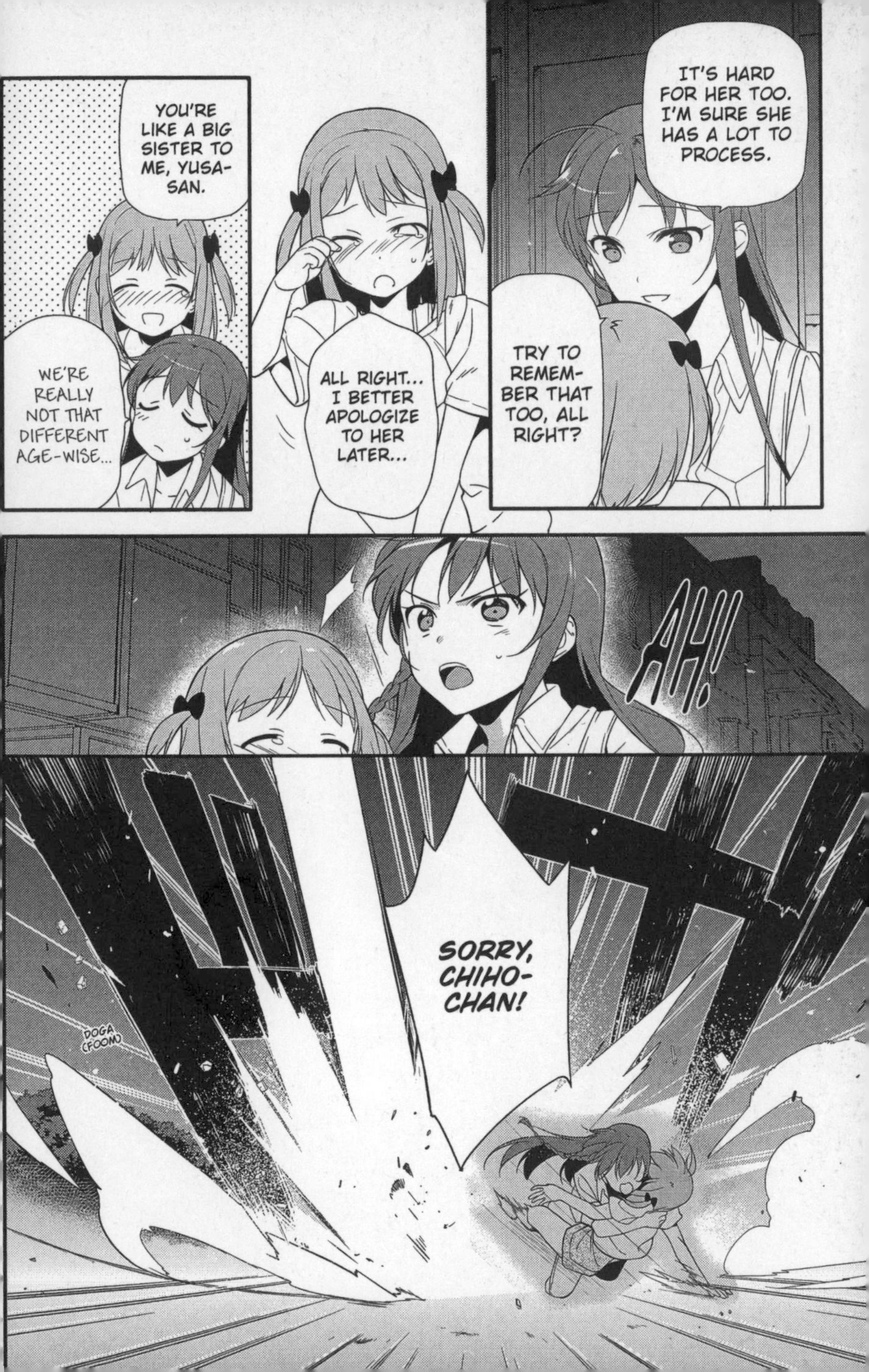
IT'S HARD FOR HER TOO. I'M SURE SHE HAS A LOT TO PROCESS.
TRY TO REMEM-BER THAT TOO, ALL RIGHT?
ALL RIGHT... I BETTER APOLOGIZE TO HER LATER...
YOU'RE LIKE A BIG SISTER TO ME, YUSA-SAN.
WE'RE REALLY NOT THAT DIFFERENT AGE-WISE...
AH!
SORRY, CHIHO-CHAN!
DOGA (FOOM)

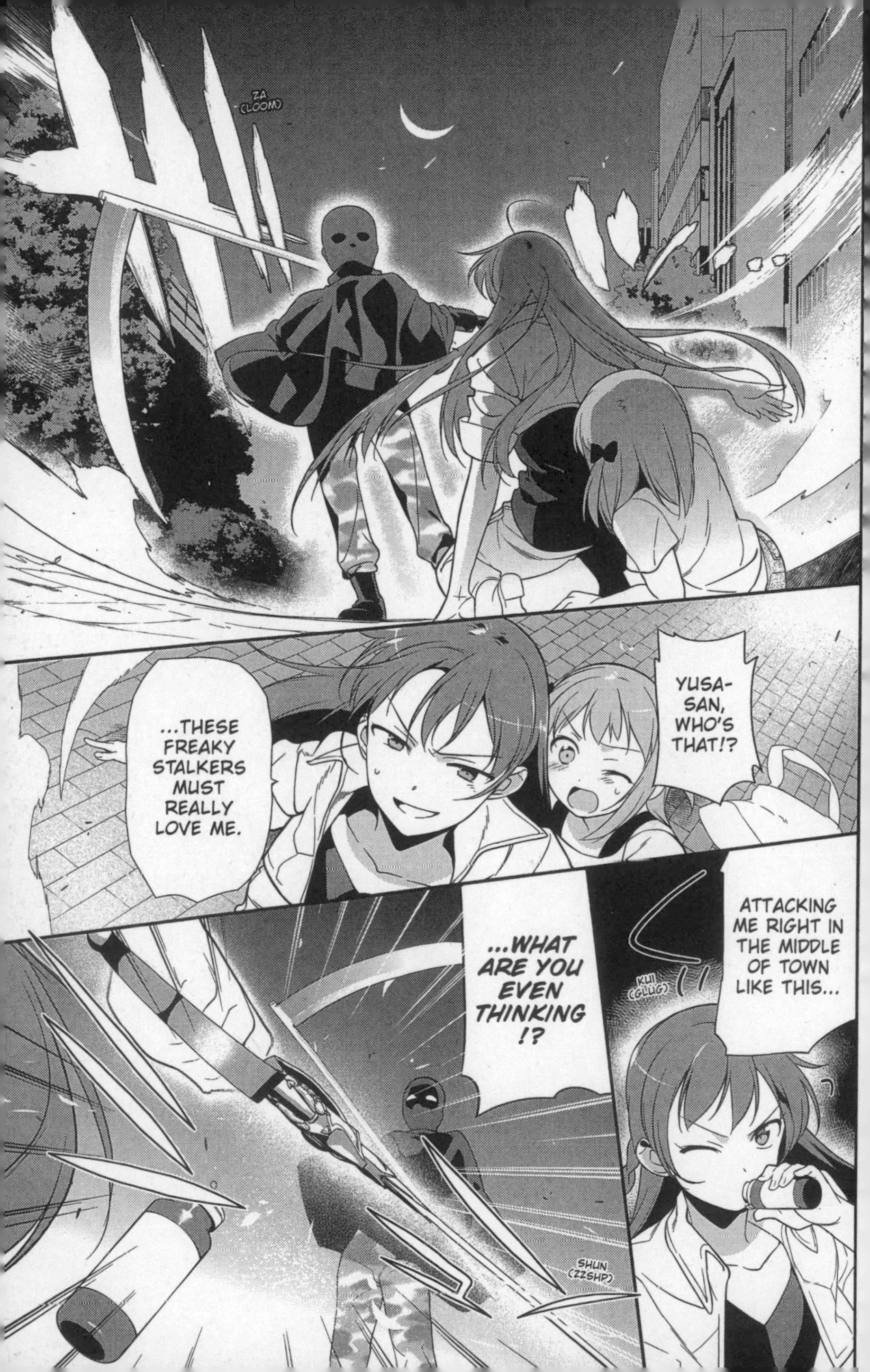
ZA (LOOM)
YUSA-SAN, WHO'S THAT!?
...THESE FREAKY STALKERS MUST REALLY LOVE ME.
ATTACKING ME RIGHT IN THE MIDDLE OF TOWN LIKE THIS...
KUI (GLUG)
...WHAT ARE YOU EVEN THINKING !?
SHUN (ZZSHP)

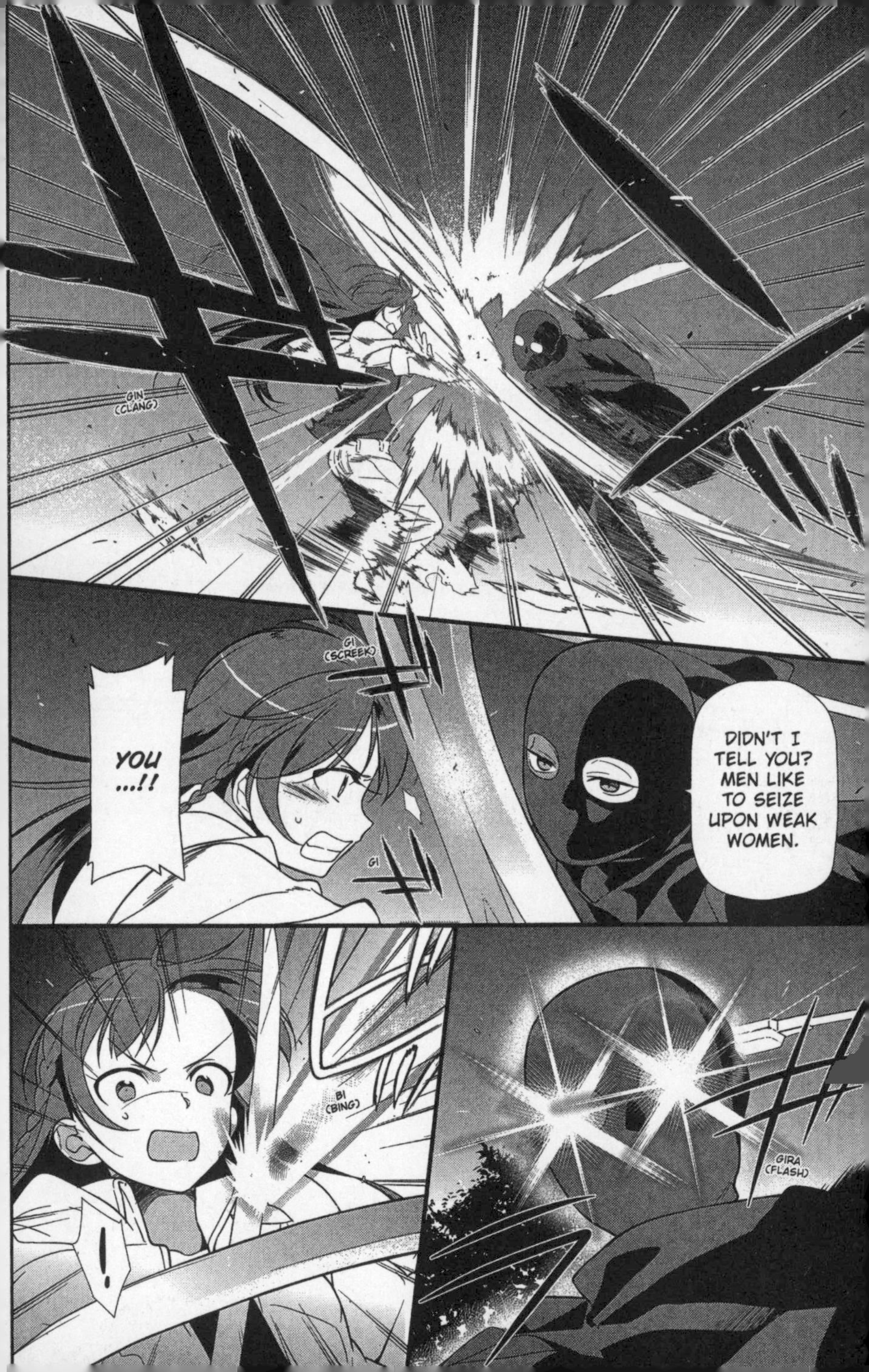
GIN
(CLANG)
DIDN'T I TELL YOU? MEN LIKE TO SEIZE UPON WEAK WOMEN.
GI
(SCREEK)
YOU ...!!
GI
GIRA
(FLASH)
BI
(BING)
!

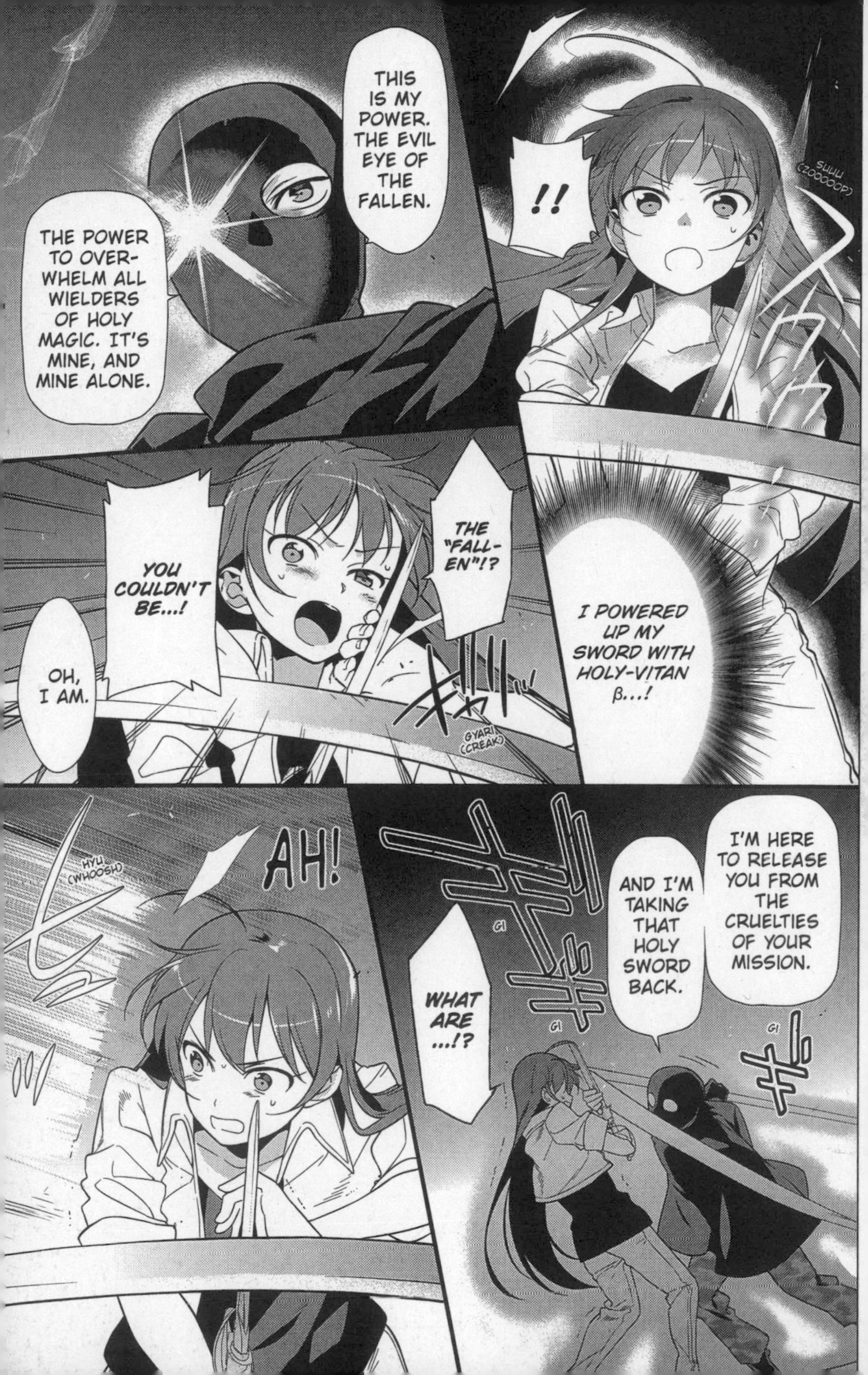
!!
SUUU (ZOOOOOP)
THIS IS MY POWER. THE EVIL EYE OF THE FALLEN.
THE POWER TO OVER-WHELM ALL WIELDERS OF HOLY MAGIC. IT'S MINE, AND MINE ALONE.
I POWERED UP MY SWORD WITH HOLY-VITAN β...!
THE "FALL-EN"!?
YOU COULDN'T BE...!
OH, I AM.
GYARI (CREAK)
I'M HERE TO RELEASE YOU FROM THE CRUELTIES OF YOUR MISSION.
AND I'M TAKING THAT HOLY SWORD BACK.
GI
GI
GI
WHAT ARE ...!?
AH!
HYU (WHOOSH)

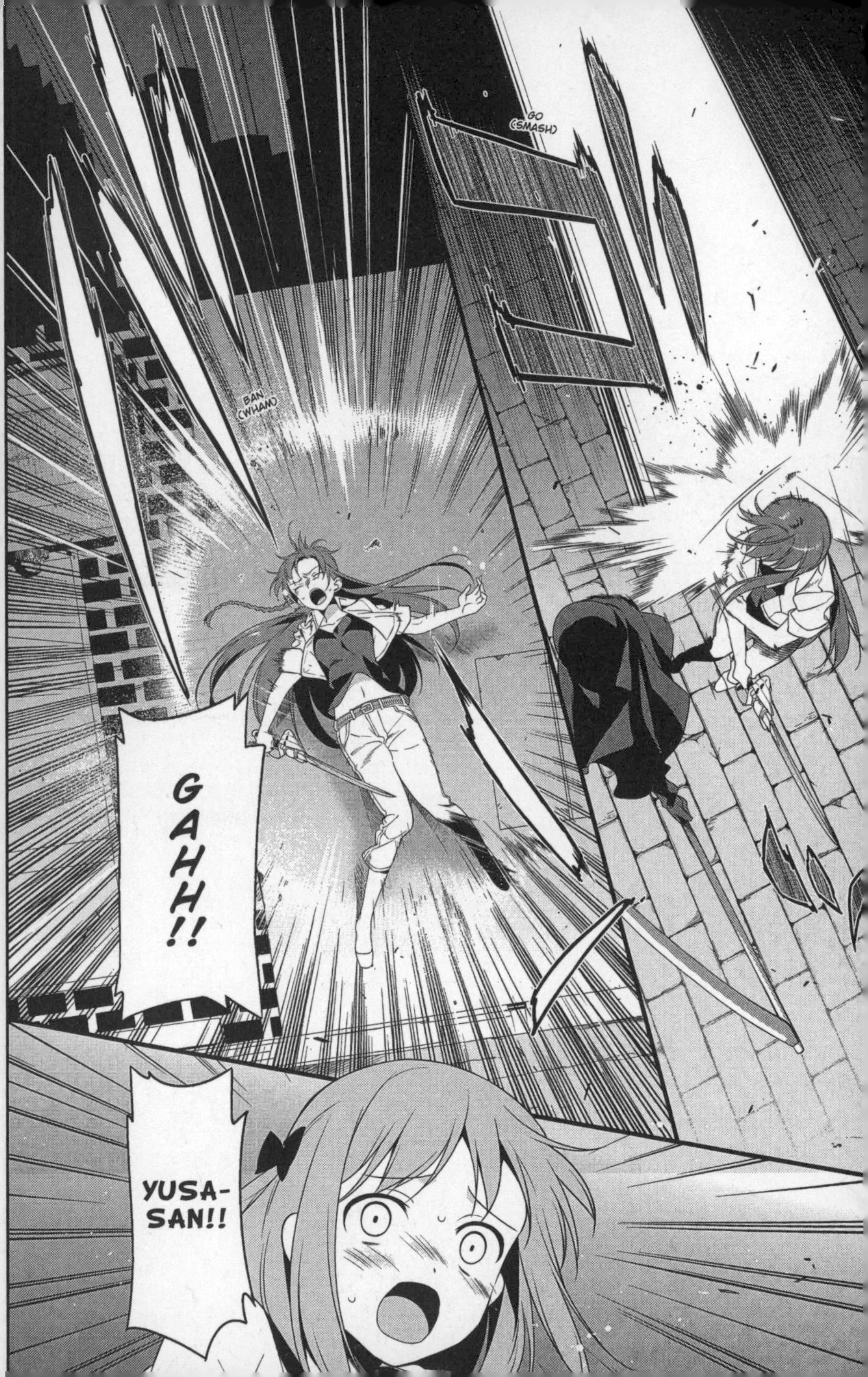
GO (SMASH)
BAN (WHAM)
GAHH!!
YUSA-SAN!!

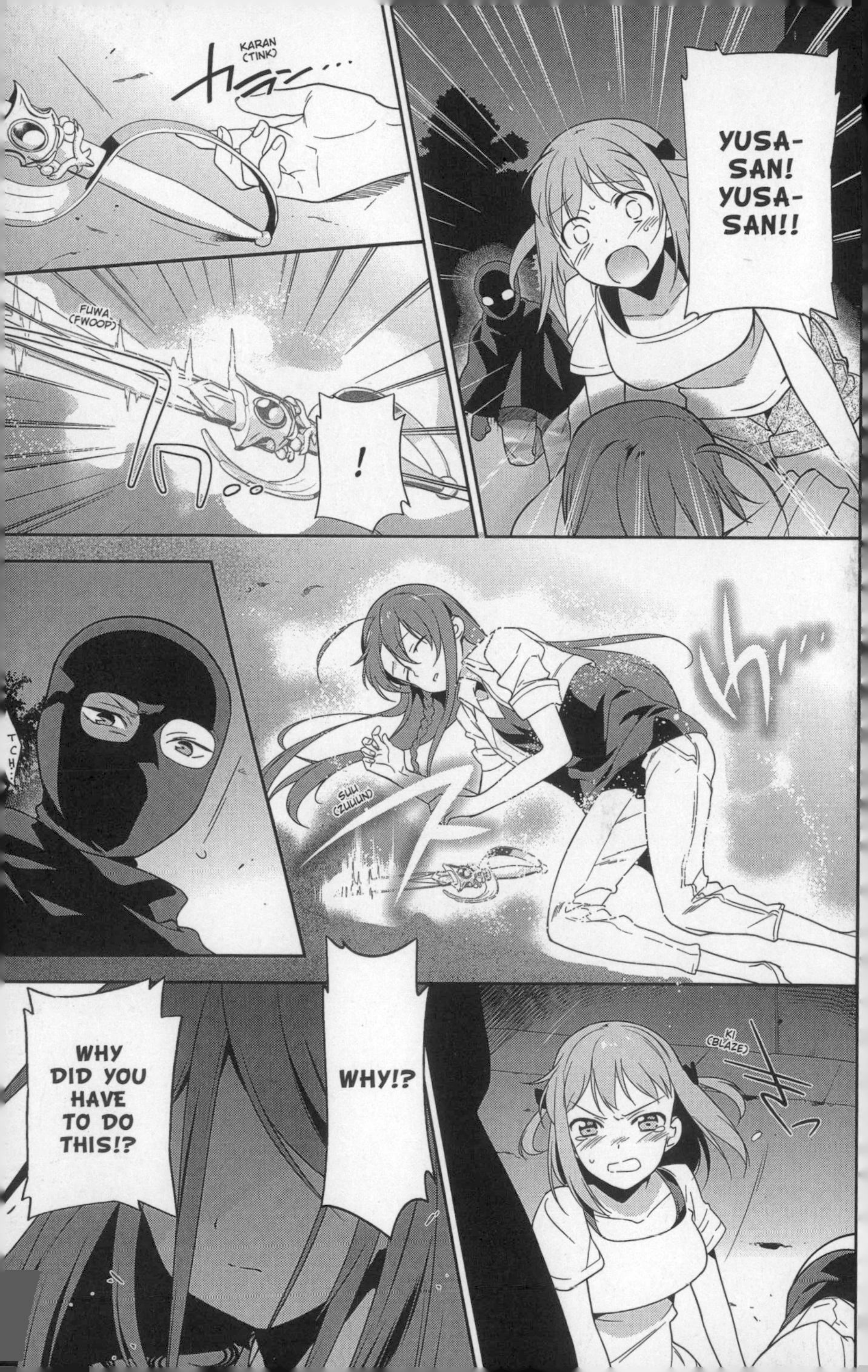
YUSA-SAN! YUSA-SAN!!
KARAN (TINK)
FUWA (FWOOP)
!
SUU (ZUUUN)
TCH...
KI (BLAZE)
WHY!?
WHY DID YOU HAVE TO DO THIS!?

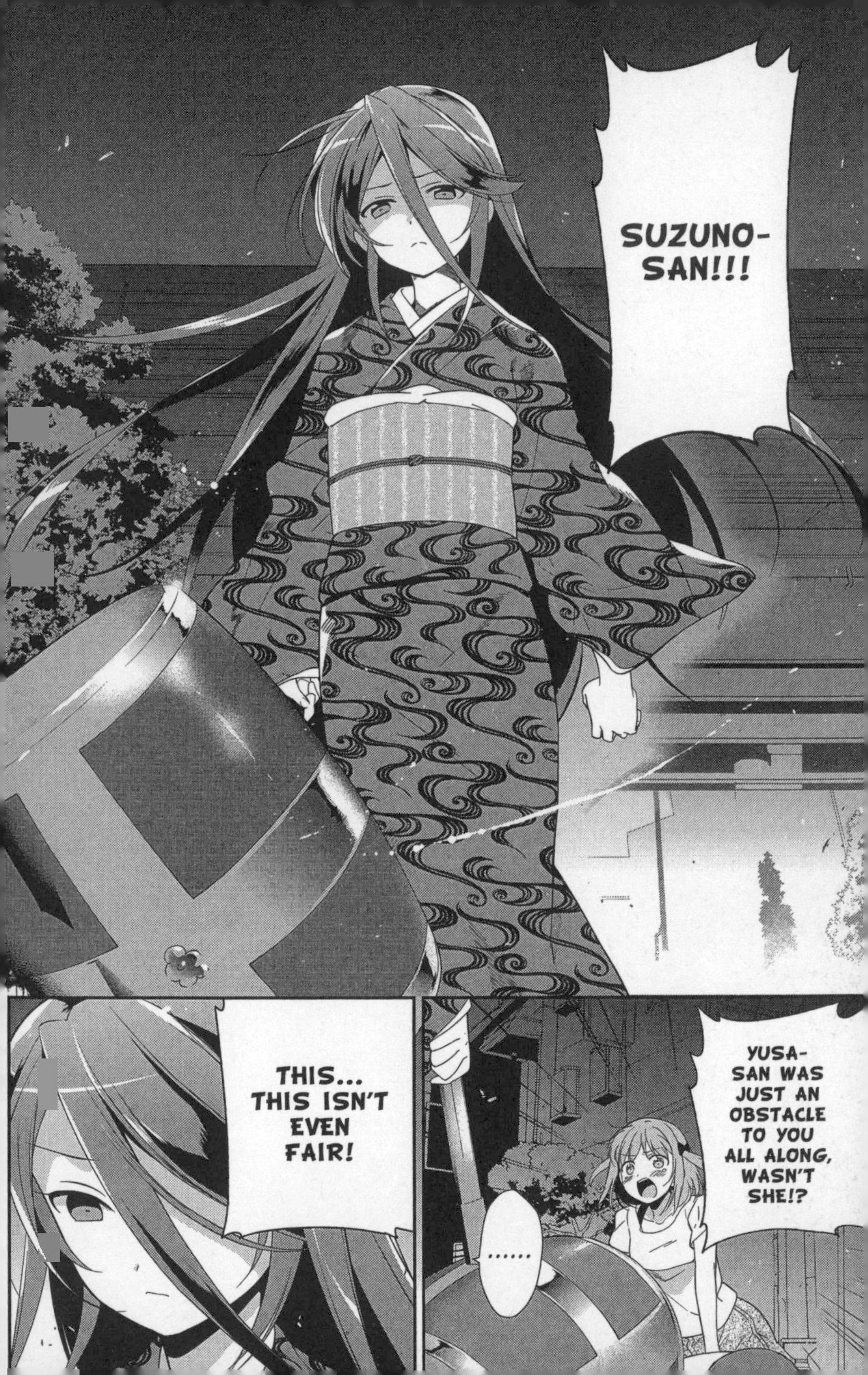
SUZUNO-SAN!!!
YUSA-SAN WAS JUST AN OBSTACLE TO YOU ALL ALONG, WASN'T SHE!?
......
THIS... THIS ISN'T EVEN FAIR!

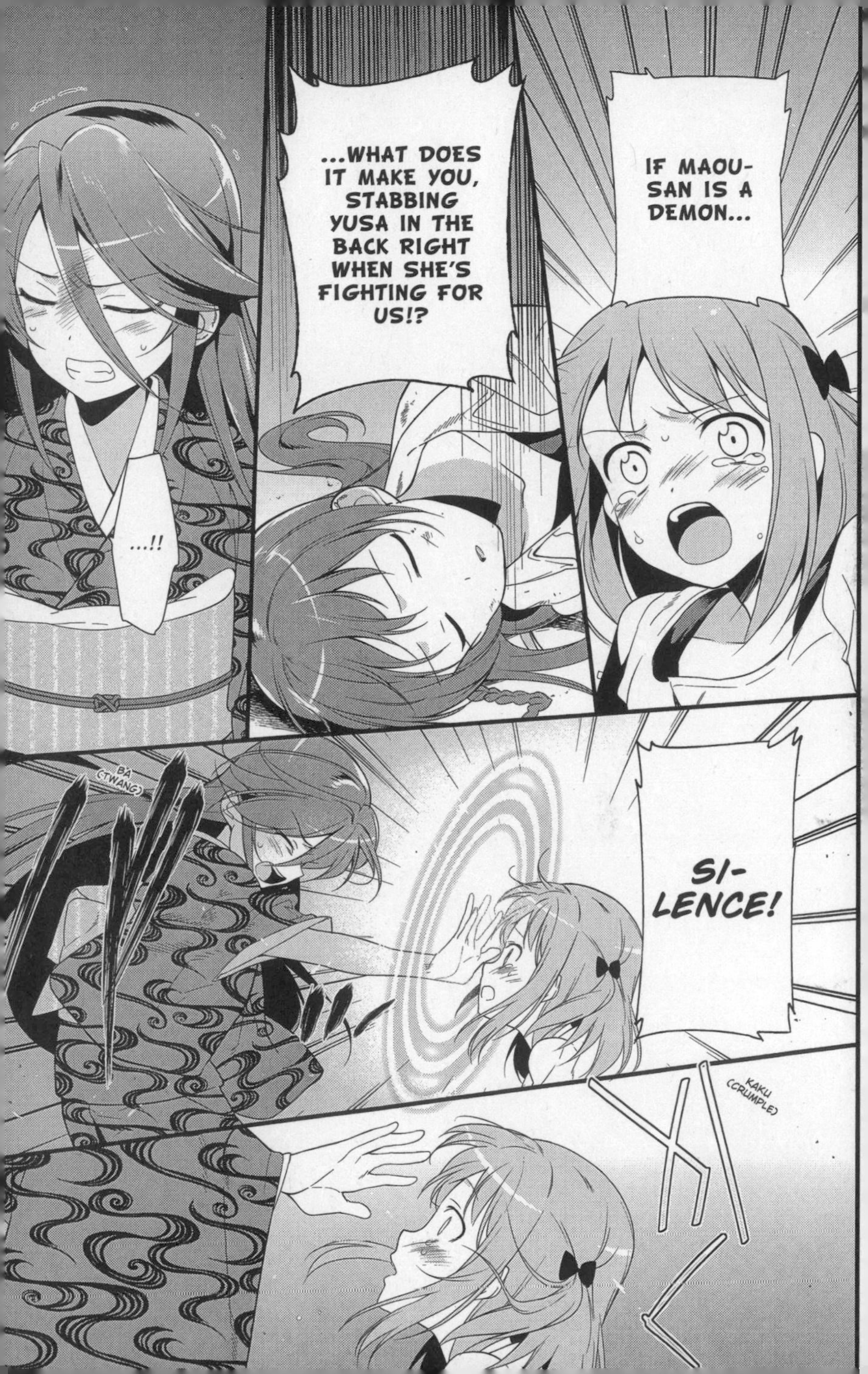
IF MAOU-SAN IS A DEMON...
...WHAT DOES IT MAKE YOU, STABBING YUSA IN THE BACK RIGHT WHEN SHE'S FIGHTING FOR US!?
...!!
SI-LENCE!
BA (TWANG)
KAKU (CRUMPLE)

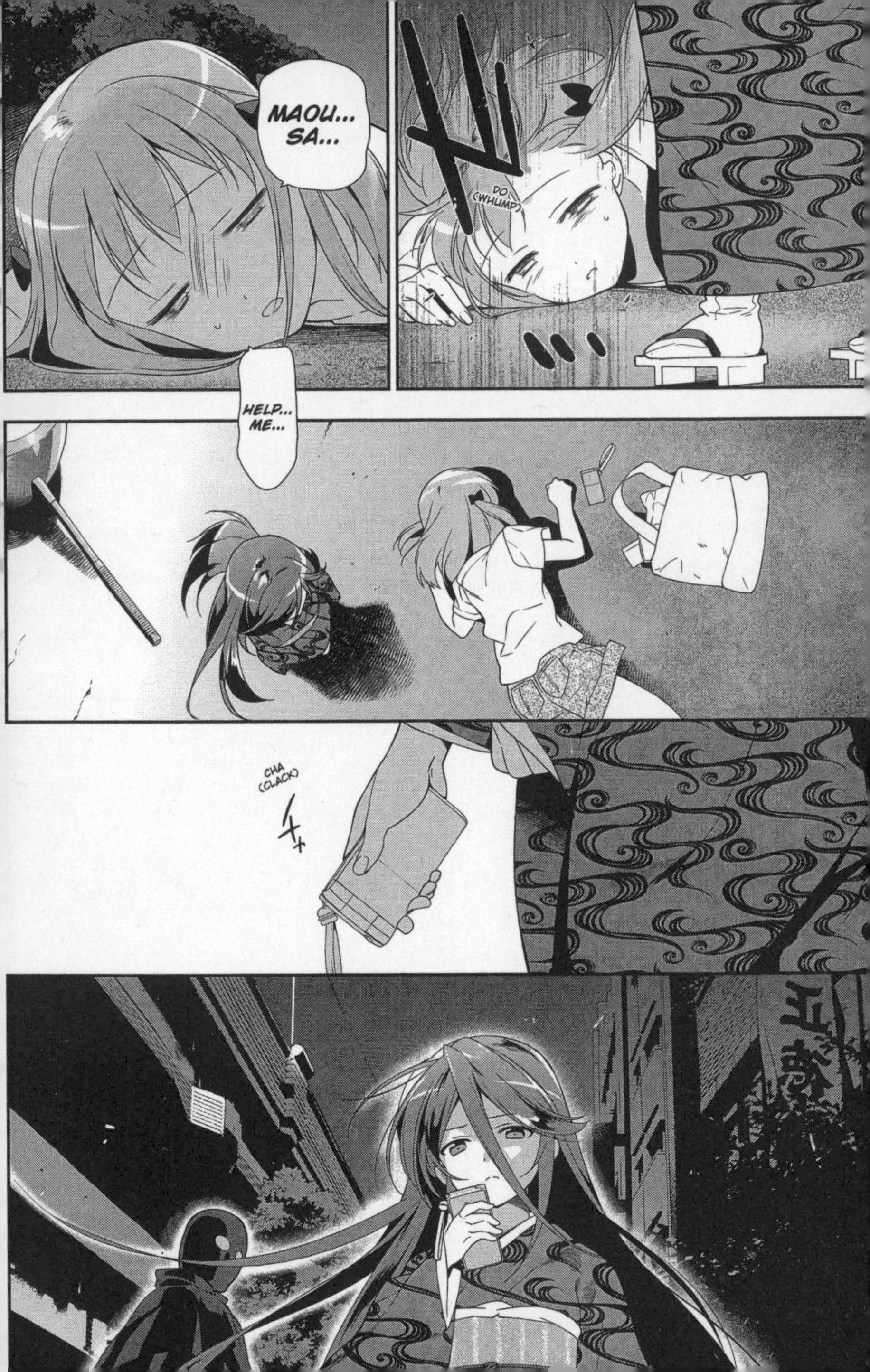
DO (WHUMP)
MAOU... SA...
HELP... ME...
CHA (CLACK)

Chiho
Sasaki

# THE DEVIL IS A PART-TIMER!

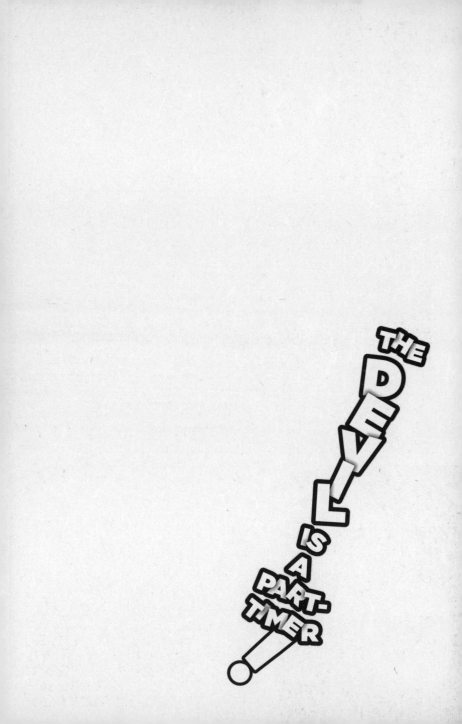

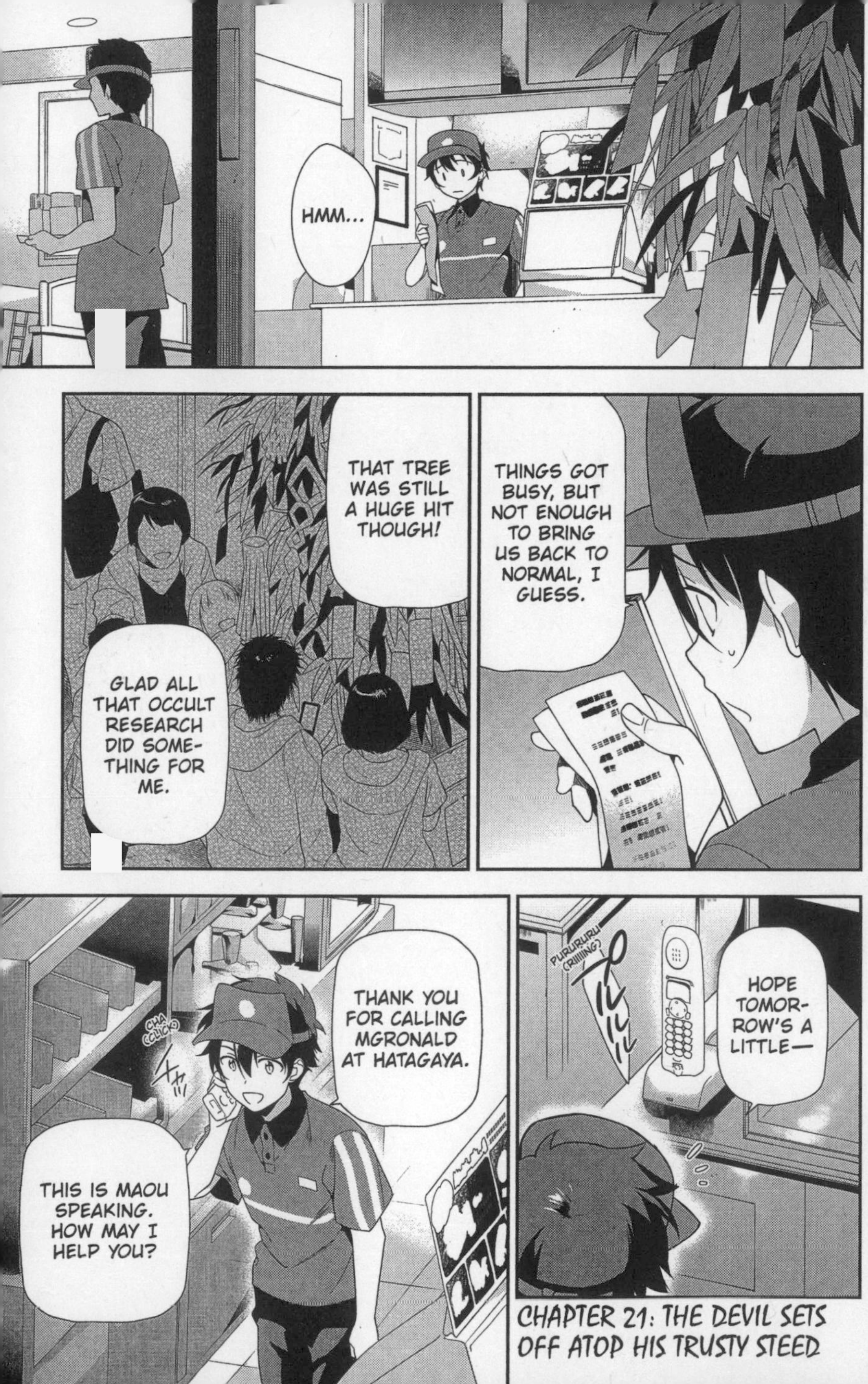
HMM...
THINGS GOT BUSY, BUT NOT ENOUGH TO BRING US BACK TO NORMAL, I GUESS.
THAT TREE WAS STILL A HUGE HIT THOUGH!
GLAD ALL THAT OCCULT RESEARCH DID SOMETHING FOR ME.
PURURURU (CRIIIING)
HOPE TOMORROW'S A LITTLE—
CHA (CLICK)
THANK YOU FOR CALLING MGRONALD AT HATAGAYA.
THIS IS MAOU SPEAKING. HOW MAY I HELP YOU?

## CHAPTER 21: THE DEVIL SETS OFF ATOP HIS TRUSTY STEED

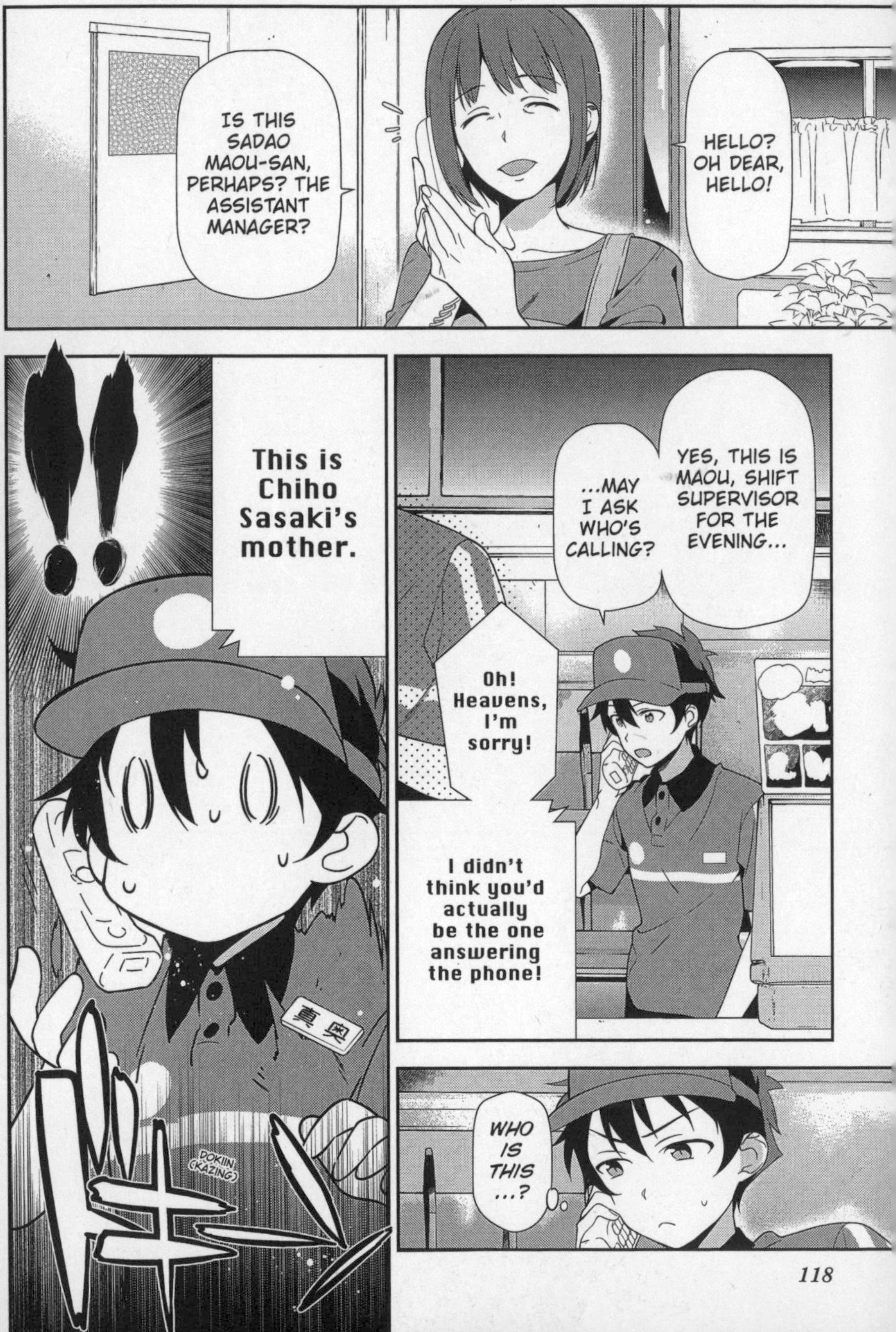
HELLO? OH DEAR, HELLO!
IS THIS SADAO MAOU-SAN, PERHAPS? THE ASSISTANT MANAGER?
YES, THIS IS MAOU, SHIFT SUPERVISOR FOR THE EVENING...
...MAY I ASK WHO'S CALLING?
Oh! Heavens, I'm sorry!
I didn't think you'd actually be the one answering the phone!
WHO IS THIS ...?
This is Chiho Sasaki's mother.
DOKIIN (KAZING)

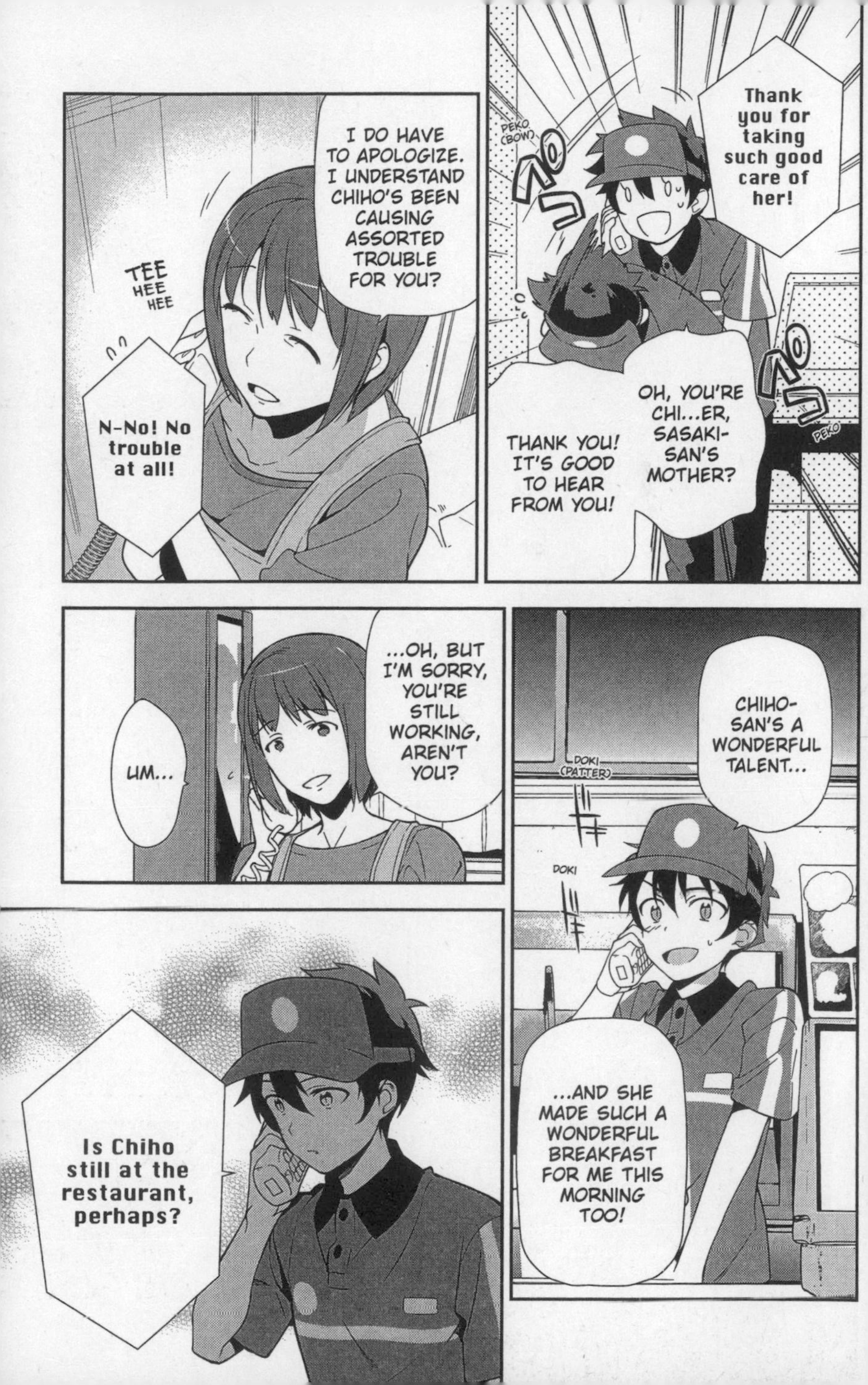
OH, YOU'RE CHI...ER, SASAKI-SAN'S MOTHER?
Thank you for taking such good care of her!
PEKO (BOW)
PEKO
THANK YOU! IT'S GOOD TO HEAR FROM YOU!
I DO HAVE TO APOLOGIZE. I UNDERSTAND CHIHO'S BEEN CAUSING ASSORTED TROUBLE FOR YOU?
TEE HEE HEE
N-No! No trouble at all!
CHIHO-SAN'S A WONDERFUL TALENT...
DOKI (PATTER)
DOKI
...AND SHE MADE SUCH A WONDERFUL BREAKFAST FOR ME THIS MORNING TOO!
...OH, BUT I'M SORRY, YOU'RE STILL WORKING, AREN'T YOU?
UM...
Is Chiho still at the restaurant, perhaps?

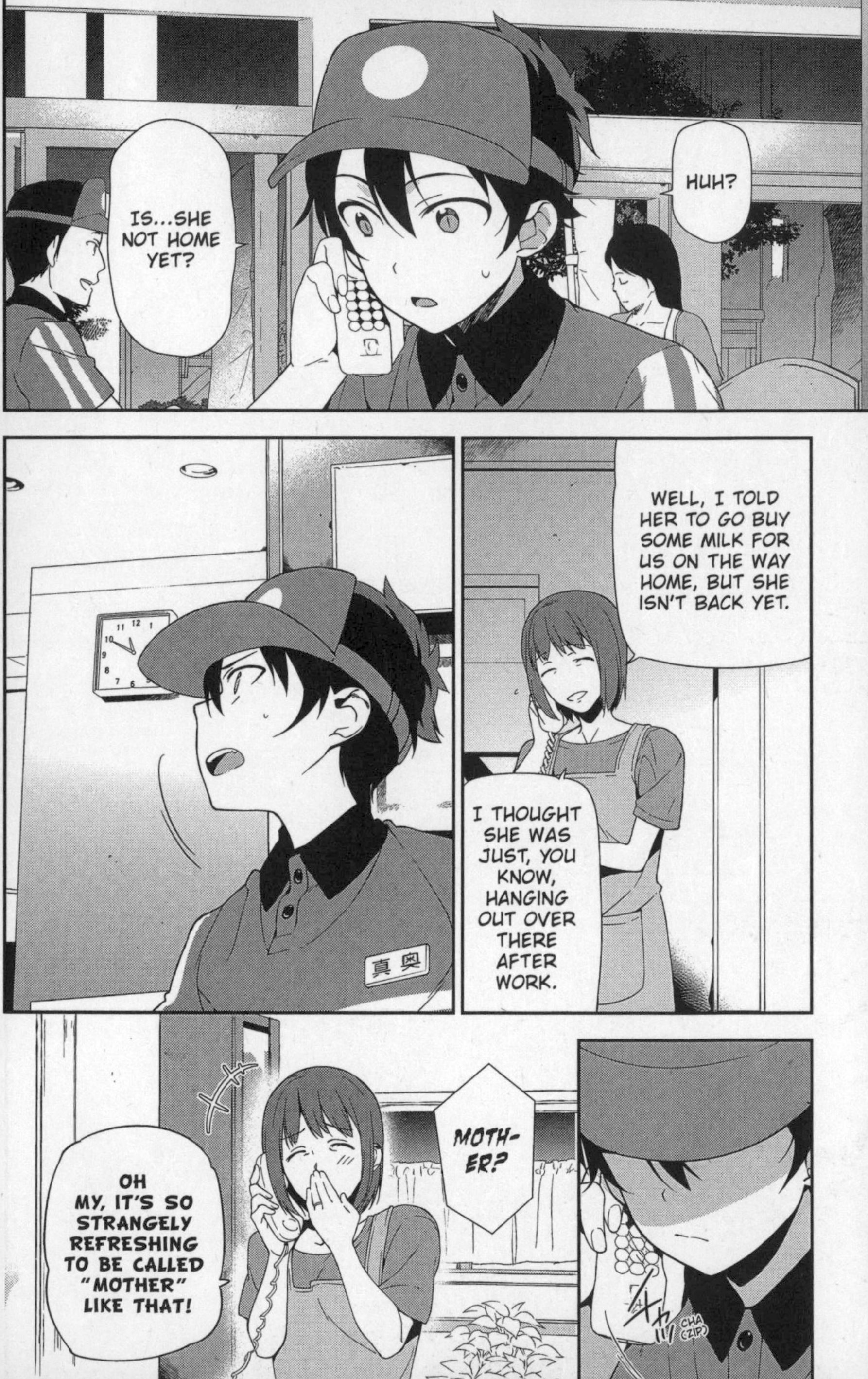

HUH?
IS...SHE NOT HOME YET?
WELL, I TOLD HER TO GO BUY SOME MILK FOR US ON THE WAY HOME, BUT SHE ISN'T BACK YET.
I THOUGHT SHE WAS JUST, YOU KNOW, HANGING OUT OVER THERE AFTER WORK.
真奥
CHA (ZIP)
MOTH-ER?
OH MY, IT'S SO STRANGELY REFRESHING TO BE CALLED "MOTHER" LIKE THAT!

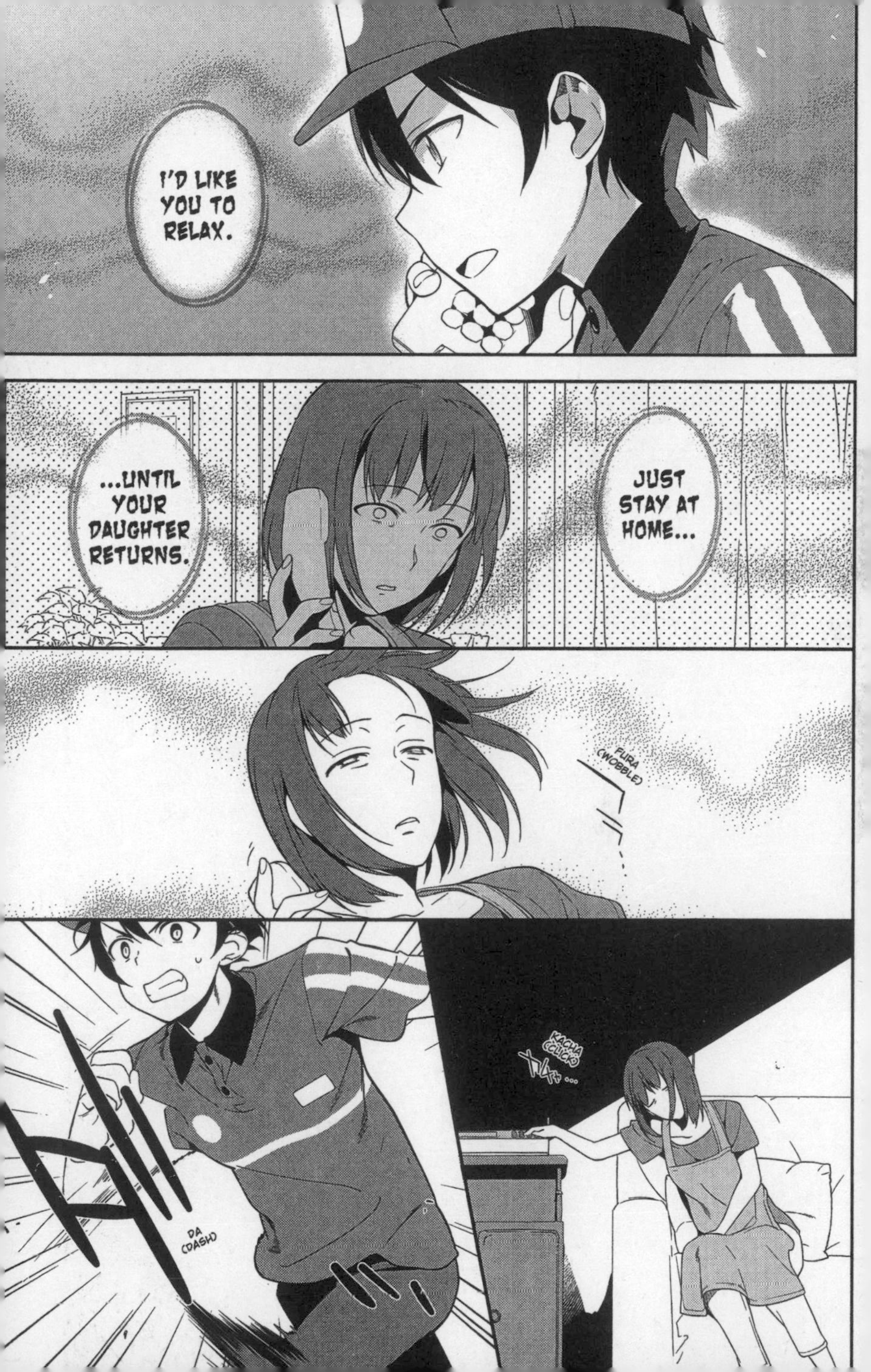
I'D LIKE YOU TO RELAX.
JUST STAY AT HOME...
...UNTIL YOUR DAUGHTER RETURNS.
FURA (WOBBLE)
KACHA (CLICK)
DA (DASH)

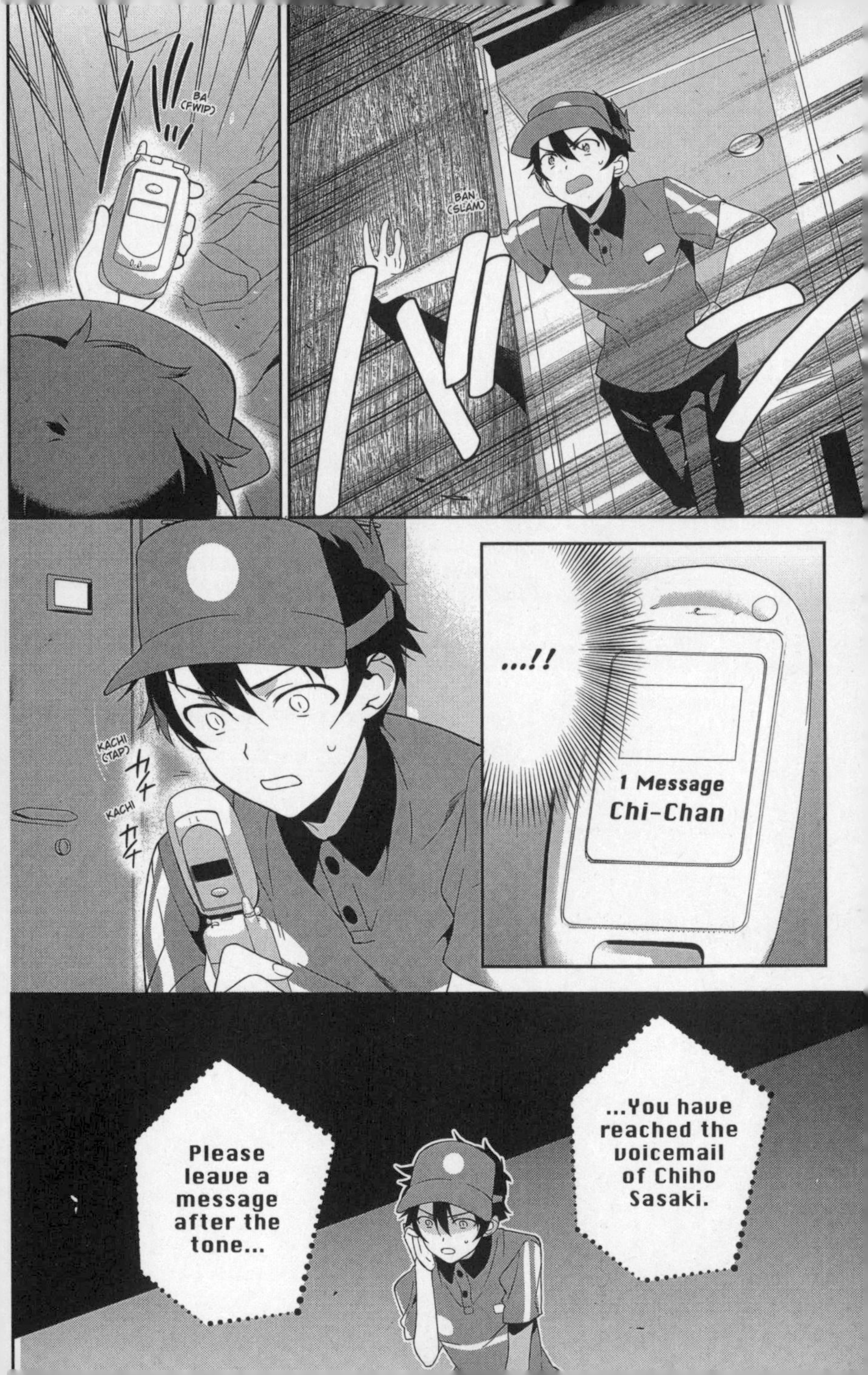
BAN (SLAM)
BA (FWIP)
...!!
1 Message
Chi-Chan
KACHI (TAP) カチ
KACHI カチ
...You have reached the voicemail of Chiho Sasaki.
Please leave a message after the tone...

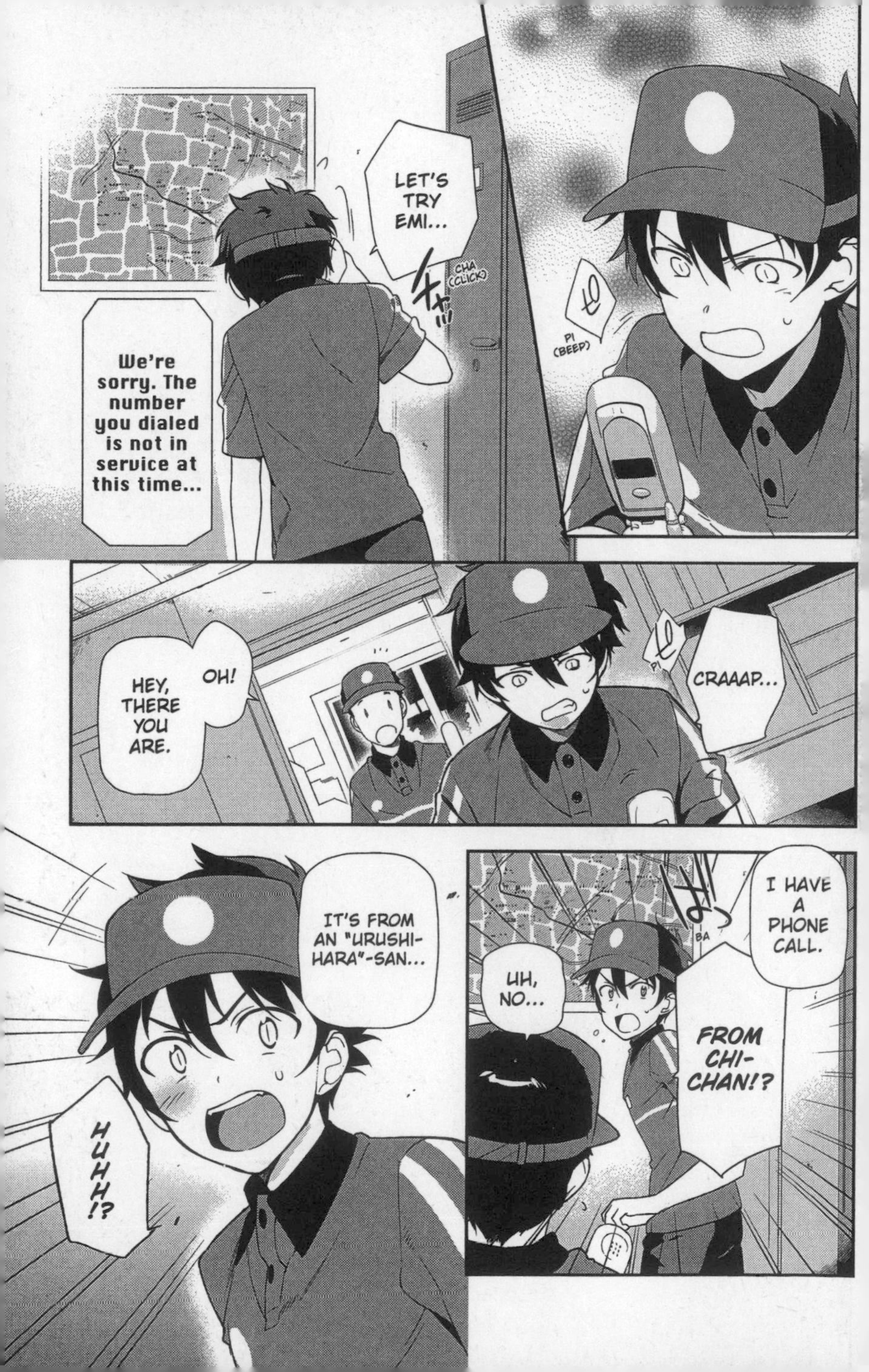
PI (BEEP)
LET'S TRY EMI...
CHA (CLICK)
We're sorry. The number you dialed is not in service at this time...
CRAAAP...
PI
OH!
HEY, THERE YOU ARE.
I HAVE A PHONE CALL.
BA
FROM CHI-CHAN!?
UH, NO...
IT'S FROM AN "URUSHI-HARA"-SAN...
HUHH!?

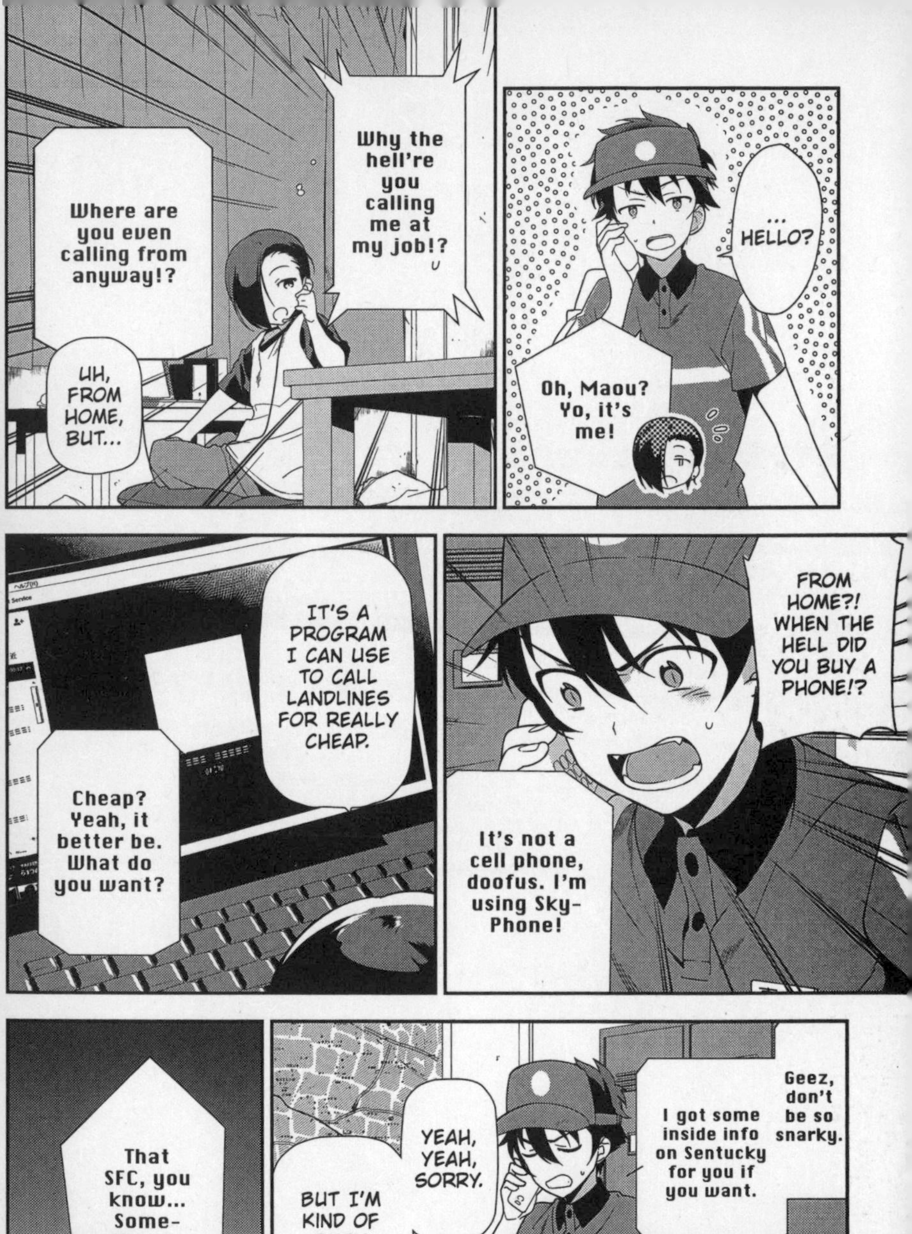
... HELLO?
Oh, Maou? Yo, it's me!
Why the hell're you calling me at my job!?
Where are you even calling from anyway!?
UH, FROM HOME, BUT...
FROM HOME?! WHEN THE HELL DID YOU BUY A PHONE!?
It's not a cell phone, doofus. I'm using Sky-Phone!
IT'S A PROGRAM I CAN USE TO CALL LANDLINES FOR REALLY CHEAP.
Cheap? Yeah, it better be. What do you want?
Geez, don't be so snarky.
I got some inside info on Sentucky for you if you want.
YEAH, YEAH, SORRY.
BUT I'M KIND OF BUSY RIGHT NOW...
That SFC, you know... Some-thing's effed up with it.

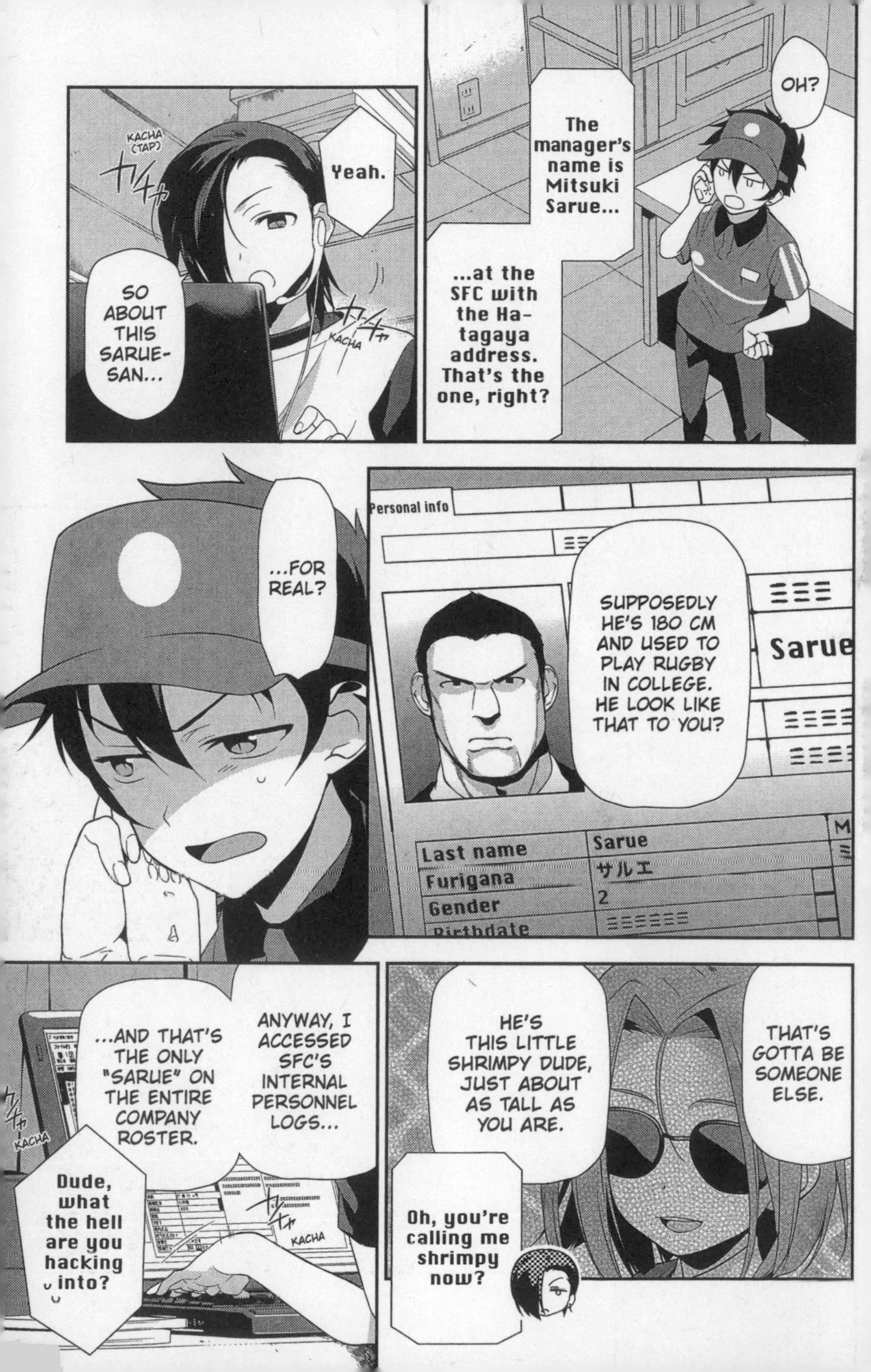
OH?
The manager's name is Mitsuki Sarue...
...at the SFC with the Hatagaya address. That's the one, right?
Yeah.
KACHA (TAP)
KACHA
SO ABOUT THIS SARUE-SAN...
Personal info
Sarue
Last name
Sarue
Furigana
サルエ
Gender
2
SUPPOSEDLY HE'S 180 CM AND USED TO PLAY RUGBY IN COLLEGE. HE LOOK LIKE THAT TO YOU?
...FOR REAL?
THAT'S GOTTA BE SOMEONE ELSE.
HE'S THIS LITTLE SHRIMPY DUDE, JUST ABOUT AS TALL AS YOU ARE.
Oh, you're calling me shrimpy now?
ANYWAY, I ACCESSED SFC'S INTERNAL PERSONNEL LOGS...
...AND THAT'S THE ONLY "SARUE" ON THE ENTIRE COMPANY ROSTER.
KACHA
KACHA
Dude, what the hell are you hacking into?

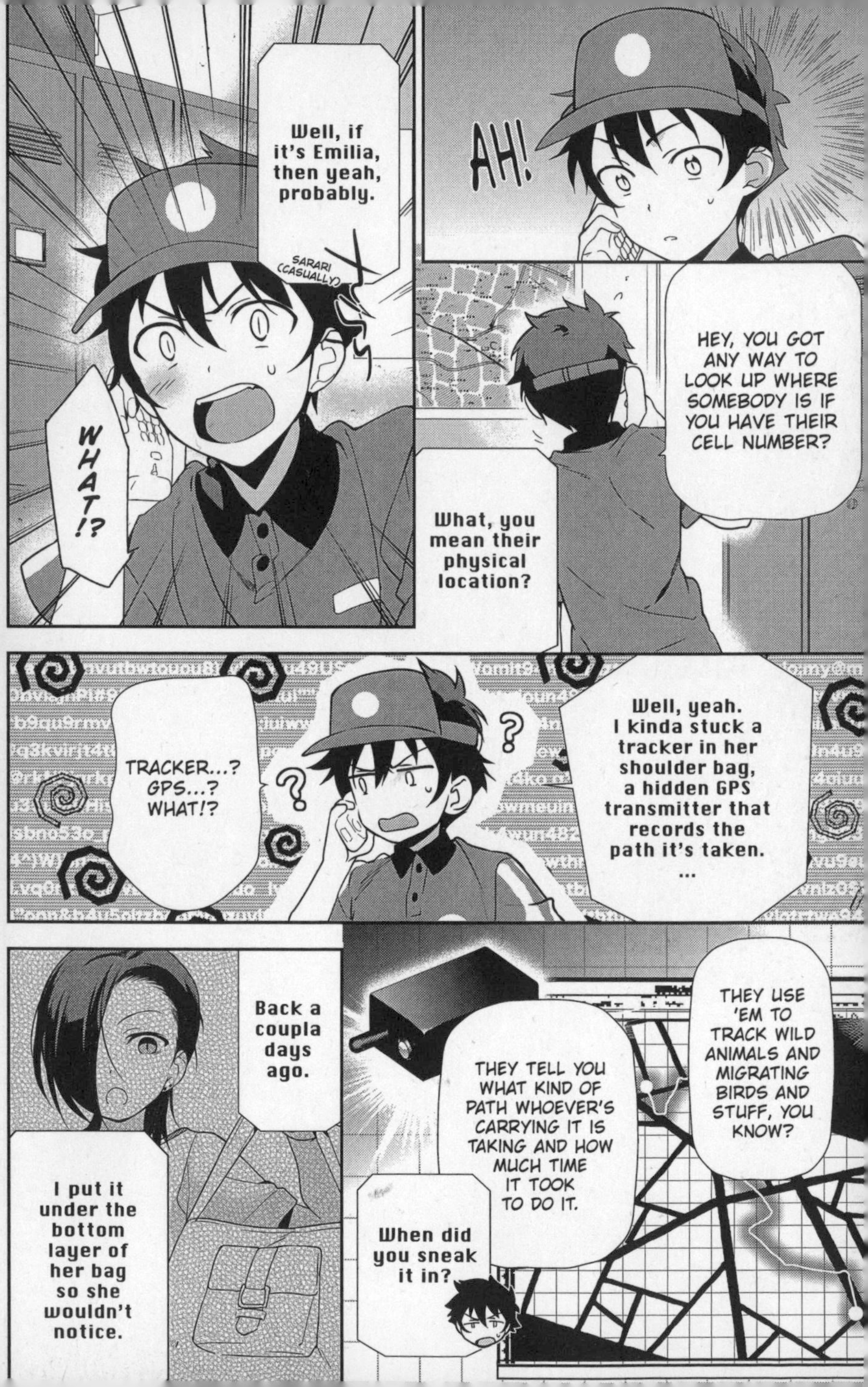
AH!
HEY, YOU GOT ANY WAY TO LOOK UP WHERE SOMEBODY IS IF YOU HAVE THEIR CELL NUMBER?
What, you mean their physical location?
Well, if it's Emilia, then yeah, probably.
SARARI (CASUALLY)
WHAT!?
Well, yeah. I kinda stuck a tracker in her shoulder bag, a hidden GPS transmitter that records the path it's taken. ...
TRACKER...? GPS...? WHAT!?
THEY USE 'EM TO TRACK WILD ANIMALS AND MIGRATING BIRDS AND STUFF, YOU KNOW?
THEY TELL YOU WHAT KIND OF PATH WHOEVER'S CARRYING IT IS TAKING AND HOW MUCH TIME IT TOOK TO DO IT.
When did you sneak it in?
Back a coupla days ago.
I put it under the bottom layer of her bag so she wouldn't notice.

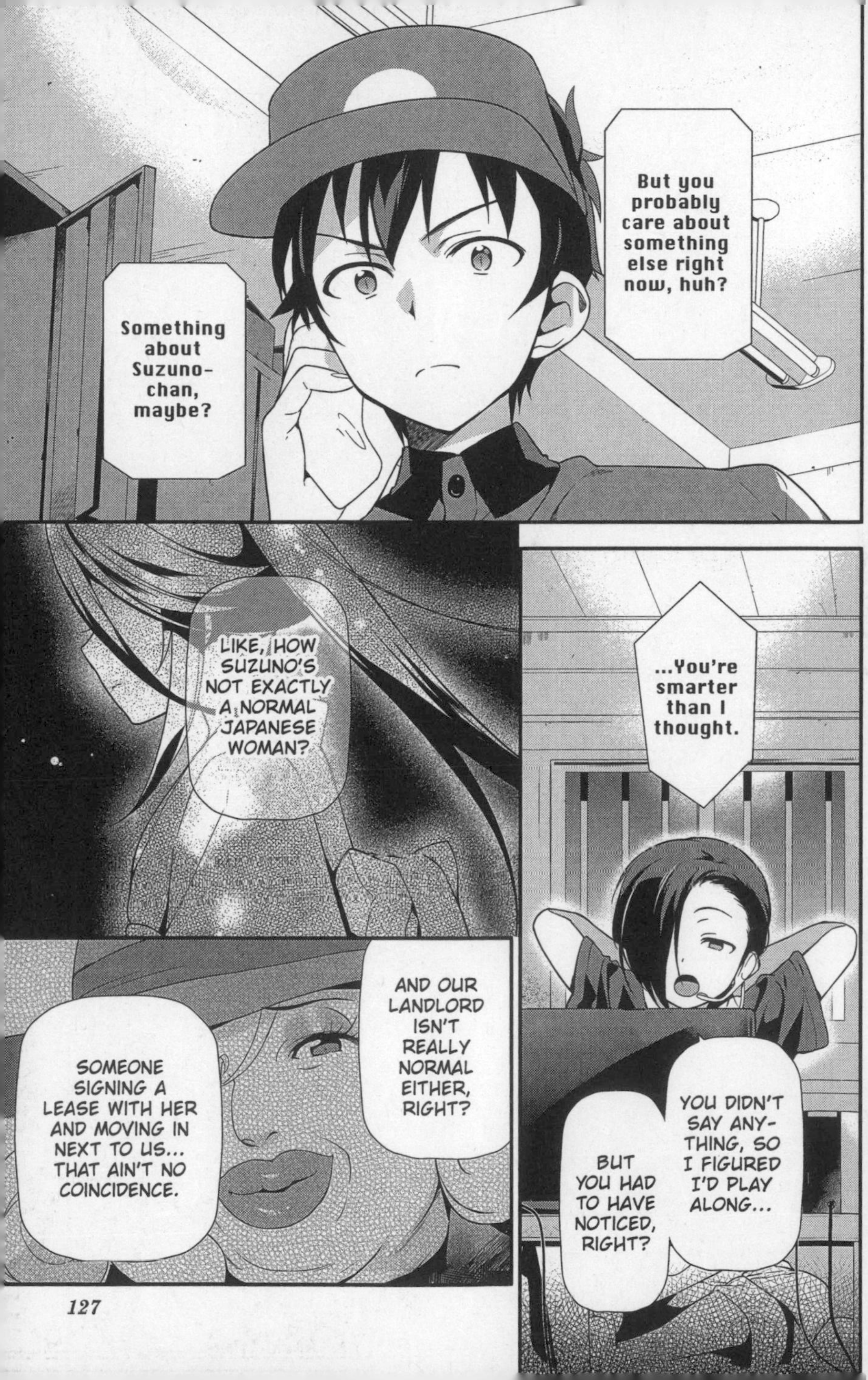
But you probably care about something else right now, huh?
Something about Suzuno-chan, maybe?
...You're smarter than I thought.
YOU DIDN'T SAY ANY-THING, SO I FIGURED I'D PLAY ALONG...
BUT YOU HAD TO HAVE NOTICED, RIGHT?
LIKE, HOW SUZUNO'S NOT EXACTLY A NORMAL JAPANESE WOMAN?
AND OUR LANDLORD ISN'T REALLY NORMAL EITHER, RIGHT?
SOMEONE SIGNING A LEASE WITH HER AND MOVING IN NEXT TO US... THAT AIN'T NO COINCIDENCE.

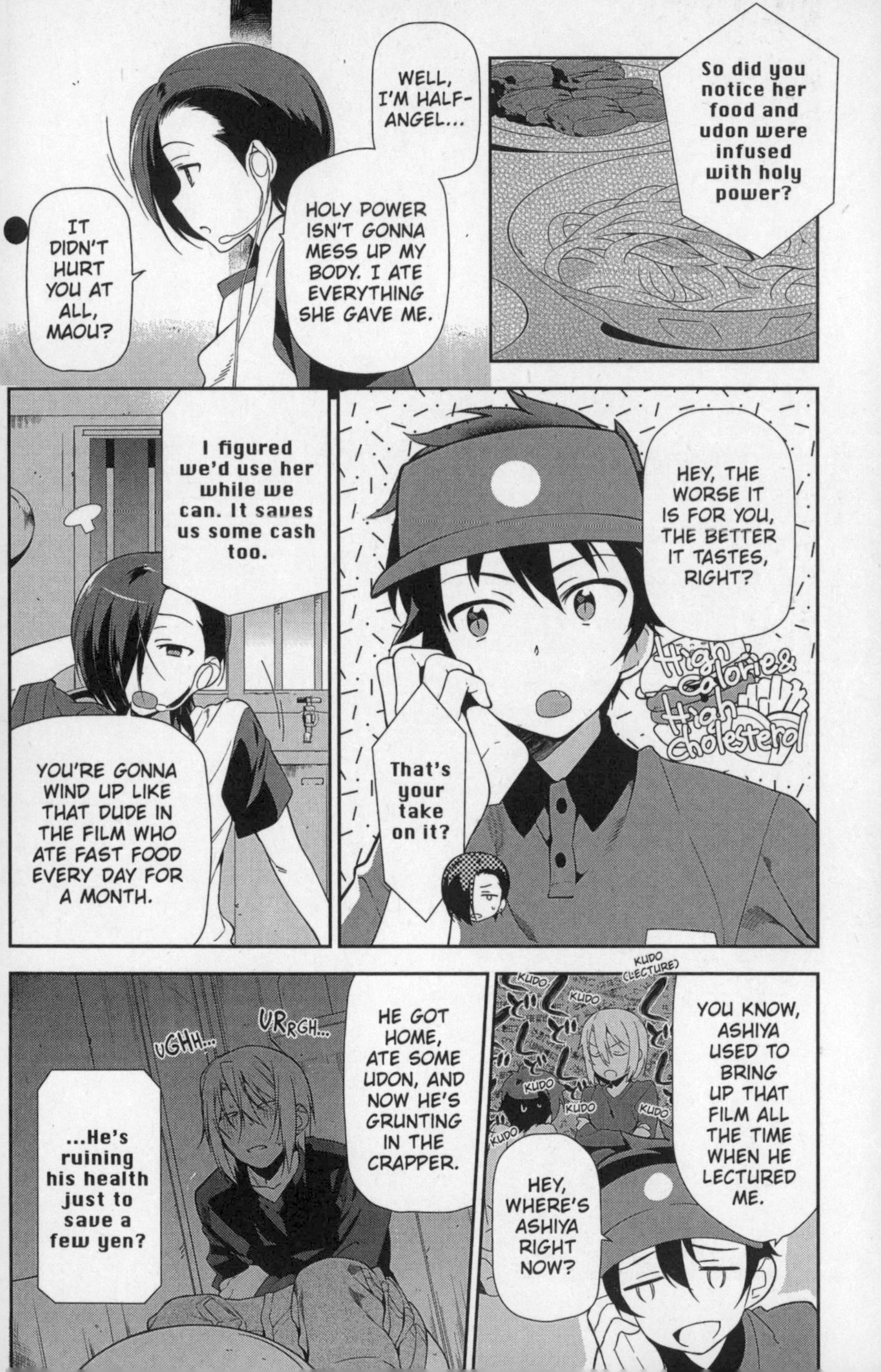
So did you notice her food and udon were infused with holy power?
WELL, I'M HALF-ANGEL...
HOLY POWER ISN'T GONNA MESS UP MY BODY. I ATE EVERYTHING SHE GAVE ME.
IT DIDN'T HURT YOU AT ALL, MAOU?
HEY, THE WORSE IT IS FOR YOU, THE BETTER IT TASTES, RIGHT?
High Calories & High Cholesterol
That's your take on it?
I figured we'd use her while we can. It saves us some cash too.
YOU'RE GONNA WIND UP LIKE THAT DUDE IN THE FILM WHO ATE FAST FOOD EVERY DAY FOR A MONTH.
YOU KNOW, ASHIYA USED TO BRING UP THAT FILM ALL THE TIME WHEN HE LECTURED ME.
KUDO (LECTURE)
KUDO KUDO KUDO KUDO KUDO KUDO
HEY, WHERE'S ASHIYA RIGHT NOW?
HE GOT HOME, ATE SOME UDON, AND NOW HE'S GRUNTING IN THE CRAPPER.
URRGH...
UGHH...
...He's ruining his health just to save a few yen?

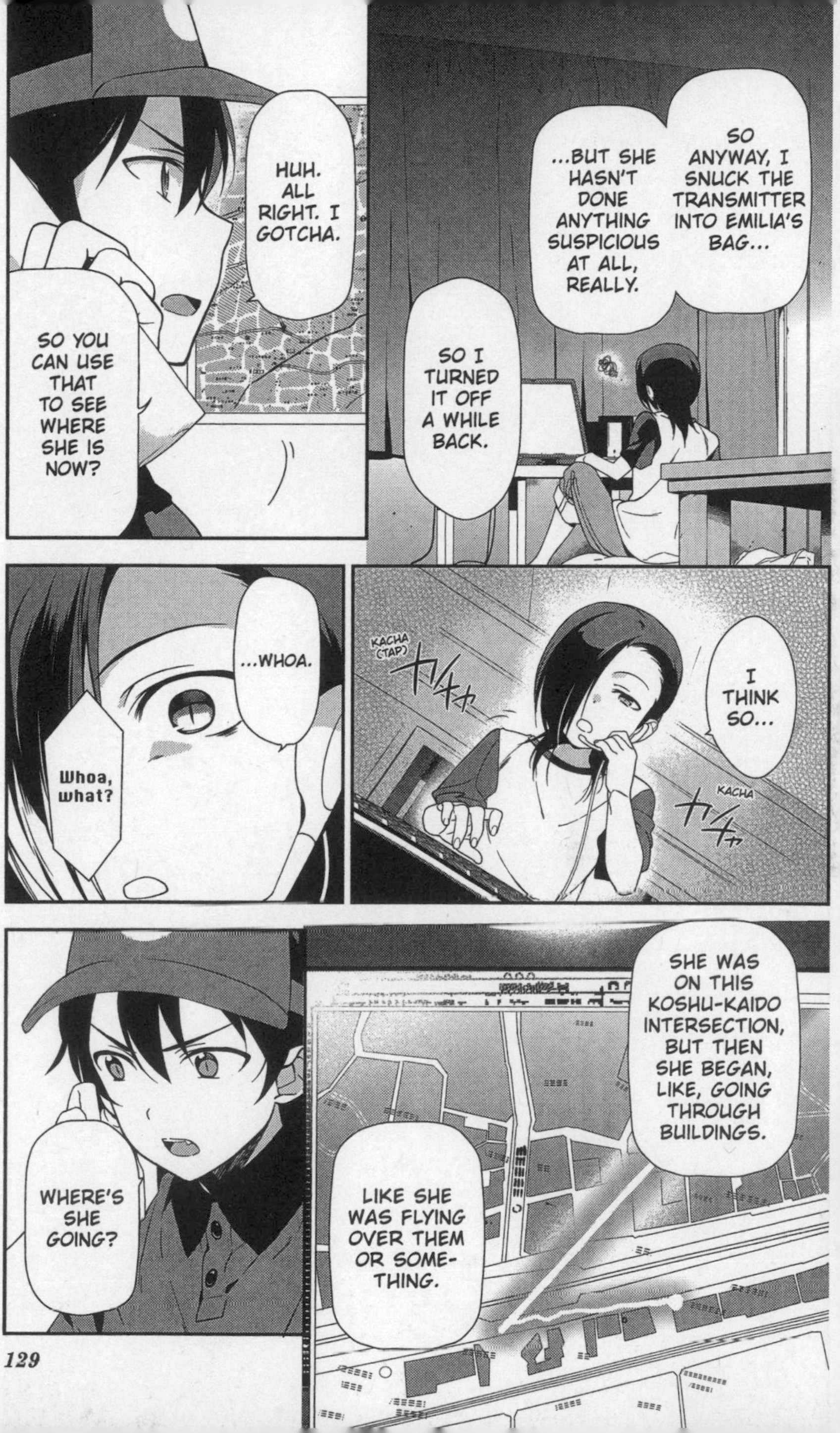
SO ANYWAY, I SNUCK THE TRANSMITTER INTO EMILIA'S BAG...
...BUT SHE HASN'T DONE ANYTHING SUSPICIOUS AT ALL, REALLY.
SO I TURNED IT OFF A WHILE BACK.
HUH. ALL RIGHT. I GOTCHA.
SO YOU CAN USE THAT TO SEE WHERE SHE IS NOW?
KACHA (TAP)
I THINK SO...
KACHA
...WHOA.
Whoa, what?
SHE WAS ON THIS KOSHU-KAIDO INTERSECTION, BUT THEN SHE BEGAN, LIKE, GOING THROUGH BUILDINGS.
LIKE SHE WAS FLYING OVER THEM OR SOME-THING.
WHERE'S SHE GOING?

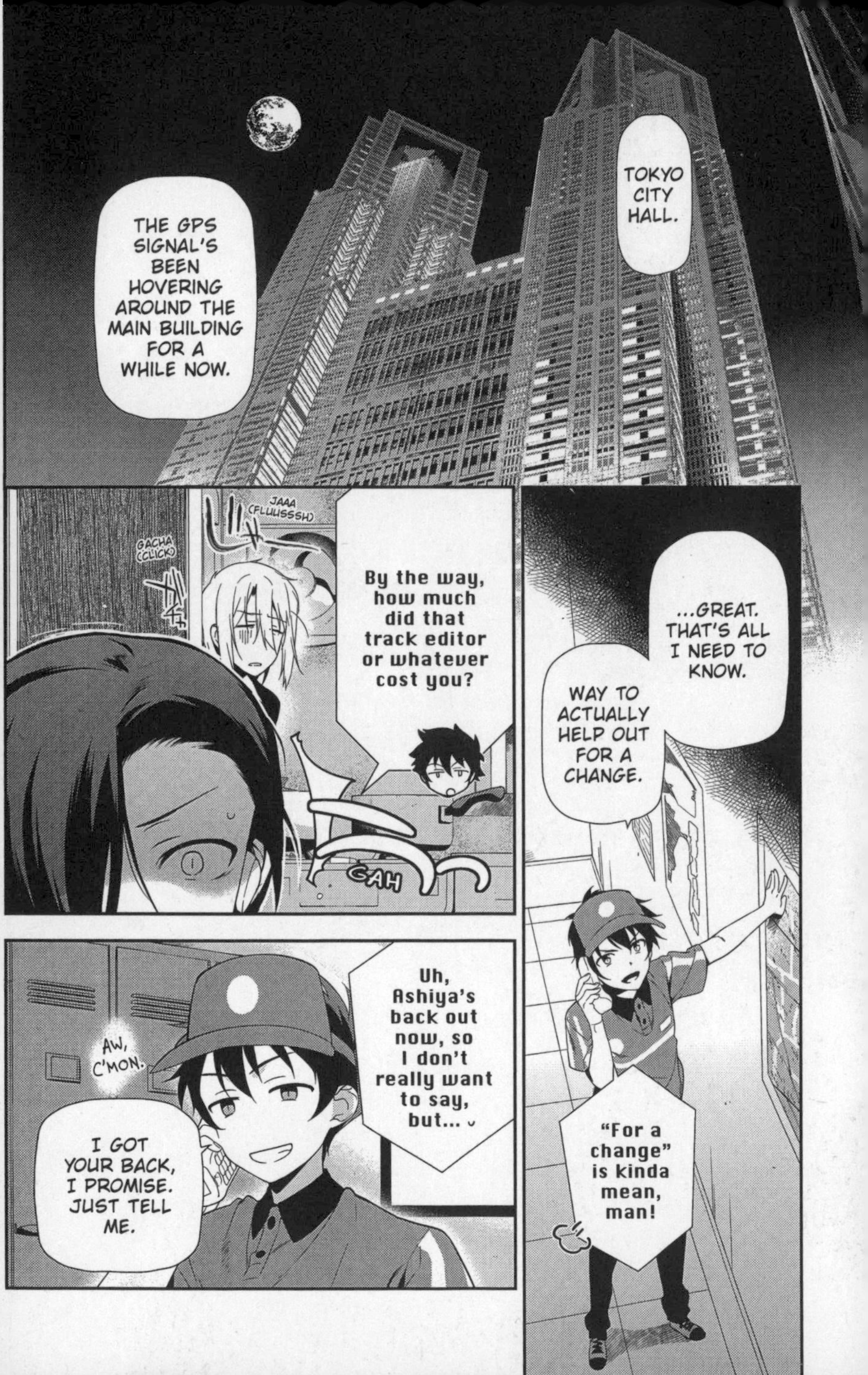
TOKYO CITY HALL.
THE GPS SIGNAL'S BEEN HOVERING AROUND THE MAIN BUILDING FOR A WHILE NOW.
...GREAT. THAT'S ALL I NEED TO KNOW.
WAY TO ACTUALLY HELP OUT FOR A CHANGE.
"For a change" is kinda mean, man!
JAAA (FLUUSSSH)
GACHA (CLICK)
By the way, how much did that track editor or whatever cost you?
GAH
Uh, Ashiya's back out now, so I don't really want to say, but...
AW, C'MON.
I GOT YOUR BACK, I PROMISE. JUST TELL ME.

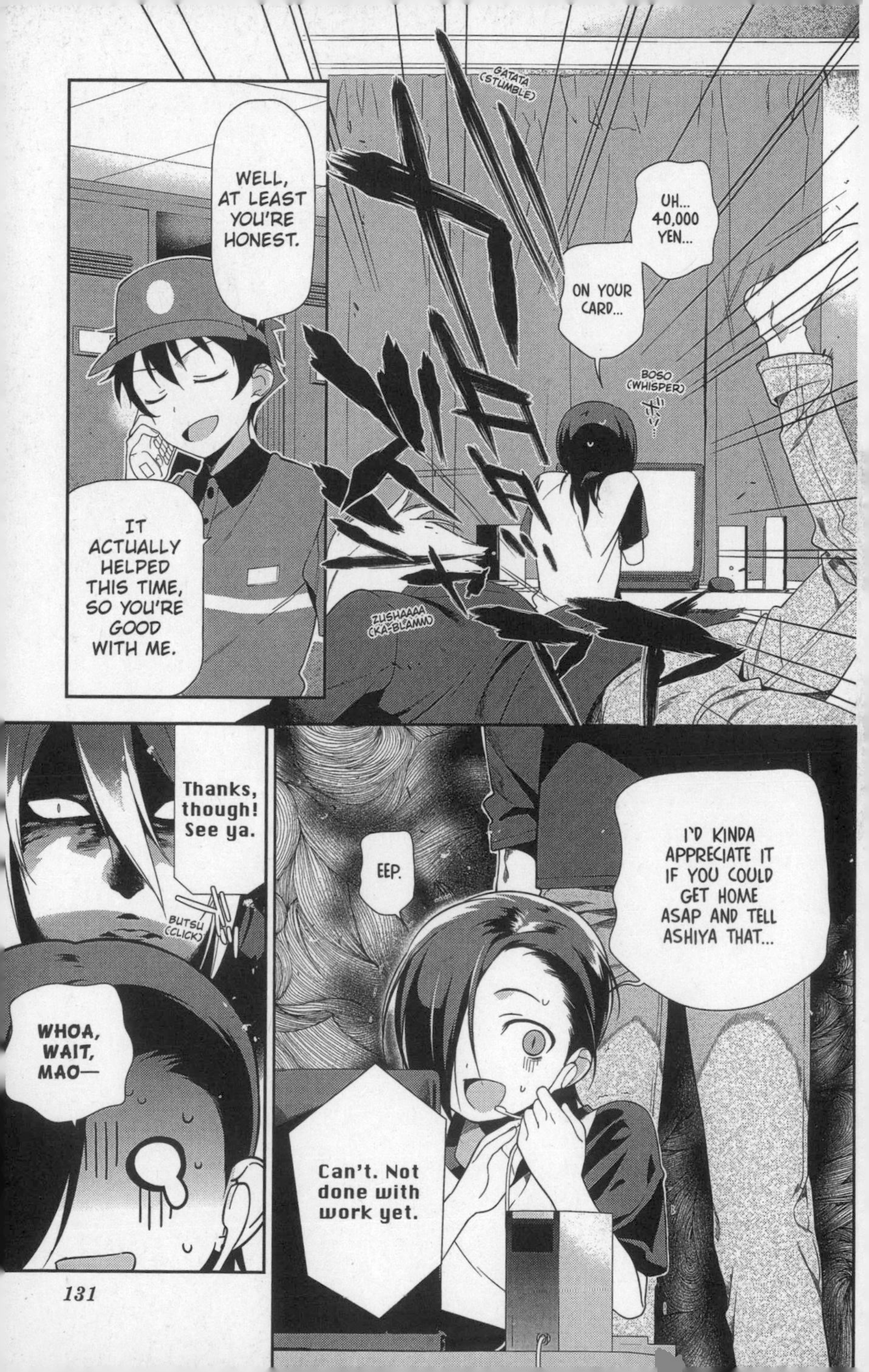
GATATA (STUMBLE)
UH... 40,000 YEN...
ON YOUR CARD...
BOSO (WHISPER)
ZUSHAAAA (KA-BLAMM)
WELL, AT LEAST YOU'RE HONEST.
IT ACTUALLY HELPED THIS TIME, SO YOU'RE GOOD WITH ME.
I'D KINDA APPRECIATE IT IF YOU COULD GET HOME ASAP AND TELL ASHIYA THAT...
EEP.
Can't. Not done with work yet.
Thanks, though! See ya.
BUTSU (CLICK)
WHOA, WAIT, MAO—

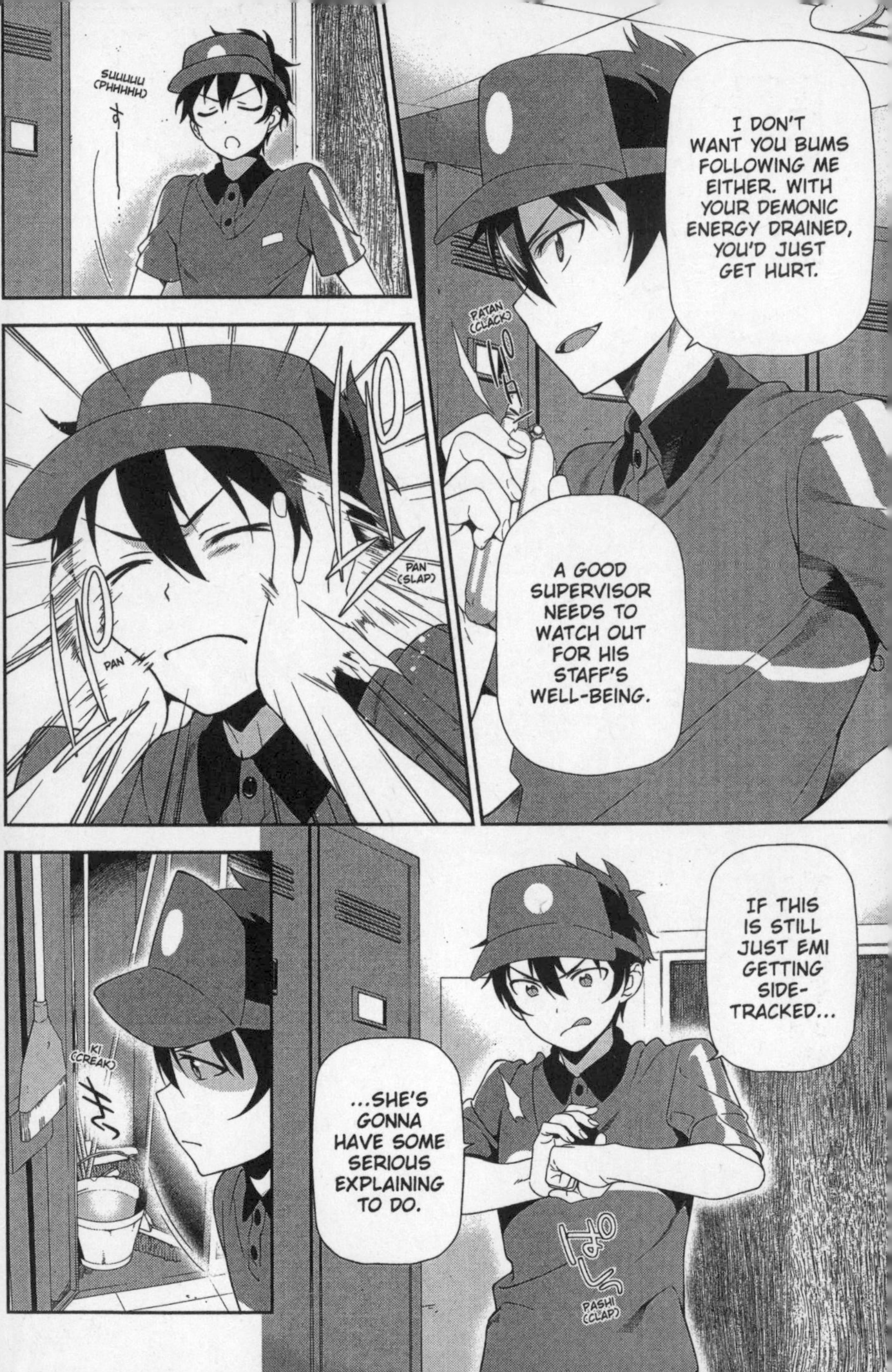
I DON'T WANT YOU BUMS FOLLOWING ME EITHER. WITH YOUR DEMONIC ENERGY DRAINED, YOU'D JUST GET HURT.
PATAN (CLACK)
A GOOD SUPERVISOR NEEDS TO WATCH OUT FOR HIS STAFF'S WELL-BEING.
SUUUUU (PHHHHH)
PAN (SLAP)
PAN
IF THIS IS STILL JUST EMI GETTING SIDE-TRACKED...
...SHE'S GONNA HAVE SOME SERIOUS EXPLAINING TO DO.
PASHI (CLAP)
KI (CREAK)

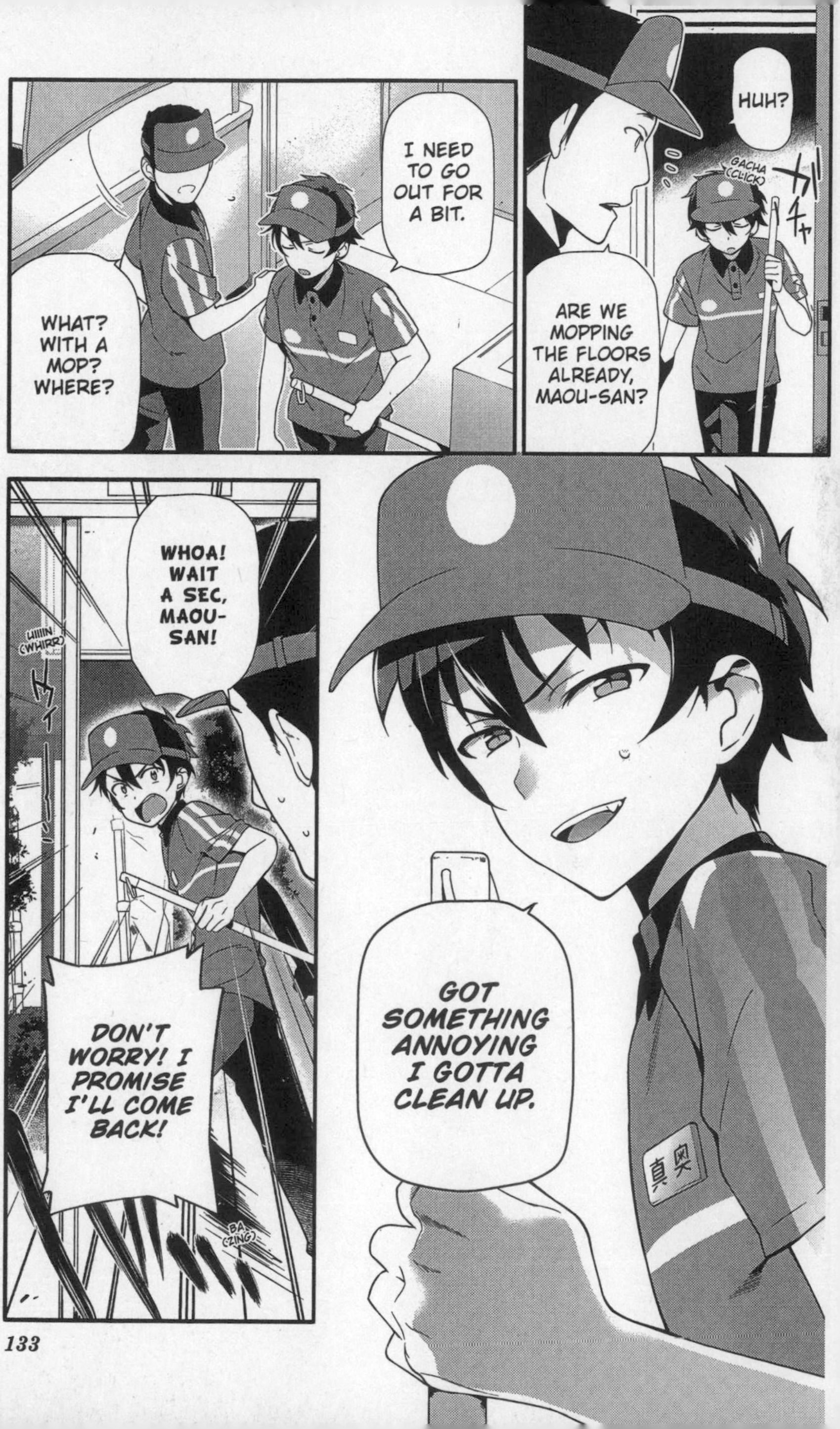
HUH?
GACHA (CLICK)
ARE WE MOPPING THE FLOORS ALREADY, MAOU-SAN?
I NEED TO GO OUT FOR A BIT.
WHAT? WITH A MOP? WHERE?
GOT SOMETHING ANNOYING I GOTTA CLEAN UP.
WHOA! WAIT A SEC, MAOU-SAN!
UIIIIN (WHIRR)
DON'T WORRY! I PROMISE I'LL COME BACK!
BA (ZING)

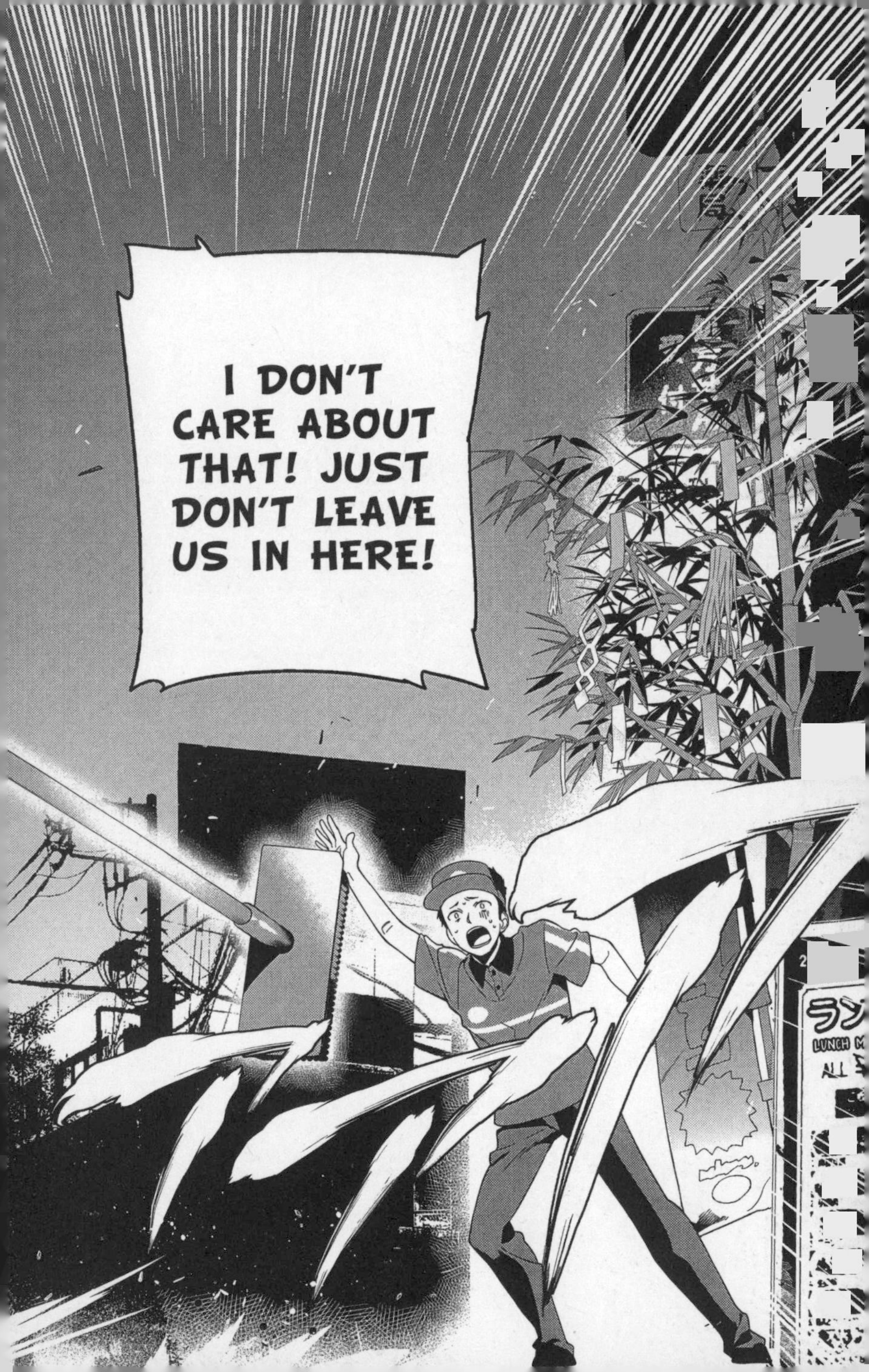
I DON'T CARE ABOUT THAT! JUST DON'T LEAVE US IN HERE!

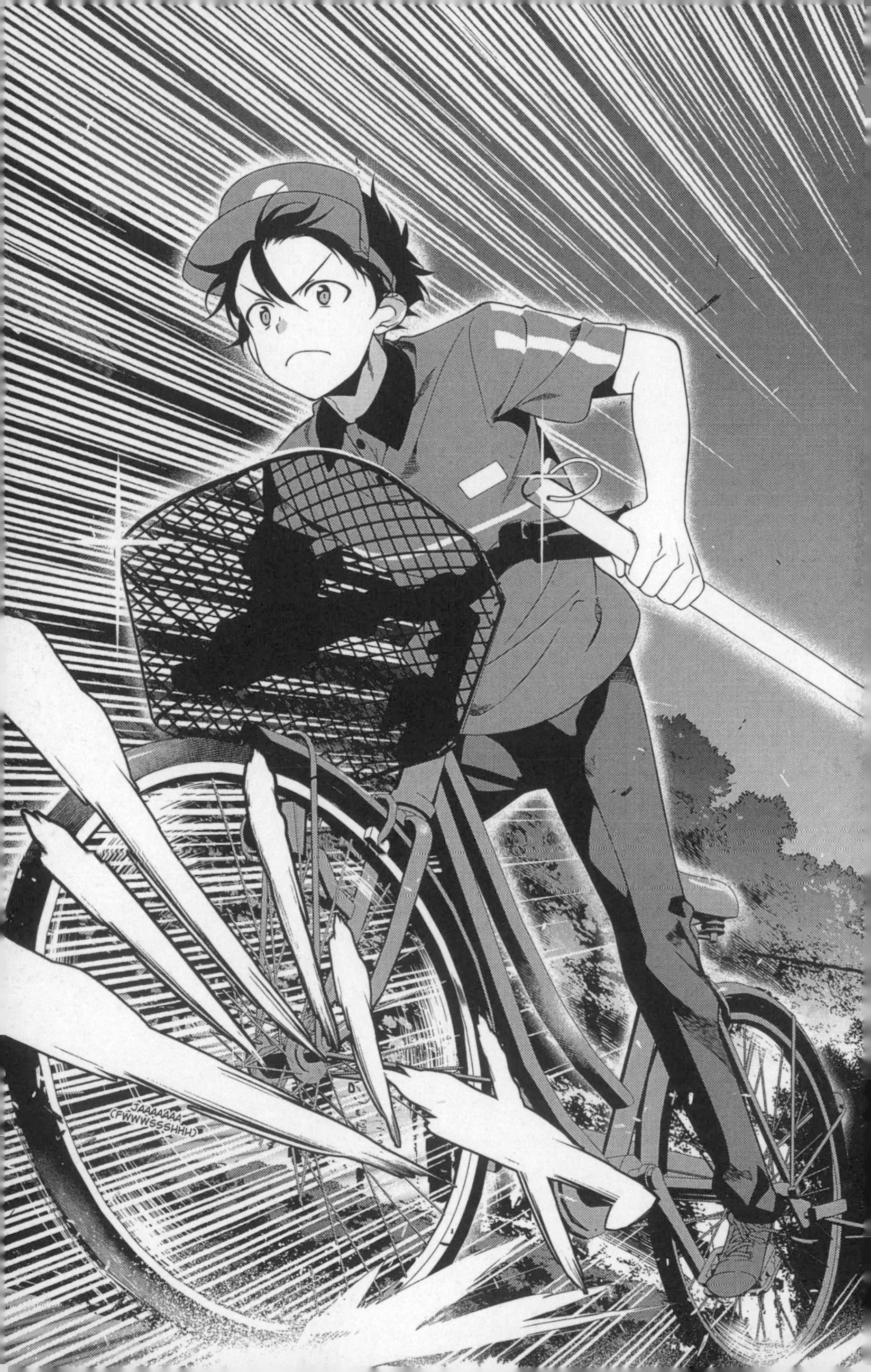
JAAAAAAA
(FWWWSSSHHH)

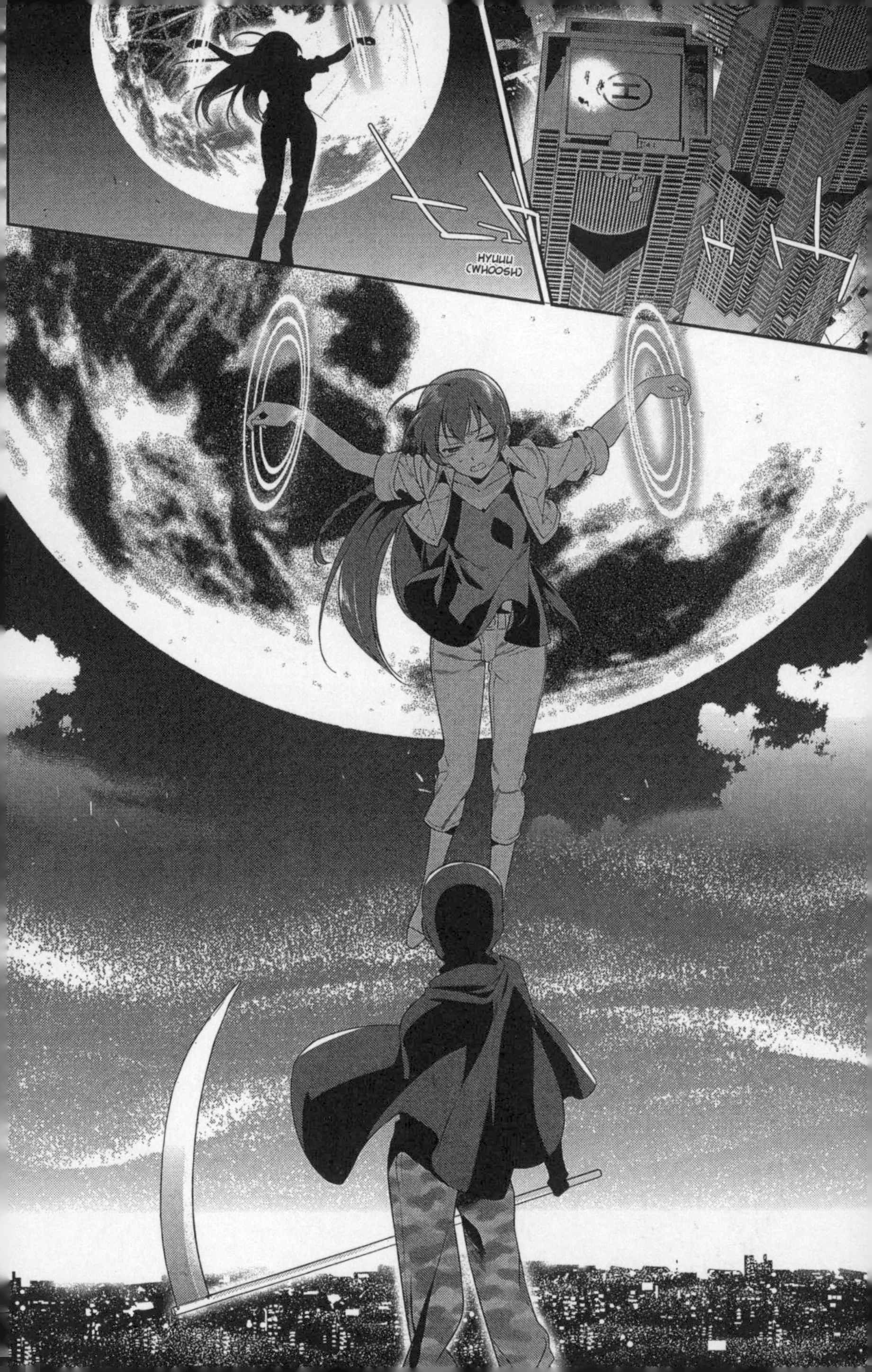
HYUUU
(WHOOSH)

Sadao
Maou

# THE DEVIL IS A PART-TIMER!

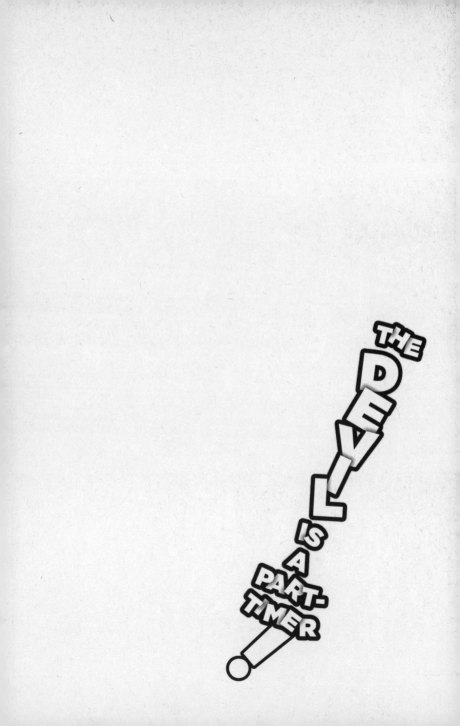

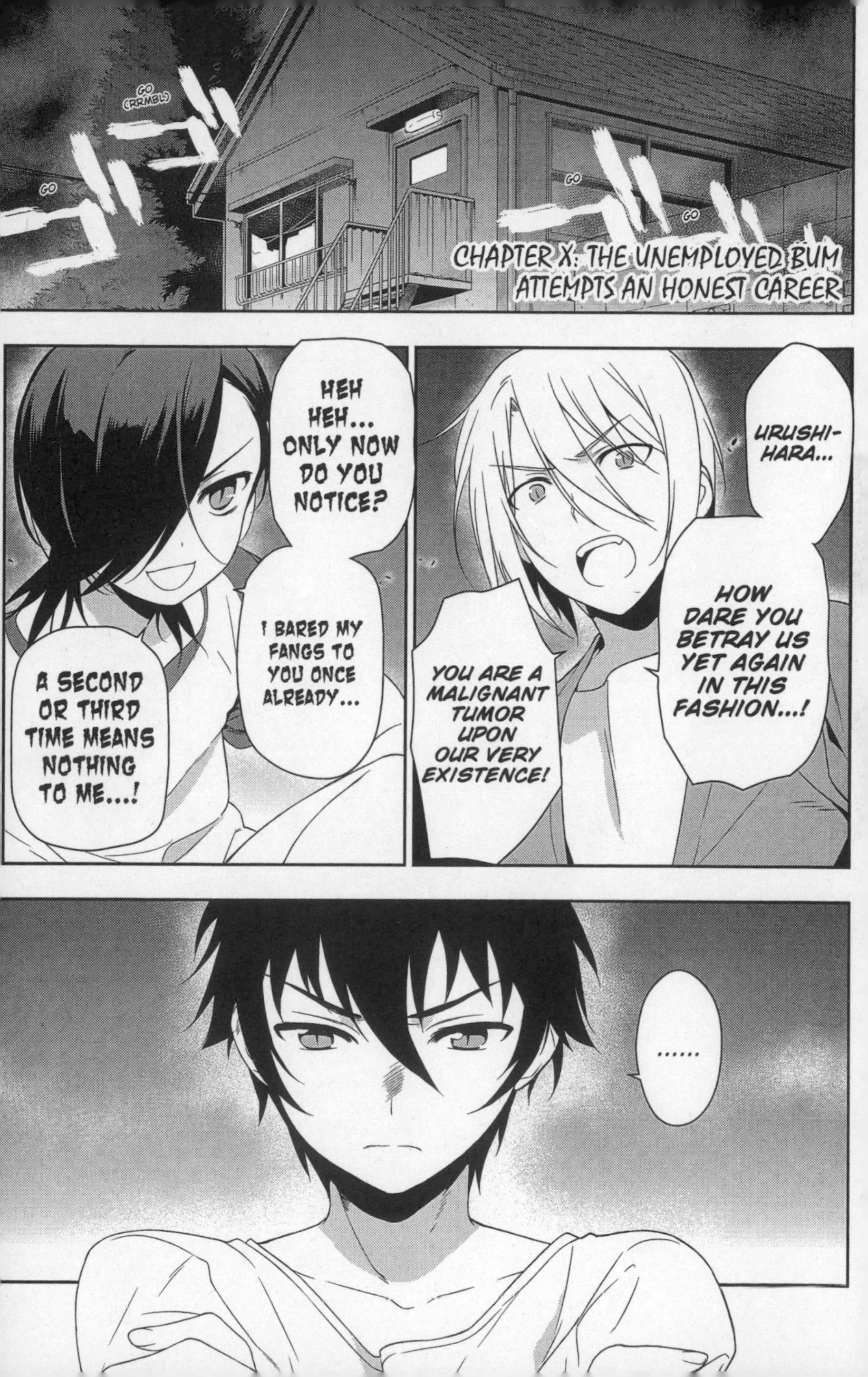
GO
GO
CHAPTER X: THE UNEMPLOYED BUM ATTEMPTS AN HONEST CAREER
GO (RRMBL)
GO
URUSHI-HARA...
HOW DARE YOU BETRAY US YET AGAIN IN THIS FASHION...!
YOU ARE A MALIGNANT TUMOR UPON OUR VERY EXISTENCE!
HEH HEH... ONLY NOW DO YOU NOTICE?
I BARED MY FANGS TO YOU ONCE ALREADY...
A SECOND OR THIRD TIME MEANS NOTHING TO ME...!
......

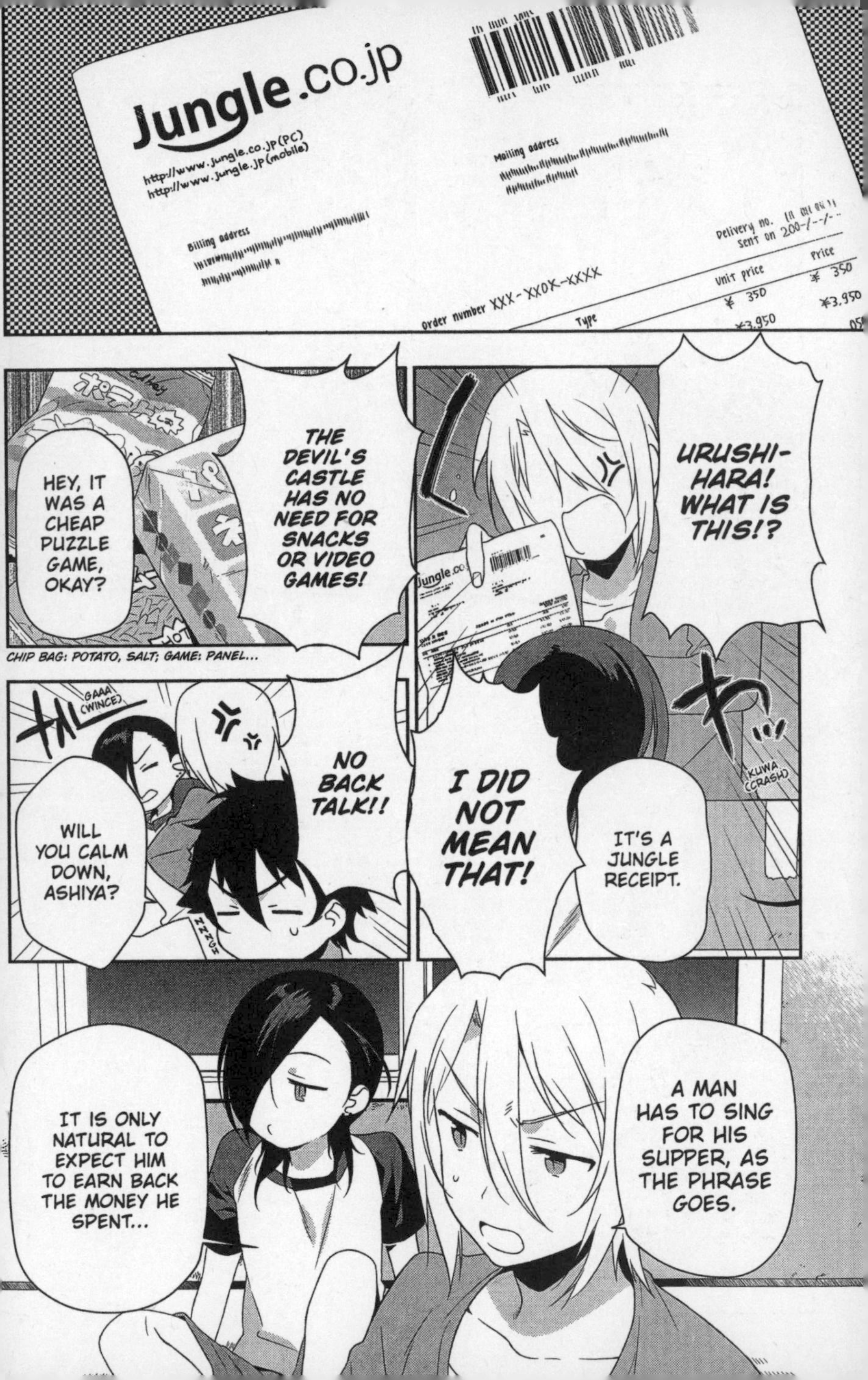
Jungle.co.jp
http://www.jungle.co.jp(PC)
http://www.jungle.jp(mobile)
Mailing address
Billing address
Delivery no.
sent on 200-/--/--
Order number XXX-XXOX-XXXX
Type
Unit price
Price
¥ 350
¥ 350
¥3,950
¥3,950
URUSHI-HARA! WHAT IS THIS!?
THE DEVIL'S CASTLE HAS NO NEED FOR SNACKS OR VIDEO GAMES!
HEY, IT WAS A CHEAP PUZZLE GAME, OKAY?
CHIP BAG: POTATO, SALT; GAME: PANEL...
KUWA (CRASH)
IT'S A JUNGLE RECEIPT.
I DID NOT MEAN THAT!
NO BACK TALK!!
GAAA (WINCE)
WILL YOU CALM DOWN, ASHIYA?
NNNGH
A MAN HAS TO SING FOR HIS SUPPER, AS THE PHRASE GOES.
IT IS ONLY NATURAL TO EXPECT HIM TO EARN BACK THE MONEY HE SPENT...

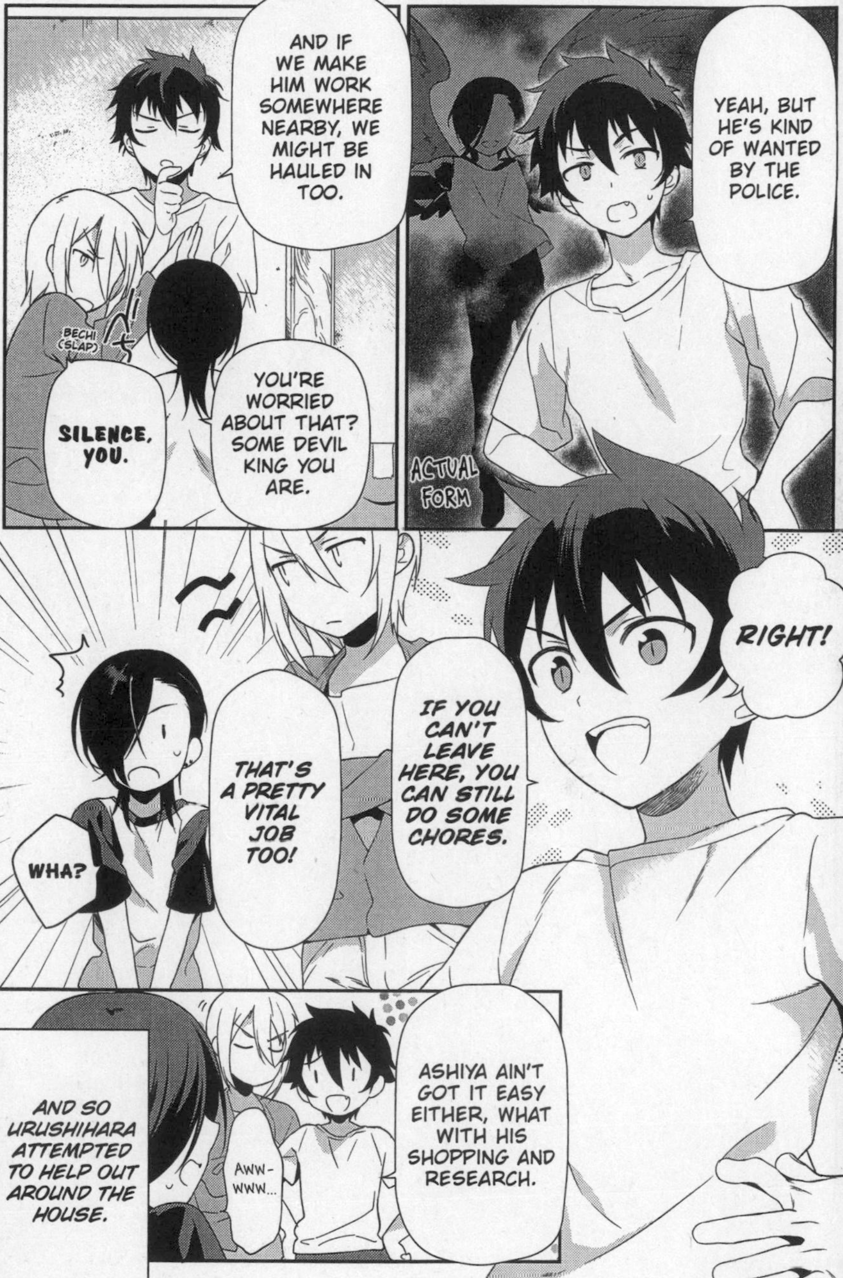
YEAH, BUT HE'S KIND OF WANTED BY THE POLICE.
ACTUAL FORM
AND IF WE MAKE HIM WORK SOMEWHERE NEARBY, WE MIGHT BE HAULED IN TOO.
YOU'RE WORRIED ABOUT THAT? SOME DEVIL KING YOU ARE.
BECHI (SLAP)
SILENCE, YOU.
RIGHT!
IF YOU CAN'T LEAVE HERE, YOU CAN STILL DO SOME CHORES.
THAT'S A PRETTY VITAL JOB TOO!
WHA?
ASHIYA AIN'T GOT IT EASY EITHER, WHAT WITH HIS SHOPPING AND RESEARCH.
AWW-WWW...
AND SO URUSHIHARA ATTEMPTED TO HELP OUT AROUND THE HOUSE.

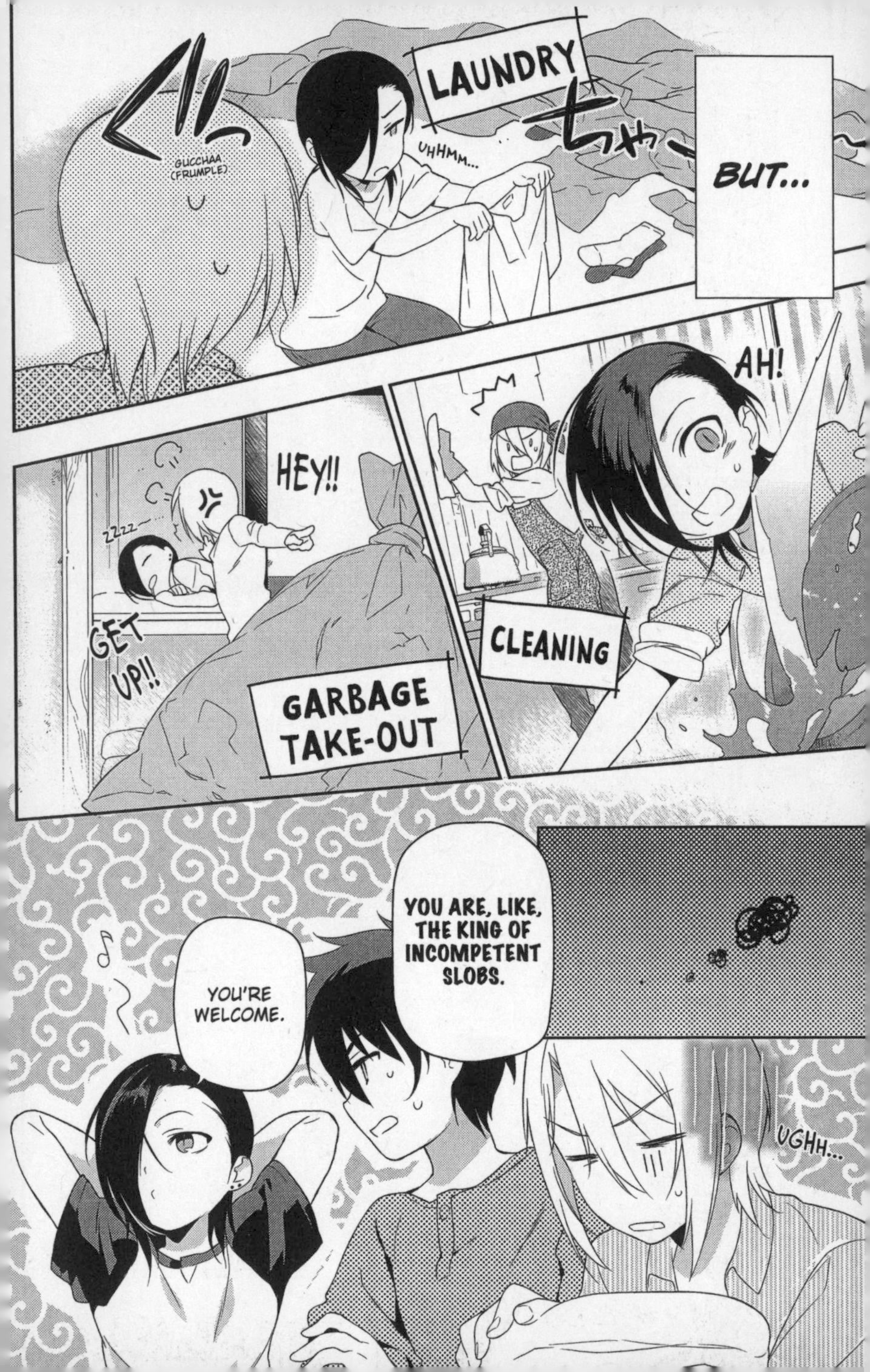
BUT...
LAUNDRY
UHHMM...
GUCCHAA (FRUMPLE)
AH!
CLEANING
HEY!!
GET UP!!
GARBAGE TAKE-OUT
UGHH...
YOU ARE, LIKE, THE KING OF INCOMPETENT SLOBS.
YOU'RE WELCOME.

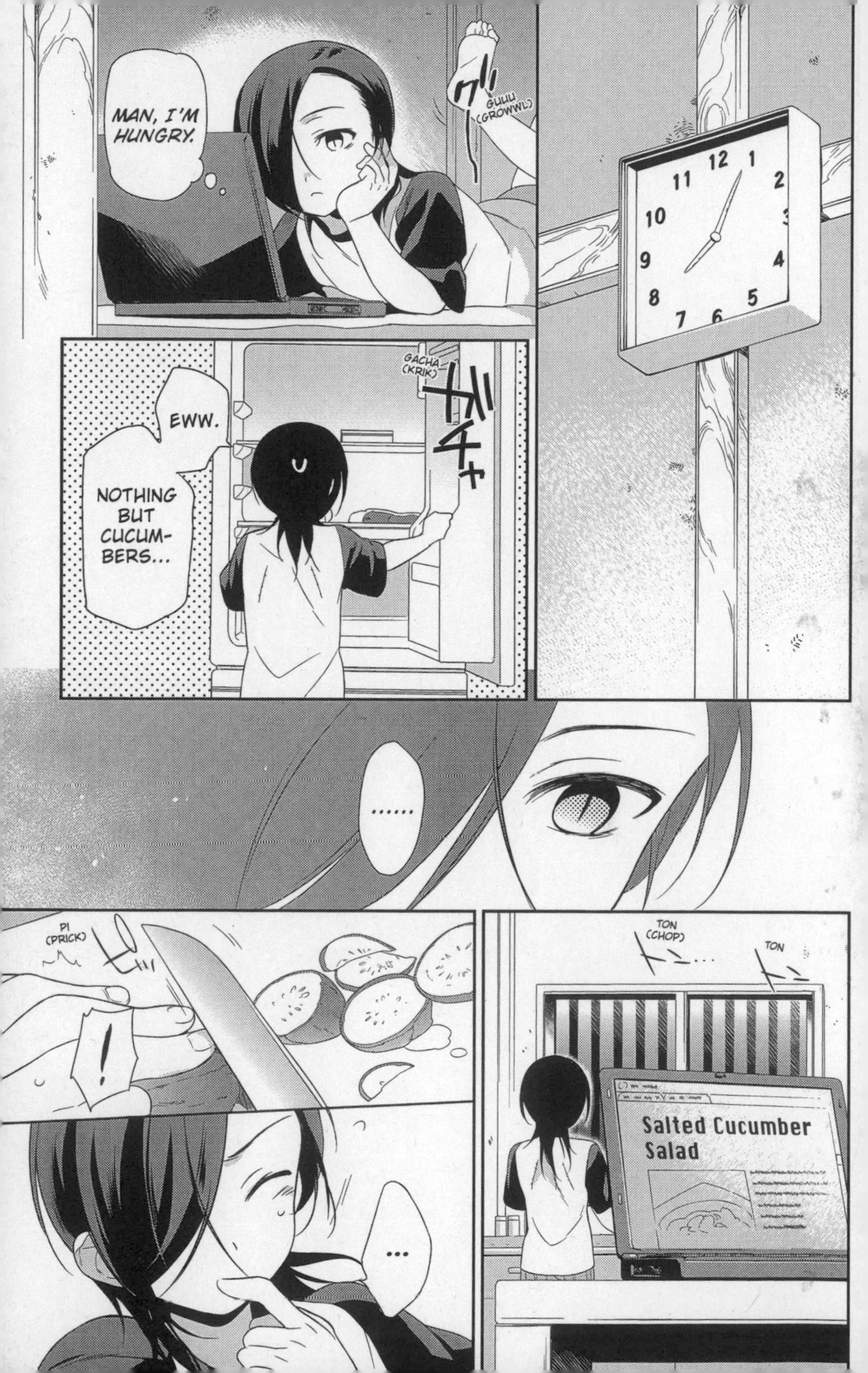
GUUU (GROWWL)
MAN, I'M HUNGRY.
GACHA (KRIK)
EWW.
NOTHING BUT CUCUMBERS...
......
TON (CHOP)
TON
Salted Cucumber Salad
PI (PRICK)
!
...

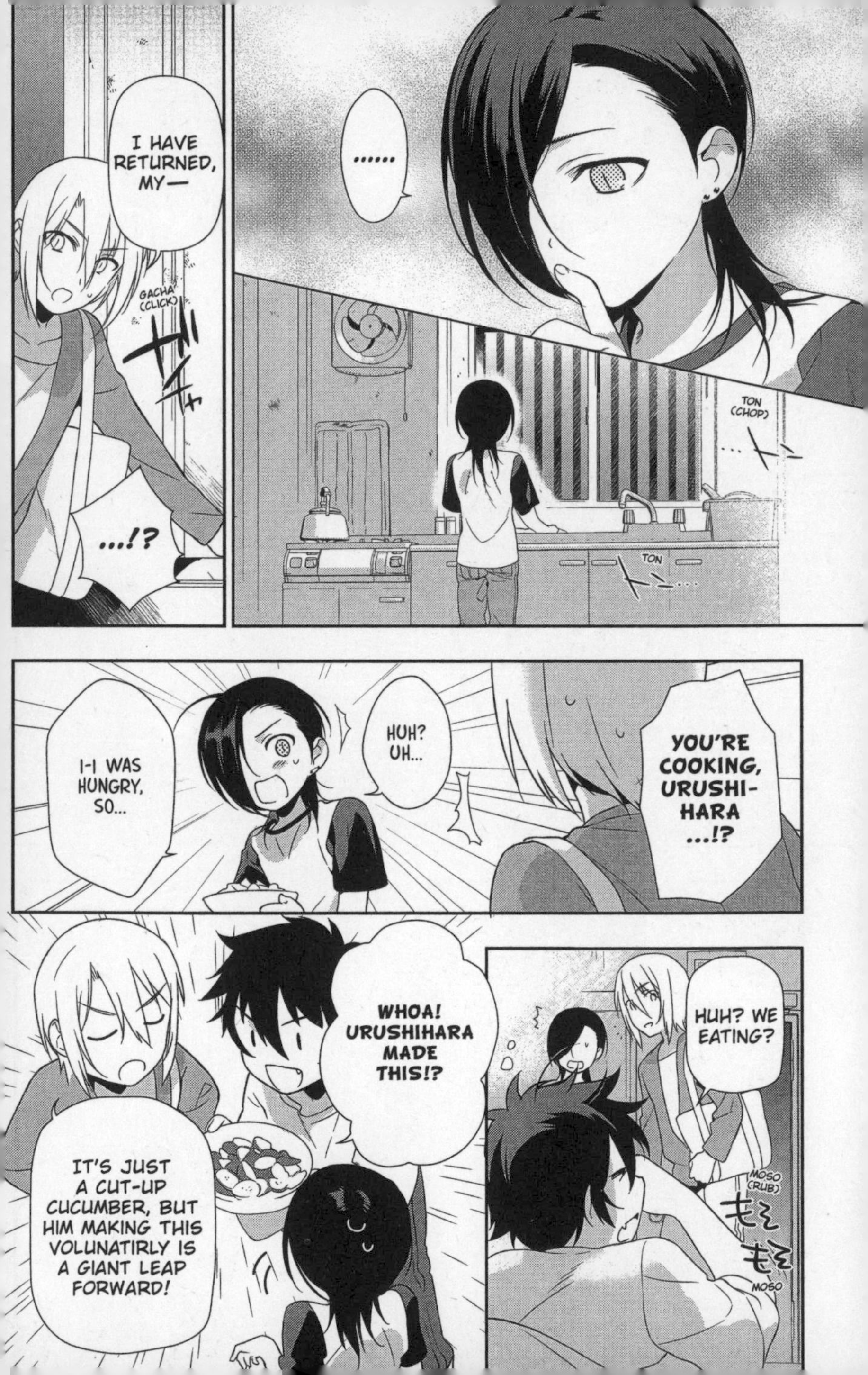
......
TON (CHOP)
TON
I HAVE RETURNED, MY—
GACHA (CLICK)
...!?
YOU'RE COOKING, URUSHI-HARA ...!?
HUH? UH...
I-I WAS HUNGRY, SO...
HUH? WE EATING?
MOSO (RUB)
MOSO
WHOA! URUSHIHARA MADE THIS!?
IT'S JUST A CUT-UP CUCUMBER, BUT HIM MAKING THIS VOLUNATIRLY IS A GIANT LEAP FORWARD!

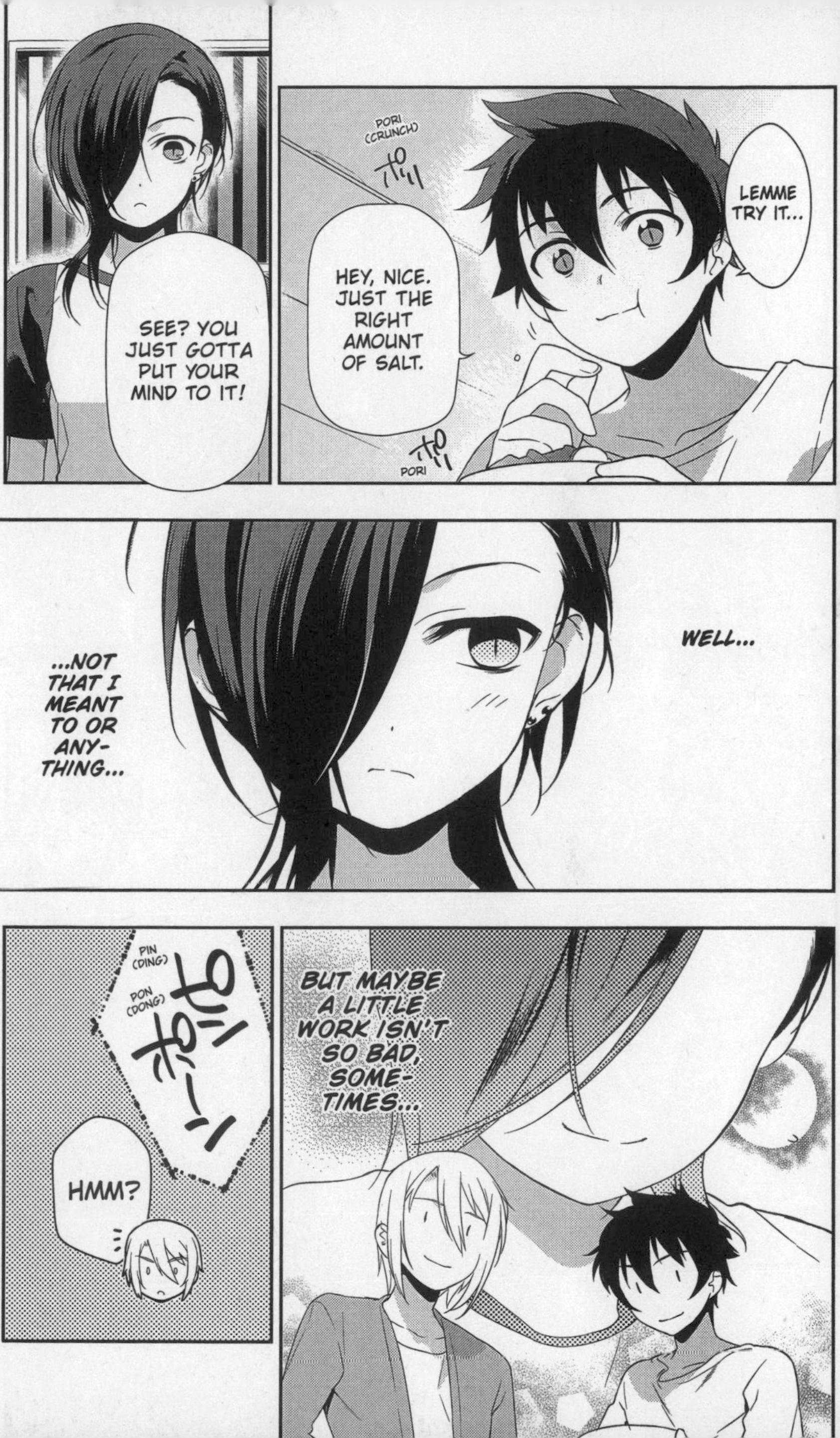
PORI (CRUNCH)
LEMME TRY IT...
HEY, NICE. JUST THE RIGHT AMOUNT OF SALT.
PORI
SEE? YOU JUST GOTTA PUT YOUR MIND TO IT!
WELL...
...NOT THAT I MEANT TO OR ANY-THING...
BUT MAYBE A LITTLE WORK ISN'T SO BAD, SOME-TIMES...
PIN (DING)
PON (DONG)
HMM?

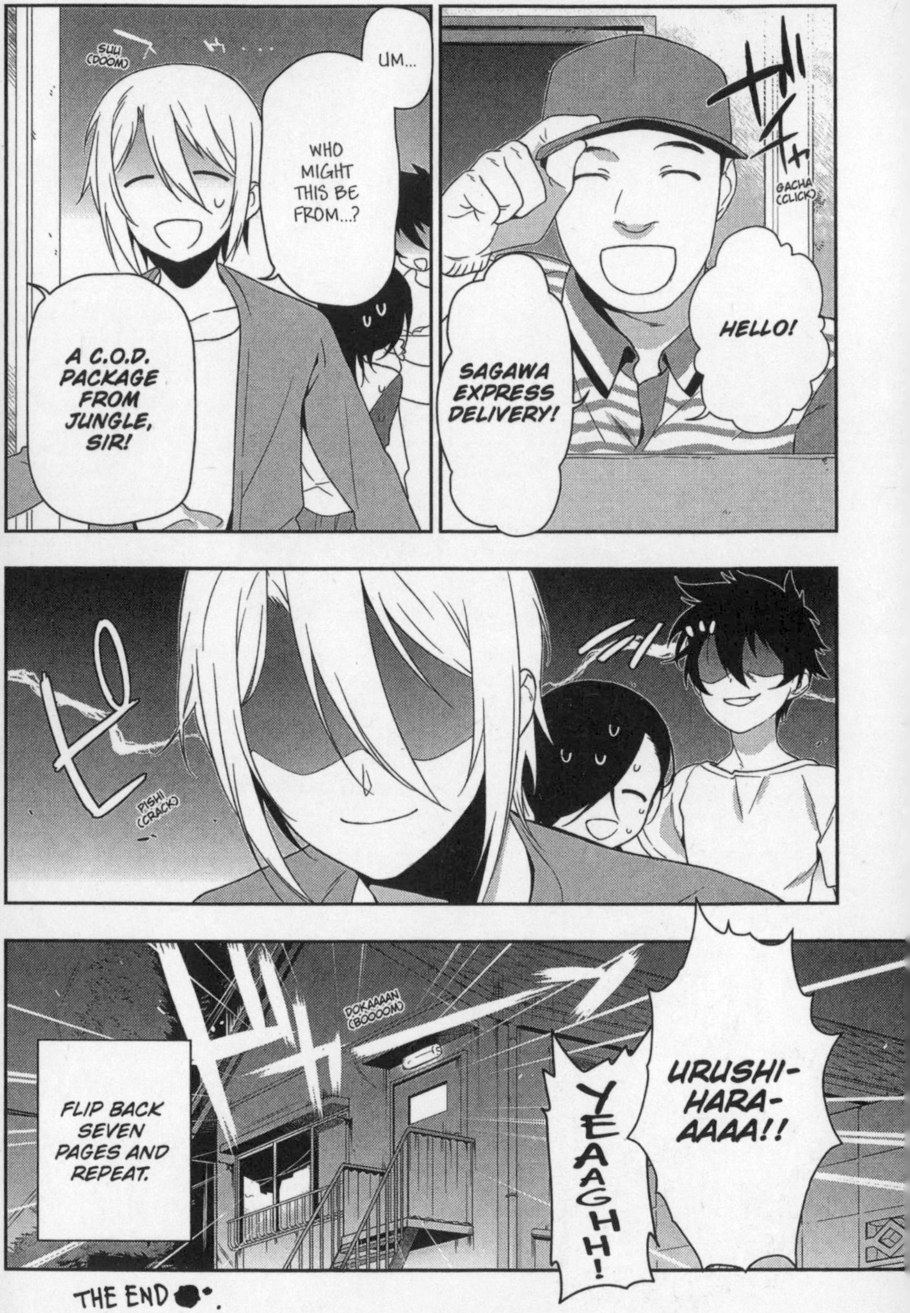
GACHA (CLICK)
HELLO!
SAGAWA EXPRESS DELIVERY!
SUU (DOOM)
UM...
WHO MIGHT THIS BE FROM...?
A C.O.D. PACKAGE FROM JUNGLE, SIR!
PISHI (CRACK)
URUSHI-HARA-AAAA!!
YEAAGH!
DOKAAAAN (BOOOOM)
FLIP BACK SEVEN PAGES AND REPEAT.

THE END.

Emi
Yusa

THE DEVIL IS A PART-TIMER!

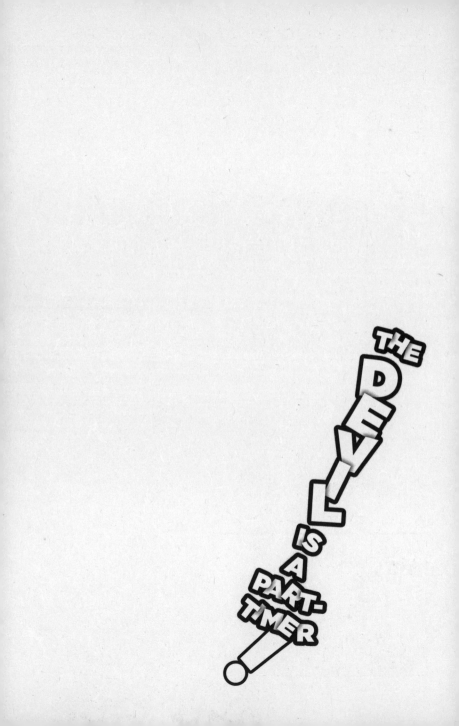

# CHAPTER X: THE TEENAGE GIRL PREPARES FOR HER HOT DATE

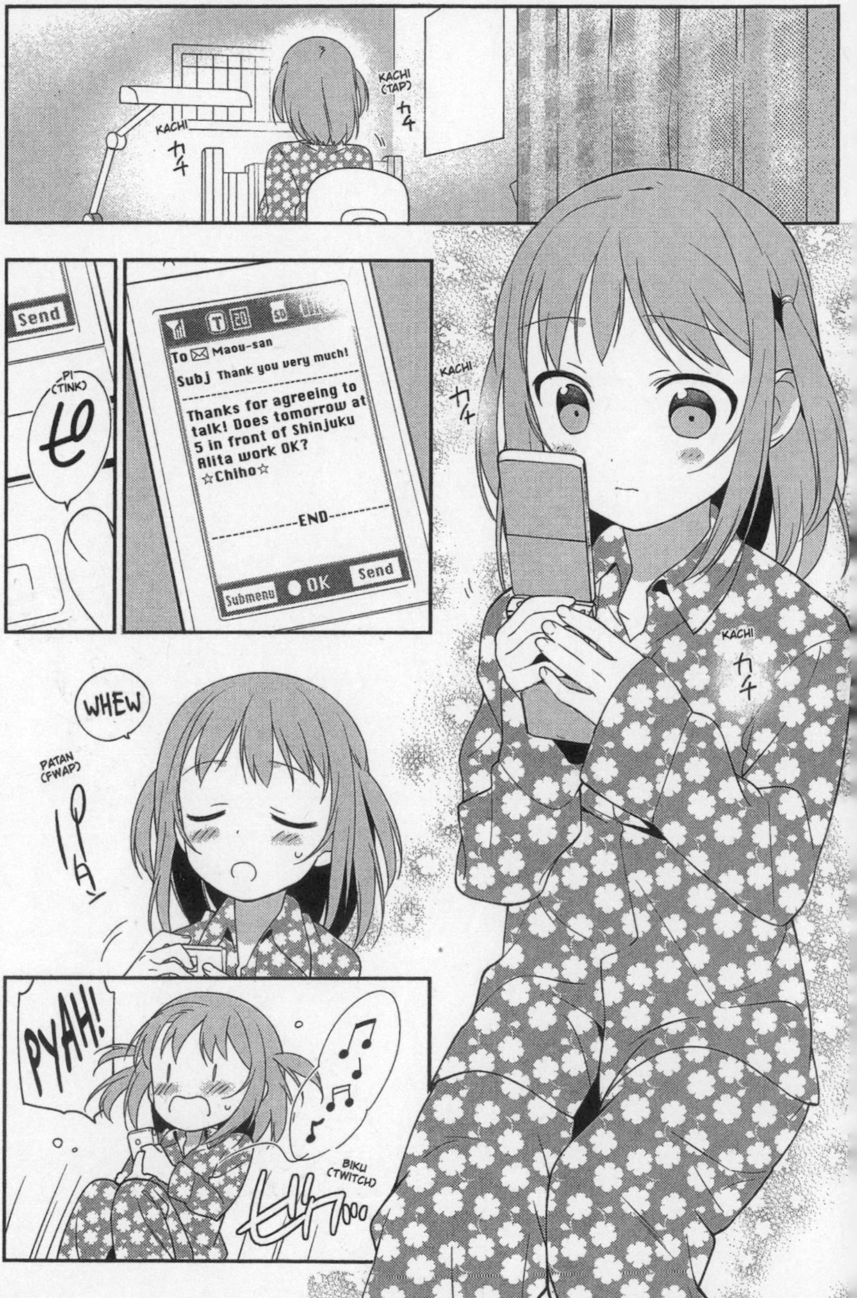

KACHI (TAP)
カチ
KACHI
カチ
KACHI
カチ
KACHI
カチ
To Maou-san
Subj Thank you very much!
Thanks for agreeing to talk! Does tomorrow at 5 in front of Shinjuku Alita work OK? ☆Chiho☆
END
Submenu
OK
Send
Send
PI (TINK)
ピ
WHEW
PATAN (FWAP)
PYAH!
BIKU (TWITCH)

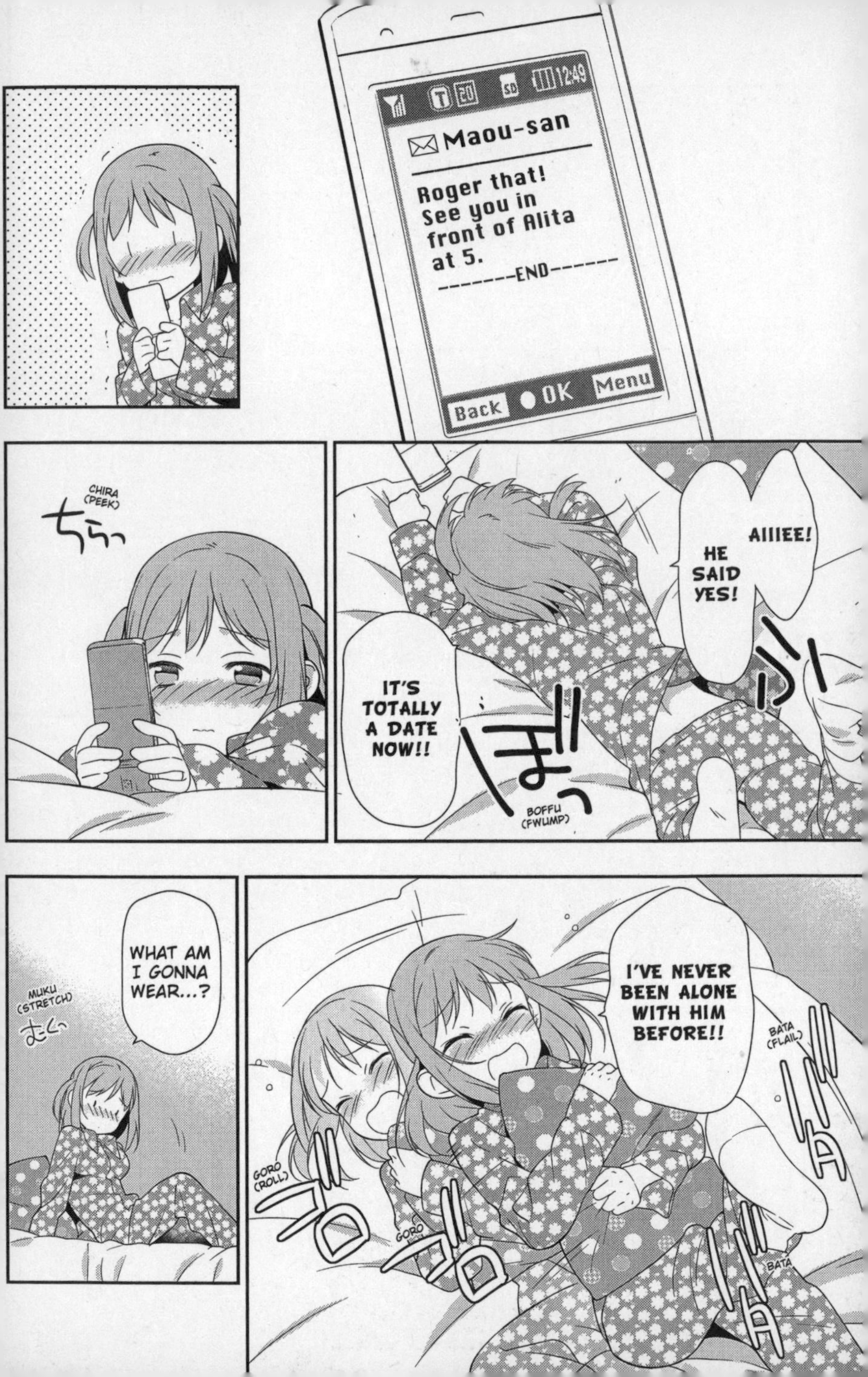
Maou-san
Roger that! See you in front of Alita at 5.
--------END--------
Back
OK
Menu
AIIIEE!
HE SAID YES!
IT'S TOTALLY A DATE NOW!!
BOFFU (FWUMP)
CHIRA (PEEK)
ちらっ
I'VE NEVER BEEN ALONE WITH HIM BEFORE!!
BATA (FLAIL)
GORO (ROLL)
GORO
BATA
WHAT AM I GONNA WEAR...?
MUKU (STRETCH)

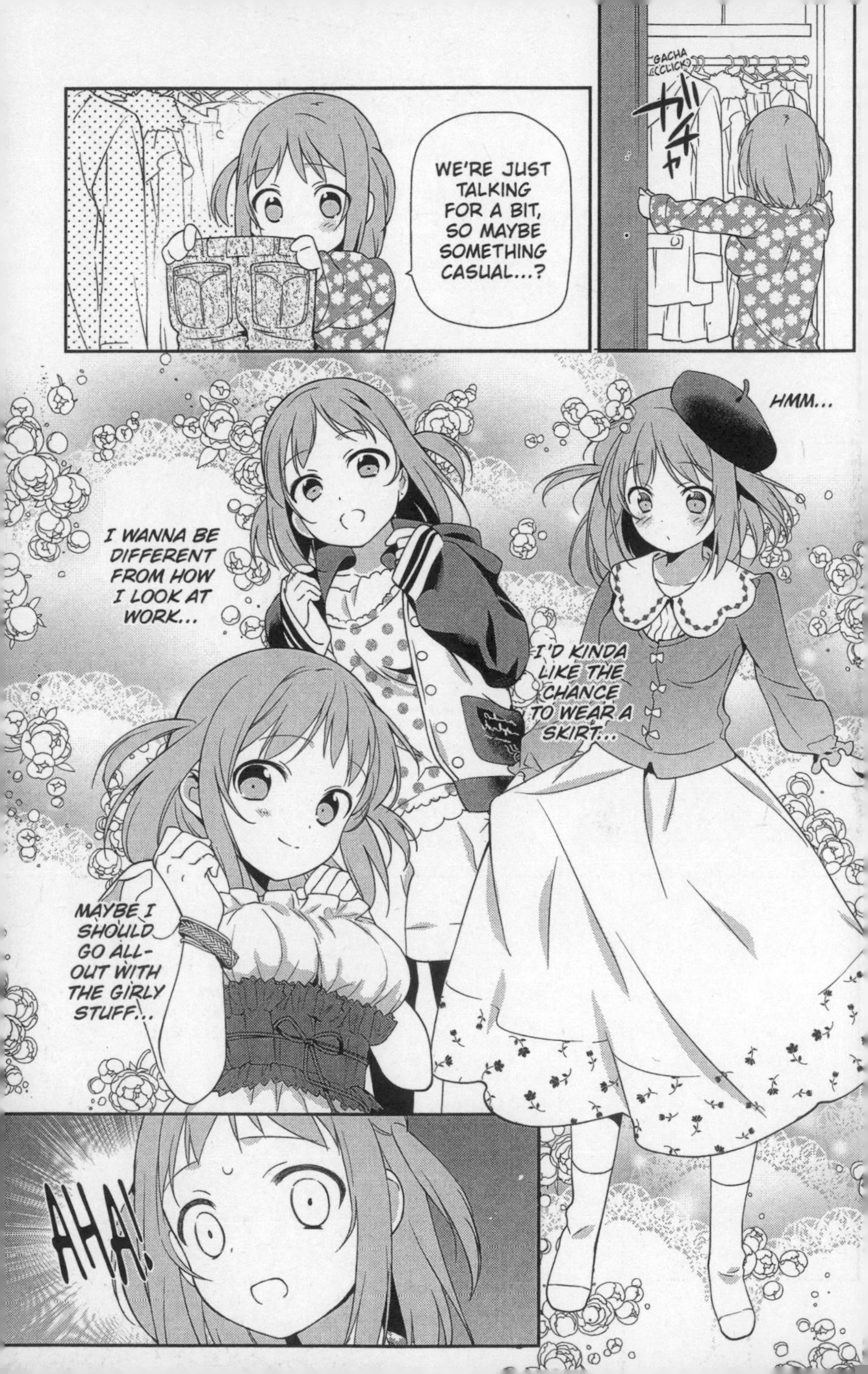
GACHA (CLICK)
ガチャ
WE'RE JUST TALKING FOR A BIT, SO MAYBE SOMETHING CASUAL...?
HMM...
I'D KINDA LIKE THE CHANCE TO WEAR A SKIRT...
I WANNA BE DIFFERENT FROM HOW I LOOK AT WORK...
MAYBE I SHOULD GO ALL-OUT WITH THE GIRLY STUFF...
AHA!

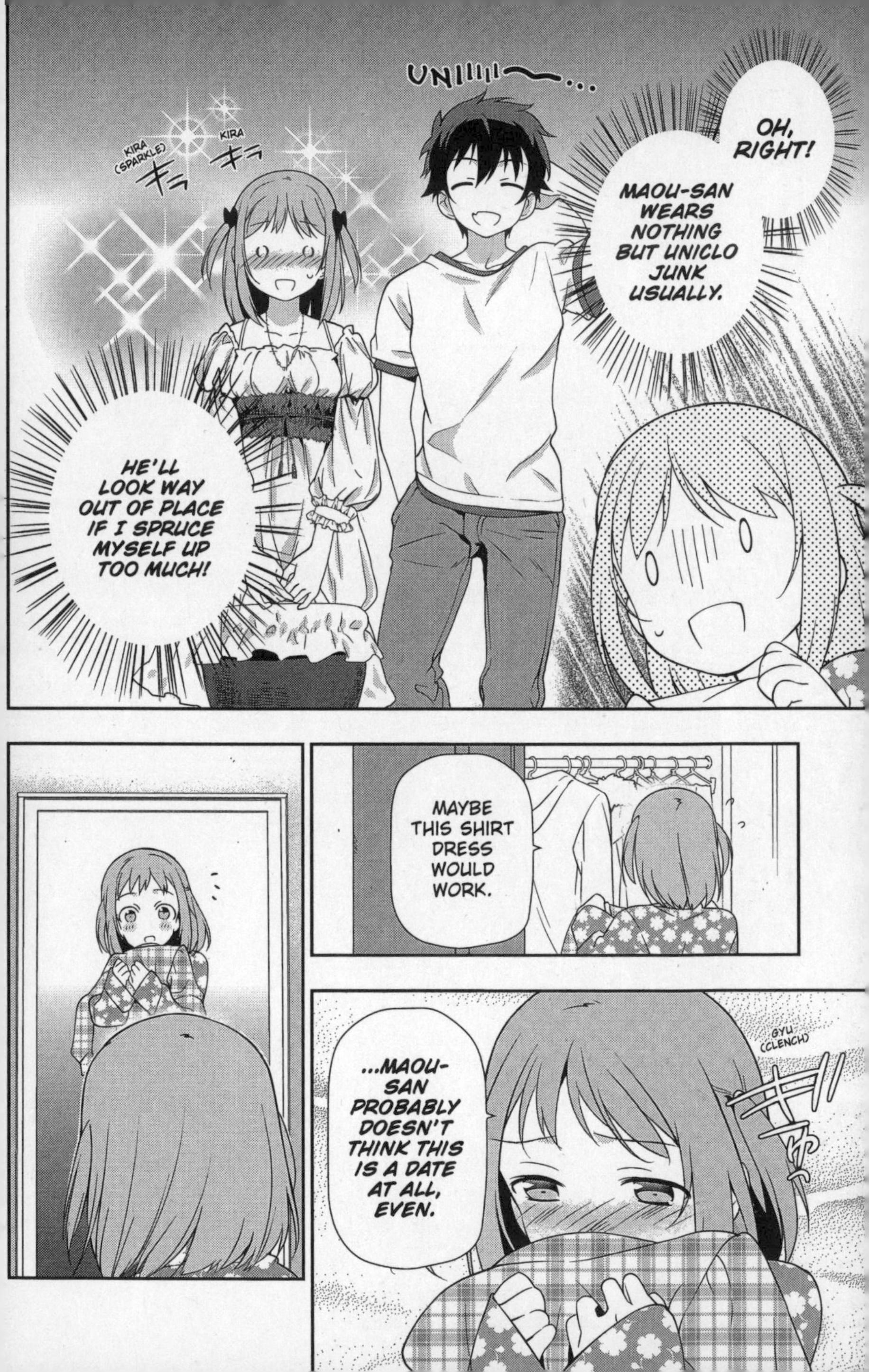
OH, RIGHT!
MAOU-SAN WEARS NOTHING BUT UNICLO JUNK USUALLY.
UNIIIII~...
KIRA
KIRA (SPARKLE)
HE'LL LOOK WAY OUT OF PLACE IF I SPRUCE MYSELF UP TOO MUCH!
MAYBE THIS SHIRT DRESS WOULD WORK.
GYU (CLENCH)
...MAOU-SAN PROBABLY DOESN'T THINK THIS IS A DATE AT ALL, EVEN.

MAGAZINE: 100 NEWEST HAIRSTYLES

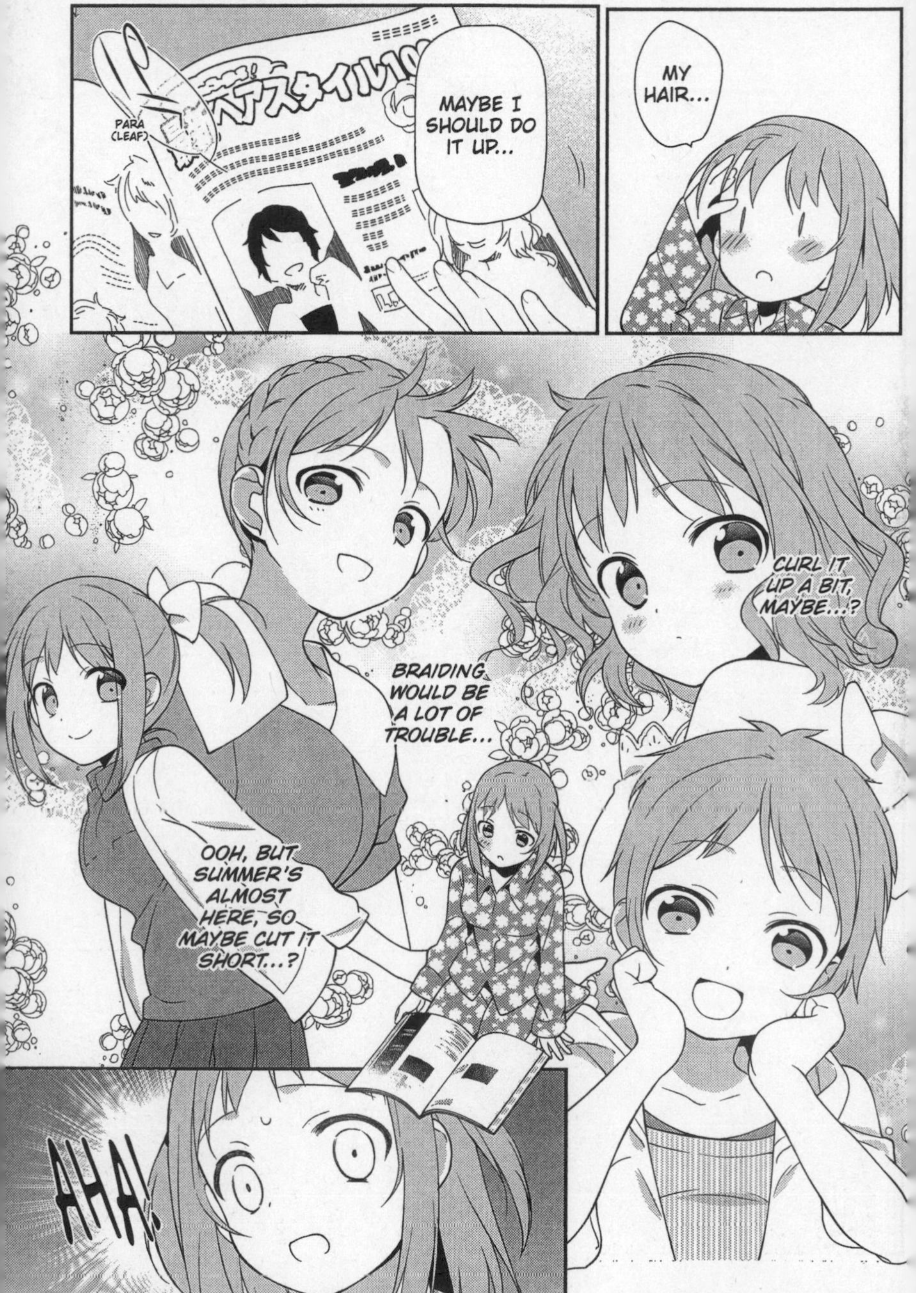
MY HAIR...
MAYBE I SHOULD DO IT UP...
PARA (LEAF)
CURL IT UP A BIT, MAYBE...?
BRAIDING WOULD BE A LOT OF TROUBLE...
OOH, BUT SUMMER'S ALMOST HERE, SO MAYBE CUT IT SHORT...?
AHA!

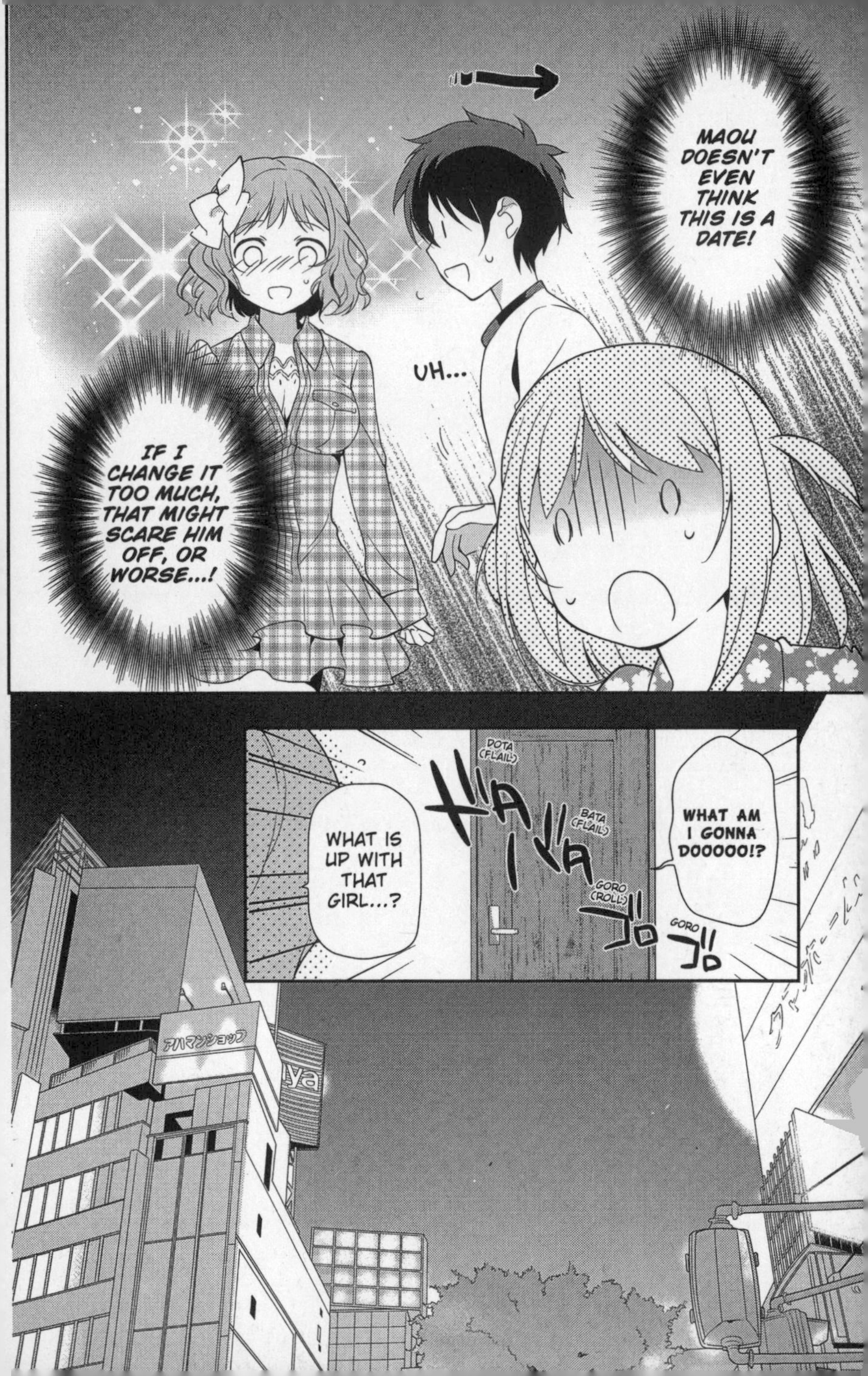
MAOU DOESN'T EVEN THINK THIS IS A DATE!
UH...
IF I CHANGE IT TOO MUCH, THAT MIGHT SCARE HIM OFF, OR WORSE...!
WHAT AM I GONNA DOOOOO!?
GORO
GORO (ROLL)
BATA (FLAIL)
DOTA (FLAIL)
WHAT IS UP WITH THAT GIRL...?
アハマンショップ

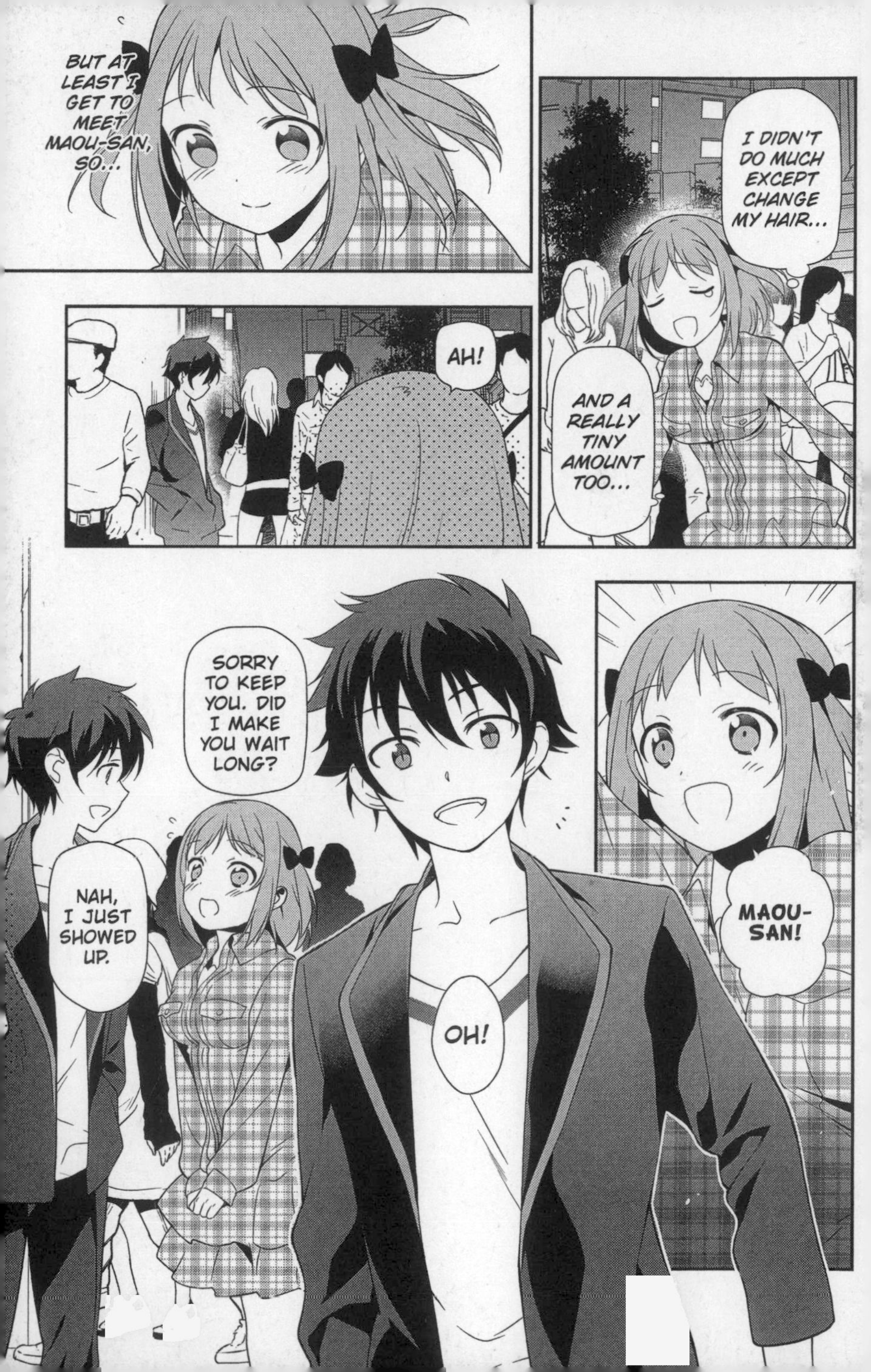
I DIDN'T DO MUCH EXCEPT CHANGE MY HAIR...
AND A REALLY TINY AMOUNT TOO...
BUT AT LEAST I GET TO MEET MAOU-SAN, SO...
AH!
MAOU-SAN!
OH!
SORRY TO KEEP YOU. DID I MAKE YOU WAIT LONG?
NAH, I JUST SHOWED UP.

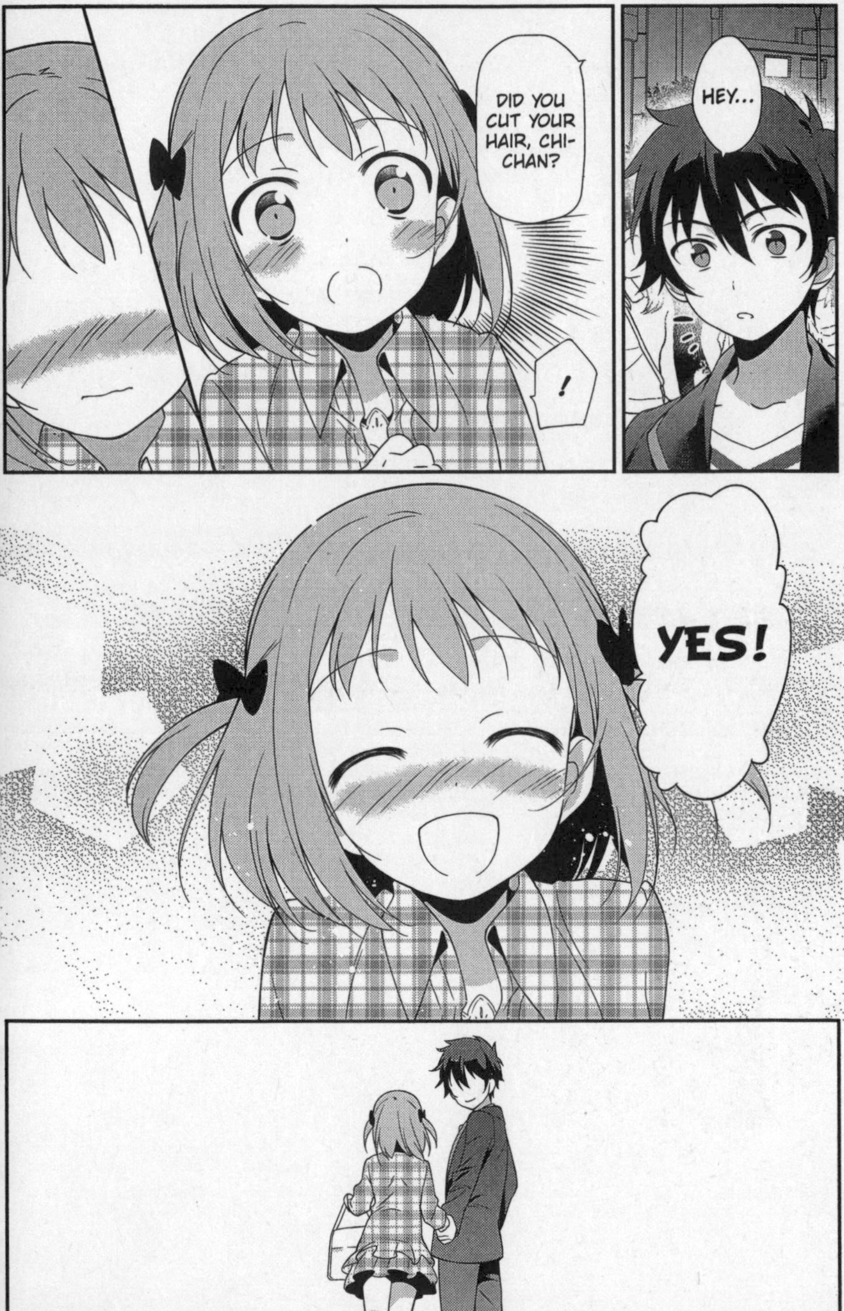
HEY...
DID YOU CUT YOUR HAIR, CHI-CHAN?
!
YES!

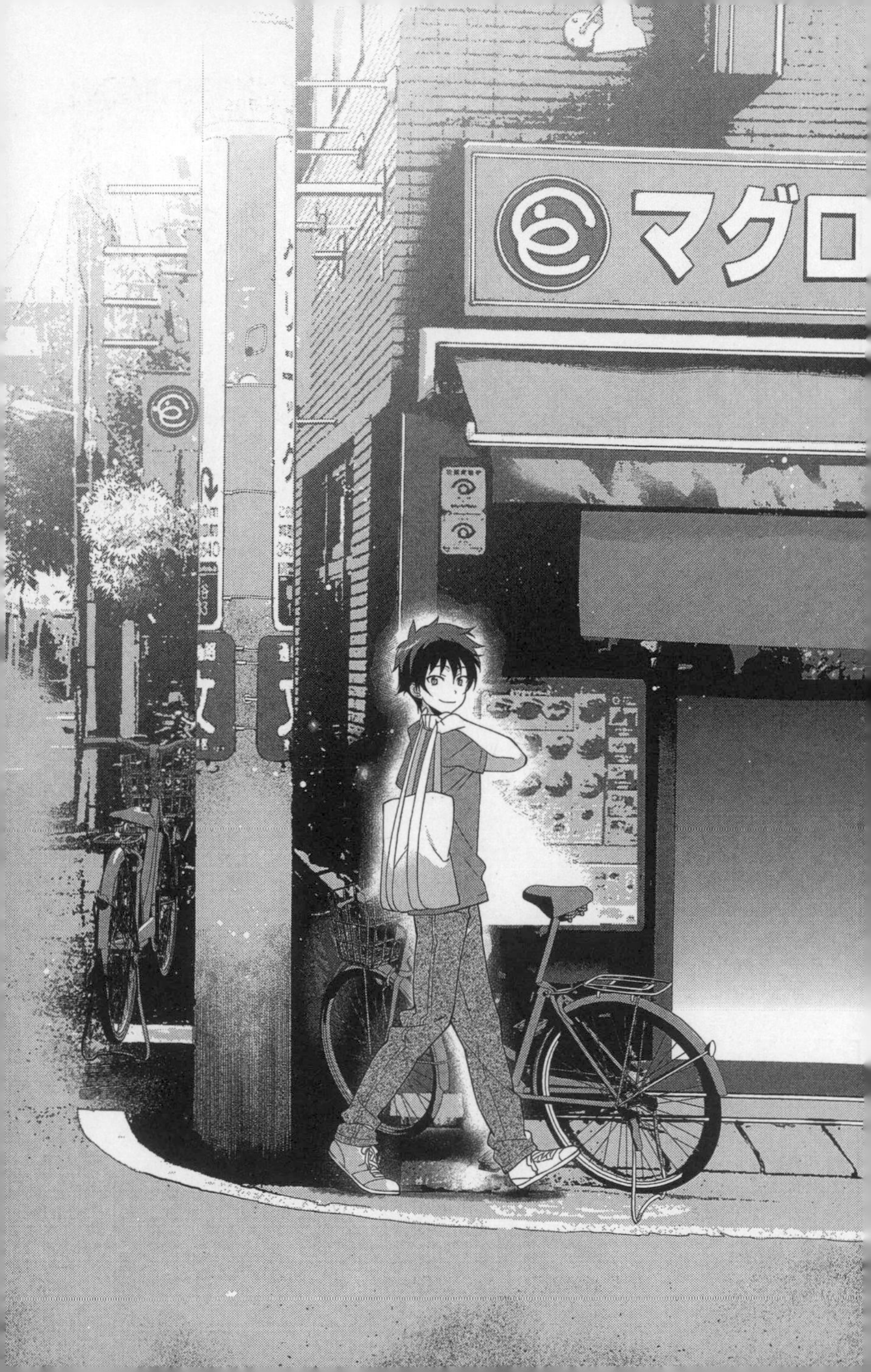
マグロ

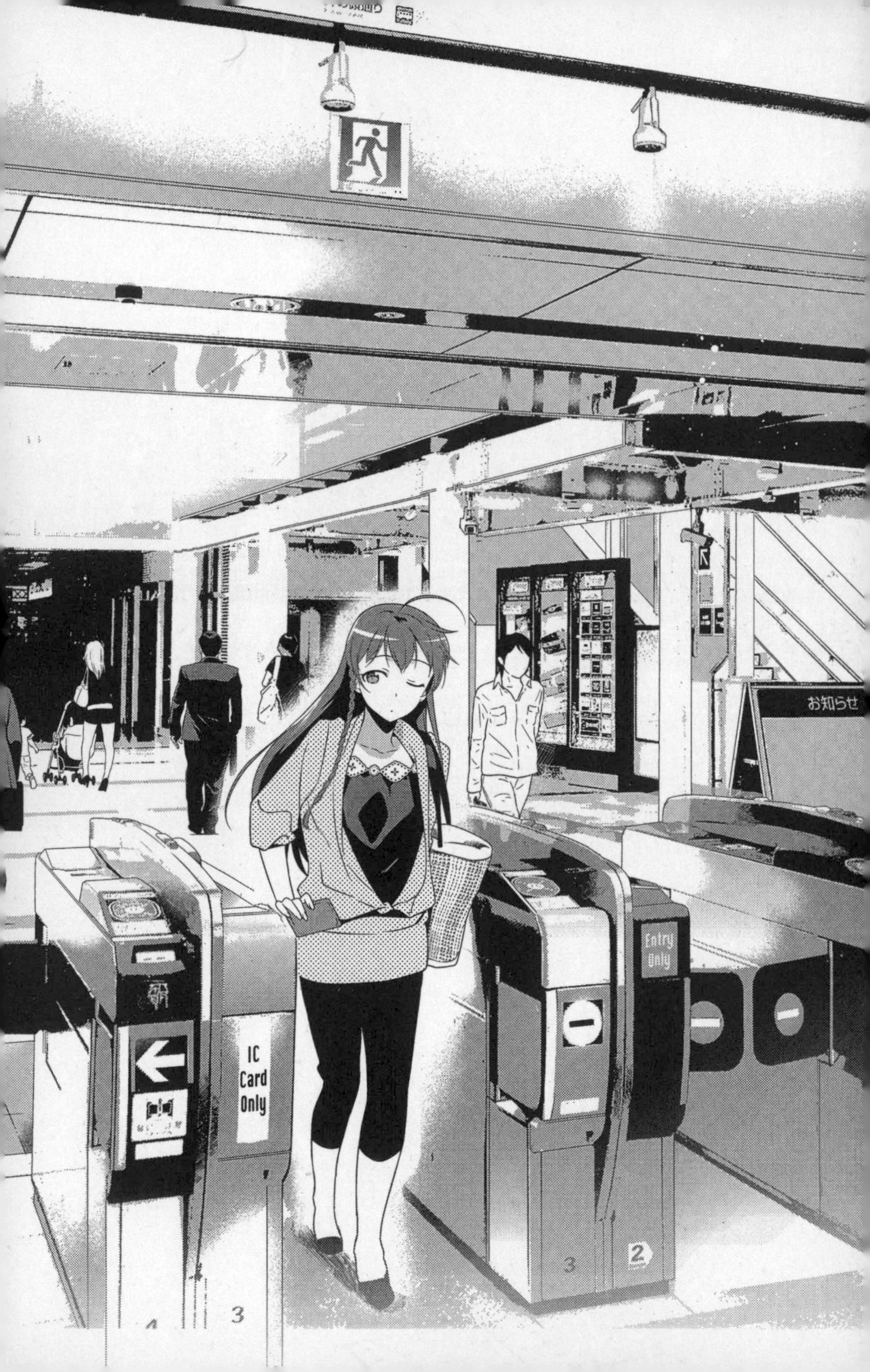
お知らせ
Entry Only
IC Card Only

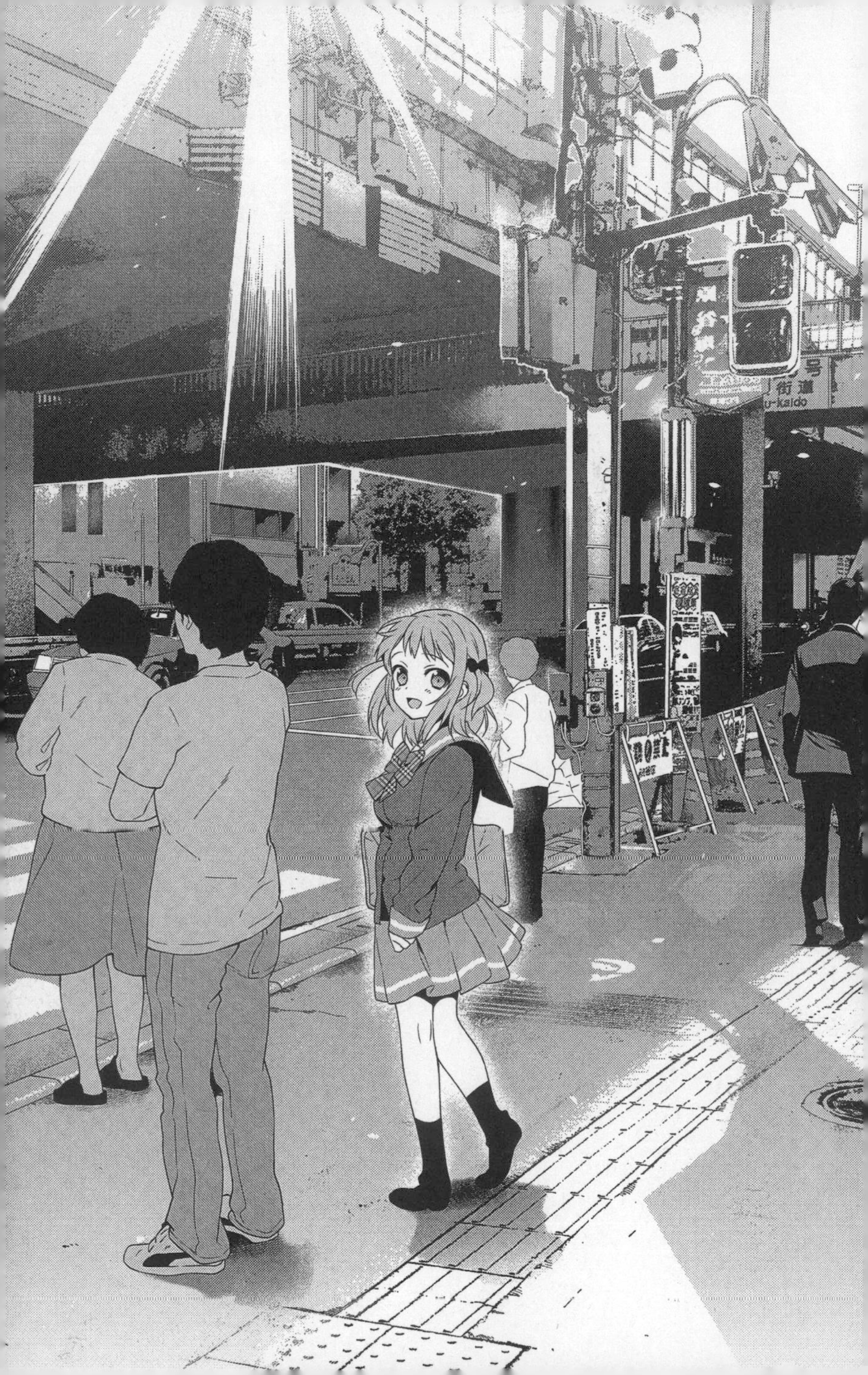

## BACKSTAGE AT THE TANABATA PREPARATIONS

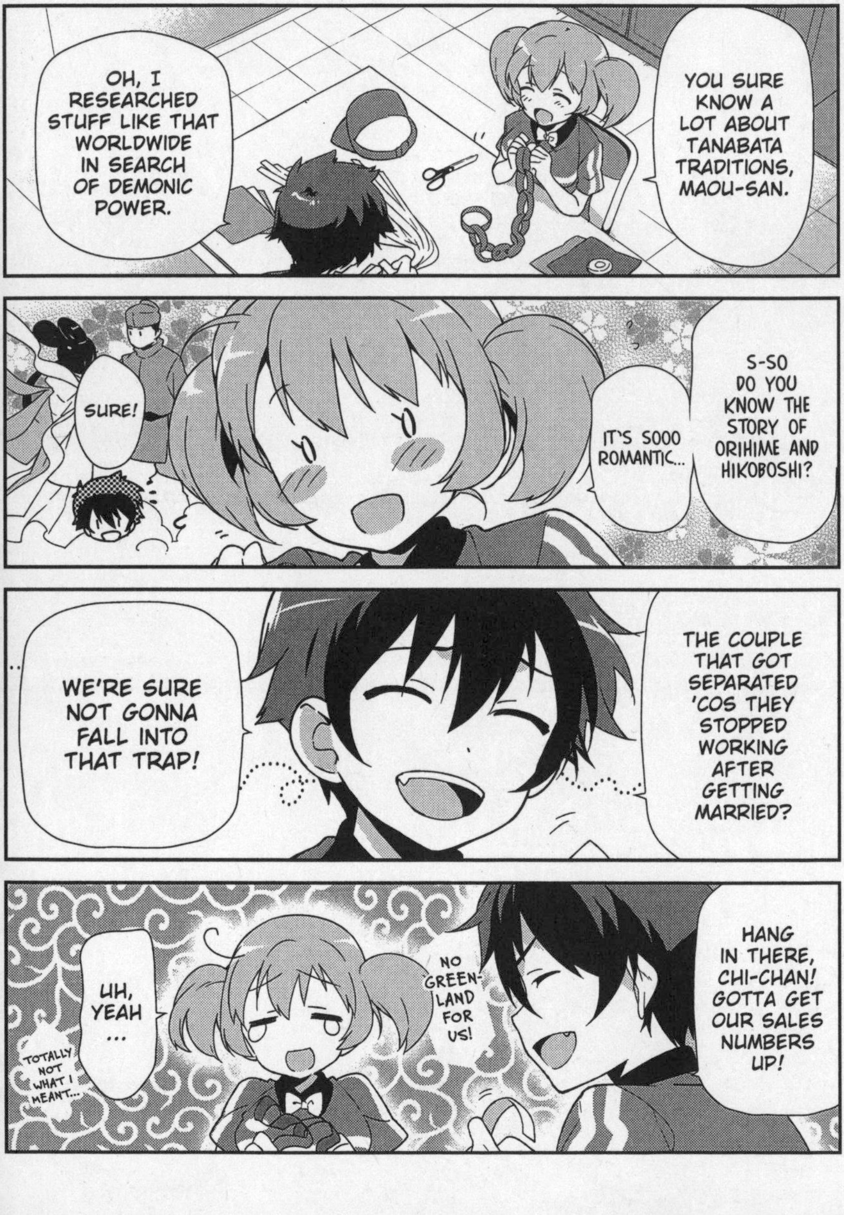
YOU SURE KNOW A LOT ABOUT TANABATA TRADITIONS, MAOU-SAN.
OH, I RESEARCHED STUFF LIKE THAT WORLDWIDE IN SEARCH OF DEMONIC POWER.
S-SO DO YOU KNOW THE STORY OF ORIHIME AND HIKOBOSHI?
IT'S SOOO ROMANTIC...
SURE!
THE COUPLE THAT GOT SEPARATED 'COS THEY STOPPED WORKING AFTER GETTING MARRIED?
WE'RE SURE NOT GONNA FALL INTO THAT TRAP!
HANG IN THERE, CHI-CHAN! GOTTA GET OUR SALES NUMBERS UP!
NO GREEN-LAND FOR US!
UH, YEAH ...
TOTALLY NOT WHAT I MEANT...

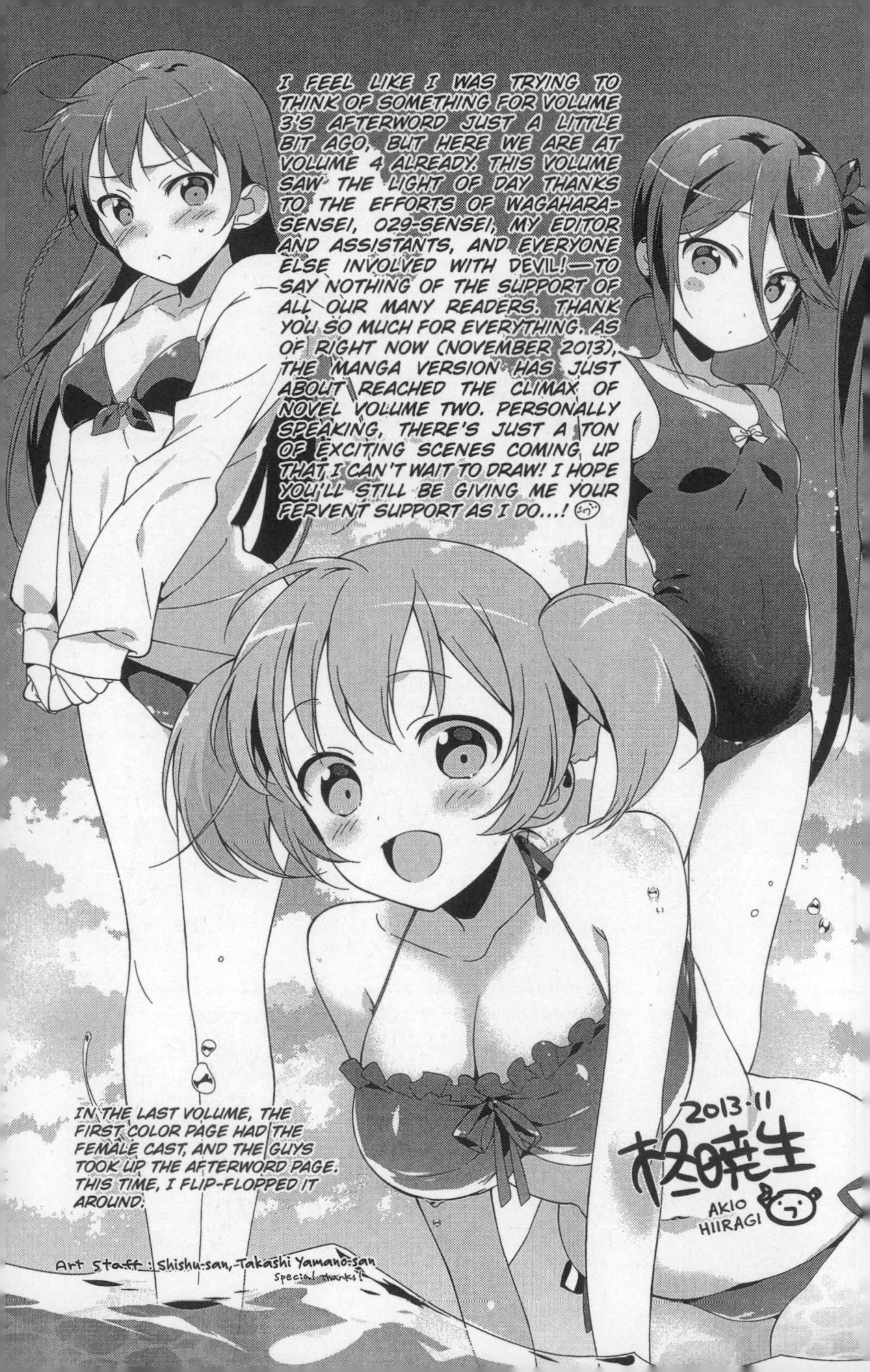
I FEEL LIKE I WAS TRYING TO THINK OF SOMETHING FOR VOLUME 3'S AFTERWORD JUST A LITTLE BIT AGO, BUT HERE WE ARE AT VOLUME 4 ALREADY. THIS VOLUME SAW THE LIGHT OF DAY THANKS TO THE EFFORTS OF WAGAHARA-SENSEI, 029-SENSEI, MY EDITOR AND ASSISTANTS, AND EVERYONE ELSE INVOLVED WITH DEVIL!—TO SAY NOTHING OF THE SUPPORT OF ALL OUR MANY READERS. THANK YOU SO MUCH FOR EVERYTHING. AS OF RIGHT NOW (NOVEMBER 2013), THE MANGA VERSION HAS JUST ABOUT REACHED THE CLIMAX OF NOVEL VOLUME TWO. PERSONALLY SPEAKING, THERE'S JUST A TON OF EXCITING SCENES COMING UP THAT I CAN'T WAIT TO DRAW! I HOPE YOU'LL STILL BE GIVING ME YOUR FERVENT SUPPORT AS I DO...!
2013.11
柊暁生
AKIO HIIRAGI
IN THE LAST VOLUME, THE FIRST COLOR PAGE HAD THE FEMALE CAST, AND THE GUYS TOOK UP THE AFTERWORD PAGE. THIS TIME, I FLIP-FLOPPED IT AROUND.
Art Staff : Shishu-san, Takashi Yamano-san
Special thanks!

# THE DEVIL IS A PART-TIMER! ④

**ART: AKIO HIIRAGI**
**ORIGINAL STORY: SATOSHI WAGAHARA**
**CHARACTER DESIGN: 029 (ONIKU)**

**Translation: Kevin Gifford**

**Lettering: Lys Blakeslee**

This book is a work of fiction. Names, characters, places, and incidents are the product of the author's imagination or are used fictitiously. Any resemblance to actual events, locales, or persons, living or dead, is coincidental.


Edited by ASCII MEDIA WORKS
First published in Japan in 2013 by KADOKAWA CORPORATION, Tokyo.
English translation rights arranged with KADOKAWA CORPORATION, Tokyo, through Tuttle-Mori Agency, Inc., Tokyo.



Yen Press
Hachette Book Group
1290 Avenue of the Americas
New York, NY 10104

www.HachetteBookGroup.com
www.YenPress.com

Yen Press is an imprint of Hachette Book Group, Inc. The Yen Press name and logo are trademarks of Hachette Book Group, Inc.

The publisher is not responsible for websites (or their content) that are not owned by the publisher.

First Yen Press Edition: January 2016

Library of Congress Control Number: 2015952592

ISBN: 978-0-316-38509-1

10 9 8 7 6 5 4 3 2 1

BVG

Printed in the United States of America